W9-BAJ-162

THE THE REBIRTH OF EUROPE
WALTER LAQUEUR

The Rebirth of Europe is the first attempt to trace in one volume, political and cultural, economic and social developments in Europe since 1945. As such, and because of its comprehensiveness and clarity, The Rebirth of Europe, *by one of the world's most distinguished historians, is an essential and highly readable reference work.*

"There were parades, laughter, and dancing in the streets all over Europe on Victory Day, but on the morning after, Europeans began to take stock of the consequences of the war." With this picture of a night of joy and a dawn of foreboding, Walter Laqueur commences this unique history.

In four sections, Professor Laqueur covers the period from the end of World War II to Stalin's death, the main postwar economic and social trends, cultural developments since the middle '50's and politics from 1955 to the Czech crisis.

He concludes, "Far from dying in convulsions as Sartre had predicted, Europe has shown a new vigour which has astonished friends and foes alike. In a wider sense the European age has only begun."

THE REBIRTH OF EUROPE

by Walter Laqueur

HOLT, RINEHART AND WINSTON
New York   Chicago   San Francisco

CONTENTS

PREFACE

'The man who ventures to write contemporary history,' Voltaire wrote to Bertin de Rocheret, 'must expect to be attacked both for everything he has said and everything he has not said.' The present book is, to the best of my knowledge, the first attempt to trace in one volume, political and cultural, economic and social developments in Europe since 1945. Europe still consists of thirty-odd, more or less independent, countries. A work dealing only with the common features and patterns in the continent's recent history would at best be incomplete, while a survey of each separate country would be impracticable. I have tried to combine the two approaches. The first part of this book covers, roughly speaking, the period from the end of the second world war to Stalin's death. Part II deals with the main economic and social trends, and Part III with cultural developments in Europe since the middle fifties. In Part IV, European politics since 1955 are described and analysed. The bibliography does not purport to be complete; it is a guide to further reading.

London – Boston, June 1969

PART I

THE POSTWAR PERIOD

Introduction

The second world war ended in Europe with the surrender of the Germans on 7 May 1945. The document was signed in Rheims by Field Marshal Jodl on behalf of the *Wehrmacht* and by Lt General Bedell Smith on behalf of the American and British forces, with French and Russian officers as witnesses. Later on there was a similar ceremony in Berlin between the Russians and Germans, and all hostilities ceased on 8 May. The longest and most destructive war in modern history was over. A Frenchwoman, Micheline Maurel, who had been an inmate of a concentration camp, describes the unreality of the first hours of freedom: 'I passed the whole day in a sort of paralysing ecstasy. I tried to persuade myself that I was free. I tried to write a poem. But I never got further than: Free, free, free at last. Freedom as yet did not mean much to me. . . .' For the millions of soldiers this was the end of the road; the Russians, who had fought their way after initial defeats through half Europe, from Stalingrad to Berlin; the western armies which had advanced from the Normandy beachheads the year before. Soon they would be demobilised, return home, rejoin their families and resume their peacetime occupations. For millions of German soldiers it was the beginning of the long road to captivity.

Most of France, Belgium, and Italy, almost all of eastern Europe, had been liberated well before May 1945. When the armistice was signed nazi rule was limited to a small section of Germany, to Norway, Denmark and parts of Czechoslovakia. The Third Reich, which its leader had predicted would last a thousand years, was at the end of its tether. 'Do you want total war?' Dr Goebbels had asked in 1943. Now there was total defeat.

The Allied leaders exchanged messages of congratulation. Stalin cabled Churchill: 'This historic victory has been achieved by the joint struggle of the Soviet, British, and American armies for the liberation of Europe.' Churchill in a victory broadcast that evening told the British people: 'I wish I could tell you tonight that all our toils and troubles are over.' But it was Victory Day only in Europe; the Japanese were still fighting; and even though the end in the Pacific was now in sight, it was already clear that there could be no relaxation in the efforts to tackle the tremendous problems of the postwar world facing victors and vanquished alike.

On that long-awaited day of victory few people chose to think of the challenges and problems of the future. In London there were floodlights for the first time after six years of blackout; everyone was cheerful, happy, and orderly; not a single drunk was to be seen or heard. Big Ben was floodlit, so were the Clock Tower, Speakers Corner, and County Hall, the Horse Guards, the Lake in St James's Park and Buckingham Palace. There was the joyous roar of the crowds, songs and fireworks. In Moscow the news was received at 2 a.m. 'I looked out of the window,' Ilya Ehrenburg wrote; 'almost everywhere there were lights in the windows – people were staying awake. Everyone embraced everyone else, someone sobbed aloud. At 4 a.m. Gorky Street was thronged.' There were salvoes from a thousand guns. There was great joy and deep sadness. 'That evening,' writes a Russian, 'there could not have been a single table in the Soviet Union where those gathering round it were not conscious of an empty place.' On the afternoon of the 8th, General de Gaulle went to the Arc de Triomphe. The place was very full; after the General had saluted the tomb of the Unknown Soldier, the human torrent broke through the barriers. But, with all the demonstrations, the official speeches, the sound of church bells and the artillery salvoes, the rejoicing of the people was grave and measured: 'Comme ils sont obscurs, les lendemains de la France!'

The German reaction was one of stupor and apathy. There had been fears that the young soldiers would not surrender, that fanatical partisan and guerrilla units would fight on. But nothing of the sort happened; the last act of the *Götterdämmerung*, the twilight of the Nordic Gods, had already taken place, and no one wanted to prolong the agony. Hitler had committed suicide a few days before in his bunker; Mussolini had been caught trying to escape and was hanged by partisans; their dreams of power had been buried with them. Germany was utterly exhausted. Hitler had said that if Germany did not win the war, it would be a sign of weakness, of inferiority, and the country might as well perish. His death wish was almost coming true.

There were parades, laughter, and dancing in the streets all over Europe on Victory Day, but on the morning after, Europeans began to take stock of the consequences of the war. It was a horrifying balance, enough to fill with despair even the staunchest hearts. Not since the seventeenth century had a war in Europe been fought so ferociously and caused so much destruction. Peace had now returned, but many felt, like the poet at the end of the Thirty Years War, that it was the peace of a churchyard. It had come too late. Not a few feared that Europe would never again rise from the ashes. Europe had never fully recovered from the terrible bloodbath of the first world war and its ravages; but now, in retrospect, that war seemed almost insignificant. There had been eight million victims in 1914–18; now there were four times as many. France with 620,000 victims and Britain with 260,000, had suffered less in the second war, but the loss of life in central and eastern

Europe was enormous. Poland had lost more than 20 per cent of its total population (including the millions of Jews murdered), and Yugoslavia ten per cent. Soviet losses were estimated between 12 and 20 million, German (again including civilian losses) at more than five million. Even a small country like Greece had suffered grievously.

Material losses, too, were incomparably greater than during the first world war. Large parts of Europe had been directly affected; Poland and Russia, Yugoslavia and Greece, Italy and northern France, Belgium and Holland, and, in the last stages, Germany. There had been massive air raids; both Russians and Germans had in their retreat followed a scorched earth policy. Hardly a major city in Europe had escaped altogether un-scathed; some, such as Warsaw, had been destroyed to such an extent that it was uncertain whether they could be rebuilt. In 1935 Hitler had said that ten years later no one would be able to recognise Berlin. His prophecy had come true, though not in the sense intended. Some thought it would take 15 years to clear away the rubble in the former German capital; others were less opti-mistic. The coastal and northern regions of France had been ravaged during the last year of the war and immense damage had been done in cities like Boulogne, Le Havre, Rouen, and Brest. Parts of Holland had been inundated – the Walcheren had been flooded and the land area south of the Zuyder Sea had been submerged. In Italy Naples, Milan, and Turin, centres of industry and commerce, had suffered badly; Pisa, Verona, and Lyons, Budapest and Leningrad, Kiev and Cracow, and many other cities were partly destroyed. All visitors to central Europe reported a feeling of unreality: lunar landscapes dotted with enormous heaps of rubble and bomb craters, deserted and stink-ing ruins that had once been business centres and residential areas. To find housing for the survivors was the most urgent problem, but in Germany about a quarter of all houses were uninhabitable, and almost as many in Poland, Greece, Yugoslavia, and the European part of the Soviet Union. Many more had been damaged. The problem was particularly acute in the cities. In Düsseldorf 93 per cent of all houses were thought to be uninhabitable. In the American zone of Germany 81 per cent of all houses had been destroyed or damaged. In the German-occupied parts of the Soviet Union the homes of six million families had been destroyed, leaving about 25 million people without shelter.

The spectre of famine appeared all over Europe. During the early stages of the war farming had prospered, but later on, with the loss of manpower and the lack of machinery, fertilisers, and seed, harvests were severely reduced and there were heavy losses in livestock; the situation deteriorated further as the result of a severe drought in 1945. The harvest of cereal crops in continental Europe (excluding the Soviet Union) fell from a prewar average of 59 million tons to 31 million. In France, normally a rich agricultural country, the crop of food grains had fallen by more than half. Denmark had not suffered much material damage, but it could not resume food deliveries to its regular customers such as Germany and Britain because these were now unable to pay. All over Europe strict food rationing was in force, and in most places the rations were now smaller than in wartime. A year after the end of the war it was estimated that about 100 million people in Europe were being fed at a level of 1,500 calories a day or less. One thousand five hundred calories or less is recommended for reducing weight; it is not an ideal level of nutrition for those doing heavy physical work or for growing children, or in general for people who have been underfed for years. But even this level could not always be maintained; the authorities in the American and British zones of Germany had to cut the rations in 1946 to 900–1000 calories. There were desperate food shortages in the Soviet Union; he who lost his ration book faced starvation.

Those living in the destroyed cities lacked clothes, shoes, domestic equipment and tools. As winter approached fuel became a question of life and death. Coal production had fallen drastically all over the continent; it was now only 42 per cent of the prewar level. The Ruhr coal industry was producing only 25,000 tons a day compared with 400,000 before the war. But even if larger supplies had been available, there would have been no way of transporting them to where they were needed most. Perhaps the gravest result of the war in the sense of material damage was the destruction of the network of communications on which Europe depended: 740 out of 958 important bridges in the American and British zones of Germany had been destroyed; France had only 35 per cent of its railway locomotives left and about the same share of its merchant fleet. In Holland all bridges on and north of the Leopold Canal were destroyed, completely paralysing for six months the main Dutch and Belgian canal system. Northern France and western Germany traditionally depended on inland waterways for bulk transport, but these, too, were now out of action. Many ports could not be used: Toulon was blocked by the French ships that had been scuttled there; Calais, Boulogne, Bordeaux and Dunkirk were paralysed. For many months after the liberation there was only one adequate bridge across the Rhine (at Nijmegen), only one across the Elbe (in Hamburg). In Germany railway transport had virtually come to a standstill and it took many months before the trains could move again. The experts now realised, as one of them reported, that the bombing of cities had not created as much distress and dislocation as the destruction of the vital rail and water routes.

Even now it is impossible to establish with any degree of accuracy to what extent industry was still working at the end of the war; in the prevailing chaos statistics did not receive top priority. It was perhaps at 35 per cent of the prewar level in France, higher in the neutral countries and those which had not suffered greatly (like Denmark and Czechoslovakia), but much lower in Germany, Austria, and Greece. The few reliable figures speak for themselves: pig-iron output in 1946 in the countries that now make up the EEC (France, Germany, Italy and Benelux) was less than a third of the 1938 figure, crude steel output – about a third. But 1938 had not been a very good year; in most European countries the depression had not been completely overcome: in France industrial production in 1938 was more than 20 per cent below the level of 1929. Throughout the continent the financial system had been disrupted, with consequent inflation. The amount of money in circulation in Germany was seven times as high as in 1938. Prices in France during the war had increased fourfold. In Hungary and Greece the currency collapsed. Soon after the war Belgium and Norway had to devalue and to reform their currencies immediately to ward off a similar fate. In short, the European economy in 1945 had ceased to be viable; the continent was faced with economic collapse, hunger, and disease. Before recovery and reconstruction could even be contemplated, massive first aid and disaster relief was needed. This was supplied by UNRRA, the United Nations Relief and Rehabilitation Administration, financed mainly by the United States, which provided food, raw materials, and equipment, and helped to install essential services in Italy, Yugoslavia, Greece, Austria, Czechoslovakia, Poland, and parts of the Soviet Union. UNRRA by its charter was to assist only those peoples who had opposed the Axis; in Germany supplies were provided directly by the occupying powers. Whole countries were now living on charity and to say that economic prospects were uncertain would have been a gross understatement in the summer of 1945. There seemed to be no prospects.

Those who ought to have planned for these postwar emergencies were doubly mistaken in their assumptions; they underrated the gravity of the economic crisis and they were not aware how desperately acute it really was; in other words, how close Europe stood to collapse. But once they did realise this they became far too pessimistic about the long-term chances of European recovery. The various economic blueprints prepared in Washington and London during the last year of the war make strange reading today. The problems facing the planners after the defeat of Germany were of a very different order of magnitude from what they had imagined: the loans they thought would be sufficient to cover Europe's immediate postwar needs were but a drop in a seemingly bottomless bucket. Yet once the experts understood how near to collapse Europe really was, the tendency was to underrate national resilience and to exaggerate the permanence of the damage that had been caused. In parts of Europe, paralysis was almost total, but already after a few months some visitors found that though industrial production had come to a standstill, under the debris, equipment was often intact; only 15 to 20 per cent in the heavily bombed Ruhr area was damaged beyond repair. Two decades later, when the economists tried to explain the astonishing economic revival in Europe, some of them belatedly reached the conclusion that the war years had not been wholly years of economic waste, but a time when productive capacity expanded, in Britain and in Germany alike. Many plants had been bombed or destroyed or (in Germany) dismantled, but even so fixed assets in German industry in 1946 were higher than they had been ten years before.

The preconditions for a spectacular recovery existed in 1945 but were hidden beneath the surface; not even the most sanguine expected rapid economic expansion. It was difficult not to be overwhelmed by the extent of the catastrophe, which, after all, was not only, and not mainly, economic in character. The psychological shock seemed to have created a state of general paralysis.

Europe had lost its self-confidence. Before the first world war it had indisputably been the dominant factor in world politics; it had the strongest armies, it was the world's banker; 83 per cent of all the world's investments were made by the three leading European powers – Britain, France, and Germany. America was even before the war the first industrial power in the world, but its interests in world politics and world trade were still limited. There were stirrings of revolt but on the whole European colonial rule was still undisputed. Before 1914 London, Paris, and Berlin had been the cultural centres of the world and few scientific discoveries of importance had been made outside Europe. The general feeling was one of optimism; even those critical of the social order were aware of the steady improvement that had taken place over the years.

The first world war put an end to all this; its consequences – the postwar economic crisis, the victory of bolshevism and the rise of fascism – contained, moreover, the seeds of another war. America's position was immensely strengthened, and eventually also Russia's, but both these powers were almost totally absorbed in their domestic problems; their global ambitions and the ability to pursue them were limited. The second world war brought a profound change. The eclipse of the Axis powers, the occupation of Germany and Italy, put an end to their dreams of world domination. But Britain and France were almost equally weakened. To survive, Britain had to sell about one third of her overseas assets. At the end of the war her annual income from overseas investment was less than half that before the war; the merchant fleet was reduced to threequarters of its prewar size and only two per cent of British industry was producing for export. To win the war Britain had had to incur large debts, and its currency had been undermined. Although a victor, Britain in 1945 was as poor as most other European nations, and her people were certainly no better fed. Since her economy depended on the import of two-thirds of the food required and the bulk of her raw materials, and since she was now unable to pay for these imports, her prospects seemed very bleak indeed. Even the strictest controls and rationing, which remained in force for some years after the war, seemed unlikely to be of much help in the long run.

The situation was more hopeful in France, which was less dependent on imports. But it was hopeful only potentially, in a long-term view. Torn by internal convulsions and unsure of herself, the country had to grapple for many years with economic difficulties and inflation, with structural social problems and with political instability at home and complications abroad. Like England, Belgium, and Holland, France was soon to lose its colonial empire. The economic effects of decolonisation were less than anticipated; those who in the past had argued that Europe could not exist without colonies were proved mistaken. France tried to resist the rising tide of Asian and African nationalism, and became involved in colonial wars before realising that the time had come to cut her losses. But this was because French prestige was involved; from an economic point of view the French colonies were a dead loss.

Above all, the self-confidence of the European powers had collapsed. Many now realised (to quote Paul Valéry) that there had been nothing more stupid in history than the competition between the European states and that European politics had not matched in depth and quality European thought; the radiance and staying power of its civilisation had been destroyed by its internal squabbles. The political future of Europe was now decided between Washington and Moscow; its economy faced ruin but for massive American aid. Europe's cultural predominance had been undermined by the exodus to America of many scholars from Germany in the thirties, by the stifling of cultural life and scientific research by the totalitarian powers, and by the ravages of war. True, the war had given fresh impetus to discoveries and to technological advance in many fields, but only the richest countries could now afford to engage in research that had become steadily more expensive. American universities succeeded to the position once held by European institutes of higher learning, and New York became more important than any European capital as a centre of literature, music, and the arts.

This loss of self-confidence certainly did not extend to the Soviet Union. Its position had been enormously strengthened as a result of the war. Hitler had attacked Russia in June 1941 to 'save Europe from Bolshevism', to destroy it, or at least to drive it into Asia, where he thought it belonged. As one outcome of the war, Soviet troops were now one hundred miles from the Rhine, and occupying the whole of eastern Europe and most of the Balkans. The Soviet Union had not only successfully resisted the German onslaught, it had now emerged as the strongest military power in Europe. Communists had taken a prominent part in the resistance movements in most nazi-occupied countries, and there was a good deal of sympathy for the Soviet Union. In the years immediately after the war the prospects of a victory for communist parties in west and central Europe seemed brighter than ever before. But the problems of economic reconstruction facing the Soviet Union were no less formidable than those in the West. Industrial and agricultural production in 1945 was considerably below the prewar level; the western regions were in ruins, many millions had been killed. With all its military might, Russia in 1945 was still a desperately poor country. It was clear that healing the wounds and rebuilding the national economy was a gigantic task that would take many years and demand a colossal effort.

The New Political Map

The political map of Europe, or to be precise, of central and eastern Europe, was radically changed. Several countries disappeared; others that had ceased to exist, such as Poland, Austria and Yugoslavia, were now restored. The greatest gains by far were made by the Soviet Union; it reoccupied the three Baltic states (Lithuania, Latvia and Estonia) which it had first seized in 1940; it annexed most of East Prussia, it took the Petsamo district and part of the Karelian isthmus from Finland, acquired the Subcarpathian region from Czechoslovakia, Bessarabia and parts of the Bukovina from Rumania. In September 1939, on the basis of the pact with Germany, the Soviet Union had occupied eastern Poland. This territory had been lost during the war, but was reoccupied in 1944 and now remained firmly in Soviet hands. Poland was compensated by large stretches of formerly German areas up to the Oder-Neisse line. These were the major changes – the others were comparatively insignificant: France, of course, recovered Alsace-Lorraine, Yugoslavia received part of Venezia Giulia, Rumania had to surrender Southern Dobrudja to Bulgaria. There were minor border rectifications elsewhere and the future of the industrially important Saar region was left in abeyance for a number of years. Elsewhere the prewar frontiers were re-established. All this of course occurred only gradually; during the first weeks and months after the war there was a great deal of uncertainty about the future. The peace treaties with Italy, Rumania, Bulgaria, Hungary, and Finland were signed only in 1947, the treaty with Austria only in 1955 – and about Germany there was no agreement at all between the Allies, and consequently no treaty.

Of all the changes those concerning Poland were the most far-reaching. The country, as defined by its frontiers, was moved bodily more than two hundred miles to the west. The Western Allies had agreed in principle at the wartime conferences that Poland should be compensated in the west for its losses in the east – but the solution envisaged by Washington and London was less far-reaching than the one carried out by the Russians. There was a genuine conflict of interests: from the Russian point of view it was only fair to let Germany compensate Poland for the eastern territories Poland had to cede to Russia; it also served Russia's purpose since it meant that the new Poland would have to lean heavily on Moscow for protection against the Germans who would not easily accept the loss of such a large part of their territory. From the Western point of view, the Polish advance into what was once Germany went too far. It created immense problems for the administration of Germany, such as the uprooting of many millions of Germans now driven from their homes and the creation of an enormous new refugee problem. The territorial changes were moreover bound to be a source of perpetual political unrest in the heart of Europe. At Potsdam the Western powers reluctantly accepted the new *de facto* frontier and left the final boundaries of Poland to be determined at the peace settlement which was never held.

Germany (and Austria) were divided into zones of occupation as had been agreed before the end of the war. The Russians were in control of the eastern provinces: Saxony, Thuringia, Brandenburg and Mecklenburg; the British took over part of the Rhineland, the Ruhr, Lower Saxony, and north Germany. The American and French zones were in south Germany. Berlin, wholly within the Russian zone, was also divided into four sectors. These frontiers did not exactly correspond to the armistice lines; the Americans and the British had reached positions further to the east, and had stopped their advance towards Berlin only in order to allow the Russians to capture the former German capital. But the wartime alliance was still in effect, and in accordance with decisions previously reached the Western armies retreated from their forward positions once the Russians had arrived.

There was a great difference between the way the map of Europe was redrawn in the peace treaties of 1919, and its redivision after the second world war. In 1919 there was a great deal of haggling about territorial issues, ethnic and language frontiers and so forth. An effort was made to ascertain the wishes of the population directly affected, even though in the end some of the decisions taken were clearly unjust and in violation of the declared principle of self-determination. After the second world war ethnic considerations hardly counted; no one bothered to find out what the local population wanted; the balance of power, the West-East relations, were the overriding consideration. Once it had emerged that the Soviet Union would have the decisive influence all over eastern Europe it was of little importance for the world at large whether the border between Poland and Czechoslovakia or between Hungary and Rumania followed the ethnic or any other line. The Soviet Union usually saw to it that these conflicts were rapidly solved. This is not to say that a solution of territorial disputes not based on ethnic considerations was necessarily unjust and cynical. The ethnic map of eastern Europe and the Balkans was such that simply to trace new frontiers could not always restore justice. Both Rumania and Hungary had good claims on Transylvania, a region that had several times changed hands. But the Hungarian settlers were in the eastern part of Transylvania, the one furthest from the Hungarian border whereas the regions nearer to Hungary were largely settled by Rumanians. Only by some form of compromise, or alternatively by the establishment of a large number of mini-states, could justice have been done. Ethnic considerations, in any case, were not the only ones that mattered; there were geographic and economic factors to be considered, not to mention the part played by the respective country in the war. When Czech and Hungarian interests clashed, Jan Masaryk, Prague's foreign minister, asked: 'Who won this war – Hungary or the United Nations?' Hungary and Rumania had both been on the losing side; after the war they quarrelled about certain territories but the Rumanian government was at the time more acceptable to Moscow and so Bucharest got a better deal than it would have obtained a year or two later, when Hungary was already much more closely linked with the Soviet Union. Again, a case could be made for restoring the South Tyrol to Austria. This had been lost to Italy in 1919 and was still predominantly Austrian in character; but Italy had to cede some territory to Yugoslavia – a claim strongly backed by the Soviet Union, for Tito had not yet quarrelled with Moscow. In these circumstances, and since Austria lacked a strong backer among the powers, the Western Allies thought Italy should not be pressed too hard, and it was allowed to keep South Tyrol.

Altogether some 40–50 million people were expelled from their homes and became refugees, the greatest migration Europe had known since the *Völkerwanderung* fifteen hundred years earlier. There were millions of prisoners of war and forced labourers brought to Hitler's Reich between 1940 and 1944 who began to stream back once hostilities ceased. Some six million of these displaced persons were counted in Germany when the war ended; three months later two-thirds of them had been repatriated, but at the same time an even bigger wave of new refugees began to arrive and migration continued in almost every direction. Some had been uprooted for the second or third time: 250,000 Finns living in Soviet Karelia had taken refuge in Finland at the time of the first Russo-Finnish war in 1939, returning to their homes when Finland recovered Karelia in 1941. Ethnic Germans (Volksdeutsche) living in eastern Europe, some since the thirteenth century, had been evacuated by the nazis in 1939–40 and brought to Germany; they were resettled in Poland after 1941 only to be evacuated again when the tide of war turned. Some ten million Germans fled from the German provinces east of the Oder-Neisse line and from Czechoslovakia and Hungary, mostly into West Germany. There was also a substantial internal migration from the Soviet zone to West Germany which continued right up to the erection of the Berlin wall in 1961. There were in addition hundreds of thousands of Poles, including 160,000 in General Anders' army, Ukrainians and Latvians, who found themselves at the end of the war far from their homeland and who, for political reasons, could not or would not go back. There was also the movement of many thousands of Jews, the remnant of their people, the former inmates of death camps and ghettoes who wanted to leave a continent that had become a slaughter house and cemetery for their communities and families.

Agreements were signed between the Soviet Union, Yugoslavia, Rumania, Czechoslovakia and Hungary about the exchange of minorities following the redrawing of the political map. As a result there were further migration waves in eastern Europe: hundreds of thousands of Poles from the regions now transferred to the Soviet Union streamed to the newly acquired western ·territories: peasants from Eastern Galicia were settled in Pomerania and Silesia, the University of Lwow was transferred to Breslau, now renamed Wroclaw. The northern regions of Czechoslovakia, formerly inhabited by more than three million Sudeten Germans, were now taken over by Czechs and Slovaks. In the Soviet Union 'suspected' minorities such as the Volga Germans, the Crimean Tartars, and several Caucasian peoples had been expelled beyond the Urals during the war; some of them were permitted to return in the nineteen-fifties. The tribulations of the Soviet prisoners of war in Germany did not end with their repatriation in 1945; almost all were immediately sent to forced labour camps in the far north and far east of the USSR. They joined several millions of Soviet citizens, politically undesirable elements or just suspects in camps whose very existence was staunchly denied by Western communists. After Stalin's death in 1953 most of these camps were gradually dissolved and the survivors released.

As the result of these migrations the ethnic map of central and eastern Europe was redrawn. About a thousand years of German history, of steady colonisation in the east, was erased; so was the eastward movement of Poles and Lithuanians that had lasted several centuries. It was replaced by a Russian westward drive. Within its much reduced frontiers, the new Germany found itself saddled with a refugee problem on an unprecedented scale: more than ten million newcomers. The presence of these millions in Europe was to be a heavy burden for the host countries for many years; a large proportion of them were either very old or very young, but even those able to work found it difficult to assimilate the new cultural and social *milieu*, and in many cases to learn a new language. Relatively few migrated overseas, mainly to America and Australia.

There had been nothing like it since the Huguenots were expelled from France in the seventeenth century, except perhaps the exchange of populations between Turkey and Greece after the first world war. But this was on a far smaller scale, and it happened on the border of Europe and Asia and was largely ignored at the time. With all its ravages, the first world war had not caused a total breakdown of the conventional standards of civilisation, which included the understanding that the civilian population was not to be killed off or uprooted. The second world war, on the other hand, had witnessed barbarities on an unprecedented scale; after several years of nazi rule in Europe the expulsion of millions of civilians after the war passed almost without notice. There were protests, but mainly on practical grounds; the British and Americans now responsible for West Germany, in which millions of refugees were dumped, were unable to cope with the problem. But protests against the very principle of expelling people from their homes were few and they carried little weight against the background of Auschwitz and the hecatombs of victims throughout central and eastern Europe.

The New Balance of Power

The new political map reflected the new balance of power. The shift in world politics had started in the early nineteenth century with the development of modern means of communication: the steamship, the railway network, the telegraph. The European system was gradually giving way to a world system, but all that seemed to happen at first was the transformation of the balance of power in Europe into a balance embracing the whole world, as one writer has put it. The ultimate decisions were still taken in Europe. The second world war brought the Russians into the heart of Europe; eastern Europe and most of the Balkans was now under Soviet domination. Western and southern Europe as well as Germany were now almost totally dependent on American help. The European peoples were paying a heavy price for their internecine quarrels.

The first world war had broken out as a result of the tension between Russia and Austria in the Balkans, of the nationalist passions that were running high in Europe, and of a breakdown in diplomacy. German militarism, vanity, and arrogance had played a baneful role, but one could not in fairness apportion all the blame (as was done in the Versailles peace treaty) to Germany and its allies. All the big and many of the small European powers had territorial claims and colonial ambitions, but the influence of the lunatic fringe consciously working for war was limited; not one major European power had deliberately provoked the war, but all had manœuvred themselves into a situation from which followed a war which most people thought would be both brief and not very destructive.

Its outbreak in 1914 has been explained as the result of imperialist conflicts between Germany on the one hand, and Russia, Britain, and France on the other. Such conflicts did indeed exist, but were they more serious than the rivalry between Britain and France and Russia – not to mention the competition between Britain and the United States? Others have explained it with reference to the aggressive aims formulated by German politicians and publicists well before 1914; these are indisputable, but so are the speeches and writings of Russian Panslavists and French 'revanchists'. Not everyone in Germany was unaware of the possible consequences of the war. In a memorandum to the Emperor dated 28 July 1914, the General Staff said that the clash between Austria and Serbia was a local affair in which no one in Europe would have been interested had not Russia interfered, and correctly predicted that once mobilisation had been ordered it would lead to a war that would destroy European civilisation for many decades. Germany entered the war against the better judgment of many of its leaders, not because there was a major territorial issue that could not be peacefully settled, but because there was too much apocalyptic talk about conspiracies and a final struggle between Teutons and Slavs. There was a strong suicidal urge in German policy; to discuss its origins in terms of blindness and madness will probably take one further than explanations referring to 'objective conflict of interest'.

The first world war was not inevitable, but the second could not have been prevented once Hitler had seized power in Germany. The origins and the character of this movement and of fascism in general have been discussed for a long time and at great length; fascist and semi-fascist movements emerged in the nineteen-twenties in several European countries; wherever they came to power, they distinguished themselves by the leadership principle, the suppression of all democratic freedoms, rabid nationalist propaganda, and, in most cases, an aggressive foreign policy. The rise of fascism had more than one cause; there was the patriotic fever stirred up by what many Germans regarded as the unjust peace treaty of 1919, the resentment of the 'have-nots' (Italy, Germany) against the 'plutocrats' (Britain, France), the economic and social consequences of the great depression, the fear of bolshevism, the breakdown of liberalism, and the impotence of the social-democratic parties. It is doubtful whether Italian fascism by itself would have provoked a new world war, not because it was opposed to war, but simply because it was not strong enough. Left to his own resources, Mussolini was not capable of engaging in anything more ambitious than another colonial war on the Abyssinian scale. It took the triumph of nazism in Germany in 1933 to make a new war almost a foregone conclusion. Nazism was not only more aggressive than other European fascist movements, it also had the most far-reaching aspirations, and it had (or so it seemed to its leaders) the ability to challenge the whole world. From the day he came to power Hitler was firmly resolved to rearm Germany and he worked methodically not merely for the extension of German *Lebensraum* but for a new war. The Western powers tried to appease him by territorial concessions, by promising economic help and colonies. But Hitler wanted German hegemony in Europe and he was aware that this aim could not be attained by peaceful means. He prepared therefore, systematically and relentlessly, for a war which he was sure he would win and which he imagined would lead to a 'New Order' in Europe. After his early easy successes he threw all caution to the winds and tackled at the same time the British Empire, the Soviet Union and the United States, all this on the basis of a racial doctrine that, unlike communist ideology, had no universal appeal but, on the contrary, regarded all other peoples as in various degrees inferior. In the future world order, as the nazi leaders saw it, Germany would have satellites but no real allies. Hitler's early victories made the enterprise seem much less hopeless than it appears in retrospect; the element of surprise played an important role and so did the shortsightedness and weakness of Hitler's enemies. In early 1942 he seemed very near to attaining his aims; after so many striking victories, German military power appeared irresistible. At the height of Germany's triumph, Hitler's 'New Order' extended all over mainland Europe. Spain and Portugal were not involved in the war, and Sweden and Switzerland had stayed neutral, but the rest of the continent was in his hands; Soviet power had been pushed back to Moscow, the Volga, and the Caucasus. As an attempt to unite Europe under German leadership, the second world war was in some respects reminiscent of the Napoleonic campaigns, but Napoleon waged war against governments, not peoples. In the wake of his victories some of the achievements of the French Revolution were transplanted to other European lands. The benefits, if any, which the peoples of Europe derived from German occupation were purely incidental, such as factories established to increase German industrial output in areas beyond the range of Allied bombers and the roads built to improve communications with the front. What did these count against the suffering of the peoples, the atrocities committed by the occupiers, the general humiliation, the profound hatred of nazism and the Germans?

During the long nights of the war people all over Europe pondered the causes of the war and the reasons for the defeat. That nazism was unprecedented in its cruelty no one doubted, but how to explain the quick and total defeat of France and the other European countries? What were the lessons to be drawn for the postwar world? The old ruling classes had failed; if so, how to ensure that the old system (and the 'old gang') would not make a comeback after the end of hostilities? This mood was by no means limited to the occupied countries. It was equally strongly developed in England, which shared the general disgust with the past; after the war there would have to be a more just, more democratic society. Already the first world war had caused a minor social revolution, affecting, for instance, the status of women. If women had taken such an active part in the war effort they could clearly no longer be refused the right to vote. During the second world war many barriers of caste and convention had fallen. Millions of soldiers had seen foreign countries and had drawn comparisons with their own way of life at home. Their horizon had broadened, their expectations increased. They would be less easily satisfied in future. Some of the resistance movements developed fairly clear and detailed programmes for the postwar world, others remained vague. But there was a common denominator in the emphasis on sweeping change, the abolition of class privileges and the full restoration of freedom. Communists all over Europe profited from the new mood. Their unfortunate record during the years of the German-Soviet pact was forgotten, whereas the prominent role they had later played in the resistance movements was vividly remembered. Communist policy after 21 June 1941, had coincided with the national interests of the occupied European countries, and the communists had made the most of it. The 'bourgeois' parties were usually loosely connected factions, whereas the communist organisations were far more tightly knit and therefore in a much better position to survive suppression and resume their activities under the occupation. The Soviet Union had gained tremendous prestige after the tide of war had turned. The communists had always preached the superiority of Soviet society and all their predictions seemed to have come true. Communist influence was stronger in western than in eastern and central Europe, partly because communist traditions there were more deeply rooted, partly because western Europe was not exposed to direct contacts with the Soviet Union at the end of the war. Pro-Soviet enthusiasm in Europe usually grew with distance.

The war brought to the fore new policies and new men. Who would have believed in spring 1940 that ten years later a little known Brigadier General named de Gaulle, and two obscure teachers named Bidault and Mollet, would be among the central political figures in France? That two retired gentlemen, Adenauer and de Gasperi, living respectively near Cologne and in Vatican City, would emerge as the new leaders of their countries, inaugurating a new era in the history of Germany and Italy? Einar Gerhardsen, who was to be Norwegian prime minister for 16 years after the war, worked as a navvy during the German occupation, repairing roads. Kurt Schumacher, leader of the German socialists, Léon Blum, once and future prime minister of France, Novotny, the future Czech prime minister and Cyrankiewicz, the future Polish prime minister, were all in German prisons or concentration camps. Some of the old leaders had escaped to London, and the communists to Moscow; they now returned with the Allied armies. But even among the communists, where the question of succession was not usually decided by election, there were many new faces in addition to the long-established leaders of the Communist International such as Dimitrov, Rakosi, and Gott-wald, who seized power in Bulgaria, Hungary, and Czechoslovakia. There were those who had risen from the ranks and who had not been to Moscow during the war, men like Gomulka, Rajk, Kadar, and Tito. In Moscow they were slightly suspect from the very beginning but they were the representa-tives of a new generation of communists and Moscow could not altogether do without them.

Up to 1939 there had been a traditional equilibrium in Europe. War had broken out because one country, Germany, tried to upset that balance, annexing more and more neighbouring territories in an attempt to establish its hegemony over the whole of Europe. The end of the war brought the downfall and the complete destruction of nazism. But in the process the traditional balance of power in Europe was also destroyed. Britain, France, and the other European countries were greatly weakened. The Berlin-Rome axis had been defeated mainly owing to the military efforts of the new super-powers, America and the Soviet Union. Russia, as the result of the war, advanced far into the heart of Europe, and the old prewar alliances between France and eastern Europe were replaced by a much closer association between the new 'popular democracies' and the Soviet Union. Britain, France, Germany, and Italy were for years to become dependent on American assistance. The old European equilibrium was replaced by the global balance of power between America and Russia. Europe paid a terrible price for its disunity; its division into so many nation-states with conflicting interests. The fate of the continent was now being decided in Moscow and Washington. The eclipse of the old world seemed complete.

The Purge of the Collaborators

One immediate problem facing the victors was how to deal with those who had unleashed the war, and brought untold suffering to Europe. The cry to punish the losers had been heard after many a war; in 1918 there was a general demand to hang the Kaiser. But the second world war had not been fought in accordance with established rules. Nazism had been out to defeat not only the military forces of its opponents, it had sought to enslave and, in some cases, to destroy the civilian population. The German leaders were guilty, not only of the preparation of aggressive war, but also of war crimes (first used as a term in international law in 1906) and of crimes against humanity. The Allies formally agreed in July 1945 to prosecute and punish the main war criminals.

They soon realised the complications involved in this task. It was easy enough to establish the identity of the main war criminals, but what about the many others lower down in the hierarchy who had been instrumental in carrying out their policies? What to do with the rank and file members of organisations such as the fascist parties and the storm troopers? Were they all to be punished, and if so, by whom and in what way? The demand for punishment received fresh impetus in the Allied countries after the discovery of the extermination camps during the last weeks of the war. It seemed a matter of elementary justice, and at the same time a precondition for rebuilding a new Germany, that those responsible should answer for their crimes. But the Nazi Party in Germany had counted eight million members; it included most of the higher civil servants, almost the whole business and intellectual élite. How could a new Germany (or Austria or Italy) be built without the active cooperation of these men and women? Moreover, it soon appeared that denazification alone was not sufficient; it would be necessary to re-educate millions of people. But who would be in charge of this operation? The Allied armies had been trained to win a war, not to take up legal or educational assignments. It seemed inevitable that the Germans and the other peoples concerned should take an active part in purging their own ranks.

Denazification and the treatment of nazi collaborators varied greatly from country to country. The Americans and the British tackled it in a slow but methodical way: in the British zone more than two million cases had been examined when denazification ended in 1948. The Russians and French were more inclined to concentrate on the main criminals and to let the small fry escape punishment. Nor were they as particular in their choice of instruments to build the new Germany. Stalin distrusted the Germans, but he was willing to try out men who, regardless of their political past, would carry out instructions. In some countries the purges were short and violent. In Italy and in France thousands of fascists and suspected collaborators were lynched at the time of the liberation or executed on the basis of death sentences pronounced by self-appointed courts. Within a year or two the purge was virtually over in these countries, whereas in Germany, where it had got under way only slowly, it went on for many years. It took a long time to find some of the criminals and even longer to locate the surviving witnesses and the evidence. One of the most important trials, against the Auschwitz personnel, began only in 1963.

The severity of the purge, too, varied. In Belgium some 634,000 cases were opened after the liberation, an enormous figure for a country with eight million inhabitants; eventually only some 87,000 were brought to trial, of whom 77,000 were sentenced. In Austria, where nazism had been far more deeply rooted and much more widespread, only about 9,000 people were brought to trial, and there were only 35 death sentences. Among those who administered justice and among the police, there were few who had not been associated with nazism in one form or another. Frequently they were inclined to let those charged escape with nominal punishment. In Italy and France on the other hand the purge was sometimes used by individuals as a welcome occasion to settle accounts with political or personal enemies. Austrian justice was perverted on more than one occasion by a conspiracy of silence; no one had seen or heard evil. In the Netherlands about 150,000–200,000 men and women were detained after the war as suspected collaborators; to have dined in public with a German or to have subscribed to a collaborationist journal was sufficient reason for lodging charges. In Germany, and particularly in Austria, on the other hand, the mere fact that someone had been a high Gestapo official was not sufficient reason to bring to trial, unless specific crimes could be proved against him. It was argued that they had after all only carried out instructions. The question of obeying orders played a central role in the most famous of all war crime cases – the Nuremberg trial of 24 major German war criminals which was opened in August 1945 and went on for over a year. Among them were the main surviving nazi leaders such as Goering, Ribbentrop the Foreign Minister, Rosenberg the ideologist, and army commanders (such as Keitel and Jodl) and Doenitz. Hundreds of people took part in the preparation of the trial and the typewritten records cover more than five million pages. Many Germans were at first inclined to regard the trial as a travesty of justice, but the sheer weight of evidence had a considerable impact. Millions of innocent people had been murdered, and the account had to be settled. One of the Nuremberg defendants, Hans Frank, former Governor-General of Poland, said that 'a thousand years shall pass and this guilt of Germany will not be erased'. Others remained defiant to the end. When Julius Streicher, the leading Jew-baiter, mounted the steps of the gallows, his last words were 'Heil Hitler'. Hermann Goering, for many years the second most influential man in nazi Germany, described himself as essentially a man of peace and committed suicide a few hours before he was to be executed. Most of the accused were neither defiant nor repentant; they had not really known what was going on, and anyway they had obeyed orders. In the Third Reich, they said, it was only the word of the Fuehrer that had counted. Ten of the Nuremberg defendants were sentenced to death and executed, three were acquitted, the rest received prison terms of varying length. Twenty years after the end of the trial only one, Rudolf Hess, was still in prison at Soviet insistence, and there had been doubts about his sanity all along. The Nuremberg verdict concerned not only individuals; entire organisations were found guilty of crimes against humanity.

The trial has been criticised, and not only in Germany, for a variety of reasons. The list of the accused was to a certain extent arbitrary; in the dock, alongside the most powerful political and military figures, was a radio commentator and in one case a son was substituted for the father. The defendants were assisted by counsel, but not all the evidence could be introduced. When discussing German aggression against Poland in 1939, the lawyers could not mention the secret protocol under which Poland was divided between Germany and the Soviet Union. There were more basic misgivings: the accused had been charged with violations of international law, but such law was binding only on states, not on individuals. Individuals, it was maintained, could be brought to justice only under the laws of their own country, not on the basis of a new order established only after a war.

There were serious inconsistencies in the Nuremberg trial which caused much concern to legal experts whose main preoccupation was with international law rather than political necessities. But what other course was open? The crimes committed by the National Socialists were in many ways unprecedented, and it would have been unthinkable not to punish the perpetrators simply because there were no legal precedents. It was imperfect justice, but there was no alternative.

Many other trials followed, of army leaders charged with war crimes (such as von Manstein), and of those running economic enterprises which had employed slave labour or been in other ways actively involved in Hitler's policy of aggression (I.G. Farben, Flick, Krupp), of senior officials of the German Foreign Ministry, and, of course, those in charge of police and other special units involved in the final solution, the murder of five million Jews. These trials went on for many years. Some of the main criminals disappeared without trace, re-emerging after a few years in another country. Some had stayed behind, but the evidence against them was almost impossible to assemble; their victims were dead and their accomplices unlikely to break silence. Yet the German legal machine, whatever its other shortcomings, worked with great persistence and thoroughness. Once a case had been opened, it was not easily given up. Originally it had been decided that 20 years would be sufficient to complete investigations and trials, but in 1965 thousands of cases were still unfinished and it was decided, against considerable opposition, to prolong the term.

Denazification was not an unqualified success; not infrequently a lowly official was severely punished while his superior got away scot free or with a mere fine. There were other anomalies which strengthened the belief of many Germans that at Nuremberg and in the subsequent trials justice had not been done; the victors had simply taken their revenge. The full horrors of the extermination camps were brought home to the public only as a result of the trials of the late fifties (including the famous Eichmann trial) and it was then that the majority of Germans accepted the facts and tried, each in his fashion, to come to terms with the past. Eichmann, who had been in charge of the Gestapo department dealing with the final solution, escaped to Latin America after the war. He was traced and kidnapped by the Israelis and brought to trial in Jerusalem. These revelations had a profound impact on the younger generation who refused to accept the arguments so often used by their elders that they had not known, and that in any case in a totalitarian régime there was no way of resisting the state. The moral issues became a subject of wide public debate, preoccupying writers and theologians as well as ordinary citizens.

It was up to the German people to confront its own past. Re-education by the Allies was bound to remain a dead letter, for even if they had been much better prepared for such an assignment, they would have found it impossible to re-educate a people of more than 70 million. The Western Allies had decided – to quote one of the directives – that 'Germany will not be occupied for the purpose of liberation but as a defeated enemy nation'. Fraternisation was strictly forbidden in the early days even with the not too numerous Germans who had been active opponents of the régime and had suffered for it. Yet the Allies soon realised that to run the essential services they had to employ specialists and administrators most of whom had been in one way or another connected with nazism. Later on, when an independent German administration emerged, first on a local basis and then state-wide, there was a fairly high percentage of former members of the Nazi Party among those in key positions. True, no leading nazi could hope to re-enter German political life, but rank and file members or fellow travellers usually regarded their past as a youthful aberration; they had long shed their nazi beliefs. Some sincerely tried to make amends. But the very fact that such people were permitted to take up key positions in public life so soon after the downfall of the Third Reich aroused much distrust outside Germany.

The other European countries faced similar problems on a lesser scale. In eastern Europe and in the occupied sections of Russia there had been no major quislings. There the Germans had not looked for collaborators as they had in western Europe; they imposed their own direct control over what they regarded as racial inferiors. There had been low level collaboration, thousands had volunteered to take part in the final solution, but no political or intellectual leaders were compromised; there was no native nazi movement whose members had to be prosecuted. Hungary and Rumania were exceptions, but even there the purge did not constitute a major problem. In Italy the repression of fascism was violent but short-lived. Special courts established after the liberation dealt with the cases of high-ranking and politically active fascists; those who had merely been rank and file members found it relatively easy to re-enter political life or to resume their professional careers. Of the 800,000 civil servants, many of whom had been members of the Fascist Party, no more than a few hundred were removed from their posts. There were only a few major trials, the most important of military leaders like Roatta (who escaped in the middle of his trial) and Graziani. Some fascists, or suspected fascists, were lynched or sentenced to death by partisan tribunals during the first weeks after the liberation of northern Italy where Mussolini made his last stand in 1944–5. Their exact number is not known. The official figure of '1,732 murders and disappearances' is probably too low; the numbers given by neo-fascists grossly exaggerated. After the amnesty of October 1946, only 3–4,000 former fascists or war criminals remained in prison.

Italy and Austria were by far the most lenient in their treatment of fascism and national-socialism. Since so many citizens had been involved, it was thought that only the most prominent could be eliminated from public life. But there were other reasons as well: Mussolini had not been able to establish a fully totalitarian régime in Italy; its language had been extreme, its practice less so. Neither the army nor the state administration had been completely penetrated by fascism, and there were many leading intellectual figures who had not belonged to the party. The régime had not been noted for its humanitarian character, but it had killed far fewer of its opponents than Hitlerism. In contrast to nazism, there had been in fascism a comic opera element which found its expression during the liberation. When the partisans took over a village or a small town, the *Casa del Popolo* became the new communist (or socialist) headquarters; there were violent scenes, but the few prominent fascists usually escaped, while the rest simply denied having belonged to the blackshirts. The scene was repeated all over Italy.

The French purge was much more radical. According to the official figures there were 170,000 cases, resulting in 120,000 sentences, including 4,785 death sentences of which almost 2,000 were carried out. But these figures do not tell the whole story; according to official estimates some 4,500 collaborators were killed by partisans during or after the liberation; unofficial sources give considerably higher figures. These summary executions were particularly numerous in the Midi, the partisan stronghold. Those affected were usually local police chiefs or Gestapo agents who had collaborated with the occupiers and caused the death of Frenchmen, but there were also cases of political and private vengeance. Later on the purge became systematic. The most famous trials were those of Pétain and Laval, the Vichy Head of State and Foreign Minister respectively. Laval was condemned to death and executed; Pétain, in view of his advanced age, was imprisoned.

Among those executed there were writers and journalists, while some of the main pillars of the Vichy régime were not even brought to trial. A well-known admiral (Estava) was given a long prison term, but his superior, whose instructions he had carried out, had meanwhile been reintegrated into the French army. Many observers thought that Laval, whatever his crimes, should have been given a fuller chance to defend himself. In a few cases it appeared that the record of the judge or the public prosecutor during the occupation was no better than that of the accused. There had been relatively few active resisters, in contrast to the truly staggering number of those who after the liberation claimed to have resisted from the first hour. Feelings of guilt were widespread, and at least some of those brought to trial in 1945 had to serve as scapegoats for the collective bad conscience of their compatriots.

In France more death sentences were imposed than elsewhere, but the other liberated countries took the purge no less seriously. More than 150,000 arrests were made in Holland, 18,000 in Norway, where collaboration had been rare. In these two countries, as well as in Belgium and Denmark, the purge was more systematic than in France and Italy: thousands were deprived of their civil rights and banned from pursuing their professions. Leading writers, like Hamsun and Charles Maurras, were also arrested, but their lives were spared on the ground of their advanced age and diminished responsibility. Some of the leading collaborators and nazi agents, such as Degrelle, the Belgian, and Ante Pavelić, the Croat dictator, escaped and were not apprehended.

No one was completely satisfied with the way the purge was carried out. In some ways it went too far, in others it was not radical enough. But conditions were still far from normal: the war was just over, the new governments were faced with a great many urgent tasks, their authority was not yet firmly established. Everyone agreed that nazism had to be eradicated and the collaborators punished, but in the prevailing circumstances, and with passions still running high, no one could expect exemplary justice.

Postwar Politics

Political developments throughout western Europe followed certain common patterns. Immediately after the war there was a marked trend towards the left. In France and Italy the communists polled more votes than ever before, and for the first time they were represented in government. In 1945, too, the Labour Party came to power in one of the greatest political landslides in recent British history. There were communists in the first postwar governments of Belgium, Denmark, and most of the German Länder; in Norway the merger between the Labour and Communist Parties was mooted, but the idea was abandoned. Monarchy was under heavy fire: in Italy, after a referendum, it had to go; in Greece and Belgium it just survived, but only after concessions had been made to make it more palatable. The right wing was everywhere on the retreat; the extreme right had been compromised through collaboration with nazism and the moderate conservatives, too, were identified with the old order that had suffered defeat and which few wanted restored. In the given economic situation there was little scope for the traditional advocates of *laissez-faire* liberalism; planning and the demand for nationalisation had many powerful supporters. There was considerable pressure for sweeping reforms in politics and society; in Italy this was the famous *vento del nord* (the north wind), northern Italy having been the scene of most of the fighting between fascists and anti-fascists towards the end of the war. The mood did not last: within two or three years the centre parties had established their ascendancy on the continent and the communists were again in opposition. In Britain, too, Labour was voted out of office in 1951. Partly it was the result of the stabilisation of conditions generally and of economic improvement. The communists did not always play their cards well: in Belgium, and on a much larger scale in Greece, they had made a frontal attack on the government immediately after the end of the war and had been defeated. International relations also had a considerable impact; as the Cold War developed and the Stalinist era reached its height, European communists had to pursue extreme policies which left them in almost complete isolation. But this split was not widely foreseen in 1945 and it is to the immediate postwar period that we must now turn.

BRITAIN: THE LABOUR REFORMS

Since the critical days of 1940 Britain had been ruled by a coalition government, dominated by the Tories, but in which Labour had considerable influence. The two parties were agreed that after the war new elections should be held, and so in May 1945 the wartime coalition was replaced by a caretaker government. In the general elections of July 1945, Labour gained a sweeping victory, a majority of 145 over all other parties. There was general admiration for Churchill the great war leader, but Churchill was also the leader of the Conservative Party, identified with the old England of dole queues and hunger marches, slums and millions of unemployed. Churchill's election call to 'leave these socialist dreamers to their Utopias of nightmares' left his listeners unmoved. There was a general urge for radical change, for greater social justice. The wartime government had in some ways taken account of these aspirations; it had paved the road to the welfare state by sponsoring the Beveridge Report on the extension of social services after the war. But Churchill and the other conservatives strongly doubted whether a country facing bankruptcy could afford these benefits. They were worried about the revolution of expectations that had taken place during the war, but their doubts, justified or not, were very much out of line with the national mood, as the election results proved; sections of the middle class and much of the white collar vote went over to Labour. Of the 393 Labour Members of Parliament, 253 had been elected for the first time. A whole new generation was now entering politics, the wartime captains and majors, many young teachers, lawyers and civil servants, among them Hugh Gaitskell and Harold Wilson, two future leaders of the party.

The Labour Party differed in essential respects from the continental socialist parties. It was gradualist in inspiration, not revolutionary; pragmatic in its approach and it united in its ranks people of various political persuasions such as liberals, Christian socialists, and a few orthodox Marxists. This was perhaps not conducive to doctrinal clarity, but it made Labour a people's party, unlike either the social-democratic or the communist parties on the continent, whose social bases were narrower. Parochial rather than internationalist in its outlook, it had never played a very active part in the international socialist movement. To the revolutionaries it was a typical reformist party, drab, lacking direction and perspective, aiming at piecemeal change and ultimately a welfare state, not at a real socialist society. But with all this the Labour Party enjoyed considerable prestige abroad. Other parties had perhaps more sophisticated programmes, but the Labour Party was the one example of a movement trying in its policy to combine democracy, parliamentary action, and social justice. The continental social democrats had been less successful, while the communists preached a socialism without democracy which was not attractive to the west European working class with its deep-rooted democratic traditions and its instinctive opposition to dictatorship of any sort.

The great problem facing the Labour Party in 1945 was to build a welfare state in a nearly bankrupt country. Direct war damage was comparatively small, but for more than five years the great majority of the adult population had either been in uniform or had worked in war industries or other unproductive enterprises. Britain had always been basically a poor country; without significant sources of raw material (other than coal) it had made its living by its industrial skill and its position as a centre of world trade and finance. For its livelihood it had to rely largely on imports of food and raw materials, but as a result of the war it had become far more difficult to pay for these imports: Britain's income from foreign investments was now only a fraction of what it had been. The inescapable conclusion was that Britain would have 'to export or die'. But how to export, unless there was sufficient money to pay for the raw materials in the first place? The gold and dollar reserves were down to about 450 million pounds sterling against an external debt of 3,500 million pounds accumulated during the war. It was a vicious circle, and a major American loan was needed to save the country from insolvency. Eventually, a loan of 1,100 million pounds was arranged with the United States; 'No comparable credit in time of peace has ever been given before,' said Lord Keynes, who had negotiated it. But this was no more than first aid, a massive injection, a 'springboard not a sofa' (in Churchill's words). The same problem, the dollar shortage, was to recur time and time again in the following years.

The new Labour government, unlike the parliamentary group of the party, included few new faces; the average age of the ministers was over 60; they had all been in politics for many years. Its inner core were men of considerable strength and experience. Initially there were doubts whether Clement Attlee was the best man to be Prime Minister; quiet, self-effacing, avoiding all histrionics, he was in many respects the very antithesis of Churchill. Instead of the flamboyant gestures and the rolling memorable phrases, the public was now treated to short factual statements, lacking sparkle or inspiration. Attlee, one of his contemporaries said, was such a modest man because there was so much he had to be modest about. But he had a great deal of common sense; he was tough in his own quiet way, and was probably better equipped to cope with the problems of the postwar world than Churchill or any other leader inside the Labour Party. He had the strong support of Ernest Bevin, who had been appointed, somewhat surprisingly, Foreign Secretary. Bevin, representing the trade union element in the party, had been one of its main pillars for many years, serving in the wartime coalition as Minister of Labour. He tackled his new assignment with great enthusiasm. Relations with Washington were traditionally cordial and he was certain that ties with Russia would be equally friendly: 'Left would be able to speak to Left'; they had after all a common language. On Britain's other postwar problems such as India and Palestine he envisaged compromise solutions; these could be reached, given a minimum of reason and goodwill.

Soon Bevin realised that Britain's overseas problems were much less tractable than he had thought, that the Russians usually did not speak the same language, and that there was no meeting of minds even when they did. He came under heavy criticism from the left wing of the party for not pursuing a 'socialist foreign policy'. But what scope was there for a socialist foreign policy in the postwar world dominated by America, the bulwark of capitalism, and Russia, which though socialist in name pursued a foreign policy that had surprisingly little in common with the ideals of British left wingers?

It began to dawn on many of them that there was far less freedom of action for that 'third force' between America and Russia which they had so often discussed.

Herbert Morrison acted as Foreign Secretary after Bevin's death, but during most of the Labour government's span he devoted his time to domestic affairs. He had been the leader of London's socialists for many years and done much to reform the London County Council. Like Bevin he did not have the benefit of a higher education and distrusted intellectuals in politics; he believed they lacked a sense of reality. At the 1946 Labour Party conference he said: 'The government has gone as far left as is consistent with sound reason and national interest.'

The left wing was represented in the cabinet by Sir Stafford Cripps and Aneurin Bevan, the former as President of the Board of Trade and subsequently Chancellor of the Exchequer, the latter as Minister of Health, responsible for establishing Britain's National Health Service. It would be difficult to imagine two political figures more dissimilar in character and background: Cripps an eminent lawyer, rich and impeccably upper-middle class, a vegetarian and teetotaller, austere, even Spartan, in his whole way of life. A man of very powerful intellect, he notably lacked the common touch; in the past he had often quarrelled with his party, whose policy he considered insufficiently radical. A devout Christian and a lay preacher, he had advocated close collaboration with the communists in the nineteen-thirties, and as a result had been temporarily excluded from the party. Bevan, a miner's son from Wales, had worked in the pits as a boy. He once wrote that he hated the Tory Party with a deep burning hatred; his 'lower than vermin' speech (referring to the Conservatives) probably cost his party hundreds of thousands of votes. A man of great vitality and passion and a brilliant speaker, he combined a belief in fundamentalist socialism with considerable personal charm, diplomatic talent, and an ability to win over reluctant opponents to his schemes. This he showed in his dealings with Britain's general medical practitioners, deeply distrustful of the new health scheme. With all his left wing militancy he had few illusions about the character and aims of Stalinism, and during the Berlin blockade he was one of the leading hawks in the cabinet when the question of breaking the blockade was discussed. Unlike Cripps, he did not despise the good things in life. With his comparatively early death, the left wing in the Labour Party lost its one leader of stature.

These then were the men who set out in August 1945 to build a new Britain. Within less than a year they had introduced 75 bills, a giant programme of nationalisation and of social service. In December 1945 the Bank of England was nationalised, and, later, civil air transport. The coal industry was nationalised in 1946–7, so were public transport, electricity and gas, the railways, road haulage, and the steel industry. (Road haulage and steel were denationalised by the Conservative government which replaced Labour.) The main National Insurance bill became law in 1946. Compulsory and universal in its scope, the whole adult population was insured for sickness, unemployment, and retirement benefits; there were widow pensions, maternity and death grants. In the same year medicine was nationalised, a somewhat crude but accurate term, for under the National Health Service free medical services were provided for all. It cost far more than originally anticipated: within a year after it had become law more than five million pairs of spectacles had been issued and almost two hundred million free prescriptions filled. The National Health Service became the second largest item in Britain's expenditure, exceeding £500m. a year. Soon the British became accustomed to free medicine; there were controversies as to how to run the Service, but the principle was universally accepted. The National Health Service was in many ways a symbol of Labour's postwar reforms; long overdue, they were exceedingly difficult to finance. The Labour government tried at one and the same time, in the words of John Strachey:

—to eliminate gross want from the population;
—to eliminate the major economic hazards of working-class life – unemployment, sickness, old age;
—to endow the family by children's allowances;
—to undertake both in the public and private sector a massive programme of investment, amounting to a general re-equipment of sections of British industry and absorbing over 20 per cent the national income;
—to build 200,000 houses a year, year after year;
—to raise the school leaving age;
—to raise the volume of British exports to over 170 per cent of their prewar volume;
—to maintain a rearmament programme of some £1,500m. a year.

Such a programme strained the resources of an impoverished country to the utmost.

Nineteen forty-five and 1946 were hard years for Britain. The hope had been expressed during the war that 'things would not be the same again' but in fact many old worries continued to beset the country; life certainly did not become any easier. The ugliness of the big cities, the poor food in the restaurants and the limited selection of goods in the shops depressed both natives and foreign visitors. In some respects control and rationing became even stricter in this postwar period of austerity.

Housing, too, was a major problem. A White Paper published in 1944 stated that 758,000 new houses would have to be built; it seemed an enormous figure at the time, but the fact soon emerged that even this was quite insufficient. When the government failed to provide flats and houses, some militant groups decided in favour of self help: squatters invaded empty houses and blocks of flats and, often for days, refused to move until alternative accommodation was found. Army camps were converted for civilian use, hardly a desirable solution. The squatters' movement succeeded in dramatising the plight of many people, and compelled the government to give high priority to new housing schemes and to ban temporarily all non-essential building.

The transition to a peacetime economy was hampered by many obstacles; productivity was low and there was an increasing number of labour disputes. Raw materials, even coal, were in short supply. These difficulties reached a climax during the winter of 1946–7, when there were massive snowfalls in this, the most severe winter of the century, which disrupted the whole life of a country unprepared for near arctic conditions. Transport stopped, power stations were now and again closed down for lack of fuel. Electricity was drastically cut. The acute fuel crisis came on top of the permanent convertibility crisis, and as a result two million workers were without employment. Electric fires were banned for many hours during the day, there was no greyhound racing and even television, just outgrowing its infancy, was drastically cut. The old 'Keep left' and 'Let us face the future' programmes of 1945 vintage seemed inappropriate in this national emergency, which lasted for many weeks and in March 1947 the snows came back, and when everyone thought that the worst was over, the flood waters hit Britain. There was great gloom and a tendency to make the government responsible for natural catastrophes over which they clearly had no control: 'Starve with Strachey and Shiver with Shinwell' became the new slogan, referring to the ministers of food and fuel respectively. When Mr Shinwell argued that the crisis was really a blessing in disguise, the reaction of the public was not too friendly even though, in retrospect, Shinwell was not far from the mark. Only as a result of this acute crisis did many people begin to realise what they were up against. During the previous 18 months they had been preoccupied with remembrance of things past or dreams of the future, oblivious of the stark realities of the present. After the winter of 1946–7 no one could doubt any longer that postwar recovery would be an uphill struggle and that short of a major effort Britain would hardly find its place in the postwar world. The great wave of enthusiasm began to ebb and many early illusions were shattered.

These illusions had not been limited to domestic issues, for there had also been a great deal of wishful thinking on world affairs. 'Particularly when the Labour Party is in office, foreign policy becomes the last refuge of Utopianism' (Denis Healey). Few people were prepared for the postwar confrontation with communism; when British troops had been used against communist partisans in Greece not only the left had been up in arms; public opinion, including The Times and most of the press, had protested. Communism, it was generally thought, was after all only a radical democratic and social reform movement. It had some unlovely aspects but all things considered was eminently suited for countries that lacked a democratic tradition of long standing. This belief persisted for several years after the end of the war; Orwell's *Animal Farm* was read by many when it appeared in 1945 as an amusing fairy tale that had no bearing on contemporary issues. The reports on forced labour camps in Stalin's Russia were dismissed as slanderous fabrications. It was thought to be the western statesmen's fault if they failed to get along with Stalin and his representatives; had they shown more friendship and sympathy, most of the difficulties could have been removed. Churchill said in a famous speech in Fulton in March 1946:

> From Stettin on the Baltic to Trieste on the Adriatic, an iron curtain has descended across the continent. Behind that line lie all the capitals of the ancient states of central and eastern Europe – Warsaw, Berlin, Prague, Vienna, Budapest, Belgrade, Bucharest and Sofia. . . . From what I have seen of our Russian friends and allies during the war I am convinced that there is nothing they admire so much as strength and nothing for which they have less respect than military weakness.

This was, of course, a mere statement of fact, but Churchill was bitterly attacked for it; had he not advocated intervention in Russia back in 1918? Was he not responsible for the growing tension between West and East? There was mounting evidence during 1946 and 1947 that Soviet policy was perhaps not as altruistic and peaceful as many had believed, but a real change in public opinion came only in 1948 after the communist takeover in Prague, the Berlin blockade, and the excommunication of Tito by Moscow. If a staunch communist like Tito could not get along with Stalin, even the Labour left wing was willing to admit that there was perhaps a grain of truth after all in Ernest Bevin's complaints about the Russians.

The determination of the early postwar period not to rest until social justice prevailed in Britain evaporated as the formidable obstacles to radical change were more fully understood. In later years there has been a tendency to belittle the achievements of 1945–47: 'The nationalisation of half a dozen major industries, the construction of an all-in system of social security and a free health service, and the tentative application of planning to the national economy – the achievement of these reforms seemed to have exchanged the content of British socialism' (Richard Crossman). But these reforms carried out in a few years were a major social achievement, and they initiated a long-term shift of political power and influence. It was not a dramatic revolution and its effects were not immediately visible. The results certainly fell short of expectations, but all things considered it was a substantial achievement with far-reaching consequences and it served as a model for many other countries in the postwar world.

FRANCE: THE FOURTH REPUBLIC

Soon after the fall of France in June 1940, leaflets were published, signed by a virtually unknown Brigadier General: 'France has lost a battle, it has not lost the war.' It was the beginning of the Free French movement, which in France's darkest hour carried on the struggle. 'Honneur et patrie, voici la France!' In 1940 it seemed a hopeless venture; four years later General Charles de Gaulle returned to Paris and became the head of the provisional French government. The history of the Fourth Republic thus begins on 18 June 1940, with de Gaulle's first broadcast from London.

De Gaulle was born in Lille in 1890 and chose the career of a professional army officer. He fought in the first world war and commanded an armoured division in 1940. In the years between he developed interesting new concepts about the army of the future and the role of the tank forces. In June 1940, at the time of the defeat, he was serving as Secretary of State for the Army in Paul Reynaud's government. He was not at all widely known and no one assumed at the time that his desertion (for his refusal to return to France from London was technically desertion) was to inaugurate a new chapter in the history of France. The policies of de Gaulle, one of the most striking figures in the history of postwar Europe, evoked mixed reactions from the very beginning: admiration and total acceptance on the part of his followers, suspicion and violent antagonism on the part of many others. Frenchmen and foreigners alike have been repelled by his colossal egocentricity and his dictatorial and capricious style even when he was at his best. But everyone agreed that there has been no one quite like him in recent French or European history. What he said on one occasion about the Jews applies to himself with even greater justice; he was absolutely sure of himself and domineering. De Gaulle was totally convinced that he had a historical mission to save France, to restore its honour and dignity, to make it again a great nation. Everything else had to be subordinated to this belief; it was always *la France seule* and he her only legitimate representative; 'J'étais la France', he wrote later; politicians, parties and the Allies, existed for him only in relation to his own image of eternal France and his mission on her behalf. It was an outdated, romantic vision of eighteenth-century or earlier vintage, but it was of considerable relevance at a time when there was no leadership and when many other Frenchmen despaired. Churchill and de Gaulle never got along well; perhaps they had more than a few traits of character in common.

In London in 1940 a few followers gathered around him: Cassin, Maurice Schumann, Pleven, Soustelle, Palewski, Raymond Aron. Little known then, the names were to recur frequently in the annals of the Fourth and Fifth Republics. The political and social character of the Free French movement was vague: de Gaulle was impeccably bourgeois and Catholic, tending towards traditional right-wing attitudes; certainly not a fervent republican. He took a poor view of the *république des camarades* whose corruption had contributed so much to the 1940 débâcle. His style was authoritarian; he never pretended to be a democrat or a socialist. Yet his movement, setting itself in deliberate opposition to Vichy, was driven by the very logic of events towards a *rapprochement* with the left and left-of-centre groups which were its natural allies. Gradually, most of the resistance groups that had been organised in France accepted his leadership and some of their representatives joined him in London.

The years of exile were unhappy ones for the General. The British and the Americans gave him help, but refused to treat him as an equal; in their eyes he was a deserving French patriot, but his claims to be recognised *de facto* and *de jure* as head of the French government in exile were not taken seriously. He was ordered around by the Allies: to make a trip, to give a speech on a certain day, to be silent on another. It was a galling experience, and his self-esteem was deeply wounded; as a result he behaved more imperiously than ever, refusing to compromise, regarding himself as the sole authority for all decisions concerning the future of France. Churchill and Roosevelt found him quite insufferable.

After the landing in North Africa in November 1942 the centre of the French political scene shifted from London to Algiers where, in the following year, a Consultative Assembly was established. For a little while the future of the Free French movement seemed in the balance; Giraud, a higher-ranking general than de Gaulle, who had escaped from a German prison camp, staked his claim to be the leader of all Free French forces. But de Gaulle's position had already become so strong that the Allied leaders, albeit somewhat reluctantly, had to opt for him. De Gaulle had now around him a group of distinguished advisers; some of them well-known politicians such as Vincent Auriol, Pierre Cot, Henri Queille, others as yet relatively unknown: Pierre Mendès-France and Jean Monnet. The communists, too, were represented, and three days before the Allied landings in Normandy a Provisional Government was established in Algiers. Its aims, other than the liberation of France, were not made very clear. In de Gaulle's many speeches the vision of a future France always figures prominently but, the idea of French grandeur apart, no one had a clear notion of what kind of régime the General envisaged; was it to be a parliamentary democracy more or less on the pattern of the Third Republic? This seemed unlikely in view of the general criticism levelled against its shortcomings. The future of France depended, of course, to a considerable extent on the changes that had been taking place inside France.

The various local resistance groups inside the country had joined forces in

May 1943 in a National Council (CNR – Conseil National de la Résistance). All political groups were represented in the CNR, which was headed by Georges Bidault, then a left wing Catholic. The communists had at first kept out of the resistance movement, but with Hitler's attack on the Soviet Union in June 1941 the 'imperialist' war (as they had called it) turned into a patriotic, anti-fascist war from the Soviet point of view and they joined it wholeheartedly. Because of their devotion and their superior organisation, they soon gained a dominant position within the main partisan group, the FFI (Forces françaises de l'Intérieur). There was tension between them and other resistance movements and the communist attempts to seize all key positions and to impose their will on other groups aroused suspicions. But the situation in France did not resemble that in Greece or Yugoslavia, and the country was spared a civil war. An attempt was made to work out a common political programme, in the Charter of the CNR. It was not clearly defined, but the general trend was obvious: opposing 'economic and financial feudalism', the programme called for the nationalisation of some of the key industries and services and stressed the need for a plan. It stood for the establishment of 'true economic and social democracy', the introduction of comprehensive social services, the principle of merit as the only criterion in education. It was very much an expression of the general demand for sweeping changes in the postwar world, 'la révolution par la loi', in the words of Bidault.

On 25 August 1944, de Gaulle returned to Paris. The General's path along the Champs Elysées turned into a moving demonstration; Parisians gave him a hero's welcome amid scenes of mass enthusiasm. France was free again! French flags, the Cross of Lorraine, the symbol of French patriotism, and portraits of de Gaulle appeared now in every window, replacing the picture of the old Marshal of Vichy who, with the remnants of his government, had escaped to Germany. A fortnight later a new government was constituted; de Gaulle refused to proclaim a new republic as his advisers had suggested. He argued that he had represented France all along, that continuity had been preserved. It was typical of the man and his style. The government was a mixture of the old and the new France. The 22 members, of whom 13 represented political parties, included most of the men who were to play leading roles in the annals of the Fourth Republic: Bidault, Mendès-France, René Mayer, Pleven, Teitgen, Lacoste, and de Menthon. There were also two communists, one of them, Tillon, a well-known partisan leader.

The new government faced a number of most urgent tasks. The war against Germany had not yet been won, not even the whole of France had been liberated. France was expected to make a real contribution to the war effort in the last phase of the struggle. Eventually a million Frenchmen were enlisted but more than twice that number of forced labourers and prisoners of war were still in German camps. The economic situation had gone from bad to worse; the output of coal, to give but one example, was down to a fraction of the level of 1938. There was no shortage of food in the provinces, but communication between town and country had broken down. For Christmas 1944 Parisians could buy apples but little else; even bread was in short supply.

Politically, the country was on the brink of anarchy; outside Paris the decisions of the central government were largely ignored. Partisan leaders and local chieftains effectively ruled large parts of France. De Gaulle began to tour the country almost immediately after his return to restore the authority of the central government. In October 1944 the 'Patriotic Guards' (the self-appointed local militia) were dissolved and the central organs of administration and security took over. Financial problems were pressing and inflation was severe. Mendès-France, the French Stafford Cripps, wanted to apply drastic measures and to introduce a régime of austerity: to block bank accounts, to tax illicit profits, to devalue the currency, as had recently been done in Belgium. René Pleven, his main antagonist, proposed easier remedies such as floating a loan instead of introducing stringent controls. De Gaulle and the cabinet opted for Pleven's policy, whereupon Mendès-France resigned in April 1945. In later years many realised that this was a fateful mistake, for the failure to apply drastic measures at that turning point was to bedevil the French economy for a long time to come.

France also faced crises in some of its overseas territories: Indo-China, Syria, and the Lebanon. The country had still to regain its status as a big power; much to de Gaulle's chagrin, France had not been represented at the conferences of Yalta and Potsdam. The General put most of the blame on the West, and snubbed the new American and British ambassadors, singling out for favourable attention Bogomolov, the Soviet ambassador, thus establishing a pattern that he was to follow for many years. But the Russians were not particularly forthcoming; when de Gaulle went to Moscow in January 1945 Stalin, too, had found him a very difficult interlocutor. Since France was no longer in Stalin's eyes a country of great consequence, de Gaulle and his ministers were largely ignored.

It was de Gaulle's ambition to take a position in world affairs somewhere in between the Anglo-Saxons and the Russians, but the time was not yet ripe for such grand designs. The General was not greatly interested in economic affairs, even though these had to be given priority in the early postwar period. The average Frenchman did not want to hear about a policy of grandeur; the General admitted as much in his *Memoirs*: 'Which are the immediate preoccupations of Frenchmen? The majority above all wants to survive!' Problems of supply and transport and the reorganisation of agriculture and industry figured high on the list of priorities. Electricity was down to half the prewar output; rationing, unlike that in Britain, was very badly organised. The newspapers for the most part were given new names and new editors. Some of the reforms contemplated during the war were now carried out. In December 1944 the coal mines were nationalised, and shortly after, the four biggest banks, Air France, and certain large factories, such as the Renault motor works. In some cases the decision on what was to be nationalised was made dependent on the behaviour of the owners during the occupation.

Considerable shifts had taken place in French political life. Some of the leaders of the Third Republic, such as Herriot, Léon Blum, and Paul Reynaud, were still in German prisons. None of them was held in high esteem despite the fact that they had suffered during the occupation; only Léon Blum was again to play a leading part in French politics. The whole domestic line-up had changed; the communists were now the strongest party with some 900,000 members. Their dubious behaviour during the first two years of the war was forgotten. Thorez, their leader, returned from his Moscow exile and became a minister of state. The communists had an almost unassailable position in some parts of France, and could probably have seized power if they had so wanted in the anarchy of the first months after the liberation. But the wartime alliance was still in force and the communists were not encouraged by Moscow to pursue such revolutionary aims. Their ambition, on the contrary, was now to be part of the government coalition and to be accepted by the other political parties. De Gaulle distrusted them because of their dependence on Moscow's guidance, but he could not ignore them. The socialists did not in principle reject cooperation with them, but they were not particularly enthusiastic either. They were afraid of being swallowed up by the communists with their much superior monolithic organisation; events in eastern Europe, and in particular the fate of the socialist parties behind the Iron Curtain, seemed to justify their suspicions. Léon Blum had written during the war that without socialism, democracy was imperfect; without democracy, socialism was helpless. The communists certainly demonstrated that a non-democratic party was not necessarily helpless, but their ruthless efficiency did not make them any more attractive. Soon, most of the good will and the wartime solidarity disappeared and gave place to bitter strife on the left.

Meanwhile the socialists were preoccupied with putting their own house in order and the leadership was gradually taken over by new men. Some of their traditional working-class support had passed to the communists, but the socialists who in October 1945 obtained 24 per cent of the vote (in comparison with the 26 per cent of the communists), still had their proletarian base in the country and also considerable support among white-collar workers and the intelligentsia. The MRP was a new party; its leaders were left-of-centre

Catholics like Bidault, but much of its support came from regions that had been traditionally conservative (Normandy, Alsace, Brittany). There was no strong right-wing party at the time except for a group of 'Independents', and millions of conservative votes went for that reason to the MRP. The Radical Socialist Party, the main pillar of the Third Republic, was now only a shadow of its former self, polling six per cent of the total. It was moreover a house divided, for there was nothing in common between the left-wing planned economy advocated by Mendès-France and the old fashioned *laissez-faire* liberalism such as proposed by René Mayer. De Gaulle had no organised political support during these early days. The old socialist and radical leaders refused to work under him, objecting to his dictatorial style. The communists demanded key positions in the cabinet such as foreign affairs, defence, and domestic affairs, which he refused to give them; he offered them five other posts which were not acceptable to them. In October 1945 a referendum was held on the character of the new Consultative Assembly to be elected. The results at first sight seemed to reinforce de Gaulle's position; there was to be no return to the anarchy of the Third Republic. But the unanimity was more apparent than real. The three parties which claimed to be the legitimate heirs of the Resistance (communists, socialists, MRP) polled 75 per cent of the vote and elected de Gaulle head of the new government. But they wanted strict limitations of his power. Relations between the government and the Assembly were strained; the General had been deeply offended by the demand to reduce the military budget by 20 per cent made by a socialist parliamentarian. On 20 January 1946, he called a cabinet meeting; appearing in full uniform and without any forewarning, he told his ministers that he had decided to resign. The transition from war to peace was over, the political parties, he said, could now assume full responsibility for affairs of state; de Gaulle was no longer needed.

In his heart the General did not, of course, feel so optimistic about the ability of the political parties. He was in fact not at all happy about the way things had turned out. He was fairly certain that the parties would fail again, as they had in the Third Republic, and that his hour was still to come. But for the time being he had to concede defeat. The first chapter in the history of postwar France had been closed with the rejection of the war leader by the politicians.

ITALY: CHRISTIAN DEMOCRATS AND COMMUNISTS

Italy, like France, faced a revolutionary situation at the end of the war. Its liberation took place in several stages: after the setbacks of the Axis in North Africa, the Allied powers had invaded Italy in July 1943. On 25 July of that

year, much to everyone's surprise, the Fascist Grand Council deposed
Mussolini who was arrested shortly after. A new government was established
under Marshal Badoglio which, while ostensibly continuing the fight on
Germany's side, wanted to end the war as soon as possible. The meeting of
the Grand Council showed that Italy, unlike Germany or the Soviet Union,
had never blossomed into full totalitarianism, as opposition to the supreme
leader still existed. Mussolini had weakened the position of the court, the
army, the church, and the bureaucracy, but he had not crushed them; at a
time of crisis his enemies made common cause and overthrew his régime.

The Germans were taken unawares by the sudden turn of events and it
took them a few weeks to react. During August they moved troops into Italy
and on 9 September reoccupied Rome. Badoglio had started negotiations
with the Allies, but progress was slow and only on 8 September did Italy
decide to surrender. In the muddle of the '45 days' (as this curious interlude
came to be called), the Germans disarmed some 60 Italian divisions, rescued
Mussolini from his prison and occupied most of Italy. The Allies, reacting
slowly to the challenge that had suddenly arisen, could not match the German
performance. By September Italy was divided into two, the agricultural
South from which the Allies were slowly advancing, and the industrial
North, occupied by the Germans, in which Mussolini established a new, more
radical, fascist régime, the 'Republic of Salò'. Mussolini intended to learn
from past mistakes; his appeal was now mainly directed to the 'common
people'. The Duce and his assistants fulminated against the plutocrats, the
aristocracy, and the military leaders who had betrayed him.

In the south meanwhile political life was resumed. It appeared, again to
everyone's surprise, that the nucleus of the leading parties had somehow
managed to survive 20 years of fascist suppression; they were all revived
within a few weeks. Even their old leaders were still present, men in their
seventies and eighties like Croce, Orlando, Nitti, Bonomi, Don Sturzo, and
Sforza, anxiously waiting for their turn to re-enter politics. There was in
many ways more continuity in Italian political life than in other European
countries which had suffered years of dictatorship. The partisan movement's
inspiration was overwhelmingly communist and socialist, but these units
were mainly active in the north. By the time the north was liberated a new
political structure had been established in central and south Italy, traditionally
more conservative in its attitude, which could not easily be dislodged.

Badoglio's government was replaced by one headed by Bonomi, who had
been a socialist before the first world war but had subsequently moved to the
right. Under him three major and three minor parties participated in the
coalition. The strongest was the Christian Democratic party, not unnaturally,
in which the clergy still played such an important role. It united in its ranks
people of very different political persuasions, from the moderate left to the

far right; its leadership was, on the whole, more to the left than its rank and file. The socialists, the oldest of all surviving parties, were heirs to a great tradition, but all too often they showed poor judgment, an inability to take decisions in a critical situation, and they gradually lost influence to their rivals on the right and left. They soon split into a left wing (under Nenni), which for many years favoured close collaboration with the communists, and a right wing which opposed it. The Communists had managed to preserve their cadres even under fascism; they had been very active in the Resistance and now reaped the fruits of their perseverance. In Togliatti they had a leader of considerable stature; an excellent tactician who helped to make his party the strongest of all European communist parties outside the Soviet bloc. It had 400,000 members in early 1945; later this figure passed the two million mark. Of the smaller parties, only the Action party deserves mention, for it was the one attempt to infuse a new element into Italian politics. Under the name *Giustizia e Libertà* it had developed among anti-fascist emigrés in Paris as a small activist democratic socialist group of intellectuals, dissatisfied with the record of the established parties whose failures had led to the victory of Mussolini. The Action party took a leading part in the Resistance, and after Bonomi's resignation in June 1945, their leader, Parri, became Prime Minister. But while the Action party had a strong position among the intelligentsia, it had no influence on the trade unions or other working-class institutions; it lacked both the political know-how and the resources of the Christian Democrats and the communists and failed to gain a mass basis.

The future of the monarchy was one of the main issues facing the country. It had been traditionally opposed by the Left, and was further compromised by its collaboration with the fascist régime. The ranks of Christian Democrats and of the liberals were divided. Even in the eyes of erstwhile supporters the monarchy had now become a liability. The socialist and Action parties opposed the King, the communists were in principle against the monarchy but announced their willingness to compromise and to postpone a decision. The situation was further complicated by the conflicting attitudes of the occupying powers: American policy was that King Emmanuel III ought to go, while Churchill wanted to keep him. Meanwhile the King had resigned in favour of his son, Umberto II. But the problem persisted. In a general referendum on 2 June 1946, 54 per cent of all Italians voted for a republic. Support for the monarchy was unexpectedly strong, especially in the south, where a majority of voters continued to favour it. Others were no doubt influenced by a speech of the Pope (Pius XII) who, in a radio broadcast on the eve of the election, had called all Italians 'to choose between the supporters and the enemies of Christian civilization'. But his intervention, too, did not decisively affect the outcome: Umberto II left for Portugal, and the House of Savoy ceased to rule Italy.

Other political issues were not tackled in the same decisive way. Bonomi's government was weak in almost every respect; it neglected to purge fascist elements, and did little to promote economic reconstruction. A great many hopes had been put on the purer, juster, and more democratic society that was to be built after the overthrow of fascism. But liberation came as an anti-climax. While the fascist tyranny disappeared, the realisation of the dreams of yesteryear seemed as remote as ever. The whole atmosphere of 1945, the inefficiency, cynicism, corruption, and hopelessness have been realistically described in the novels of Pavone, Moravia, and others, and in the films of the period; they provide a more vivid picture than any historical account. As in France, there was great dissatisfaction, especially among the left and the resistance, about the way Italian politics were drifting. In May and June 1945 there had been a real chance for them to seize power; effective control, after all, was in many places in the hands of the partisans or local militias that had been organised under communist or left-wing socialist leadership. But there was also the warning example of the Greek civil war. The communists knew that the British and American armies would have intervened against any attempt to seize power by force. They opted therefore for democratic action within the newly-established political framework. There was some 'direct action' in the industrial field as factories in northern Italy were taken by the workers who assumed control by means of factory councils. The old owners had often collaborated with fascism and the former managers had disappeared or were turned out. But these attempts to establish workers' control did not last long either. The factory councils did not prove efficient, productivity was low and still falling, and the Allied powers threatened to cut off raw materials unless normal conditions were restored.

In June 1945 Bonomi was replaced by Parri, the leader of the Action party; his was the only radical government in Italian postwar history. It was received with enthusiasm by the former members of the resistance movement, who hoped that it would at last cope with the problems which Bonomi had been so slow to tackle. Parri devised a scheme which favoured medium and small industrial enterprises in preference to the big firms. He also intended to introduce other economic and financial reforms, such as a more efficient income tax, that would have brought about structural changes in the country's economy. Such measures naturally provoked the opposition of vested interests which, recovering from the shock of 1944–5, rallied in defence of their cause. Parri was in many ways a tragic figure, a man of 'unquestioned integrity and lofty aspirations, and with a conscience tempered by long suffering' (H.Stuart Hughes). Scrupulous to a fault, he lacked practical political experience and the ability to take quick decisions. But the defeat of his government was due in the last resort not to personal shortcomings but to the weakness of his party. The Action party was after all a minority group which had never really sought to become a mass party. The situation facing it in 1945 was not exactly promising'; there were many signs of anarchy and general disintegration; separatist movements had sprung up in Sicily and other parts of the country; there was growing unemployment, a weakening of the authority of the central government, and a breakdown in public order as the police had almost ceased to function. At the same time major foreign political decisions had to be taken. In Parri's cabinet all parties were represented, but the Liberals and the Christian Democrats largely sabotaged his policy which they considered far too radical. The communist attitude was little better; they exploited the situation to strengthen their own position throughout the country. Parri fell in December after six months in office. On resigning he said at a press conference that the 'fifth column' inside his government, having 'systematically undermined his position, was now preparing to restore to power those political and social forces that had formed the basis of the fascist régime'. It was not, of course, a return to fascism, but the re-emergence of the forces that stood for tradition and order; it was also the end of the dreams about radical social and political change in postwar Italy.

The fall of the Parri government inaugurated the rule of the Christian Democratic Party. De Gasperi, its leader, headed a government in which at first communists and socialists were also represented. A man of great personal integrity and considerable stamina, gentle and conciliatory in his approach, he combined shrewdness with an extraordinary firmness of purpose. Gradually he outmanœuvred the socialists and communists, and as the authority of the state was slowly re-established throughout the country, the economic situation improved. The socialists split and the communists eventually found themselves in isolation. When their press attacked de Gasperi, the Prime Minister used the opportunity to resign and form a new cabinet in May 1947 from which the communists found themselves excluded for the first time since the war. They threatened to react violently, but their hour had passed with the ebbing of the revolutionary enthusiasm of May–June 1945. The Christian Democrats were now by far the biggest political party – polling 48 per cent of the total vote in the elections of 1948. De Gasperi proudly introduced his new coalition as a 'government of rebirth and salvation'. In Scelba he had a capable minister of the interior who thwarted the attempts of the communists and the left-wing socialists to attain their aims by extraparliamentary means, such as riots and other disorders. From now on decision making was in the hands of the Christian Democrats, divided into a left and a right wing, and to a lesser extent of the small parties which were their coalition partners. The communists and the left-wing socialists were out in the wilderness.

The Italian economy was in poor shape at the end of the war. Industrial output was down to one quarter of the prewar figure, the output of electric energy, usually a good indicator, was only 30 per cent of that of 1941. Fortunately it emerged subsequently that the war damage was not as extensive as had at first appeared. Italian industry, concentrated for the most part in the north, had suffered comparatively little; its productive capacity had been reduced only by five to ten per cent. The fall in production was mainly due to the general dislocation, transport difficulties, the lack of foreign exchange and the consequent inability to buy foreign raw materials. Galloping inflation was another major impediment on the road to economic recovery; the amount of money in circulation in 1946 was 20 times as great as in 1938. A currency reform and a project for a tax on property were hotly debated but, as in France, ultimately defeated. As a result, economic recovery was slowed down, an inflationary spiral developed, and Italy became the last major European country to benefit from the great economic boom of the nineteen-fifties.

The pattern of postwar developments in Italy resembles in some respects that of France: there was a rapid succession of cabinets and strong communist parties emerged in both countries which, after 1947, were no longer represented in the government coalitions. But in some ways the parallel with Germany is even closer. In both countries after a transitional period political power passed firmly into the hands of Christian Democratic parties. These provided reasonably effective leadership and their position became virtually unassailable for many years. The close identification of the communists with the Soviet Union, at first a source of strength, gradually became a liability. Most Italians wanted a government capable of tackling the urgent economic problems; political issues played a minor role. It was difficult to work up violent passions against de Gasperi and Adenauer and absurd to compare them with Mussolini and Hitler. But the failure to carry out radical reforms in 1945 perpetuated a deep internal division in the country; a large part of the population, the majority of the working class, was not just pushed into opposition; it found itself outside the political system. Whether such a development was inevitable in view of the cold war is still a matter of controversy. Seen in wider perspective it was certainly a national misfortune for Italy, and a source of much tension and internal weakness.

THE SMALLER COUNTRIES

The problems faced in 1945 by governments and political parties all over Europe were broadly speaking similar: the transition from war to peace, the purge of collaborators in the occupied countries, the reintroduction of democratic institutions, the challenge of communism and the reconstruction of the national economy. In some countries the transition was smoother than in others, Belgium had suffered much less than neighbouring Holland during the last phase of the war and its economic situation was much better in 1945-6.

But economic well-being did not necessarily imply political stability. Belgium was plagued by internal dissension to a far greater extent than its neighbour. The old conflict between the French-speaking Walloons, radical in politics, anti-clerical, and gravitating towards France, and the Catholic and conservative Flemings, reappeared, the former accusing the latter of insufficient zeal in resisting the Germans. The position of the King was a major bone of contention; he was criticised for staying behind in 1940 and above all for contracting a second marriage at a time of national misfortune; this was considered frivolous by many of his subjects. The country was evenly divided on this issue and eventually the King abdicated in favour of his son Baudouin. But the struggle dragged on for a long time and poisoned relations between the parties.

Holland faced problems of a different sort. The revolt in the Dutch East Indies spread within weeks after Japan's surrender and the Dutch government found little support in Washington and London for its attempts to reimpose its control. There was a widespread belief, quite mistaken as later appeared, that without Indonesia the Dutch economy would collapse. There were internal difficulties too; the political parties did not find it easy to adjust themselves to the postwar climate. Most enterprising were the Dutch Social Democrats, who decided to transform their party into a Labour movement, broadly speaking on the British model. They gained considerable influence and were to play an important part in Dutch postwar history.

Denmark and Norway had suffered less than Holland during the war, and the transition to peace (and a peace economy) was relatively brief, involving no major complications. In Denmark both King and Government had stayed behind, having been caught by the unexpected German attack, but their behaviour during the occupation was beyond reproach, and though some of the resistance leaders were now co-opted into the government, the political parties were able to pick up the threads where they left them in 1940. The Norwegian King and government had been in exile in London and returned soon after the end of the war. The Norwegian merchant fleet, the country's greatest economic asset, had been severely reduced by wartime operations, and a major effort was needed to rebuild it. In domestic politics the Social Democrats were still, as in Denmark, the strongest party. During the occupation the communists had won many new adherents, but this was not to be a lasting achievement. The Norwegian Socialist Party, traditionally one of the most radical in Europe, still had a much wider electoral appeal. The Norwegian communists moreover had committed the mistake of not joining the general resistance movement but had established their own separate group. Once the war was over they found themselves deprived of all political influence.

While the occupied countries faced many common problems after the liberation, conditions in those which had been neutral varied greatly. Sweden and Switzerland, even Spain and Turkey, had lived in fear of invasion and much of their effort had been devoted to national defence. Their political structure differed enormously: Sweden had a Social Democratic government, Switzerland was predominantly liberal in an old-fashioned way, Spain was ruled by a right-wing military dictatorship, and the definition of the Turkish system presented difficulties even to the most seasoned political observer – a relatively enlightened dictatorship gradually transformed itself into a democracy of sorts. There were few recriminations on the part of the Allies against Sweden and Switzerland; they had been exposed to a real threat and could not have behaved very differently towards the Germans. Inside these countries, however, not everyone took such a lenient view. Had not the spirit of compromise been carried too far? Had it really been necessary to turn back thousands of refugees who had knocked on their doors before and during the war? Had not some circles inside the country adjusted themselves by embracing quasi-nazi views? The general inclination was to let bygones be bygones, but some thought that these disturbing questions should not be brushed aside and they were indeed to occupy many Swedes and Swiss for years to come. There were no second thoughts about the wisdom of having stayed neutral; it was a question of how to interpret neutrality. Switzerland decided after the war not to join the newly-founded United Nations because it might divert the country from its time honoured neutrality.

Spain, on the other hand, was severely criticised. General Franco had cooperated closely with Hitler and Mussolini, and a division of Spanish volunteers had participated in the war in the east. But when it came to the decisive question whether Spain should join the war on Germany's side, the Caudillo had baulked. After three years of destructive civil war that had cost hundreds of thousands of lives, the country was not strong enough. Nevertheless the general feeling in the west in 1945 was that the Franco régime, a remnant of the fascist thirties, should be ostracised. Spain was excluded from the United Nations and France shut its border with Spain in February 1946 and kept it closed for two years. The United Nations frequently discussed sanctions against Spain, and at one stage many states withdrew their diplomatic representatives from Madrid. But the decisive impulse for the overthrow of the régime had to come from within, and this failed to materialise. There was much grumbling inside Spain about the economic stagnation, a social policy that favoured the rich, the corruption of the bureaucracy, and the dominant position of the church. But the opposition was itself a house divided, and after the terrible blood-letting of 1936–9 political apathy was widespread. Franco was bad, but a new civil war would be worse. However objectionable the régime which kept about a quarter of a million of its subjects under police surveillance, it was neither fair nor correct to define it as fully-fledged fascist in the accepted sense. The hold of the Falange, the Spanish fascist party, was not remotely comparable to that of the fascist parties of Germany and Italy; after 1946 its importance steadily declined, whereas the influence of the army and church became stronger. In March 1947 Spain received a new constitution, which in some respects was quite unprecedented: it was to be a monarchy without a king, with General Franco as permanent head of state. Visitors to Spain at the end of the war were struck by the strangely non-European character of the country; one of them defined it as a detached portion of Latin America. Spanish politics, too, like those of neighbouring Portugal, resembled the military régimes of certain Latin American countries.

It seemed even less certain whether Turkey should be considered part of Europe. Once the war had ended the country found itself under considerable pressure; the Soviet Union renewed its old demand for control over the Black Sea Straits, and for good measure also pressed for the cession of some border provinces. Turkey in 1945 was still a backward agricultural country with a one-party system. In the nineteen-twenties and thirties far-reaching social reforms aimed at modernisation had been introduced, but Kemal Ataturk, the father of modern Turkey, had died in 1938, and while his successors had not on the whole deviated from the basic tenets of Kemalism, this movement had lost much of its momentum. Leading politicians, such as Menderes and Bayar, split away from the Kemalist People's Party and founded their own group, the Democratic Party, which in the elections of 1950 gained a crushing victory over its opponents and was to rule the country for the next decade.

Visitors to Europe soon after the end of the war were also struck by the fact that almost immediately after the fighting was over the various nation-states, big and small, retreated into their own shells, and that domestic affairs became far more important than foreign policies. It seemed an anachronism: for how could these small separate units survive in the postwar world? There were, of course, well-known historical reasons: the nation-state had always been for most people the natural entity; 'Europe' was a vague concept for all but a few statesmen and intellectuals. And yet perceptive observers also sensed that there was a movement in the opposite direction: a recognition of common political interests, the understanding that economic recovery in Europe would succeed only if it was based on close cooperation. In addition, there was the growing danger from the East. It is easy to belittle this danger in retrospect; the acquisitive appetite of the Soviet Union was after all not unlimited, nor was Russia strong enough in 1945 to pursue a policy of aggression beyond the lines that had been agreed upon in Yalta and Potsdam. But the Russians had allies in the West and it is not certain that, but for the resolute resistance of the nations of western, central and southern Europe, some would not have succumbed. The fate of eastern Europe was there for all to see. The Soviet Union, the great hope of the resistance movement during the war, had become the main danger, and this too made Europe close its ranks.

RUSSIA UNDER STALIN

Stalin was at the height of his power at the end of the second world war. Soviet forces had occupied eastern Europe and most of the Balkans. In the Far East, Russia had taken revenge for its defeat by Japan 40 years earlier, a fact which Stalin did not fail to recall. Most of the traditional aims of Russian foreign policy had been achieved; it seemed only a question of time before Russia would control the Dardanelles and gain a permanent foothold in the Middle East. This was not the result of some great design: before the war Stalin had followed an isolationist policy ('Socialism in one country') since the country was not strong enough to pursue a more militant course. But the end of the war opened new opportunities to extend the borders of the Soviet Union and to promote the cause of communism, and Stalin grasped them with both hands.

The Soviet Union emerged from the war as one of the two super-powers, but it was still much weaker than the United States which had suffered hardly at all. The ferocious onslaught of the German armies, and the Russian defeats of 1941–2, had left deep wounds. About 20 million Soviet citizens had been killed or had died of starvation and exposure. Entire cities – Kharkov, Kiev, Minsk – had to be rebuilt; Leningrad, the former capital, besieged by the Germans for two years, was a mere shadow of the beautiful and active city it had once been. Absolute priority was given to the rebuilding of the national economy as the occupied territories were liberated. Even so, steel production was only half the prewar level as the war ended, and agricultural output was down to 60 per cent. The great decline in production was caused not only by enemy action. Though the Germans never reached the oil fields of Baku, production there, too, was halved during the war. The general dislocation, the lack of skilled workers, of transport, of food and shelter, affected output in every field. Soviet citizens had not been exactly spoiled before the war; they had been accustomed to many privations and had put up with conditions that were unthinkable elsewhere in Europe. But the postwar years were the darkest, most difficult period in recent Russian history.

Great changes had taken place in the Soviet economy: whole industries had been transferred to the east during the war, but only half of them returned after 1945 consequent upon the decision to industrialize Siberia and Soviet Central Asia. Russians had to work even harder than before the war; the 40 hour week introduced in certain branches of industry in 1937 had long been abolished, food rations were pitifully small. Workers were not permitted to move from one job to another; they were tied to their place of work like serfs in feudal Europe. The food supply did not improve as both 1946 and 1947 were years of drought; the ravages of the war quite apart, Soviet agriculture had not yet recovered from the terrible setback it had suffered during collectivisation in the late twenties and early thirties. Even in 1953 there were fewer cattle in Russia than 25 years earlier. There were not enough tractors and agricultural machines, the peasants had to sow and harvest by hand, and sometimes even to put themselves to harness. Russia had a socialist planning system, and in theory it should have been possible to prevent inflation, but the rouble rapidly lost its purchasing power and in 1947 a currency reform had to be carried out.

There was more abject poverty in Russia than in war-ravaged Europe. To soldiers in the Soviet occupation army even postwar Germany seemed almost a paradise as far as housing, food, consumer goods, and living standards in general were concerned. To catch up with the West a giant effort was made to rebuild the national economy, with the stress, as before the war, on heavy industry. The rate of recovery was most impressive; by the end of 1945 the production of coal was almost 90 per cent of the prewar level, of oil 62 per cent, of steel 67 per cent. Not much advance was made in 1946, a year of economic reorganisation and conversion, when there were power shortages and other bottlenecks. But by the end of the following year, 1947, Russian industry had reached the prewar level, and in 1950 it exceeded it by 40 per cent. It had been widely believed that the war had set back the Soviet economy by several decades, but in fact its growth was retarded only by a few years. Enormous power stations were established in Kuibyshev, Stalingrad and elsewhere; the Volga-Don Canal was built, giant new industrial concerns, such as the Zaporozh steel plant, were established, and others greatly expanded. The coal mines were mechanised, and new oil fields developed beyond the Volga and in the Urals. A new five year plan was adopted in 1946, to be fulfilled in less than five years. In a speech in February 1946 Stalin had announced that in 15 years the Soviet Union would produce 500 million tons of coal and 60 million tons of steel and oil. These seemed almost fantastic figures, outstripping in some respects the United States. But all these targets were achieved, some in considerably less time.

The Soviet Union did not accomplish this single handed. During the first postwar years Russia received massive help from the West, and extracted raw materials at nominal prices from its new satellites in eastern Europe. Two million German prisoners of war constituted a welcome addition to the labour force. Goods and equipment to the value of many billion dollars were shipped to Russia from Germany, Manchuria, and other places in lieu of reparations. Without this the recovery of the Soviet economy would not have made such rapid progress, but in the last resort it was the great efforts of the Soviet people which made the economic recovery possible.

Some of the postwar planning was misdirected. There was Stalin's giant project of afforestation to prevent erosion; 15 million acres of trees were to be planted, but the scheme was abandoned after the death of the dictator. During the war a relatively liberal policy had been pursued in agriculture; the peasants had been permitted to devote much of their time to the cultivation of their small private plots (which had imperceptibly grown in size). After the war, especially after 1950, much stricter controls were introduced. According to a plan mooted by Khrushchev, the number of *kolkhozy* (the collective agricultural settlements) was reduced by merging several small units into one agricultural town (*agrogorod*). It was assumed that as a result a more efficient unit would emerge and, incidentally, political control would become easier. In 1947 there had been 250,000 *kolkhozy*; by the end of 1950 only 125,000 were left; by 1952 their number was reduced to 94,000. Some of them were relatively affluent, especially those on rich soil or those producing technical crops such as cotton. But the great majority were very poor and their members lived in extremely primitive conditions. When the peasants grew old their families had to take care of them; unlike the workers and employees in the cities they were not eligible for old age pensions. The migration from the countryside to the cities continued; the labour force in agriculture in 1950 was about ten per cent smaller than before the war.

During the war years everything had been subordinated to the war effort, and the general political climate was relatively liberal – certainly in comparison with the purges, the trials, the constant indoctrination and the strict orthodoxy of the nineteen-thirties. The emphasis had been on patriotism and the fatherland; the traditional heroes of Russian history – from Alexander Nevsky to Suvorov and Kutuzov – made a spectacular comeback. The Communist International had been dissolved while the persecution of the Russian Orthodox Church had ceased, and it was permitted to contribute to the war effort. In the army dual control was abolished; the political commissars had only an advisory function. The composition of the ruling élite, the Communist Party had changed; it counted 3.4 million members on the eve of the war, almost six million when it ended. Every other party member in 1946 had joined during the war; they and most of the Russian citizens had great expectations for postwar Russia. There was a general conviction that things would not be the same again, that the bureaucrats and the apparatchiki would lose their power, that the squalor, the injustices and the inhumanity would give way to more humane conditions, that no one would now have to fear the notorious knock on the door in the early hours of the morning. The great sacrifices, it was argued, could not have been in vain, the super-human efforts that had been demanded of the Russian people would have to be rewarded. During the war Soviet citizens had become accustomed to greater freedom; soldiers on the eve of a battle in which many of them would undoubtedly be killed were no longer intimidated by the secret police. Millions of Russian soldiers had been abroad during and after the war and their experiences were not likely to be forgotten. Would they react like the Decembrists, the young officers who under the impact of their experience in France in 1814–5 had engaged in a revolutionary conspiracy? The authorities thought there was a real danger that foreign political and cultural ideas would infiltrate the Soviet Union and act as a revolutionary ferment, an element of decomposition within the established order. Against this strict measures were taken; indoctrination was strengthened and controls made much more severe. There were additional reasons for this policy: the Soviet Union had acquired at the end of the war a great many territories and millions of new citizens. These included the following:

	Sq. miles	Population
Lithuania	24,000	3 million
Latvia	20,000	2 ,,
Estonia	18,000	1.1 ,,
Eastern Poland	68,000	10 ,,
Bessarabia and Bukovina	19,000	3.7 ,,
Moldavia	13,000	2.2 ,,
East Prussia	3,500	0.4 ,,
Carpatho-Russia	5,000	0·8 ,,
Karelia	16,000	0.5 ,,
Petsamo	4,000	0.004 ,,
Tannu Tuva	64,000	0.06 ,,
Kurile Islands	4,000	0.004 ,,
Southern Sakhalin	14,000	0.4 ,,

The gains in territory amounted to an area larger than Spain and Portugal together, and there were millions of new citizens who had to be re-educated. In the areas temporarily occupied by the Germans millions of Soviet citizens had collaborated with the enemy – they had now to be punished. Some of the smaller nationalities or, to be precise, those which had survived the rigours of the transfer, had been resettled in the Soviet east. Stalin would probably have taken similar measures against the Ukrainians, but for the fact (as one of his assistants later remarked) that there were so many of them. All indications in 1946 pointed to the return of the prewar political orthodoxy and the terrorisation of the population. A Soviet history textbook summarised developments on the domestic scene:

The Stalin personality cult took deep root after the war. It tainted all aspects of party work, and the work of its central bodies. The Leninist principles of collective leadership went by the board. Only one plenary meeting of the Central Committee was held in postwar years, and no party congress was convened, although none had been held for14 years. In the circumstances, many fundamental questions of party policy were not given deep enough study, and the solutions took no account of what the party membership thought. Mostly, decisions were taken by Stalin on his own.

In the ideological field the Stalin cult created a rift between theory and practice. The collective thought of the party was ignored. Stalin thought no one but he was qualified to deal with matters of theory. The works of Marx, Engels, and Lenin were, in effect, relegated to relative obscurity. No written works of any worth appeared in the fields of political economy, philosophy, and history. (*A Short History of the USSR.* part II, p. 270, published by the Academy of Sciences of the USSR, 1965.)

It is a severe indictment, but it still omits some essential aspects of Stalinism. It mentions that Stalin did not consult the party on his decisions, but it does not comment on the character of his decisions. It notes some of his misdeeds *vis-à-vis* the Communist Party, but not with regard to the country at large. Above all, it explains the whole phenomenon as a freak, purely accidental, a temporary aberration from the canons of bolshevism, the result of the negative character traits of one single man. But bolshevism is founded *inter alia* on the belief in historical laws and the question arises therefore whether the Stalin phenomenon was accidental, or whether it was inevitable. This was a disturbing question. Communism, as everyone in Russia knew, was the dictatorship of the proletariat. The proletariat would be in power until such time as a classless society would emerge, and the state with its repressive function would no longer be needed. But the dictatorship of the proletariat had always meant, in practice, the absolute rule of a handful of people, and from them power had passed into the hands of one man. Stalin concentrated more power in his hands than any ruler in modern history, and he had been deified like the Pharaohs of ancient Egypt. There were in other words striking contradictions between official theory and practice, between the task the country was asked to fulfil and the political system under which its 200 million inhabitants were forced to exist. Stalin was convinced that the people were far too backward to be given more freedom; they needed iron discipline and a hard taskmaster. All this, however unpleasant, would have been easier to digest for Russians and foreigners alike had it been stated in so many words. Instead, official propaganda maintained that the Soviet Union was the happiest and freest country in the whole world.

These postwar shocks did not come as a total surprise, for many political observers, including some leading socialists, had from the beginning of the revolution given warning that dictatorship was not a political system that could be adopted and discarded at will. Once chosen it would have a lasting impact on the state and on society; it would not be a 'transient phenomenon'. Rosa Luxemburg had predicted with astonishing foresight that the dictatorship of the working class would gradually turn into the dictatorship over the working class – first by a small group of people, and ultimately by one man, firmly convinced that they knew what was best for the party and the people at large. But it was not just a question of Stalin's style; there were elements of madness in many of his actions. Some could no doubt be explained in rational terms. The breakneck speed of economic development (and the price that had to be paid for it), or the exclusive stress on heavy industry, were attacked by some and defended by others; these were issues of legitimate controversy. Other policies were not merely wrong and self-defeating but plainly irrational: the purges and mass arrests for instance, which struck down Stalin's closest collaborators. Towards the end of his life these irrational measures became more and more frequent. Some reflected the corruption through total power of the supreme leader who had lost touch with realities; some can be explained as the result of progressive paranoia and other manifestations of mental disease. Whatever the explanation, the political system that emerged in postwar Russia was very different from that 'higher form of democracy' that successive generations of Rusian revolutionaries had dreamed about and fought for.

Stalin was in his middle sixties when the war ended, and he had been in power for more than 15 years. All opposition, even all potential opposition, had been eliminated long before. A prodigious worker and still full of energy, he ran the country practically single handed; morbidly suspicious of rivals, he delegated authority as little as possible and played off his lieutenants against each other. While professing great belief in mankind in general, he despised human beings and was convinced that without him the country and the communist system would go under. He was a firm believer in the revolution from above, the imposition of policies by decree, and distrusted any spontaneous movement from below. In the nineteen-twenties he had opted for 'socialism in one country' because he realized that, other reasons apart, Russia was simply not strong enough to pursue a policy of world revolution. But in 1945 he was presented with the great opportunity, which he could not let pass, to impose the Soviet system on the countries of eastern Europe and the Balkans. Systematically he proceeded to export his political system to Poland, Hungary, Rumania, and other countries. There was hardly any pretence that the people of those countries wanted to adopt Stalinism; it was simply the inexorable course of history, with him, Stalin, as the instrument of providence.

Stalin's lieutenants, the members of the politburo and the central committee secretariat, obeyed the Boss (as they called him) unquestioningly. Any deviation, however slight, would not just have cost them their jobs; their very lives would have been in danger. The Old Bolsheviks who had made the revolution in 1917 had disappeared in the trials and purges of the nineteen-thirties. Only a handful now remained, Kalinin (1875–1946), the titular head of state, a peasant by origin and a metal worker in his youth. He had supported Stalin in his fight for power in the twenties and was rewarded by a post that was purely honorific. Two other survivors of the pre-Soviet period were the faithful Molotov and Voroshilov, Marshal of the Soviet Union. Molotov was second only to Stalin; for ten years (1939–49), and again after Stalin's death, he served as Foreign Minister. A bolshevik fundamentalist, he unflinchingly carried out all orders; his belief in Stalin's wisdom was not shaken even after he was virtually eliminated from the leadership in 1949, and despite the fact that his wife was arrested. Voroshilov had been a Red Army leader in the early days, but his record during the war was less than brilliant. He, too, was now a mere figurehead. Far more powerful were the younger members of the politburo – Beria, Zhdanov, Malenkov, and Khrushchev. Beria, like Stalin a Georgian by origin, was head of the secret police, a state within the state, with a standing army of several hundred thousand. Beria's empire embraced not only all the normal secret police functions, but also activities as diverse as irrigation and agricultural projects (on which the inmates of the labour camps were employed), the State archives, nuclear research, etc. In theory, the secret police were subject to the instructions of both the government and the Communist Party. In practice it was omnipotent, and even the highest functionaries of party and state trembled when they had to face Beria's acolytes. Beria was subsequently made responsible for all the evils of the 'cult of personality'. Andrei Zhdanov (1886–1948) was one of the central figures in the early postwar period, secretary of the party central committee, and the supreme authority (next to Stalin) on all ideological issues. He also played an important role in the coordination of the activities of communist parties outside the Soviet Union. Malenkov, the youngest member of the politburo, had risen very quickly after 1939 and was for a while the main contender for power after Stalin's death. His field was party organisation but he also had a close interest in the management of industry. Khrushchev rose to the top more slowly; for many years he was a leading party organiser in Moscow and the Ukraine. Of peasant origin, he had worked in his youth as a locksmith in the Donets region. Like so many of his generation in the higher echelons of the party, he was an all-round man, dealing in the course of his work with problems in the spheres, among many others, of agriculture and industry. Of the rest Kaganovich should be mentioned; an old comrade-in-arms of Stalin, his position in the leadership was gradually declining. There was also Bulganin, the perfect bureaucrat, chairman of the State Bank, minister of defence, chairman of Moscow City Council, another all-rounder. Last but not least, Mikoyan, the wily Armenian who was to outlast them all, a specialist in foreign and internal trade and in his later years, by sheer staying power, an 'elder statesman'.

While the dictator was alive there hardly seemed to be any differences between the men around Stalin; they all acted as his instruments and spoke with one voice. Only after his death did it appear that they had personalities and policies of their own. During Stalin's lifetime there was a great deal of jockeying for position and in-fighting, but it was next to impossible to explain such internal warfare in terms of political or ideological differences. Usually it was a struggle for power and the issues involved hardly ever concerned basic principles. Bitter fighting took place between the Zhdanov and the Malenkov factions; Malenkov had gained considerable power during the war through his department of cadres which was in charge of all appointments and nominations. Zhdanov, who resented the success of the upstart and disliked some of his policies, managed to reduce his rival's influence immediately after the war. But in 1947, when Zhdanov fell ill, Malenkov launched a counter-offensive, and after Zhdanov's death succeeded in ousting most of his rival's followers from their positions. As in medieval Europe, everyone in the hierarchy owed his position to someone else – *nul homme sans seigneur*. When the seigneur fell from grace his protégé, too, was in grave danger, unless of course he managed in good time to transfer his loyalties to a new master. Thus when Malenkov's star was in eclipse, his protégé Professor Alexandrov, head of the important propaganda department (*agitprop*), was deposed only to return to grace a few years later when Malenkov's star shone brighter again, and to disappear finally into oblivion when his master lost his position in the party leadership. Zhdanov's followers were in even more serious trouble after the death of their boss; the whole Leningrad party leadership, men like Kuznetsov and Rodionov (who was also chairman of the Russian Republic's Council of Ministers), were sentenced to death on trumped up charges. This so-called 'Leningrad affair' was kept secret at the time though it involved also Voznesensky, a member of the supreme party body, the politburo, who was executed probably without benefit of trial. All this in complete secrecy; from one day to the next a member of the politburo had become an 'unperson'. Purges went on throughout the entire country; in some places in the course of one year up to 25 per cent of the local leaders were deposed. Sometimes this only meant transfer to another party job; if there was any purpose behind these changes (which is by no means certain), it was to prevent the bureaucratisation of Soviet life. If so, it was not very successful, for the system itself presupposed the existence of a gigantic bureaucratic machine, and changing the bureaucrats from time to time did not have a profound effect on the essence of the system.

The Communist Party had gradually changed in character: originally it had been a group of like-minded intellectuals and professional revolutionaries with a sprinkling of working-class members. As a state party, it became more and more 'white collar' in character; everybody in a leading position in society had to belong to the party, whose vast army of professional organisers constituted its backbone. The position of the party was not undisputed: the political commissars had to give way to professional officers in the army and to a new breed of technocrats in industry and agriculture. With Pervukhin and Saburov, representatives of this stratum entered the top party leadership. They were faithful communists; in education and mental make up they did not differ from the regional party secretary. But by assuming responsibility for the national economy, they developed certain specific characteristics and, as a group, common interests; their influence was to grow in subsequent years. Mention has been made of the unlimited powers enjoyed by the secret police, in theory an instrument of party and state, but in practice totally independent, an authority against which there was no appeal. In one sphere, however, party activities were greatly strengthened after the end of the war: propaganda became much more concentrated, ideological control far stricter, and the heresy hunts which had been discontinued during the war were renewed. Great stress was put on education; the number of students in higher educational institutes grew from 800,000 before the war to 1,200,000 in 1946. A Higher Party School and an Academy of Social Sciences was established in 1946. In the postwar intellectual climate their main assignment was to popularise the Marxist classics and, above all, the works of Stalin.

Party propaganda put heavy emphasis on Russian superiority to the West, not just during the Soviet period, but all along throughout history. Claims were put forward to many Russian 'firsts' in science, technology, and most other fields of human cultural endeavour, including the invention of the telephone, the automobile, and the aeroplane. Many writers and composers, philosophers and painters, came under fire for 'slavishly imitating Western patterns' and 'cosmopolitanism' became one of the main sins in the Soviet calendar. Others were condemned for having produced work that was not sufficiently optimistic in mood; it was not enough to be a communist or to accept communist ideology in principle; the party line had to be reflected down to the last detail. This campaign of total regimentation of the arts and sciences was initiated by Andrei Zhdanov, but it was not the personal whim of one Soviet leader; in fact it gained further momentum after Zhdanov's death. The ideological line was laid down in a number of party decrees in 1946 concerning the performance of two literary magazines (one of which, *Leningrad*, was closed down) and the state of Soviet music. Evgeni Varga, a leading economist, was severely criticised for having suggested that within the next ten years or so a major economic crisis in the West was not a foregone conclusion, that, on the contrary, a new boom was not inconceivable. He even suggested that the ruling classes in the West might make certain concessions to the workers; and he thought it not impossible that they would give up their colonies. Such views were emphatically rejected, for they were incompatible with Stalin's policy which was based on the assumption that an armed conflict between capitalism and communism was sooner or later inevitable.

No field, no aspect of life in the Soviet Union was exempt from control, and the results were usually disastrous. In genetics the Lysenko school, which denied the laws of traditional genetics, took over, only to be denounced in later years as a group of charlatans and forgers. The Soviet cinema (to provide another illustration) had produced interesting films in the nineteen-twenties, some of which had won world acclaim. After the end of the war film makers had to conform strictly to the new canon, but hard as they tried they could not satisfy the authorities. As a result the number of films released steadily dropped until in the year before Stalin's death it reached the all time low of five (compared with the hundreds of films released each year not only in the United States, but also in Japan and India). Conditions in other fields were similar: Einstein and Freud were bitterly denounced as spokesmen of imperialism and reaction, and a leading Soviet writer said in a solemn and widely publicised statement that if a jackal could write, he would do so like Sartre and T.S.Eliot.

Russia had always been a country of contrasts, but in the postwar period the contradictions became more glaring than ever. Economic recovery was impressive. The nation as a whole, though still desperately poor, was growing richer each year, but the individual standard of life hardly improved. The average Russian family still lived in one room, food was scarce, clothing and other necessities of daily life difficult to obtain and substandard. More and more Soviet citizens were acquiring a higher education, yet at the same time ideological control became more rigid and severe than ever before. According to the official doctrine the régime was the freest, most democratic on earth, yet the individual had no political rights and was quite helpless *vis-à-vis* the authorities. Stalin would have never dreamed of consulting his colleagues, let alone his subjects, whenever any decision of importance had to be taken. The all-pervasive, absurd and mendacious propaganda was an insult to the intelligence and the maturity of Soviet citizens. According to official doctrine proletarian internationalism remained the great lodestar of Soviet policy, domestic and foreign. But in fact the country was deliberately isolated from the outside world; all foreign influence, however innocuous, was denounced. A country in which industrialisation and the general educational level were making rapid strides was run like a kindergarten presided over by strict disciplinarians. Marxism-Leninism preached the unity of theory and prac-tice, but in fact, theory and practice became more and more divorced from each other. The war had given rise to great hopes in the Soviet Union; the postwar era was a period of even greater disappointments.

EASTERN EUROPE AND THE SOVIET IMPACT

All eastern Europe and the Balkans with the exception of Greece and Albania were in Soviet occupation as the war ended, and all the countries in the area, again with the exception of Greece, became, to use the official term, 'Popular Democracies', or, as less kind observers put it, Soviet satellites. Political developments in these countries during the first postwar decade were very similar and it became the custom to regard them as a unit. But apart from belonging to the Soviet sphere of influence and being subjected to the same treatment after 1945, there were considerable differences that should not be ignored. The Poles, Czechs, Serbs, and Bulgarians were 'brother Slavs' – the Hungarians, Rumanians, and East Germans were not. Most of the peoples in this area had lived for centuries under foreign rule, and attained national independence only during the nineteenth century or after the first world war. They were all intensely nationalist in spirit and, with the exception of Czechoslovakia, preponderantly agrarian in character. But their agrarian structure was unsound; much of the land was in the hands of comparatively few families, while the great majority of peasants had little or no land. There had been sporadic agrarian reforms after 1918 in some countries, but in Hungary and Poland this problem was far from being solved. There were substantial national minorities: the presence of millions of Ukrainians and Jews in Poland, of Germans and Hungarians in Czechoslovakia, the co-existence of Serbs, Croats, and other peoples in Yugoslavia, to name but a few, gave rise to severe political and social problems. There were no major armed conflicts between the countries of eastern Europe and the Balkans between the two world wars but neither was there much goodwill and most had territorial claims with regard to one or several neighbouring countries. Twenty years is a short time to judge the performance of any country, but the interim balance was not encouraging. Only Czechoslovakia, traditionally the most advanced country of eastern Europe, provided reasonably efficient government, tackled successfully its social and economic problems, and did not depart from parliamentary democracy. In the history of the other countries democratic régimes were only brief interludes; for most of the time power was in the hands of a small oligarchy which ruled with the help of the army. In Hungary governments were fairly stable; in other countries there were frequent violent overturns.

The incapacity of the ruling classes of these countries to manage their domestic affairs reasonably efficiently, and above all their constant internecine disputes, their inability to join forces, was a basic source of weakness. For from a geopolitical point of view their situation was precarious; they were situated between superior and much more powerful forces, Germany to the west and the Soviet Union to the east. They had attained independence at a time when these neighbours had been temporarily weakened. Once the two powers recovered their strength, the future of the smaller nations of eastern Europe was again in the balance. During the nazi era all of eastern Europe passed under German control; some countries were occupied (Poland, Czechoslovakia, Yugoslavia), others became co-belligerents on Germany's side (Hungary and Rumania). Bulgaria, while an ally of Germany, managed to stay out of the war against Russia. In Yugoslavia and Albania major resistance movements emerged, a fact which was to be of great relevance in the postwar world, for these countries showed more independence than those of their neighbours who owed their liberation entirely to the Red Army. There were resistance groups in Poland too, but for geographical and other reasons these never attained the same importance as in Yugoslavia. In other east European countries there was little or no resistance, either because the population was by and large pro-German and anti-Russian, or because it was apathetic and in any case geographical conditions did not favour guerrilla warfare.

The occupation of eastern Europe and the Balkans by the Soviet army took place between summer 1944 and spring 1945. The Russians came as brother Slavs to Poland and Czechoslovakia, as enemies to Hungary and Rumania. But the difference in Soviet behaviour was less marked than might have been expected. It is never easy to keep an occupying army from committing excesses and the commanders of the Red Army did not try very hard. After years of bitter fighting and much suffering, the battle had at last moved beyond the borders of the Soviet Union; it seemed unrealistic to expect the veterans of many battles to behave with exemplary discipline. The excesses did not last very long, nor were they organised, but there was a great deal of violence; civilians were shot, women were raped, looting and plundering was an everyday occurrence. Such incidents were more frequent in the former enemy countries, but Poland and Yugoslavia, and Czechoslovakia were not spared, and the age-old feeling of superiority of the Poles and other east European peoples *vis-à-vis* their eastern neighbours received fresh fuel: the Russians, they said, were still part of Asia; European civilisation had not yet reached them.

Poland and Yugoslavia were the countries hardest hit by the ravages of the war. Six million Polish citizens had been killed, half of them Jews; Yugoslavia, a smaller country, lost about two million. Damage to Yugoslav industry was estimated at one-third of its prewar value. Damage in Poland was even more extensive; in 1945 almost half its arable land was left uncultivated, and agricultural output was down to 38 per cent of the prewar level. A million farms were left without a horse, and there were, of course, no tractors. Above all, the communication system had broken down almost completely. Hungary and Rumania had suffered less and they had many resources: Hungary's industry was second only to Czechoslovakia's in eastern Europe and it had always exported much of its agricultural produce. Rumania had oilfields and also a considerable agricultural surplus. But the economic outlook in these countries in 1945 was in some ways even bleaker than in Poland and

Yugoslavia. The former was compensated for its losses by the East German territories, and both Yugoslavia and Poland received substantial help from UNRRA, the United Nations Agency for Relief and Reconstruction. Hungary and Rumania as former enemy nations did not get such assistance; on the contrary, they had to pay reparations, 300 million dollars in each case, mainly to the Soviet Union. The Hungarian currency collapsed; in August 1946 the dollar was worth 29.667 million pengoe, and a new currency, the forint, had to be introduced. Rumania, largely dependent on its agricultural crops, suffered disastrous droughts in 1946 and 1947. Bulgaria and Czechoslovakia, on the other hand, were comparatively little affected by the war; their economic difficulties stemmed from the general dislocation of the postwar period, the breakdown in trade and communications between them and their neighbours.

Political developments in eastern Europe after 1945 followed a very similar pattern. At first all-party coalitions were established from which only the fascist and extreme right-wing parties were excluded. These gave way after a year or two to new coalitions, in which the communists obtained all the commanding positions, while their partners were reduced to the status of mere satellites. Eventually these 'Popular Fronts' were replaced by one-party communist régimes. But the process did not stop at this point, for the purges continued inside the communist parties. The first victims were party leaders accused of 'national communist' deviations (such as Rajk in Hungary, Gomulka in Poland, Patrascanu in Rumania, and Traicho Kostov in Bulgaria). After this heresy had been stamped out, other targets were chosen, and as the purge continued the pattern became more and more obscure. It turned into a struggle between various communist factions in which ideological attitudes or even the degree of loyalty to Moscow no longer played a decisive role.

There were local variations: in Yugoslavia and Albania the communists had seized power without outside help and the prewar democratic parties were weak or non-existent. There was therefore no need for real or bogus coalition governments and power was in communist hands from the very beginning, the few non-communists having been removed in summer 1945. The purges, too, were of varying intensity in the different countries. But except for Yugoslavia, political developments in all of them were so strikingly similar that most observers came to believe at the time that they followed not only an agreed pattern but also a timetable that had been fixed in advance. This, in retrospect, appears less certain. There was no doubt agreement about the ultimate aim and, broadly speaking, about the interim phases. The communists knew that cooperation with non-communist parties was not to last forever, that the socialist parties were to be taken over, or if not, then crushed. They were well aware what key positions they needed and what techniques should be used in preparation for the takeover. But there is no reason to believe that a strict timetable ever existed, or that there were instructions concerning, for instance, the duration of the quasi-democratic phase before the ultimate seizure of power. Such decisions were taken more or less spontaneously, and usually depended on a great many factors. The Bulgarian communists seized full power in 1945; their Czechoslovak comrades could have done so with equal ease at the same time but preferred to wait almost three years.

There had been a strong Communist Party in prewar Czechoslovakia and it was no great surprise therefore that in the first free elections in that country (in May 1946) it polled slightly more than a third of the total. Elsewhere communist parties had before the war been illegal and numerically very weak, counting at most a few hundred or a few thousand members. Their growth in the postwar period was favoured above all by the presence of Soviet troops. In Bulgaria there was also a strong traditional pro-Russian sentiment; in Yugoslavia the partisans under Tito had gained much popularity as the patriotic force *par excellence*; their fight against the enemy had attracted sympathisers from all sections of the population, including the peasants. By and large, however, the communists were still a tiny minority at the end of the war and ethnically many of them belonged to minority groups. This had a direct influence on their policy, for instance with regard to collaborators and ex-fascists. The purge among these elements was on the whole less severe than in western Europe. The leaders were usually eliminated, but the rank and file were not punished, and many of them found their way subsequently into the Hungarian and Rumanian Communist Parties. In Rumania and Bulgaria, the communists did not immediately abolish the monarchy. King Michael of Rumania was forced to abdicate only in December 1947, three years after the Soviet occupation; King Simon II of Bulgaria, aged nine, went into exile in September 1946. General Kimon Georgiev was Prime Minister of Bulgaria for more than two years even though the communists had fought this 'military fascist' in the twenties and thirties. In Rumania the communists collaborated with Tatarescu, who had been a right-of-centre Prime Minister before the war. Piasecki, a pro-fascist youth leader in prewar Poland, became one of the communists' most trusted allies after 1945. They preferred right-wing leaders willing to cooperate, to socialists reluctant to do so, for these were potentially dangerous rivals. They knew that ultimately the outcome of the struggle depended on seizing control of the secret police, the army, the radio, the press, and the Ministry of the Interior. Aware of their lack of mass support, the communists advocated whenever possible postponement of elections because, as they argued, conditions were not yet ripe. Wherever free elections took place the results were not encouraging from the communist point of view. In Hungary, in November 1945, the Smallholders Party polled almost four times as many votes as the communists; in Berlin in October 1946 the communist vote (despite massive Soviet support) was below 20 per cent, less, in fact, than they had polled before Hitler came to power.

The Communist Parties proceeded cautiously with their programme of social change. Firms formerly owned by Germans were immediately taken over by the authorities, but otherwise there was little change during the first year after liberation. During 1946 most banks, insurance companies, iron and steel foundries, mining, and some other industries were nationalised, and many big factories were taken over by the state. (In Poland, for instance, this applied to all factories employing more than 200 workers.) In Hungary and Czechoslovakia nationalisation at first proceeded very slowly. Banks and most of the retail trade in Hungary were taken over by the state only in 1948.

There were differences in the speed of land reform. While the very big estates in Rumania had already been distributed as the result of agrarian reform after the first world war, the opponents of land reform in Hungary had prevented land reform, arguing that since Hungary was mainly producing wheat the preservation of large units was an economic necessity. Less than one per cent of the landowners in Hungary owned almost half the land; there were, on the other hand, hundreds of thousands of landless peasants. In 1945 all Hungarian political parties agreed that agrarian reform was to be tackled immediately. The polarisation of land tenure was less extreme in the other east European countries and the redistribution of property was made easier as the result of the acquisition of new territories (in Poland) and the expulsion of three million Germans from Czechoslovakia. But from the communist point of view agrarian reform was merely the first step towards the collectivisation of agriculture on the Soviet model. At first they pursued this aim slowly and cautiously. There was not enough machinery to make collectivisation a success and the Russian example had shown that undue haste in this respect could have disastrous consequences. Some countries began to experiment in 1946 on a limited scale with agricultural cooperatives which were voluntary in character. The first decisions about the forced collectivisation of agriculture were taken only in summer 1948.

Communism in eastern Europe thus initially pursued social policies that were likely to have a wide appeal. The communists were fully aware that more radical change could be introduced only after they were themselves politically firmly entrenched. This aim, the consolidation of their political influence, they pursued relentlessly and with much less restraint. They did not, however, attack their rivals frontally but used what Rakosi, the Hungarian leader, later called the 'salami technique', gradually undermining the positions of their competitors. Some of the leaders of the parties opposing them were won over by bribes or flattery; those who did not yield to this treatment were threatened with violence or arrested and silenced. Some were removed on the pretext that they were not acceptable to the occupying power, others were arrested on trumped up charges. In Poland, Hungary, and Rumania, the Peasant Parties were the communists' main rivals because they had a far broader mass basis. The Polish communists benefited from the reluctance of their rivals to join the provisional government established in July 1945. Mikolajczyk, leader of the Peasant Party, was then in London; by the time he reached Poland the communists had seized most key positions. When the Peasant Party resumed its activities, the communists, already firmly entrenched in the police, constantly disrupted its work and harassed and arrested its local leaders, banned its meetings and ultimately manipulated the elections in such a way that Mikolajczyk, fearing for his life, fled from Poland in October 1947.

In Hungary the communists were at first in a weaker position as some of the key offices, such as the prime ministership, were not in their hands. The Smallholders Party, as the elections had shown, was by far the strongest political group. They were, in fact, entitled to form a government without communist participation, but were willing to compromise, demanding only that the party secretary, Bela Kovacs, should become minister of the interior. Faced with this demand, Rakosi threatened that his party would refuse to join the coalition. He implied that as a result the occupying power would install a government of its choice. The Smallholders retreated and made it possible for the communists in the course of two years to destroy a party far bigger than their own, by applying various forms of repression and terror. The communists agreed to collaborate only with those non-communist politicians who were willing to accept their leadership; others were dismissed from their posts or arrested. The usual charge against them was that they had made their party a 'haven for fascists and reactionaries'. Thus the Smallholders lost all power; Bela Kovacs, the party secretary and most dynamic leader, was arrested in February 1947 and his party colleagues in the government, still nominally constituting the majority, were unable to obtain his release. In Poland and Hungary, the Socialist Parties were taken over by the communists (in 1947 and 1948 respectively) after all the socialists who opposed the merger had been excluded from membership. The same happened to the smaller and less influential Rumanian Socialist Party under Titel Petrescu in 1946, and a similar pattern was followed in Czechoslovakia in 1948. In Rumania there was open Soviet intervention: Vyshinsky, the Soviet representative, demanded in March 1945 the dismissal of the Prime Minister, General Radescu; he was to be replaced by Petru Groza, a wealthy landowner who had no specific policy of his own and was willing to serve under the communists. The Peasant Party and the other oppositionists were persecuted, their leaders Maniu and Michalace were arrested in June 1947 and given life sentences. In Bulgaria the transition to full communist rule was the most rapid of all. Dr Dimitrov, the left leader of the Peasant Party, was forced to resign and his party was taken over by the communists even before the war had ended. The technique they applied was simple and effective: they delegated several hundred of their members to join the Peasant Party; by various manipulations these elected themselves local leaders, deposed the central leadership (Petkov and Lulchev) and then decided to merge with the communists. The social democrats were silenced in May 1945 when the police seized their newspapers and transferred them to the communists. Several opposition leaders courageously continued to speak up in parliament; some of them were subsequently even asked to join the government, for the transition had been carried out (the Russians thought) in indecent haste. This they refused to do, and it would hardly have affected the final outcome of the unequal struggle. In August 1947 Nikolai Petkov was sentenced to death and the communists announced that they would no longer tolerate opposition. In Yugoslavia some opposition leaders were arrested in 1945–6, but repression on the whole was less severe, simply because the communist hold on the country was much stronger from the very beginning. The partisan army had emerged victorious from the war and there was no need to go through all the formalities and niceties of coalition and national front; there was no scope for the opposition parties. In Czechoslovakia, on the other hand, the coalition functioned comparatively well for the first two years after the war. The police and the army were in communist hands, but the political parties under President Benes (whose willingness to collaborate with Moscow was above suspicion) were on the whole in agreement with the policy to be followed. There was a tug-of-war in Slovakia, and also inside the Social Democratic Party, between pro-communist elements and advocates of an independent line, but the confrontation came to a head only during the second half of 1947. The first two postwar years were the happiest in the history of the Czech Republic; they were years of relative economic prosperity and political freedom, and it was hoped that the country would escape the trend to dictatorship which was already so marked elsewhere in eastern Europe.

East European politics were decided in Moscow, but the Soviet leaders hoped to give these countries at least the appearance of an independent existence. The idea of annexing them like the Baltic countries or east Poland was rejected for the time being. Stalin strongly resisted any plan for a merger between the satellites. When Marshal Tito and Dimitrov of Bulgaria, the former secretary of the Communist International, discussed the possibility of a Balkan Union in 1946, they were sharply rebuked by the Russians who advised them that even a customs union was unnecessary; Moscow clearly preferred to deal with its clients separately rather than as a group.

The Soviet Union derived substantial economic benefit from east Europe, extracting reparations from Hungary, Rumania, and East Germany. The other countries were forced to sell much of their produce to Russia well under world market prices and to buy Soviet goods at artificially high prices. This, combined with the behaviour of Soviet troops during the occupation, the unpopularity of communism in general, and the inevitable clash between communism and the church, made the task of the local communists very difficult, hard as they tried to pursue popular policies. They displayed great energy in tackling long overdue social reforms and economic reconstruction, and remarkable skill in crushing all opposition. By 1947 the prewar level of industrial production was attained, though agriculture was still lagging behind. Most countries had adopted short-term plans, usually for a period of three years, to cope with the immediate economic problems. In their various enterprises the communists showed great initiative and resourcefulness; their political know-how was vastly superior to that of their rivals. They had a clear concept of political power, how to obtain and how to use it, and they had no scruples in dealing with their rivals. In some countries communism was more popular than in others; there was less resistance in Yugoslavia, Bulgaria, and Czechoslovakia than in Poland, Hungary, and Rumania. But everywhere communists were a minority and there was no reason to assume that they would ever get majority support in a democratic way. Therefore a régime of coercion and terror was inevitable. Ultimately, the east European communists, with all their drive and other accomplishments, were dependent on Soviet help; sometimes the presence of the Red Army sufficed as deterrent, on other occasions direct intervention was called for. It was in the last resort not the general secretary of the party nor the Prime Minister who ruled, but the Soviet ambassador, whose position was broadly speaking similar to that of a Roman Proconsul. Once it had been decided that east Europe was to belong to the Soviet sphere of influence, direct involvement on Moscow's part was inescapable; any premature withdrawal of Soviet troops, or a policy of non-interference in the satellite countries would have caused the downfall of most of these governments within a very short time. After 1948 Soviet domination became virtually total. But this in turn created growing resentment and a nationalist reaction even among the native communists, first in Yugoslavia and subsequently in the other east European countries.

Germany in Twilight

What remained of Germany was at first divided into five parts, the four occupation zones and Berlin, itself subdivided into four sectors. The three

Western zones which subsequently became the Federal German Republic (*Bundesrepublik*) had about 47 million inhabitants, the Eastern zone and the Eastern sector of Berlin about 18 million. Every fifth inhabitant of West Germany was a refugee; more than eight million had fled from East Prussia, Silesia, and Czechoslovakia. There was, in addition, a steady stream of refugees from the Soviet zone to the West, about two million between 1945 and 1952. This continued until the building of the Berlin wall in August 1961 made such escape impossible. East Germany was the only European country whose population decreased between 1945 and 1960.

There was no active political life in Germany in the immediate postwar period. There were still hundreds of thousands of prisoners of war, and many in the Federal Republic itself were debarred from playing an active part in politics because of their nazi past. In the general chaos of 1945-6 the finding of shelter and sufficient food had a far higher priority than politics. There was no time to ponder the past and little inclination to think about the future. The responsibility for the administration of Germany rested wholly with the occupying powers. Political parties were re-established in the Soviet zone almost immediately after the end of the war, and, in August 1945 in the British zone, in September in the American zone, and lastly, in December, in the French zone. But since the country was then run at every level by the occupation authorities it was not at all clear what part these parties would play. The communists in East Germany had a head start: a plane from Moscow with Ulbricht and other German communist leaders landed in Berlin even before the fighting had ended. Within a short time they established the nucleus of a party organisation; backed by the authority of the occupation army, they soon welded it into an instrument of political power. In their first manifestos they stressed that it was the task of their party to fight for democracy and to uproot the remnants of nazism; 'communism' and 'revolution' did not figure in these appeals. The presence of the Soviet army made it possible to impose from above, by decree, all the changes that were deemed necessary; there was no need to appeal to the revolutionary impulses of the masses. Walter Ulbricht was the central figure among the East German leaders and he remained at the helm for more than two decades. A typical *apparatchik* of the Stalin period, he was neither a popular charismatic leader, nor an outstanding speaker or ideologist; but he had the reputation of a capable organiser, an energetic party boss of the new style and, above all, his loyalty to the Russians was never in question. The other parties that were allowed after the war in the Soviet zone had at first far more popular backing than the communists, as far as can be established from the results of local elections, but the Russians did not want them to play an important political role and they gradually faded away, leading a mere shadow existence.

Three major parties emerged in the Western zones: the Social Democrats

(SPD), the Christian Democrats (CDU), and the Liberals (FDP). The SPD was the oldest German party; during the last years of Wilhelmian Germany and for much of the Weimar period, it had also been the strongest. But it hardly ever had a commensurate influence on German politics, for its appeal was by and large restricted to the working class. It represented the views and interests of a strong minority, but it had never been able to attract other sections and to become a truly national party. When in government, the Social Democrats had always needed coalition partners to rule; they were never in a position to carry out their own political programme for which, they thought, the time was not yet ripe. Their belief in democracy and order was deeply rooted and they lacked a sense for political power; even in 1918 they had not known how to exercise it. The idea of a revolution, though still an essential part of their ideological programme, seemed altogether unreal, and the Soviet example had acted as a further deterrent. How could a socialist and democratic society be established if the majority of the population was not yet in favour of it? The party had crumbled in 1933, unable to put up a determined resistance to Hitler; some of its leaders were discredited by their performance in the Weimar Republic, others had died. There was still a fairly strong social democratic tradition in certain parts of Germany, above all in the big cities, but unlike the communists the Social Democrats did not enjoy the active support of any occupying power. On the contrary, the Western Allies were deeply distrustful of the new party leader, Dr Kurt Schumacher, an invalid of the first world war, who had spent almost the entire nazi era in prisons and concentration camps. Schumacher, a man of high principles and inflexible character, was convinced that the socialists' readiness to compromise had been one of the main reasons of their past defeats. Under Schumacher these mistakes were not be be repeated. The party was to combine a radical socialist programme (including the nationalisation of big industrial enterprises and banks) with resistance to communist en- croachments and a firm, sometimes intransigent, line *vis-à-vis* the occupying powers.

The Christian Democratic Union, the other big all-German party, advocated at its first conference in December 1945 a federal structure for the new Germany as a form of protection against the excessive powers that would otherwise be wielded by the central authorities. Catholic influence was very strong in this party, but it was not a mere revival of the Catholic Centre Party, one of the big parties of the Weimar Republic. There was a new readiness to cross the barriers between the confessions. Nor would the political prospects of a party exclusively Catholic in character have been very bright, for though the predominantly Protestant regions of East Germany had been lost, and though the Catholics were traditionally much better organised than the Protestants, they did not constitute a majority in the *Bundesrepublik*. In its first manifestos the new party stressed its socialist beliefs, a socialism that opposed the class struggle and emphasised 'social responsibility'. 'Socialism' in the programme of the CDU gradually gave way to 'solidarity' and later, after the economic situation had improved, to a policy orientated towards a free market economy and *laissez-faire* liberalism. Such a programme was by no means unpopular. Germany had lived for many years under a system of restrictions and controls, regimented by a network of state regulations. The Nazi Party, after all, had also claimed to be socialist in character. Policies that promised little or no state interference had had a good chance of being accepted, provided, of course, that they were also effective in terms of stability and economic progress. Of the early Christian Democratic leaders only Konrad Adenauer was to play a central part in German politics. A former burgomaster of Cologne, a devout Catholic and a Rhinelander by origin, he became the undisputed leader of his party, and later of West Germany. He disliked the Prussian tradition that had been so deeply ingrained in modern German history and believed in close cooperation with the Western powers, above all in a reconciliation with France, the 'hereditary enemy'. He was convinced that a large dose of parliamentary democracy would not be healthy for Germany; in his view it had helped to destroy the Weimar Republic. Adenauer's style of work was paternalistic, if not authoritarian. He was neither a great thinker nor a great statesman in the traditional sense, but over the years his resolution, his shrewdness and persistence won the 'old man' – he was nearly 87 when he reluctantly resigned – the grudging admiration of even his adversaries.

The Free Democratic Party which also came into being in 1945 was a curious amalgam of South German radicals and right-of-centre nationalists from the North. One of their early leaders, Theodor Heuss, became West Germany's first president. For more than a decade they cooperated with the CDU in the central government, but they never gained sufficient popular support to play an important, independent role in German politics. In the first elections after the war they polled about ten per cent of the vote (about as much as the communists) and this was to remain their share for the next 15 years, until, in the nineteen-sixties, the party suffered a further decline. The electoral system adopted in the new Germany was a compromise between proportional representation and the British system, and the smaller parties complained that it was unjust, favouring the two big parties. The legislators had been influenced by the bitter experience of the Weimar Republic with its proliferation of small parties in which workable and stable majorities had been exceedingly rare.

The real political revival took place in the Western zones of 1947–8 as the parties consolidated their positions and gradually received greater freedom of action from the occupation authorities. In the Soviet zone, too, party politics began to play a bigger role, but it was the policy of one party only. The communist leaders were aware that they needed a broader mass basis to carry out their policies. They could, of course, count on the Russians, but complete identification with the occupation authorities was a mixed blessing. The harsh Soviet line during the first two years, the seizure of so much property, including factories, livestock, and art treasures, caused inevitably a great deal of hardship and antagonised not only the middle classes but also most workers and peasants. The disappointing results of the local elections in the Soviet zone in winter 1945–6 eventually induced the communists to drop all democratic pretences. This involved the creation of a party of a 'new type', truly bolshevik in character, and the elimination of all other independent political forces. The turn of the Social Democrats came first. They were systematically harassed, their leaders were arrested, while rank and file militants lost their jobs or their ration cards. Social Democratic offices and newspapers were 'spontaneously' attacked by 'angry workers'. After only a few weeks these strong arm tactics showed results: in February 1946 Schumacher recommended the dissolution of all SPD organisations in East Germany, since the communists had made it impossible for the socialists to function there. Otto Grotewohl, the SPD leader in the zone, was at that time equally bitter about communist tactics, but gradually persuaded himself that there was still hope of saving the social democratic movement in the East provided they cooperated closely with the communists. This policy was highly unpopular with the party activists; despite the terror, 82 per cent of Berlin's Social Democrats voted against a merger with the communists, only 12 per cent in favour. But the opponents of 'working-class unity', as the communists called them, could not in the long run resist the pressure exerted by the occupation authorities and the police. Their organisations were smashed and Grotewohl, with a handful of supporters, carried the day. In April 1946 the first conference of the 'Socialist Unity Party' (SED) took place and from then on it was plain sailing; the Social Democrats were absorbed in the new Communist Party. The 'bourgeois parties' had received more than half the vote in the East zone elections of 1946, but they offered no serious challenge to the well-organised communists; soon they differed from the communists only in name, and those of their leaders who were unwilling to follow the lure of the SED were forced to resign or were arrested. As a result of these developments in East Germany, the influence of the Communist Party in West Germany dwindled into insignificance. Social Democrats, Christian Democrats and Liberals were alarmed about the fate of their comrades in the East, and a militant anti-communism spread in their parties.

The gradual imposition of a communist dictatorship in East Germany during the winter of 1945–6 also brought about a change in the policy of the

Western occupying powers. At first they had been reluctant to do anything that could offend the Soviet Union. But the Russians did not reciprocate, and strongly resented any criticism, however mild, let alone interference with their policy in East Germany. Gradually the Americans and the British began to retaliate and coordinated their policy without paying undue attention to Soviet wishes and complaints. In January 1947 the American and British zones were merged into one economic unit. The French had at first opposed any step towards German reunification, but when their efforts to persuade the Russians to modify their policy failed, they too changed their line and from summer 1947 the three Western powers followed, broadly speaking, a common policy. Denazification ended, the last prisoners of war were released, and a central German government came into being, at first in the form of a Supreme Economic Council. The German political parties and their leaders were given an increasing share in running the country; foreign affairs and defence remaining in the early years the prerogative of the occupying powers. But a new economic plan was adopted, many of the restrictions on German industrial production were step by step removed. In June 1948 a drastic currency reform was carried out: ten old marks were (to simplify somewhat a highly complex operation) exchanged for one new mark. A calculated risk was taken with the decision to reintroduce the free play of supply and demand, the mechanism of a market economy. Rationing continued for a few essential goods like bread, milk, coal, and electricity. It was not at all certain whether a country that had been impoverished to such an extent would have the necessary resources to increase production and to expose itself without catastrophic results to the cold winds of the market, but the gamble paid off; the reform succeeded better than even the most optimistic had dared to hope. At first prices rose and unemployment increased, but both were brought under control and gave way to stability and full employment. Almost overnight shops were full again with goods that had not been seen for years; production rose by 50 per cent within six months, and in the following year it again increased by 25 per cent. Great energies were released by the reform: it was a most spectacular turning point in postwar German history, the beginning of the 'economic miracle' of the fifties. The reform paved the way for the subsequent triumph of the CDU, which was given the credit for these successes.

The Soviet Union had opposed the currency reform, which it regarded, not without justification, as a further important step towards the unification of the three Western zones. Two months before the reform, Marshal Sokolovsky had left the Allied Control Council in protest, adjourning its session *sine die*. Three years after the end of the war, this marked the end of formal Allied cooperation in Germany.

The Soviet Union then decided to bring pressure on the West in Berlin, at the point where it was weakest. During the night of 23 June 1948 all land traffic from the West to Berlin was stopped; the former German capital, almost entirely dependent on food and fuel supplies from the West, was to be starved into submission. Berlin had long been a thorn in the flesh of the Soviet authorities: a communist stronghold in the Weimar Republic, it had now become a symbol of resistance to the imposition of communist rule. The leader of the Social Democrats in Berlin, the strongest party by far, was Professor Ernst Reuter. Reuter had been a well-known communist after the first world war, but had subsequently resigned from the party, which did not endear him to the Soviets and his former comrades. He was the soul of the resistance and the Soviet authorities did their best to obstruct his election as Chief Burgomaster. Berlin was an island and it was also the one remaining hole in the curtain through which many refugees from the East escaped every day. The Allies faced a difficult dilemma: to supply Berlin by air was not only an unprecedented logistic operation, it was bound to be extremely costly, as well as risky from a military point of view; what if a military confrontation with the Russians ensued? But public opinion in the West, under the fresh impression of the overthrow of democracy in Czechoslovakia, was all in favour of making a stand. General Clay, the American Commander in Chief, wrote at the time that if Berlin fell to the Russians, the whole of Germany would follow and then the whole of Europe would become part of the new Soviet empire. An 'air-bridge' was improvised, and eventually worked with clock-like precision. In the course of 200,000 flights, West Berlin was supplied with almost one and a half million tons of goods, including 900,000 tons of coal. The Soviet authorities had clearly underrated the resourcefulness and determination of the West. They realised too late that the only way to stop the Western planes was to attack them, but this would have led to armed conflict and probably to all-out war. After a few months Stalin decided that the risks involved were too heavy and he began a slow retreat. On 12 May 1949, after more than 300 days, the blockade was lifted. Berliners celebrated; the general feeling was that at least in one place the Soviet advance had been halted.

The reintegration of West Germany proceeded rapidly after 1949. Membership of OEEC (the Marshall plan) in 1948 was the first step towards independence and foreign recognition. In April 1951 West Germany became a member of the newly-founded European Coal and Steel Community, and one month later it joined the Council of Europe. In July 1951 the state of war between Germany and the Western Allies was officially ended; a similar agreement with the Soviet Union was signed only in 1955. There was no formal peace treaty, for the former allies could no longer agree on essential questions. In 1951 West Germany appointed its first Foreign Minister (Adenauer) and its diplomatic representatives. With the treaties of Paris

(1954), the occupation status was ended and the Allied control authorities abolished; Western troops were to remain stationed in Germany on the basis of new agreements. Germany's own contribution towards the defence of the West was discussed for a number of years. The German parliament, against strong internal opposition, favoured the incorporation of German units in a West European defence scheme. This project had first been proposed in 1950 by René Pleven, the French Prime Minister, to prevent the revival of a separate, national German army. But Pleven's plan was rejected in 1954 by the French parliament and Germany instead joined NATO in October 1954. In 1955 Theodor Blank became the first German Minister of Defence. When the Six decided to join forces in 1957, it was taken for granted that Germany would be a founder member.

These were the main stages in the re-emergence of West Germany on the European scene in the fifties. The country rapidly moved into second place in the list of the world's trading nations; its political influence was by no means equal to its economic power, but it was clear that Germany would not remain a power vacuum for any length of time. The Cold War hastened the process of reintegration, which in the eyes of some Germans went in fact too fast. The Social Democrats opposed both entry into the Council of Europe and the creation of a new German army: *Ohne mich* (without me) was a popular slogan in the early and middle fifties. But a majority of Germans did not think this practical politics, and they accepted, albeit without great enthusiasm, the German military contribution within NATO. The general elections of 1953 showed that the CDU had improved its position; it now polled 45 per cent of the total vote, whereas the Social Democrats had fallen back to 29 per cent.

There was genuine enthusiasm for the European idea in Germany during the fifties. Hitler, too, had advocated a united Europe, and a few Germans may have regarded the new European idea as a convenient backdoor channel for establishing German hegemony over the old continent. But most Germans realised, as did a majority of Frenchmen and Italians, that in a shrinking world a divided Europe had become too small a unit and that everyone would benefit from closer cooperation. The stability of German politics in the fifties can be explained only against the background of the country's astonishing economic recovery, but the economic miracle in its turn was possible only because of the political stability. The recovery took several years to gather momentum after the currency reform had created the preconditions. There had been a surprising increase in industrial output in 1949, but there were more than nine per cent unemployed in 1950 and Germany had an unfavourable balance of payments until 1951. The statistics of industrial production indicate that growth was uninterrupted and steady: 1958=100

1948	27	1953	67	1957	97
1949	39	1954	74	1958	100
1950	49	1955	86	1959	107
1951	58	1956	92	1960	119
1952	61				

The Gross National Product (GNP) increased threefold between 1950 and 1964, faster than in any other European country, though not as fast as in Japan. Altogether industrial output increased sixfold between 1949 and 1964. There had been nothing comparable in German history; those who had predicted the downfall of capitalism in central Europe were confounded; the gains exceeded even the most sanguine dreams of the optimists. In retrospect a great many reasons can be adduced to explain the miracle: Germans had been underfed for many years, they did not have proper housing and clothing, millions wanted cars and all the new machinery that made the chores of daily life less of a burden. The result was an enormous consumer demand and many new industries had to be established to satisfy it. The chemical industry, in particular, mushroomed and the electrical and textile industries traditionally located in Berlin and central Germany had to be rebuilt in the West. Even the millions of refugees proved to be an economic asset, for without a substantial labour force there could have been no miracle. In 1960 unemployment had fallen to less than one per cent, and for everyone who wanted a job there were seven places to be filled; in addition more than a million foreign workers had found employment in Germany. It has been claimed that the recovery would not have been possible without the initial help given to Germany under the Marshall plan, 1.5 billion dollars between 1948 and 1952. But Britain and France received even bigger sums and the Marshall plan alone does not suffice as an explanation for the boom. The fact that world trade recovered much more quickly after the second than after the first world war was probably more decisive in Germany's spectacular recovery.

While West Germany became to all intents and purposes part of the Western political, economic, and military system, East Germany was accepted as a fully-fledged 'Popular Democracy' in the East. At the elections of October 1950, 99.7 per cent of all votes were in favour of the government. Developments in East Germany followed a pattern that had been established elsewhere in eastern Europe; first the non-communist parties were smashed, then the communist leadership was purged of obstreperous and undesirable elements, a process which lasted until well after Stalin's death in 1953. Agriculture was collectivised, though at a slower rate than in neighbouring countries. In many ways the tasks facing the East German leaders were more difficult than those confronting the other satellites. For the citizens of East Germany continued to be aware of events in the other, bigger part of Germany, and while they could not give vent to their feelings in free elections they voted with their feet. In one month alone (March 1953) 58,000 left their homes and escaped to the West. Some were attracted by the fleshpots of West Germany, others found the lack of freedom in their own zone intolerable. Young people were struck by the contrast between ideology and realities. The leaders were well aware of their unpopularity, but there was little they could do to counteract the attractions of West Germany. There was, on top of it all, a severe economic crisis in 1952–3: Russia continued to extract goods on a massive scale, and there was no Marshall plan for East Germany to assist it in its postwar take-off. In June 1953 a strike of East Berlin building workers sparked off a mass revolt which, but for the intervention of Soviet armed forces, would have swept away the régime. This crisis acted as a warning sign, and while it was not followed by liberalisation in the political field, a determined effort was made by the authorities to improve the standard of living. Reparations to the Soviet Union ceased and within the next ten years East Germany became the second biggest industrial power within the communist bloc in Europe. The efforts to win genuine political support for the régime by making East Germany a show case demonstrating the advantages of communist society over the other part of Germany were less successful. Gradually the population resigned itself to the status quo as the feeling grew that they would have to live with it for a long time and that an accommodation with the régime was unavoidable. After 1953 the danger of an overthrow of the East German régime from within had passed. But the communist rulers were more ambitious they wanted to win, or at least to hold their own, in peaceful competition with the Federal Republic. This uphill struggle continued for eight more years until with the building of the Berlin wall in 1961 they admitted that they had failed.

The Breakdown of the Alliance

The rift between the Allies developed even before the war ended. To some observers this break-up of the wartime alliance was inexplicable, the result of misunderstandings perhaps, or of diplomatic failure. Surely the alliance would have lasted had the leaders only shown more goodwill and imagination, had they been less influenced by suspicion and narrow egoism. Such an appraisal ignored the deep differences between Soviet and Western society and political life; it took for granted that America, Britain, and the Soviet Union had more or less the same war aims, the same concept of a postwar world, or at least that their divergent aims were somehow compatible. It also ignored the prehistory of the war. The Soviet union had not entered the war because Britain was in mortal danger and Hitler about to establish nazi rule all over Europe. Up to 21 June 1941, the Soviet Union had cooperated with Germany and bitterly attacked 'Western Imperialism'; the changes in its policy came only as the result of the German invasion. America had been committed even before Pearl Harbour, but it became a belligerent only after it was attacked. What held the wartime alliance was the common peril; but there was no valid reason to assume that it would outlast the war, and it was not surprising that the first strains began to appear soon after the tide of the war turned. The more the German and Japanese armies were weakened, the less the Allies needed each other, the more acute became the struggle for power in the postwar world. Hitler's last hope was that the Allies would fall out. His wish was realised, but he was mistaken in assuming that the split would occur in time to save his régime. The origins of the cold war lie in the last year of war, but it developed real momentum only after the defeat of Germany and Japan.

The differences between the Allies manifested themselves in disagreement about the future of Poland and later of Germany, about territorial changes, reparations, and the government of occupied (or liberated) countries. The settlement of these problems would have been difficult enough between big powers of similar character and structure; the peace treaties after the first world war had not, after all, been easily achieved. The differences between the Soviet Union and the Western Allies were of course far more deeply rooted than the differences that came to light in 1919. They did not even speak the same language, unless it was a matter of straightforward geographical fact or economic figures. When they decided on the 'democratic transformation' of a certain country, America and Britain took it for granted that this referred to parliamentary Western-style democracy, whereas the Soviet leaders had different ideas about the meaning of the term. Western-style democracy meant a restoration of capitalism which was unacceptable to Stalin, certainly as far as his own sphere of influence was concerned, for capitalism and fascism according to Soviet doctrine were birds of the same feather. The Western Allies put great stress on free elections in the liberated countries. For the Soviet Union this was an imperialist ruse because such elections were bound to bring anti-Soviet elements to power since neither the Soviet Union nor communism was popular in eastern Europe and the Balkans; the workers and peasants in these countries were not aware of their real class interests. A lengthy period of political retraining and indoctrination was therefore necessary, and, above all, a social revolution imposed from above. This, as the Russians saw it, was the historical necessity; 'bourgeois democracy' and free elections were mere red herrings.

During the latter part of the war many exchanges took place between

Washington, London, and Moscow about the future of central and eastern Europe and the Balkans. London displayed much more activity than Washington; it was still America's declared policy to get out of Europe as quickly as possible after the end of the war. In May 1944 Winston Churchill suggested a deal to Stalin according to which Rumania would be part of Russia's sphere of influence, while Greece would be under British control. The Russians agreed, but only on condition that the scheme also received President Roosevelt's blessing. But the American administration was far from enthusiastic. The whole scheme smacked too much of old-fashioned imperialism. During a visit to Moscow in October 1944 Churchill resumed this discussion with Stalin: why should we get at cross purposes in small ways? How would it do for you to have a 90 per cent predominance in Rumania, for us to have a 90 per cent say in Greece, and go 50:50 about Yugoslavia? For good measure Churchill added on a sheet of paper – Bulgaria 75:25, Hungary 50:50. Stalin took out his blue pencil, made a large tick on it and handed it back: 'It was all settled in no more time than it takes to sit down.' Churchill had some pangs of conscience and asked: 'Might it not be thought rather cynical if it seemed we had disposed of these issues, so fateful to millions of people, in such an off hand manner? Let us burn the paper.' 'No, you keep it,' said Stalin.

This scene has often been recalled. The agreement reached regulated for a while the status of Greece and Rumania, but it did not form the basis of postwar policy. The United States, opposing the idea of spheres of influence, had submitted at Yalta a 'Declaration on Liberated Europe' which, though somewhat vague in the first place, and further watered down by the Russians, established the principle of joint responsibility between the three parties. The Declaration mentioned the right of all peoples to choose the form of government under which they wanted to live, and the restoration of sovereign rights and self-government to those who had been forcibly deprived of them by the aggressors. More specifically, the three governments promised to establish conditions of internal peace, to carry out emergency measures for the relief of distressed peoples, and to form interim governmental authorities broadly representative of all democratic elements; they also promised free elections as soon as possible. It was an admirable document, quite oblivious of the military and political facts of life and therefore doomed from the outset. It ignored the fact that in the countries liberated by the Red Army, the Soviet Union would inevitably have the decisive say, and that Soviet concepts of sovereign rights, self-government, democratic elements, will of the people, were not at all identical with Western views on these same matters.

The conflict came to a head first over Poland, the main bone of contention between the Allies during the last year of war. The Soviet Union had made it clear from the very beginning that it aimed to regain all its territories, including those it had acquired as the result of the German-Soviet Pact of 1939, i.e. eastern Poland. Britain had accepted this position in principle and had tried without much success to persuade the Polish government-in-exile (in London) to accept the Soviet demand on the understanding that the new Poland would be compensated in the West. America was not in principle opposed to the idea but suggested that discussion of territorial settlements should be left to the peace conference. During 1941 and 1942, while Poland was still occupied by the Germans, the issue was largely academic, but with the advance of the Red Army in 1943 the question of Polish-Soviet relations became suddenly acute. A major crisis developed after the German announcement that the graves of some 14,000 Polish officers had been found near the village of Katyn. They had been prisoners of the Russians and were apparently killed in 1940. The Soviet Union immediately denied this as an infernal lie, designed to sow distrust among the Allies; since the Germans had committed so many atrocities, it seemed at the time more than likely that they were also responsible for the Katyn massacre. But against this was the evidence that the 14,000 had disappeared well before the Germans invaded Russia. In the circumstances the Polish government asked the International Red Cross to verify the German allegations, very much against Churchill's advice. He had told them: 'If they are dead, nothing you can do will bring them back.' The Soviet government immediately broke off relations with the Polish government-in-exile. Subsequent investigations have left little doubt that for once the German allegations were correct; the Polish officers had been killed by the Soviet secret police, perhaps as the result of a 'great mistake', as Beria said on a later occasion.

In the meetings with his allies during the war, Stalin always stressed that the Soviet Union would not be satisfied with anything less than a friendly Polish government. Poland had been part of the cordon sanitaire established around Russia; twice in a generation Russia had been attacked by the Germans through Poland. The Russian complaints about the anti-Soviet attitude of the Polish government in London were not groundless, but the Poles' distrust of their eastern neighbours was as deeply rooted in history and recent events had done nothing to weaken it. For centuries Russia had made common cause with Germany in suppressing Poland; for more than a century the country had been divided between these two and Austria, and it had regained independence only in 1918. In 1939, immediately after the German attack, Poland was invaded by the Russians according to a pre-arranged plan; the friendship between Russia and Germany had been cemented in blood, Molotov said at the time – Polish blood. Nor had subsequent events reassured the Poles; the Polish soldiers held captive in the Soviet Union had been kept in prison camps until well after the invasion of 1941. Inside Poland a resistance army had been active, but the Russians did everything in their power to weaken it. On 1 August 1944, this Polish Home Army had risen against the Germans, while the Red Army was shelling the suburbs of the Polish capital. Hitler sent five divisions to suppress the rising, but the Soviet army did not help the Polish insurgents nor did it assist the Western Allies in providing assistance. Within a few weeks the Germans had defeated the Home Army and destroyed Warsaw. The Russians washed their hands of the whole affair. They wanted to have nothing to do with an adventure about which, they said, they had not been consulted, but the Poles claimed that the communist radio station in Warsaw had called on the people of Warsaw to rise. Stalin knew that most Poles loathed the Russians and that, especially among the Polish élite, there was no willingness to collaborate with the Soviet Union. The destruction of the Polish Home Army by the nazis was not therefore a disaster in Soviet eyes. It was an attitude that did not endear the Soviet Union to the Poles.

The Western Allies, like Russia, wanted governments to be established in the liberated countries that would be friendly towards them and their political system. But each side interpreted friendliness in its own image: for Stalin the only friend that could be trusted was a totally dependant agent, a satellite; any other kind of government was suspect. Stalin made occasional exceptions, as in Finland which he thought a hard nut to crack. Finland also had the advantage that, from a geopolitical point of view, the country was less important than Russia's western neighbours. The absence of loyal communist supporters in a country such as Poland made it all the more vital to establish from the very beginning governments dominated by people on whom Moscow could really depend. But such governments could be set up only against the will of the great majority of the population.

The Russians appointed a communist government for Poland (the Lublin government) when their troops crossed the old frontiers, whereas the Western Allies continued to recognise the London government-in-exile with which the Soviet Union had broken off relations. Churchill and Roosevelt tried hard to reach a compromise, to establish a united Polish government on the basis of a merger of the London and Lublin groups. When Stalin met Roosevelt and Churchill in February 1945, the future of Poland was discussed at almost every session. Russia was in the stronger position for, as the Allied leaders were meeting, most of Poland was already occupied by the Red Army, which in its pursuit of the Germans had reached the Oder and was only about 40 miles from Berlin. It was against this background that the Allied leaders tried to work out solutions for postwar Europe.

When the Big Three met at Yalta, Franklin Roosevelt had just been re-elected, the first American President to be elected for a fourth term. His first years in office and above all the New Deal, had been the subject of bitter conflict and internal strife. But in 1944 there were no major controversies in either American domestic or foreign policy; the immediate task was to win the war – 'to finish the job and bring the boys home'. Roosevelt had a superb feeling for domestic politics; his experience in foreign affairs was more limited. In his dealings he revealed a mixture of cleverness and naïveté, and even in retrospect it is not always easy to establish where one began and the other ended. He hoped that cooperation with Russia would continue after the war; he had a hunch (he said) that Stalin would cooperate. He dealt with him (and the Soviet Union in general) as he would have treated a dissenting faction within the Democratic Party, hoping that from the usual give and take that constitutes American politics a reasonable compromise would emerge. Roosevelt was not in good health at the time of the conference: 'At this critical time Roosevelt's health and strength had faded,' Churchill wrote later. To a much greater extent than Churchill and Stalin he was influenced by his advisers. Among them there were some who had direct experience in dealing with the Russians and who advocated a tougher line – Averell Harriman, the American ambassador in Moscow, his deputy, George Kennan and General Deane, the military attaché in Moscow; there were also some policy advisers from Washington, and the counsel of the Secretaries of State, Stettinius and Byrnes, of General Marshall, and of Stimson, Secretary of War, was against toughness; the war had to be won, America was not in a position to impose its wishes about the future of territories that were already occupied by the Russians. Other advisers, such as Harry Hopkins and Joseph Davies, a former American ambassador to Moscow, went even further. Davies, as appears from his *Moscow Diary*, wholeheartedly supported all of Stalin's policies, including even the Moscow trials. He believed that the Soviet leaders were at bottom moved by altruistic impulses, and that it was their primary aim to promote peace and the brotherhood of man. These beliefs, though not perhaps in this extreme form, were by and large shared by public opinion in the United States during the war. Criticism of Russia and of Stalin's régime was thought to be in bad taste. Russia, after all, was an ally, fighting heroically against the common enemy. Stalin's victories seemed to justify all his policies in the past, however harsh and cruel. It was widely assumed that postwar Russia, united under a great and benevolent leader and no longer threatened by external enemies, would be the natural ally of the United States in shaping the 'one world' of which Roosevelt's presidential rival, Wendell Willkie, had written. At the same time there was a great deal of suspicion of Churchill and British policy: Churchill's proposals were thought to embody outworn and reactionary concepts such as the balance of power, or as designed to further traditional British imperialist interests. Roosevelt was convinced that Stalin was not an imperialist and some of his advisers told him that Churchill was more concerned with maintaining

Britain's position in Europe than with preserving peace. The President genuinely believed in the United Nations as the chosen instrument to regulate the problems of the postwar world, and in personal diplomacy, not power politics. These attitudes were praiseworthy, but they ignored both the basic character of Stalin's régime and the political realities of eastern Europe. During the last weeks of the war, when Soviet demands increased, Washington and London drew closer, but at the Yalta Conference Roosevelt was still very much concerned not to 'gang up' with Churchill against Stalin. Without American support Britain could not achieve much in resisting Soviet political and territorial demands in eastern Europe.

Winston Churchill, who had been in politics longer than the other two war leaders, was now at the apex of his career. Unlike Roosevelt, his interest in domestic affairs and party politics was limited, and his ability in this field not outstanding. His heart was in world affairs and in the conduct of the war. Not all his enterprises had been crowned with success; if his political life had ended in 1938, the verdict of history would have been that Churchill was a gifted amateur, flamboyant and full of energy and ideas, but deficient in judgment, a conservative statesman basically rooted in the eighteenth, not the twentieth century. He had realised earlier and more acutely than other British leaders the dangers of Hitlerism, and when the hour of trial came he was ready to lead his country, giving fresh courage to its people at a time of great peril. Under his leadership Britain continued the fight against seemingly overwhelming odds. His personal prestige as a war leader was tremendous, so much so that many tended to forget that the country he represented was no longer the great power it had been in the past.

Churchill's position at Yalta was not an easy one. Britain had gone to war as a result of the German attack on Poland, to which it had pledged its support. It could not stand idly by while the European balance of power was being destroyed by Hitler's aggression. But at the end of the war Poland's independence was again in danger, and Russian power constituted a threat more formidable than Hitler. Churchill's understanding of the motives of Soviet politics was unsophisticated; he had never read Marx or Lenin and relied on his own instinct. For him it was simply a big-power conflict; questions of ideology hardly came in. But he realised much earlier than the Americans and the European Left what the Russian advance into Europe meant: the whole of eastern Europe and the Balkans would be swallowed up and become part of the new Russian empire, and no one could be certain that the Soviet advance would stop at the line that had been agreed upon, for Europe in its then state of weakness was hardly in a position to resist. New dictatorships and police states would be set up and it was not to this end that the war had been fought. From the Americans Churchill could not at first expect much help; Roosevelt was still convinced that Stalin did not want annexations and that they would work together for stability and peace. There was no way to influence Stalin but friendly persuasion.

Stalin, too, was at the height of his power at the end of the war. But his power, unlike that of Churchill and Roosevelt, was unlimited; it was not to be challenged in an election. The war had done a great deal to refurbish Stalin's image both in the outside world and among his own people. He had usurped power in the nineteen-twenties and relentlessly destroyed all opposition. In some respects he pursued the policies outlined by Lenin, building socialism, as he understood it, in one country. Agriculture was collectivised, and industry built up at breakneck speed. The society and the régime, with its grotesque cult of the leader, its permanent purges, were a mixture of rationality and madness, just as Stalin himself combined sincere ideological conviction, cynicism, and unlimited personal ambition. But most of the negative aspects of Stalinism were forgotten in 1945. It seemed that his policies had been wholly justified, for he had prepared his country for the great onslaught which he had predicted would one day come, and under his leadership the Soviet people had resisted and destroyed the invader. That many of his policies both before and during the war had gravely weakened Russia's ability to defend itself was forgotten in the hour of triumph.

There were no doubts in the West about Stalin's greatness. In a speech at Yalta, Churchill declared that 'we regard Marshal Stalin's life as most precious to the hopes and hearts of all of us', and a little later, in a speech in the House of Commons: 'I know of no government which stands to its obligations . . . more solidly than the Russian Soviet government.' There was a certain guilt feeling in the West about the absence of a 'second front' before June 1944. Few people recalled what Stalin's attitude had been in 1940 when an invasion of Britain seemed imminent. Enormous quantities of war material and food had been shipped to Russia from the United States under the Lend-Lease Scheme, including almost 15,000 planes, 7,000 tanks, 52,000 jeeps and 376,000 trucks. Yet to Western public opinion all this seemed woefully insufficient. Only the Western experts stationed in Moscow knew that Soviet newspapers had not been permitted to mention these deliveries.

There was much potential friction, but it did not come out into the open until after the Yalta Conference, which was in many ways the high tide of Allied cooperation. There it was resolved that Poland's eastern frontiers would roughly follow the Curzon line, as the Russians had demanded. As the British and the Americans opposed the Oder-Neisse line, it was decided to postpone a final settlement of Poland's western borders to the peace conference. The communist Polish government was to be enlarged and become fully representative, pledged to hold free and unfettered elections. The Western powers interpreted this as the establishment of a new, democratic government, whereas the Soviets maintained that only a few non-communists would be co-opted, and these only on condition that they accepted Poland's new frontiers as defined at Yalta, which few non-communist Poles did. Stalin found the Western insistence on a democratic régime for Poland irritating; the Soviet Union after all had not been given the opportunity to share control in liberated Italy or in Greece, where Britain faced a strong left-wing resistance movement opposed to the return of the monarchy. The Western Allies regarded these territories as their own preserve; with what right were they meddling in east European affairs? The Western powers were in a better tactical position; they could be reasonably certain that from free elections democratic governments would emerge. The Russians on the other hand knew that Polish or Rumanian communists would not have stood a chance in elections, and this strictly limited their freedom of manœuvre.

A great many topics were discussed at Yalta, such as Russia's entry into the war against Japan, the organisation of the United Nations (at Russian insistence, the permanent members of the Security Council were given the right of veto), German reparations (a figure of 20 billion dollars was mentioned by the Russians) and French participation in the occupation of Germany. Some questions were left open, but on most issues agreement was reached. This did not mean much, for it still remained to be seen how the agreements would be interpreted and carried out.

The complications began almost the moment the conference was over. In Rumania a communist-controlled government was appointed following a Soviet ultimatum. In Poland, Marshal Zhukov invited 16 leaders of the Polish Home Army to lunch to discuss ways and means of cooperating in the war against Germany. At the end of the lunch they were arrested, to reappear only in a show trial in Moscow and to be sentenced to lengthy prison terms for alleged sabotage. On 4 May, Churchill wrote his foreign secretary that the 'terrible things which had happened during the Soviet advance clearly showed the kind of domination the Russians intended to impose'. The Russians meanwhile complained that the Western Allies were negotiating with the Germans behind their back, and they were greatly offended when the Lend-Lease agreement was abruptly ended a few days after the war. The honeymoon between the Allies was drawing to a close.

Roosevelt died on 12 April 1945. During the last months he had been tired, anxious to avoid further argument. Harry Truman, his successor, had little experience in foreign affairs and thought it wise to continue Roosevelt's policies at least until he was more firmly in the saddle. He sent Harry Hopkins, Roosevelt's close confidant, to Moscow in an attempt to settle the disputes that had arisen. Hopkins upon his return reported complete success, but his optimism was not justified, as it soon appeared. Truman had asked Churchill to 'forget the old power politics', but the new American President himself was not permitted to forget power politics for very long.

The Allied conference scheduled to deal with the most urgent postwar problems was convened in Potsdam during the second half of July 1945. It was the first time that Harry Truman represented the United States; in the middle of the conference Attlee and Bevin were to replace Churchill and Eden after Labour's election victory. The discussions ranged over a wide field, from Poland and Spain to Greece and Libya. But the most important topic was the future of Germany. Various schemes had been drawn up during the war to ensure that Germany would never again be a danger to its neighbours and to the world at large. In 1944, at the time of the Yalta conference, everyone seemed to agree that Germany should be broken up into a number of small states. But by the time Germany surrendered both Russia and the Western Allies had reached the conclusion that these schemes were not workable, and in any case not desirable. Germany was to be treated as one economic unit; there was to be decentralisation, but not dismemberment. In the economic field a similar change of mind had taken place: in 1944 the Americans had produced a plan for the pastoralization of Germany. The reasoning behind it was that if the Germans did not have the potential to produce arms, they would not be in a position to wage war. This, the so called Morgenthau plan, did not however become official policy; it had been based on the assumption that it would be exceedingly difficult to keep Germany down, whereas once Germany had capitulated it appeared that it was far weaker than the Allies had imagined. The real problem was to keep it from complete collapse. Soviet views, too, had changed. The official line had been violently anti-German up to 1945, but after that there was a marked shift. Ehrenburg, the most outstanding propagandist of the anti-German line, was officially rebuked, and as the Russians entered Berlin, banners were displayed with a recent Stalin quotation to the effect that Hitlers come and go, but the German people remains. There were also economic considerations: the Russians were pressing for very heavy reparations, and they realised that it would be impossible to extract them unless German industry could be set to work.

The Potsdam conference was in agreement about a number of principles: that Germany should be disarmed and demilitarised, that the Nazi Party should be dissolved, that it should be brought home to the German people that they had suffered total military defeat and could not escape responsibility for what they had brought upon themselves; that all war criminals should be brought to judgment, and that political life should be reconstructed on a democratic basis; that all democratic parties should be encouraged, and education and the legal system reorganised; and that for the time being there should be no central German government, the Allies being responsible for those central departments (such as finance, transport, etc.) that would have to be established.

There was no difficulty in drawing up such a statement of intent; the real test was in carrying out these agreed policies, for a 'democratic party' still meant different things to Stalin and the Western Allies. Two problems provoked much dissension from the very beginning: the frontiers of the new Germany and the question of reparations. America and Britain agreed to Soviet annexation of part of East Prussia, but they thought that Polish territorial claims went too far; how could the many million Germans expelled from these territories be resettled in a much smaller and poorer Germany? The Oder-Neisse line served as a basis of discussion, but there was an Eastern and a Western Neisse, about 100 kilometres apart; the Americans, as a last concession, were willing to accept the former, while the Russians and Poles would not budge from the latter. In the end the West gave way, as before at Yalta. The Poles were to retain control of the occupied territories, though the final border would be settled only in the German peace treaty. Poles and Russians had much reason to be satisfied with the outcome of the conference.

Everyone agreed that the Allied control authorities were to ensure – to quote the official formula – 'the production of goods and services essential to maintain in Germany average living standards not exceeding the average of other European countries'. But on reparations there was no end of haggling. The Russians argued that the sum of 20 billion dollars had been agreed upon at Yalta, of which they were to get half. The Western leaders replied that this had merely been a basis for discussion. They recalled that unrealistic demands for reparations after the first world war had been the source of much misfortune to victors and vanquished alike. They also argued that the annexation of a sizable part of German territory by Russia and Poland constituted reparation for war damage. They objected to fixing an overall figure for reparations, but it was in principle agreed after long haggling that the Russians would be entitled not only to reparations extracted from their own zone, but also to 25 per cent of industrial equipment from the Western zones, since it was not necessary for maintaining Germany's postwar economy on the level envisaged.

In the course of the Potsdam conference the Russians complained about the civil war in Greece and demanded the inclusion of the progressive forces in that country in the government. Much to everyone's surprise, Russia also declared an interest in Tangier and in the former Italian colonies, suggesting at one stage Soviet trusteeship for Libya. This clearly worried the Western statesmen. Russian territorial demands in Poland, Germany, Rumania, or Czechoslovakia could be explained with reference to the Soviet wish to strengthen its defences, but a strategic position in Africa was obviously not a defensive measure. Moscow also demanded the annexation of two Turkish provinces and pressed for control over the Black Sea Straits; it was intolerable that Turkey should have a 'hand on Russia's throat'. Western suspicions began to increase. Was there no end to Russian demands? The admiration for Russian achievements was dimmed by fear of Soviet ruthlessness and power, and by the realisation that Moscow's friend in the West would, if they could, destroy free governments everywhere. The Potsdam conference reached a number of decisions with regard to the future administration of Germany, but most of them were ambiguous and self-contradictory; the conference as a whole was not a success, for the spirit behind these accords was no longer one of implicit trust. The wartime alliance was in the process of disintegration. Some of the agreements remained a dead letter from the beginning; others were soon to be disregarded. The whole political climate was rapidly changing.

The conferences of Yalta and Potsdam have been, in retrospect, the subject of much criticism. At the time the decisions were on the whole welcomed, but only a few months later, when the full details became known, and with the change in the political climate, there were bitter attacks on the Western leaders, and on Roosevelt in particular. The charge was that they had been outsmarted by Moscow, had failed to foresee that the Russians would turn against the West after the war. America had been in a position to speak the only language the Russians understood – the language of power – yet Roosevelt and his advisers had surrendered to Stalin all along the line. Later, after the cold war had abated, an opposite school of thought argued that the cold war was the natural outcome of American policy. The Alliance would have remained intact had Washington been even more forthcoming, had it not indirectly used the A-bomb as a threat and had it not given the Russians any ground for suspicion. Stalin was told at Potsdam by Truman that a new weapon with an immense power of destruction had just been tried out, but he was not surprised for he had received the information from his own sources well before.

The West at Yalta did not negotiate from a position of strength as far as eastern Europe was concerned. Roosevelt, as already noted, was very ill at the time; a more vigorous American President, one with fewer illusions about Russia, the United Nations, and the postwar world in general, would have been more alert to the dangers ahead. It is likely that some mistakes would not have been committed; the West could have insisted, for instance, on a land bridge to Berlin. But the territories in dispute were occupied by Soviet forces, and in such circumstances it is unlikely that more forceful language would have greatly impressed the Russians. Opinion at home in the United States was anxious for an early withdrawal from Europe, and shortly after the end of hostilities the troops themselves began to clamour for even quicker demobilisation than envisaged in Roosevelt's undertaking to withdraw the army within two years. In the circumstances America was not in a good position to pursue a tough policy (unless indeed atomic threats were to be used, which was unthinkable). More use could have been made of economic leverage and of the Soviet need for continued American help. In January 1945 the Soviet Union had applied for a six billion dollar loan; later on, the Russian insistence on reparations was further evidence of its need for economic assistance. However, in Stalin's view Russia was in fact doing America a favour by asking for a loan, for, as he saw it, the American economy would face a postwar slump unless demand was artificially created. Roosevelt (and later on Truman) should have had a clear reparations policy and should have used economic aid as a diplomatic instrument in their negotiations with Stalin. But, however badly it needed economic aid, there is no reason to assume that the Soviet Union would have been persuaded by such means, however substantial the scale, to desist from annexations and from imposing its will on the countries of eastern Europe. Had America opposed the Oder-Neisse line more strongly at Potsdam, the border between communist East Germany and communist Poland might now run some 60 miles to the east, but this would have hardly constituted a basic change affecting the overall balance of power. Perhaps, from the Western point of view, it was all to the good, for a stronger East Germany under communist control would have presented a more formidable challenge to a non-communist West Germany and thus created another serious problem in the heart of Europe.

In short, greater Western toughness at Yalta and Potsdam would have hastened the outbreak of the cold war, but it could not have been prevented once Europe had become a power vacuum. America was committed not to become involved in European politics and to withdraw its army, while Britain alone was too weak to resist Soviet pressure. In these circumstances the Soviet advance to the west was only natural: politics, like nature abhors a vacuum. Averell Harriman, ambassador to Moscow, had realised in 1944 that if the Soviet right to penetrate her immediate neighbours in order to safeguard Russian security was accepted, the penetration of the next immediate neighbours would follow with equal logic. The real question was how far the Soviet Union would expand and how difficult, or how easy, the process of digesting its immediate neighbours would prove to be.

Stalin deeply distrusted the Western leaders despite their professions of friendship and sympathy. Even before Yalta he told Djilas: 'Churchill is the kind who, if you don't watch him, will slip a kopek out of your pocket . . . Roosevelt is not like that. He dips in his hands only for bigger coins.' Roosevelt, of all people, had done nothing to merit such suspicion. But Stalin distrusted everyone and there was no good reason to be less suspicious of Westerners than of his own subjects. There is no proof that he deliberately decided at a certain stage to turn against his allies regardless of consequences. He would no doubt have preferred to continue receiving Western economic aid, but it was even more important that his political and territorial demands should be accepted. It soon appeared that he could not attain both aims; the more extreme his demands, the more resistance they provoked. One thing led to another, and within a few months the wartime alliance had collapsed.

All this would probably have happened even if it had merely been a traditional conflict between big powers pursuing their opposed interests. But the Soviet Union was not just another state; it had an ideology and a social system sharply differing from those of the West, and it was doctrinally committed to assist the victory of communism all over the globe. As long as capitalism and socialism existed 'we cannot live in peace, one or the other will triumph,' Lenin had declared. More than two decades had passed since those lines had been written, and the Soviet Union under Stalin had undergone important changes. The messianic mission was no longer so acutely felt, and ideological motivation in Soviet foreign policy had certainly lessened over the years. But the totalitarian state that had developed still had a dynamism of its own; it was impossible to understand the mainsprings of Soviet policy while ignoring this essential feature of its character. Russia was not a traditional nation-state, not a 'static' great power; it did not pursue *realpolitik* as the West understood it.

Protestant and Catholic rulers in Europe had agreed after the Reformation on the principle that the religion professed by the individual should depend on his place of residence: *cujus regio – ejus religio*. Could an arrangement on similar lines have worked in postwar Europe? Stalin seems to have thought so; he said on one occasion that this war was different from previous ones inasmuch as the occupying power was imposing its social system on the countries under its control. He did not interfere in Greece in 1944–5; the revolutionary party in Athens could expect no help from Moscow, for the Russians regarded Greece as outside their sphere of interest. But it is doubtful whether any such arrangements would have worked in central Europe, even if America had accepted the principle of spheres of interest. Communism was ideologically committed to renew the struggle against 'Western Imperialism' once the war ended, as Jacques Duclos, the French communist leader, had written in April 1945. The renewal of the contest could have been delayed but not indefinitely postponed. In Stalin's eyes the Western proposals to establish governments that were friendly to the Soviet Union and yet representative of all the democratic elements in the country were a mere trick, a new attempt at capitalism encirclement. Only communists were acceptable to him, and among the communists only those handpicked by him could be trusted. Suspicions and misunderstanding played a certain part in the outbreak of the cold war, but below these suspicions there were real conflicts of interest. Collaboration with the West after 1945 would have involved the liberalisation of Stalin's régime and the opening of the Soviet Union to all kinds of undesirable foreign influences. Such a policy was contrary to Stalin's principles, to his entire attitude and outlook. During the war, when his country was threatened, certain concessions had to be made, but the continuation of such policies in peacetime would have endangered the very existence of the Soviet state. This was Stalin's basic dilemma, and it seems most unlikely in retrospect whether any Western concessions could have induced him in the long run to act against his best interests. His political system was based on a state-of-siege mentality; the sacrifices he demanded from his people could be justified only with reference to the unrelenting hostility of the capitalist wolves and sharks waiting for the opportunity to attack the Soviet Union. This system needed tension, not relaxation, in its relations with the outside world.

The Cold War

Three years after the end of the war Europe's main economic wounds had been healed; industrial and agricultural output had almost reached the prewar level. There were exceptions: Italy's recovery was seriously lagging behind, and in Germany it had hardly begun. The significance of the achievement should not however be overrated for the thirties had been years of depression, and regaining the level of 1938 was not in itself a reason for congratulation. There were moreover serious difficulties that had not existed before the war: Europe was not earning enough dollars to pay for its imports, and without this a lasting recovery seemed well nigh impossible. Some put the blame on the mistaken economic and financial policies of the respective governments, while others claimed that it was, in fact, a structural crisis, for Europe's place in the world had radically changed. Nor was it certain whether Europe still had the will and the ability to regain its old prosperity and influence. 'What is Europe now?' Churchill wrote in 1947. 'A rubble heap, a charnel house, a breeding ground of pestilence and hate.' He was not alone in his pessimism.

Within a year of the end of the war the Soviet Union accused its former allies of fascist aggression, imperialist expansion, and preparing a new world war. On the other hand, many people in the West felt, to quote again Churchill's famous speech at Fulton in March 1946, that the police governments established in eastern Europe did not represent the liberated Europe they had fought for, nor did such a Europe contain the essentials of peace. Many came to believe with President Truman that unless Russia was met with a strong hand and an iron fist, another world war would be in the making.

It seemed only normal that the former allies did not see eye to eye on many problems, and that there were clashes of opinion and interest. But who had expected that within two years after the end of hostilities Europe would be divided into two implacably hostile camps, and that there would be widespread fear of a new world war?

Western policy during the immediate postwar period has been severely criticised from opposed points of view. Around 1950 the general opinion was that Western policy towards the Soviet Union had been too credulous and soft. A decade later some critics argued that, on the contrary, the West had not shown enough goodwill, that there had been hysteria and a tendency to overrate both Soviet hostility and Soviet power. Stalinist Russia, they argued, was basically a conservative country in search of security, but with no desire to expand beyond its natural borders. There is some truth, though not necessarily an equal measure, in both contentions. Western statesmen, and the general public in Europe and America, had come to believe during the war in an image of Russia that had little in common with Soviet realities. Since the Soviet Union was an ally in the struggle against Hitler, any criticism of its internal régime was thought to harm the war effort. By 1946 most people were less ready to show much consideration as it became more and more obvious that Stalin's tyranny had not mellowed. Western democracy was far from perfect, but this by itself was not sufficient reason to accept the Soviet system of forced labour camps with their millions of inmates, or to welcome, in the name of the preservation of peace and human progress, the spread of such a system beyond the borders of the USSR.

In 1946 the Greek civil war was resumed from bases beyond Greece's border. The Soviet Union refused to withdraw from Persia and put growing pressure on Turkey. All opposition was gradually eliminated in eastern Europe and the Balkans, while Soviet efforts to impose its political system on its zone of Germany became more intense. At the foreign ministers' meeting throughout 1946–7 little progress was achieved towards a lasting peace settlement. The Soviet stand became more and more adamant, despite constant, often pathetic Western attempts to reach compromises and to allay Soviet suspicions. In 1947 and 1948 the situation deteriorated further; the democratic régime was overthrown in Czechoslovakia which became a fully-fledged satellite; the Berlin blockade was imposed; the Soviet Union refused to cooperate with the West in the new projects for the economic recovery of Europe that had been mooted (such as the Marshall plan), and the attempts to establish international control of nuclear weapons. The communist parties of western Europe, above all those of France and Italy, passed to the attack against governments that, they claimed, had sold out to American monopoly capitalism. Nineteen forty-eight saw the first meeting of the Cominform, a new organisation that in some ways resembled the

Communist International which had been dissolved during the war. The Western communists were criticised on this occasion for having in the past put too much emphasis on parliamentary activities; from now on their opposition would have to be far more militant. Strikes and widespread disorders occurred that summer all over Europe. There was in all probability no concerted, detailed plan behind these actions, but more and more people in the West came to believe that there was a growing Soviet threat that could be averted only by a firm stand and the application of counter-force. The West felt suddenly cheated, and in this rude awakening many wartime illusions were shattered and there was an inclination to overdramatise the conflict, to attribute to Stalin and the other communist leaders not only satanic cunning and evil but also relentless and unlimited territorial ambitions. Having ignored communist ideology for many years, there was now in the West a growing inclination to take strictly at face value all theoretical writings about world revolution and the coming inevitable conflict. There was a tendency to view largely in military terms a struggle that was essentially political in nature. On all these counts Western policy has rightly been criticised in later years. But the wisdom of hindsight should not be stretched too far, even if it may appear in a perspective of 20 years that there never was a real danger of a communist takeover in western Europe. Europe in 1947–8 was neither stable nor prosperous; not much initiative and force would have been needed by a resolute minority to impose its will. Democracy in Czechoslovakia had after all been overthrown and there were disturbing reports from Finland and other countries. The language of communist leaders was violent; perhaps they did not mean all they said but one could certainly not afford to ignore their pronouncements and predictions.

America was certainly unprepared for political warfare; it lacked the experience and the organisational weapons. There were 'Russian' parties, some big, some smaller, in all European countries, but there was no corresponding 'American' party. Above all, the West lacked a common political philosophy, the purpose and single-mindedness needed for sustained political warfare. Zhdanov, the ideologist of the Cominform was the first to popularise the idea of the existence of two hostile camps in Europe and the world. But western Europe was in fact anything but a 'camp'; rent by deep internal divisions, it contained conservative, liberal, Catholic and socialist forces as well as many others. The only unifying tie was the common threat and the wish not to succumb to it. At the height of the cold war the slogan of the liberation of eastern Europe gained some currency in the West, but there was little thought and even less conviction behind it; the posture of the West was essentially defensive; it had little to oppose to the dynamic, aggressive policy of the Soviet Union and the communist parties. There were foolish speeches and irresponsible actions on the part of Western leaders which aggravated relations with the Soviet Union, and some of the fears were quite irrational. But usually Western actions came as an answer, usually belated, to a Soviet challenge. These answers deepened the mutual distrust, for once the West had begun to suspect Soviet motives there was a tendency to dismiss out of hand all Soviet initiatives even if they might have helped to reduce tension. There were such moves even at the height of the cold war, for Soviet policy was not always consistent. After a barrage of anti-Western propaganda and action there usually came a proposal of a more conciliatory nature, such as, for instance, Stalin's suggestion in 1952 concerning free elections in a neutral Germany. Perhaps there was a feeling in the Kremlin that things had gone too far. But after their bitter disappointment of 1945–7 there was little inclination in the West to take up these Soviet initiatives. In its essential orientation, Soviet strategy was immovable; 'we shall never get out of Germany', Stalin told Kardelj, the Yugoslav Foreign Minister, in 1948. Western statesmen were to regret in later years that they had failed to probe sufficiently the more conciliatory Soviet proposals, if only because these omissions contributed to the emergence of the myth of the 'lost opportunities'.

The cold war created a far greater degree of European unity than had been thought possible, and it also brought about lasting American involvement in European affairs. These developments were highly undesirable from the Soviet point of view, and to that extent Soviet policy between 1946 and 1949 can be said to have failed. Soviet influence in Europe was no longer expanding; the borders were frozen, and a stalemate prevailed in international relations. Even France, hitherto reluctant to make common cause with the 'Anglo-Saxons', changed its course and began to cooperate in the economic and political field, and to coordinate its military efforts. From now on it was clear that the map of Europe could be changed only as the result of a major war. While the Soviets talked about such a war as an eschatological certainty, their policy remained cautious, unwilling to take major military risks. In Berlin in 1949 the Soviet leadership retreated after it had encountered resolute resistance. Aggression in Korea in 1950 is more difficult to explain; it was probably thought that a local conflict in the Far East did not involve the risk of global war; the extent of Soviet involvement in the preparation of this attack is, in fact, not fully known. Soviet suspicion of the West was often self-defeating; Western proposals from which it would have benefited and which involved hardly any political risks were rejected, such as the American invitations in 1946–7 for economic cooperation. To a certain extent this may have been deliberate, in view of the built-in need of tension of the Stalinist system. But there was an extra cutting edge in its hostility that cannot be explained with reference to domestic needs and traditional deep-seated suspicions. The Soviet attitude towards Germany had been much more friendly during the two years preceding Hitler's attack than after the war.

Was it only because it felt more threatened in 1939 than in 1947? There is no obvious explanation. In 1949 the first Soviet nuclear bomb was exploded, but the implications of warfare in the nuclear age dawned only gradually on the Kremlin; Stalin was too old and inflexible by then to revise his policy, and he continued to pursue his aims with an intransigence mitigated only by his native caution. He genuinely believed that communism as he envisaged it could not coexist in the long run with governments and societies of a different character. He did not want to settle conflicts with the outside world, but on the contrary sometimes deliberately sharpened them. At the same time he did not draw the ultimate conclusions from his own theories. The contradictions of Stalinism were partly inherent in the system but the tortuous personality of the supreme leader certainly added further complications. As the Hungarian Marxist philosopher Georg Lukacs later wrote,

> The epoch which ended with Stalin's death was not consistent . . . and this of necessity, for the fundamental axiom of Stalin's policy – the inherent need for a constant sharpening of conflicts – determined not only the internal affairs of the Soviet Union, but also involved the perspective of a third world war. Fortunately Stalin did not go right to the end in drawing conclusions from his doctrine; hence his policy also included elements of a recognition of the new epoch; but only elements.

The contradictions of American policy were of a different character. The general trend after the war was to withdraw and to cut commitments in Europe as soon and as much as possible. In April, at the Foreign Ministers Conference in London, Secretary of State Byrnes had suggested the withdrawal of all Allied troops from the continent, but he encountered stubborn resistance from Molotov, who also rejected a draft treaty on Germany and made it known that Russia was in no hurry to conclude such a treaty. Molotov refused to discuss Austria, and showed no interest in a 25 year agreement to keep Germany disarmed. In the following months the American line hardened; in a speech at Stuttgart in September Byrnes declared that 'as long as there will be an occupying army in Germany, America will be part of it'.

It was not any single event which had caused America to change its policy. Throughout 1946 there was still much goodwill towards Russia in Washington and a somewhat naïve belief that all the misunderstandings could be sorted out in direct talks at the highest level. Even Truman seems to have believed that 'Old Joe' was basically a decent fellow, a reasonable man at heart, with whom one could do business but for the unfortunate fact that every so often he was the prisoner of the politburo. Churchill's Fulton speech was not at all well received in the United States, and those few who, like James Forrestal, demanded a tougher line towards Russia were isolated. Leading Americans such as Bedell Smith and General Marshall were still in favour of moderation, so were elder statesmen like Cordell Hull. Their change of mind came only in 1947, when they realised after endless talks with the Russians that 'one cannot reach agreement with the Russians about Germany' (Bedell Smith), and that they were 'coldly determined to exploit the present state of Europe to propagate communism' (General Marshall). The Soviet refusal to withdraw their troops from Iran seemed a minor disagreement at the time, and in any case they left after a few months. Soviet territorial demands on Turkey were not followed up by action, but the support given to the insurgents in Greece was more serious. During the first phase of the civil war in 1944–5 Stalin had loyally observed the agreement with Churchill according to which Greece was part of the British sphere of influence; the Greek communists received no help in their armed struggle against the government. The decision to renew the civil war was made in May 1946; it cannot have been taken without Soviet knowledge, and in all probability Soviet support. It was a deliberate decision, not a case of automatic escalation, and it was bound to lead to a major crisis.

The Soviet leaders from Stalin down were firmly convinced that Europe would not recover from the war, and that, above all, America would be faced within two or three years with a major economic crisis on the scale of the great depression. This was the most important underlying assumption of Soviet policy; it gave Moscow a confidence that would have been otherwise inexplicable in the light of American nuclear superiority. The great crisis of the capitalist world seemed inevitable, but constant pressure had to be maintained to hasten its downfall.

These predictions seemed to be confirmed when Bevin informed Washington in February 1947 that Britain could no longer assist Greece and Turkey economically or militarily. Once again the help of the New World would be needed to redress the balance of the Old. In his emergency Truman asked Congress for 400 million dollars for economic and military aid to these countries. 'The free peoples of the world look to us for support,' Truman said. 'It must be the policy of the United States to support them resisting subjugation by armed minorities or by outside pressure primarily through economic and financial help.' The Truman doctrine was followed four months later by General Marshall's commencement speech at Harvard: 'Our policy is not directed against any country or doctrine but against hunger, poverty, desperation and chaos. The initiative must come from Europe.' Russian and eastern Europe were not excluded from the Marshall plan, but they decided, for reasons to be discussed below, not to participate. This, in June 1947, was the real turning point; collaboration between West and East was at an end, and Europe was finally split.

It has been argued that the Truman doctrine made it impossible for the Russians to adhere to the Marshall plan, that they might have cooperated but for the American promise of military assistance to certain European countries. On this view America should have provided economic help to Europe but refrained from giving military help even to countries badly needing it. But financial schemes would hardly have deterred the Russians from pursuing their course. Economic aid is not of much help to countries directly threatened with armed intervention; Greece's priorities in 1946–7 were of a different order.

Washington's decision to take a leading role in European politics was not taken at once, and it was reached with reluctance. For the first two years after the war Britain was almost alone in resisting Soviet pressure in central Europe, while America still believed in a policy of concessions. The change in Washington's policy came with the progressive disillusionment of the American representatives who were dealing with the Russians. They had hoped that at least on Germany there would be agreement; instead it now became the main battlefield of the cold war. The Soviets wanted ten billion dollars reparations from Germany, to be extracted largely from the zones occupied by the West. But the German economy was at a very low ebb, running only at a fraction of its former capacity. America was forced to provide massive help almost from the beginning of the occupation to prevent a complete collapse. The Russian demand meant, in effect, that America would have to pay even more, for without this infusion German industry would not be able to deliver goods to Russia. This America was unwilling to do unconditionally; it insisted that the Russians remove the barriers which they had erected between their zone and the others, cease its campaign of terror against non-communist political leaders and put an end to the arrests and the kidnappings. In Soviet eyes this was intolerable interference in their internal affairs.

Public opinion also played an important part in the change in American policy. Suddenly the American press woke up to the fact that Russia was still a dictatorship, a police régime which feared and repressed all internal opposition, as a *New York Times* correspondent put it after his return from the Soviet capital in July 1946. These reports should not have come as a surprise, because the state of affairs described was not exactly new, but they did come as a shock precisely because the public was so little prepared for them. There were signs of hysteria and histrionics, as well as 'threats of blustering or superfluous gestures of outward toughness', against which George Kennan warned in a famous article on 'The Sources of Soviet Conduct' (*Foreign Affairs*, July 1947). Kennan, a leading American diplomat with considerable Soviet experience, suggested that the main aim of Soviet policy was to 'make sure that it has filled every nook and cranny available to it in the basin of world power'. It was applying constant pressure in that direction, but there was no evidence that the goal must be reached at any given time. On the contrary, if Soviet policy found unassailable barriers in its path, it accepted them philosophically and accommodated itself to them. Mr Kennan advocated a long-term Western policy of containment, the 'adroit and vigilant application of counter-force at a series of constantly shifting geographical and political points, corresponding to the shifts and manœuvres of Soviet policy'. In the long run, Kennan predicted, the Soviet régime would either break up or mellow, for no messianic movement could face frustrations indefinitely without adjusting itself in one way or another to the logic of that state of affairs.

Critics of the containment doctrine argued that America was not strong enough to contain the Soviet Union on a global scale, that the American counter-force would ultimately consist of a 'heterogeneous array of satellites, clients, dependants and puppets' (as Walter Lippmann put it,) that it ignored legitimate Soviet interests and fears. There was a tendency among Western observers to overrate the extent of Soviet fears and the need to reassure Moscow. The German victories during the war had certainly been a great shock, but on the whole the Soviet leaders, aware of their country's military superiority in Europe, were quite confident; there were no Forrestals among them. True, West German rearmament was a setback for Soviet policy, but it was not a military threat, and it was in any case a direct consequence of the Korean war. The general feeling in Europe was that if military aggression on a limited scale was possible in the Far East, it could not be ruled out nearer home, and urgent measures to defend the continent had to be taken. Once there was agreement on these lines, German participation was only a question of time.

In Europe containment became official American policy in practice, if not in name, after the Prague coup and the Berlin blockade, and the United States began to rearm on a massive scale. Washington had decided to impress on Stalin that there were to be no changes in the status quo in Europe. The Russians accepted the fact; the foreign ministers who had held a series of increasingly fruitless conferences in 1948 and 1949 no longer met. Any further discussion seemed pointless; they were to assemble again only the year after Stalin's death.

The two parts of Europe were now hermetically sealed off from each other, with Berlin as the only hole in the curtain. Thousands streamed through it each week, mostly East Germans, all in one direction. There was no physical contact between West and East; trade had dwindled to a minimum, and there was of course no tourism in either direction. Western books and newspapers were banned in the East; radio stations continued their propaganda contest in the air, but the Western stations were heavily jammed. The Eastern bloc countries were shaken by deep internal convulsions; communist leaders disappeared overnight and it was not at all clear whether their successors were more firmly in the saddle. There seemed to be no purpose in trying to negotiate with Stalin's satellites, for their dependence on Moscow was by now total. The situation inside the Kremlin, too, was far from stable and indications of a new major purge became more numerous. Stalin's position seemed secure enough, but no one else's. Suddenly, in the middle of all the guessing about Soviet policies which had become more and more unpredictable, there came on 6 March 1953, the news of Stalin's death following a stroke six days earlier.

Stalin was 73 and had been in indifferent health for a number of years, but the news of his death was totally unexpected. Never in modern history had one man cast such a giant shadow over his own country and the world at large. His own subjects had certainly grown accustomed over the years to the idea that somehow the 'father of the peoples' was immortal, that for better or worse he would be with them for ever. In their first message his successors spoke of 'confusion', and there were reports from Moscow about tears and mourning. But many people all over the world breathed more freely.

Stalin's death aroused great expectations; imperceptibly at first, a thaw set in. It did not yet herald the end of the cold war. The changes in both foreign and domestic policy were less drastic and took longer than many had at first expected, but with his death a whole epoch of Soviet history came to an end. When the new Soviet leaders re-examined Stalin's foreign policy they found that both sides had kept in Europe what they already had before the cold war started. In an overall view, Stalin was certainly not the winner in Europe, for balanced against the consolidation of the Soviet empire there was NATO and, more important, the new spirit of European cooperation which but for the Soviet challenge would have remained a dead letter. There was the defection of Yugoslavia, not weighing very heavily in the global scales, but disturbing in its implications for the future; if one communist country could successfully defy the communist metropolis there was the danger that the example would spread.

The cold war was a contest without victors. Forced on the West, it had retarded and distorted its social and political development. The birth of a European community, the overcoming of the particularisms, the new friendship between old enemies such as France and Germany, were by-products of the cold war, but it was not at all certain whether these achievements, the result of a state of emergency and of great pressure, would be maintained once the immediate danger diminished or passed. If the policy of containment was part successful, it was due less to Western farsightedness and determination than to the development of nuclear weapons which revolutionised the risks of war and thus caused a general freeze up of frontiers and of political and social structures.

The Soviet Union had of course legitimate interests in eastern Europe and other parts of the world and it would not be correct to say that Stalin never showed moderation or a sense of reality in foreign policy. The declarations of the West, on the other hand, were not always dictated by wisdom. There was too much gullibility before 1948, too much inflexibility after. And yet, to establish a symmetry between East and West is to misread the origins and the character of the cold war. The claim that a more rational Western policy could have averted it can be made only if one leaves out of sight some essential factors: the intransigence of communist ideology in the postwar period, the dynamics of Stalinism and totalitarian societies in general, and Stalin's paranoia. Soviet policy was a mixture of *realpolitik* and persecution mania, of rational and irrational factors. Towards the end of his life, to quote Khrushchev, 'Stalin's persecution mania reached unbelievable dimensions'. The basic difference between the West and the Soviet Union could not have been resolved by gestures and declarations, however forthcoming, on the part of the West. The cold war could have been avoided only if the Soviet Union had not been possessed by the idea of the infallibility of its own doctrine: 'These convictions transformed an impasse between national states into a religious war, a tragedy of possibility into one of necessity.' (Arthur Schlesinger, *Foreign Affairs*, October 1967.)

The Quest for European Unity

The movement for European unity was given a decisive impetus in the post-war period as the result of the coup in Prague in 1948 and the outbreak of the Korean war in 1950. The European idea had been advocated by philosophers and statesmen for centuries, although for them military considerations had not been overriding. As far back as 1650 William Penn had called for the establishment of a European parliament; the Abbé Saint Pierre, Cardinal Alberoni and others had formulated similar plans during the seventeenth century. Romantics (like Novalis) had evoked in their writings the good old days when the whole of Christian Europe had been one nation; unromantic statesmen like Napoleon had unsuccessfully attempted to unite Europe by force. In the twentieth century the Pan-European movement had explained in detail the great benefits that would accrue to all if Europe were to unite, and Briand had tried to inaugurate a policy of little steps towards the same end. Hitler had attempted in his own way to unite Europe under German hegemony, and there had been many expressions of European solidarity among the various anti-nazi resistance movements during the war.

The idea of a European federation thus had many adherents on the left and right alike when the war ended. They were at one in the belief that after the destruction wrought by two European civil wars, the continent could be rebuilt only by a common effort. Beyond the disputes which kept them apart, the European nations had many ideas and interests, ambitions and sentiments in common. There was also the growing conviction that in the modern world, especially in the economic field, the small nation-state as an independent unit was no longer viable. Winston Churchill in a speech in Zurich in September 1946 had talked about the need for a new initiative to help this turbulent and mighty continent to take its rightful place with other groupings and help to shape the destinies of men. Europe at present was little more than a plaything of outside powers; united, it could overcome all its internal difficulties and again be a great power in the world.

The first major initiative towards European unity came in the economic field as the result of the threatened breakdown of the British and French economies in 1947. In his famous Harvard speech General Marshall, anticipating de Gaulle, talked about the need for European cooperation up to the Urals, and of the necessity for a common programme of recovery. A four-year plan of American aid such as was envisaged, and the creation of a common European market, would again make the old continent viable and relieve America of the burden of permanent economic support. The Organisation for European Economic Cooperation (OEEC) was established to act as a framework for these projects. It included 17 European nations; America at first stayed out, but later became an associate and eventually a full member. The aims of this body were limited: to close the dollar gap and to liberalise European trade. These purposes were achieved within a remarkably short period without undue difficulty. Trade between the European nations doubled within six years, a favourable balance of trade helped to close the dollar gap, and the Gross National Product (GNP) of most European countries increased at a remarkable steady rate each year. When American aid came to an end the advantage of OEEC were obvious to all, and it was decided not to abolish the organisation. But there was already a rift between the maximalists who wanted to enlarge its scope and saw it as a mere beginning, and the minimalists who pleaded special circumstances and difficulties and opposed any such initiative. British leaders argued that their country, while welcoming European cooperation, had close ties with the Commonwealth and was interested not merely in European trade but equally in a revival of world trade. For that reason Britain wanted to pursue a flexible policy and opposed a European customs union – the next logical step in the development of OEEC. By 1950 it was clear that little further progress would be made by OEEC. The original impetus had petered out and a new initiative was needed to give fresh momentum to the more ambitious aims of the European federalists.

Meanwhile, on a similar contingency basis, the first steps had been taken towards strengthening European defence. The idea that there should be some form of Atlantic union backed by America and the British Commonwealth, was pressed by British and Canadian leaders, whereas the French from the beginning put greater stress on the European character of such a scheme and also emphasised the need for closer political collaboration within the framework of a European assembly. But the prospects for cooperation in the military field were not as good as the chances for economic union, nor was there any reason to assume Europe would be able to defend itself without American help within the foreseeable future. American benevolence and good wishes were not enough; the United States would not only have to join a European defence organisation, but to take the leading part in it. Such 'entangling alliances' had been anathema to American policy-makers from the early days of the Republic, and the decision to establish NATO (the North Atlantic Treaty Organisation) signified a revolution in American foreign policy. From the outset Europe's military weakness and inability to defend itself without foreign assistance shaped the character of the treaty; it was an Atlantic, not a European alliance, and this gave rise to doubts and criticism. Was it not a mere abstraction, an alliance of limited scope and duration in which the divergent interests of the member states would always be a divisive factor? America was a global power with many interests in various parts of the world; could it be taken for granted that Europe would always receive top priority? Would America be ready to go to war and risk using nuclear weapons in response to a limited Soviet offensive in Europe? These arguments were countered by the NATO planners developing a 'forward strategy' aimed at defending Europe as far to the east as possible.

The groundwork for NATO was laid in Brussels in 1948 and the treaty was signed in April 1949; its headquarters were established in Paris. In addition to the United States and Canada, the following countries joined the organisation: the Benelux countries, Britain, Norway, Iceland, Denmark (but not Sweden!), Greece, Turkey (in 1952), Italy, West Germany, France, and Portugal. In the early days of NATO the main emphasis was on rather loose joint defence planning and the re-equipment of European armies with American arms. The real test, the unification of command and the integration of forces, came later, after the question of German participation had been solved following much heart-searching and a real crisis.

The joint economic and military measures taken during the late forties were on a strictly ad hoc basis, designed to cope with immediate dangers and problems. These steps did not, however, satisfy the advocates of political unity who, meeting in The Hague in May 1948, decided to establish a permanent European Assembly, the Council of Europe, in Strasbourg. Strictly unofficial, this body with its 130 members was consultative in character; its meetings were mainly devoted to the discussion of human rights and cultural relations and it had, of course, no power to enforce its resolutions.

Among economic planners and businessmen on the continent the conviction was growing that a new initiative was needed to advance beyond OEEC. A lasting solution to Europe's difficulties would be found only within a common market which would coordinate fiscal and monetary policies, and promote large-scale, low-cost production and a substantial rise in productivity.

The initiative for a first scheme on these lines was taken by the French in May 1950; it envisaged a coal and steel pool between France and Germany under a common authority. This was the Schuman plan, and its authors saw it as the first step towards a common European economic system. It was a pilot scheme, but it concerned one of the continent's key industries, accounting for about a quarter of the total trade of the six countries that were eventually to constitute 'Little Europe'. It was 'the first expression of the Europe that is being born', in the words of Jean Monnet, who was the real spiritual father of the project. At the beginning the plan encountered predictable opposition: the British argued that it was not compatible with their Commonwealth links, Labour saw it as a big business conspiracy, and Harold Macmillan maintained that 'our people will not hand on to any supranational authority the right to close our pits or our steel works'. Inside Germany and France, too, there was resistance on both the left and the right; the communists appeared as the true defenders of the national interest that had been betrayed by Schuman, Adenauer, and de Gasperi. De Gaulle and his movement, then in opposition, were on principle against any curtailment of French sovereignty; the German social democrats said they were in favour of real European unity – not the 'Europe Inc.' of the tycoons of heavy industry. But despite all opposition the Common Coal and Steel Market came into being in 1953, and within the next five years proved itself an outstanding success. Steel production rose by 42 per cent, trade between the six member countries flourished, there were no political or economic ill effects. This had a profound influence on the early opponents of the Common Market; the lesson that industrial production among the Six increased more than twice as fast as in Britain between 1950 and 1955, and almost three times as fast between 1955 and 1960, was not lost on them. De Gaulle and the German and Italian Social Democrats came to accept the Common Market, and even the West European communists were eventually compelled to modify their opposition, despite all Lenin's warnings against the perils of the Capitalist United States of Europe.

After the Schuman plan had been accepted, a further initiative was undertaken by the Benelux countries which suggested the elimination of tariffs and the coordination of monetary policies. Other proposals concerned the establishment of a European atomic pool to meet future power shortages. At conferences in Messina in 1955 and in Rome in 1957, it was decided to found a European market, and to establish an atomic pool (Euratom). The new European Economic Community (EEC) had certain escape clauses which reassured de Gaulle; with its emphasis on economic integration, it went beyond a mere customs union but fell short of complete economic union. Its main purpose was to bring about continuous and balanced expansion, to foster a high level of employment and raise the standard of living, to stabilise prices and to prevent lack of equilibrium in the balance of payments. These aims were to be accomplished in three preliminary stages, each lasting four years.

The EEC came into being on 1 January 1958. The founder members were France, Germany, Italy, Holland, Belgium and Luxembourg. Headed by a nine member commission ('to be chosen for their general competence and of indisputable independence'), it was based on a quasi-federal structure independent of governments and private interests – a European parliament, a Council of Ministers, a Central Commission, and a Court of Justice. These organs were to supervise the EEC and the many other agencies that were formed in its wake (the European Social Fund, the Economic and Social Committee, the Overseas Development Fund, the European Investment Bank, the Transport Committee, etc.). The founding document, known as the Rome treaty, envisaged immediate tariff cutting and the total abolition of customs barriers by 1967. External tariffs were to be retained and this became one of the main targets of criticism by non-members. But the tariffs were usually lower than in the past: almost non-existent in the case of raw materials, less than six per cent for finished goods, 13–17 per cent for capital equipment. On the whole, the Common Market contributed towards a general liberalisation of international trade; it did not simply replace the old nation-state protectionism by a new European bloc surrounded by high tariff walls.

Within five years of its foundation, EEC covering a total population of 165 million, emerged as the world's greatest trading power, the biggest exporter and buyer of raw materials. It was the second largest importer and its steel production was second only to that of the United States; total industrial production of the Six increased by 70 per cent between 1950 and 1960. These impressive achievements were not just the result of pooling resources (as some argued), or liberalising trade, and trusting the free play of market mechanisms and unregulated competition. Most of the inspiration behind the Common Market was provided by French experts (Monnet – the father of the Schuman plan, Marjolin, E. Hirsch, Pierre Uri and the

Belgian Jean Rey), who believed in *dirigisme*, in economic and social planning. They realised from the outset that not all branches of the European economy were viable; even the most fervent believers in *laissez-faire* liberalism were forced to admit that in order to survive, agriculture had to be centrally planned. Big business viewed the activities of the planners with misgivings; in its view the Eurocrats in Brussels – 3,000 by 1962, with their number still growing – had far too much power. The *laissez-faire* enthusiasts did not necessarily oppose the new common ethos and community spirit and the informal consultations between organisations and individuals on every level, but they did not agree with the social goals set by the Eurocrats in Brussels. On the part of the governments, too, there was suspicion that the supranational authority was becoming too strong and independent, that a new technocratic élite was developing whose prime allegiance was to Europe, not to their country of origin. There was every reason to assume that the importance and scope of centralised European decision-making was likely to increase even more in the years to come. Almost from the beginning there were conflicts of interest between public (European) and private (business) planning. In part these were due to structural differences, for industry in France (to give one illustration) was nationalised to a larger extent than in Germany. Such conflicts did not, however, make cooperation impossible, as the Benelux example had shown. Within its closely integrated structure Holland had put much more stress on a planned economy than Belgium, without causing lasting damage to collaboration between the two countries.

There were from the beginning considerable strains and stresses in the new European community, but there was also a welcome fresh spirit, a much needed dynamism, and the first stirrings of a new European patriotism. Frontiers remained, but seemed to shrink in importance; small placards were to be seen: 'Another border but still Europe'. The new Europe seemed big enough to accommodate both specialists and conservatives, and even de Gaulle, the opponent of a closely-linked federal union, came to accept the new structure as an 'imposing confederation'. The one real crisis facing EEC was the result of its very success. Britain and the other European countries which had at first opposed the project came to realise their mistake and belatedly asked to be admitted. The dissension among EEC members on this issue belongs to a later chapter of European history.

The efforts to achieve closer integration were less successful in the military field. Following the outbreak of the Korean War, America began to press again for a European integrated force under a centralised command with the inclusion of German units. But the impact of Korea was less strongly felt in Europe than in America, and there were still deep fears of a revival of German militarism. The French countered American pressure with a plan of their own, which provided for small national contingents in a unified

European army. There was to be a common budget, and of course supra-national control. The basic assumption in this, the Pleven plan for a European Defence Community (EDC) was that within NATO, control over German remilitarisation would be inadequate, and that more than a coalition of the old type was needed. The American reaction was at first cool; Washington was not certain whether the Pleven plan was just a manœuvre to delay German inclusion in NATO, or whether it was sincerely meant as a workable solution to a difficult problem. After initial hesitation America decided to accept EDC and by the spring of 1953 six European governments had signed the treaty which then had to be ratified by their parliaments. The project was defeated in the very country in which it had originated. Mendès-France, then French Prime Minister, demanded a lower level of supranational control and integration than at first envisaged. But even this modification did not appease the French critics who were opposed to any limitations affecting the French army, but refused to grant any such right to the German forces. The French demands were mutually exclusive and so, in a dramatic vote on 30 August 1954, Gaullists joining forces with the communists defeated the scheme. Soon after this setback, Britain made a fresh proposal, reviving an old project providing for direct German membership in NATO. To allay French fears provisions were made for tying German units closely into the NATO structure, and the British also promised to keep their forces (the British army of the Rhine) on the continent for an unlimited period to counter-balance the effects of German remilitarisation. The reaction in Paris was not enthusiastic, but it was realised that a second French vote against European military integration would simply result in Germany's admission to NATO in conditions that would be even less desirable from the French point of view. The French Parliament reluctantly ratified the new scheme in October 1954. NATO and Western defence were stengthened but only after the defeat of the idea of a specifically European defence community.

NATO had been founded to deter an outright Soviet attack on western Europe. This aim was achieved, although the resolution passed at a meeting in Lisbon in 1952 providing for a military force of no fewer than 96 divisions proved to be too ambitious and was never realised. After Stalin's death, as the immediate danger of a Soviet invasion decreased, there were first signs of disintegration of the alliance; the United States was still preoccupied with Korea and England and France were deeply involved in the Middle East and in Indo-China and Algeria respectively. In the early years of NATO, American nuclear supremacy remained the main deterrent, but this state of affairs was highly unsatisfactory from the European point of view, for NATO was dominated by America, and America was not committed to the full support of its allies. Only the United States would decide in what circumstances a nuclear response to an attack on Europe was necessary. There was much concern in

Europe about the future, for sooner or later a nuclear balance between West and East would be reached, and it was not at all clear how to prepare for the defence of Europe in these changed conditions. In France, and among some circles in other European countries, new approaches to European defence were advocated to make the continent less dependent on America. All these schemes were based on the assumption that Europe would be able to provide adequate conventional forces and, ultimately, a separate West European nuclear system. Not every threat against western Europe could be met with the massive retaliation that Dulles had announced. If not, how were the threats below this level to be met? Britain decided to develop its own nuclear armoury and France its *force de frappe*; West Germany wanted the United States to surrender its exclusive control of NATO's nuclear arsenal. These conflicting demands, the failure to stop atomic proliferation, and the inability to establish a strong, independent European defence force, caused a deep crisis in NATO in the early sixties. In the early discussions about European defence, German rearmament had been the main bone of contention; it was widely feared that a new European military alliance would be dominated by West Germany. These fears were psychologically only too intelligible, but they ignored the changed world situation. Germany after the total defeat of 1945 was not in a mood to engage in big-power policies, and, more important, it was no longer in a position to do so; the dimensions of the international scene had radically changed. The crisis that eventually shook the very foundations of NATO concerned the role of America, not of Germany, inside the alliance, and it was the result of West Europe's inability to regain in the military field a position of strength and independence even remotely commensurate with its economic achievements.

Despite the astonishing economic recovery, the interim balance sheet of the movement for European unity drawn in the late fifties was therefore bound to be disappointing to the federalists. A large measure of cooperation between the West European governments had been achieved, but the federalists wanted unity, not just collaboration. The staying power of nationalism was stronger, vested interests and particularist positions more deeply rooted than had been assumed. Britain which preferred not to become too closely entangled in European affairs was the main culprit during the early stage; once Britain had succeeded in enlisting American support for the defence of Europe it lost interest in the other schemes for European unity. Conservatives and Labour alike greatly overrated the strength of Commonwealth ties, and their estimate of Britain's political, economic, and military potential in the postwar world was far too complacent. There was the traditional distrust of Frenchmen, Germans, and other continentals; the few advocates of European unity in Britain in the early fifties faced an uphill struggle, the idea had far less appeal there than on the continent. There was an almost general belief that by the circumstances of geography and historical tradition alike, Britain was not really part of Europe. By the time a majority of British statesmen (and public opinion) had, after a delay of ten years, reluctantly reached the conclusion that at least in the economic field Britain's future lay with Europe, the gates of the new Europe had been closed to them. France under de Gaulle had emerged as the leading force in EEC, and used its veto to keep Britain out of the European community. De Gaulle now replaced Britain as the main obstacle to European unity. Driven by a conception of world affairs that was antiquated in character and dictated solely by French national interests (as the General interpreted them), he pursued a policy that was inherently contradictory: he wanted to lessen Europe's dependence on America, but he intended to keep out of his scheme half of Europe and further more opposed attempts to make the Community a more closely knit unit. By the late fifties the original impetus of the European idea had run out. The new institutions went on functioning on their own momentum, some of the old rivalries had been buried, and the economic map of the continent had greatly changed. But the achievements still fell woefully short of the dreams of the federalists, who regarded it as at best a transitional stage towards the realisation of a far more ambitious goal.

Politics in Postwar Europe

There were certain common features in political developments throughout postwar Europe: the weakness of democratic socialism, the retreat of communism after 1948, and the emergence of strong Christian Democratic parties. The history of the French and Italian Communist Parties is in many respects similar, and there are interesting parallels in the rise of Christian Democracy in West Germany and in Italy. It is tempting to single out these common features and to ignore others that do not fit into the picture. The Christian Democratic movements in Germany and Italy were incomparably stronger than the French MRP, which after a promising start lost much of its influence when Gaullism appeared on the scene. There was no parallel to Gaullism in other European countries. The German Christian Democrats faced a much easier task than their Italian colleagues; they were far less dependent on their allies, their party had greater internal cohesion, and they had a prime minister who was their undisputed leader for 14 years. In Italy within the same period, de Gasperi was followed by Pella, Fanfani, Scelba, Segni, Zolli, again Fanfani, again Segni, Tambroni, again Fanfani, Leone, and Moro; some of these leaders represented the left wing of the party, others belonged to the right or centre. The eclipse of west European communism was by no means complete; the French and Italian parties, though in total opposition and virtually isolated, kept their strength and received between 20–25 per cent of the total vote in all elections with almost monotonous regularity. Democratic socialism suffered in Italy, where the party split, and in France, where it fell into a slow but steady decline. In Germany, on the other hand, its influence increased after 1953, and in Sweden, Norway, Denmark, Austria, and Benelux, social democracy was in power throughout the nineteen-fifties either independently or within a coalition.

The emergence of Christian Democracy as a leading political force was no doubt the most important new factor in postwar European politics. There had been confessional parties in various European countries before, such as the German Zentrum, the Austrian People's Party, the Belgian Catholic Party or Gil Robles' *Accion Popular* in Spain. They had been on the whole right wing in orientation, their appeal was based on a vague religiosity: they represented conservative and ecclesiastical interests, whereas postwar Christian Democracy took great pains to stress that it stood for something essentially new, that it had no connection with political formations that had existed in the past. Only the Catholic People's Party in Holland continued to emphasise its confessional aspect; the others dissociated themselves from this tradition and were moreover far more independent of ecclesiastical control than their predecessors; left-wing Catholic trends were not uncommon in France and Italy. The prewar Christian parties had been anti-socialist and anti-liberal in inspiration, a response to anti-clericalism and laicism; this was their main *raison d'être*. Postwar Christian Democracy was a much more complex phenomenon: it had genuinely accepted democracy and carried out some important economic reforms. De Gasperi once said that the Christian Democrats were not fighting communism's economic programme. They had the support of various social classes, including a substantial working-class and peasant basis; their 'class character' defied ready-made explanations.

Christian Democracy in Italy was in the tradition of Don Luigi Sturzo's Popular Party of the early twenties – a lay party with left-of-centre tendencies, which after the rise of fascism had been unceremoniously dropped by the Vatican. The party, as it emerged in 1944, consisted of a strong conservative wing, tending towards 'authoritarian democracy', represented by Catholic Action leaders such as Gedda and Lombardo. The left wing included Catholic trade unionists who wanted to transform their movement into a genuine labour party, Gronchi (who later became President of the Republic), and Fanfani, who stood for an independent Italian foreign policy, gravitating occasionally towards neutralism. Under Segni, Prime Minister from 1955 to

1957, important political and social reforms were carried out. De Gasperi who was forced to resign in 1953 and died a year later, was of the centre, masterly at playing off left and right against each other. He had won in the 1948 election, and again in 1953, at a time of high international tension, when communism seemed the overriding danger, but he strongly resisted pressure by the right wing of his own party to pursue conservative and strictly confessional policies. He refused to cooperate with the monarchists who had emerged as a sizable force in the elections, and preferred a coalition with the small centre parties, though this involved him in almost permanent bargaining with his partners, and laid him open to constant attacks from both the left and the right within the coalition. After de Gasperi's death both the left and the right wing of the Christian Democrats attempted, without lasting success, to control the party and the government; the centre, represented by men like Scelba, tried equally unsuccessfully to find a formula (as de Gasperi had done) that would be acceptable to the whole party, and if possible also to potential coalition partners. With short interruptions, this internal tug-of-war lasted for many years and often paralysed the party. The great economic upsurge which began in the middle fifties and the consequent prosperity was only to a small extent the result of government initiative and direction (such as the Vanoni plan); it developed its own momentum despite the instability and defeatism of political life. Originally pledged to radical reform, the Christian Democrats became, at most, a party of gradualism. With all their shortcomings and apparent failures, they succeeded in clinging to power because of the split within the left. During the nineteen-fifties they provided that bare minimum of political stability which made the transformation of the Italian economy possible, and eventually had far-reaching repercussions on the structure of society.

The French *Mouvement Républicain Populaire* (MRP) was at first the only new political party of the Fourth Republic. Its ideological origins can be traced to Marc Sangnier's left-wing Catholic *Le Sillon*; its organisational predecessor was the small *Jeune République*, a left-of-centre group in the Third Republic which, to its great credit, had almost without exception opposed Pétain in 1940. But essentially it was a new movement, having been conceived in the days of the Resistance. Among its leaders, Georges Bidault had been secretary of the General Council of the Resistance movement and Maurice Schumann, de Menthon, Teitgen, and other leading figures had also played an important part in the Resistance. From the early days of the Fourth Republic and up to its very end, the party played a key role in French politics. It was represented in most cabinets; Bidault was Prime Minister in 1946 and again in 1949–50, and Robert Schumann headed the government in 1947–8. Bidault and Schumann between them monopolised the foreign ministry during the Fourth Republic, an almost constant fixture in an otherwise rapidly fluctuating system. The MRP was at first a party of the left trying, as one of its members put it, to reconcile the traditions of 1789 with Christian thought. During the early years of the Republic it voted in favour of the nationalisation of key branches of the national economy. It was MRP policy to favour nationalisation wherever business was a public service, or where private finance threatened the independence of the state, or where private initiative simply did not function. Until January 1946 the MRP collaborated closely with de Gaulle; it was strongly opposed to the polarisation in world politics represented by the cold war and tried to act as a 'third force', first between the communists and their enemies, and later between de Gaulle and his adversaries. The MRP was by no means opposed in principle to collaborating with the communists; it wanted good relations with the Soviet Union, and it was only with considerable reluctance, and as the result of heavy communist attacks, that it changed its position in 1947–8. Yet, despite the left-wing orientation of many of its leaders, support for the MRP came largely from the regions of France that were traditionally conservative. In 1946 the MRP received 26 per cent of the vote, but when de Gaulle made his first bid for power in the following year, the moderates shifted their support and the party suffered heavy losses including about 60 per cent of its share in Paris. By 1951 its vote had been halved, and it never recovered from this setback. The party continued to exist, but it gradually ceased to be a leading force in French politics; at the time of the Algerian war it was further weakened by the secession of Bidault and other advocates of French Algeria. The decline of the MRP was the result of more than a single cause. Though France was much more Catholic than West Germany, the church there had far less influence in politics than in Germany, let alone in Italy. In the Third Republic it had been exceedingly difficult for a practising Catholic to play a leading role in politics; it certainly did not help in terms of electoral appeal. In the Fourth Republic anti-clericalism was much weaker, which made it easier for a confessional party to function. But at the same time the need for the existence of such a party had lessened; its left-wing supporters could as well vote socialist, its right wing join the moderates or the Gaullists, as indeed many of them subsequently did.

1947 was the year of de Gaulle. The General had resigned the year before in disgust with the parties and the whole political system. He wanted to liberate the country from the stranglehold of the parties, as he declared in a series of speeches, asserting that parliament had ceased to be representative of the will of the nation and demanding a change in the constitution. His speeches were made at a time of economic and political crisis and they met with a warm response.

In April 1947 de Gaulle announced the formation of the *Rassemblement du Peuple Français* (RPF) which was to be a national movement, not just another political party. In the municipal elections of October 1947 it received about 40 per cent of the total vote. For de Gaulle, this was only a beginning; ultimately the RPF was to embrace the whole nation. De Gaulle's foreign political orientation was at that time anti-European and critical of American policy, which he thought far too lenient towards Germany. He had encountered American opposition when demanding the detachment of the Rhineland from Germany. Subsequently he modified his attitude towards Germany, his ultimate ambition was to bring Western Europe under French leadership and this could not be realised against German opposition.

The success of the RPF was startling; in a few months, with hardly any financial backing, a great party machine came into existence. Big business continued to support the traditional right, regarding Gaullism as radical and irresponsible. The General had to rely mainly on the enthusiasm of his early collaborators from the days of London and Algiers who now, again, constituted the backbone of his movement. His electoral success was most marked in Normandy and Brittany on the one hand, and Alsace-Lorraine on the other, the east and the west of France, but there was also substantial support in Paris, Lyons, and Bordeaux. Within a year the RPF had become a seemingly irresistible force; within another year stagnation set in, and then decline. De Gaulle had promised a great deal, and then inexplicably shied away from taking the next step. One of his closest collaborators complained that 'the General told us to go to the Rubicon – and to take out our fishing rods'. A *coup d'état* seemed on the cards, but de Gaulle, despite his contempt for the parties, hesitated to disregard altogether the rules of the parliamentary game. It was not simply a failure of nerve at a decisive moment; time, as the General realised, was not yet ripe, the crisis not deep enough. The communist disorders of 1947 were suppressed by Jules Moch, the socialist Minister of the Interior, the economic situation slowly improved after 1949 and prices were stabilised. De Gaulle's warnings against European unity ('do not abandon your soldiers, do not give up your sovereignty'), his anti-British tirades, his invocation of the treaty with the Soviet Union, fell on deaf ears; the 'European' policy of the parties of the centre and the moderate left had a wider appeal. The RPF had no press of its own to spread its message, and above all, there was not yet a television network, which was to play such a decisive part in de Gaulle's second bid for power ten years later.

The RPF wave gradually ebbed away; it lost much of its support in 1952 as the conservative electorate began again to vote for the traditional right-wing groups. By 1953 there were only ten Gaullist councillors left in the Paris municipality compared with 52 in 1947. There was also internal dissension: in March 1952 the Gaullist right wing in Parliament defied party discipline and voted for the new Pinay government and its programme of economic stabilisation. In December 1952 Soustelle, one of de Gaulle's most faithful

followers, was asked by the President of the Republic to form a new government, but there was not even a remote chance of success; since the R P F had
deliberately isolated itself, no one wanted to cooperate with it. Realising this,
the Gaullists decided not to persevere in sterile opposition; they participated
in the subsequent governments of Laniel, Mendès-France, and Edgar Faure.
Stage by stage the R P F was drawn into the parliamentary game, and became
a political party like all the others, much to the disgust of General de Gaulle.
At a press conference in July 1955 he announced for the second time his
retirement from public life. He did not exclude a comeback altogether, but,
he added prophetically, it would be only after an unusual shock. De Gaulle
retired to his house at Colombey-les-deux-Eglises to write the second part of
his autobiography, one of the most powerful, most interesting, and also most
idiosyncratic political documents of our time. He maintained contact with
some of the leading figures of the Fourth Republic during his weekly visits to
Paris, which become almost a ritual. Soustelle, Debré, Chaban-Delmas and
his other lieutenants continued to play a part of some importance in French
politics, while de Gaulle himself was biding his time. Towards the end of
1954 the latent unrest in Algeria turned into open rebellion. When de Gaulle
retired this had been only a small cloud on a distant horizon; it took three
more years for the crisis to deepen and the 'unusual shock' to arise to which
he had alluded.

Between 1948 and 1958 France had 19 different governments; their short-
lived character and lack of initiative (*immobilisme*) became proverbial. They
included both advocates and opponents of EDC, those who pressed for more
active warfare in Algeria and others who were against it. A new mass movement mushroomed for a little while on the extreme right: Poujadism, a
mixture of right-wing and populist elements. The refusal to pay taxes became
the declared policy of certain sections of the population. A 'Weimar situation'
threatened the Fourth Republic; the anti-democratic left and right increased
in strength and the centre was paralysed. The Socialists, the MRP, even the
Independents of the right split on such issues as EDC, Indo-China, and above
all Algeria. The Laniel government was broken by Dien Bien Phu, the military
disaster in Indo-China which led to the French decision to abandon its
position there. It was followed by one of the few outstanding postwar governments, that of Pierre Mendès-France. Formally a Radical Democrat, Mendès-
France pursued a policy well to the left of his party and eventually established his own group in Parliament. Lacking de Gaulle's charisma, he had
few political friends; his appeal to reason, his decisive economic policy, his
courage and new dynamic style (*gouverner c'est choisir*) won him the grudging
respect even of his adversaries, but his government could not be a lasting
success; the country needed strong leadership but was far too divided inter-
nally to tolerate it. During his eight months of office Mendès-France liqui-

dated the Indo-Chinese war and granted autonomy to Tunisia, thus removing two of the main sources of weakness in foreign politics. But he was defeated by the domestic imbroglio and the growing Algerian crisis, and those who followed him sank with every step deeper into the quagmire.

France at the time seemed to face well nigh insurmountable structural difficulties: industry was stagnating, agriculture was antiquated, there was no economic justification for the existence of a vast army of small shopkeepers and the whole system of distribution was cumbersome and wasteful. The housing situation in the drab and neglected cities was disastrous. The most enthusiastic tourist found little to admire but museums and old monuments. In this atmosphere of apathy and despair, France, in the eyes of friends and enemies alike, seemed doomed. Yet below the surface there was an imperceptible turn for the better. The population figures, which had remained static for a long time, suddenly took an upward turn. French industry expanded as many new factories were set up and the existing ones were modernised. France became the country of the fastest trains and the most advanced cars in Europe. By 1957 the industrial output was 46 per cent higher than in 1949, and agricultural production too had risen by a quarter. The construction of new buildings more than trebled between 1951 and 1957, new suburbs came into being, the French cities were given a new look. Great economic schemes were tackled in North Africa with the emphasis on investment in minerals and natural gas. Though the country was plagued by recurrent fiscal and foreign trade crises which seriously impeded its growth, the economic outlook was far more promising by 1958 than at the beginning of the decade. Economic progress – as in Italy – seemed to have its own laws and momentum, irrespective of the political immobilism. Though not all sections of the population benefited equally from the boom, what was astonishing was that a country deeply permeated by *incivisme*, lacking cohesion, self-confidence and faith, made any progress at all. Not only the outside world but the French themselves were slow to realise what great progress they were making.

The contrast between France and Germany in the nineteen-fifties was glaring. There was perhaps too much stability on the other side of the Rhine; the hold of the Christian Democratic Union (CDU) was never seriously in danger. For almost 15 years, up to his resignation in 1963, the party and the country were led by Adenauer, the imprint of whose rule was felt in every aspect of German politics. Under him Germany recovered from the deep wounds caused by the war and established close ties with the Western world. Adenauer had the self-confidence of a man whose formative years had been spent in a world less subject to uncertainties and self doubt, the pre-1914 world. Like de Gaulle and Churchill (with whom otherwise he had little in common) he regarded economics as a necessary evil, and left it largely to Ludwig Erhard, the main protagonist of a socialist market economy. By

instinct and conviction alike, Adenauer was a conservative, and this corresponded well with the prevailing mood of the nation: 'No experiments!'
But Adenauer had also learned his lesson from the bitter experience of the
Weimar Republic. He knew about the limits of liberalism and realised that
there could be no stability without social security, that the great majority of
the population had to share in the prosperity. Gross earnings almost trebled
in West Germany between 1950 and 1962, while the cost of living index
between 1950 and 1959 rose only from 100 to 121, in contrast to a rise from
100 to 147 in England, and from 100 to 167 in France. The advocates of a
'people's capitalism' drew fresh courage from the substantial increase in the
number of shareholders; the number of cars increased eightfold during the
decade. The German countryside was gradually transformed as agriculture
was thoroughly mechanised. By 1960 the distance between town and country
had shrunk; there were excellent shops and modern houses even in the smallest villages, and of course electricity and telephones. The refugees from the
east, many millions of them, were quickly integrated; the attempt to establish a separate refugee movement was not a success, and was eventually
abandoned. An ambitious housing programme was successfully carried out.
These and other achievements created a feeling of self-satisfaction in which
there was little scope for radical politics of either left or right-wing inspiration.
The neo-nazis showed some activity in Lower Saxony but their local successes
in the early fifties were a flash in the pan. Communist influence decreased
steadily after 1947; the banning of the Communist Party in 1956 by the
Constitutional Court seemed unwise and unnecessary in the circumstances.

There was not much change in German politics in the nineteen-fifties
and certainly very little excitement. From time to time the Liberals (FDP)
quarrelled with their senior coalition partners and threatened to withdraw.
The CDU polled 45 per cent of the total vote in the elections of 1953, a great
achievement, but not sufficient to allow it to rule the country single-handed.
There was dissension within the CDU between its left and right wing, and
also, to a certain extent, between its various regional organisations. Franz
Josef Strauss, the leader of the party in Bavaria, attained cabinet rank at the
comparatively early age of 38; a stormy career as Minister of Defence was
suddenly cut short in a flurry of charges and countercharges, but he made a
comeback in the coalition government of the late sixties. Schroeder, a lawyer
from Silesia, was another pillar of the conservative trend in the party; he was
in turn Minister of the Interior, Foreign Minister, and eventually Minister of
Defence. While Adenauer's anti-nazi record was above reproach, he was
less than scrupulous in the choice of his closest collaborators; there could be
but one opinion about the career of men like Oberländer and Globke in the
nazi era, but the former was dropped only after protests from all sides, and
Globke, a lawyer who had provided the official interpretation to the anti-

semitic Nuremberg laws of 1935, remained for years the Chancellor's close associate and confidant, despite heavy pressure. The motive for such stubbornness was Adenauer's feeling of loyalty to his associates, certainly not anti-semitism. For it was mainly owing to the personal intervention of the Chancellor that the Bundestag approved in 1953 the law on compensation for Israel and individual Jews who had suffered from Hitler's policies. Israel alone received loans and goods totalling 715 million dollars over a period of 12 years. Communist East Germany refused to pay any restitution claiming that since nazism had been uprooted in the German Democratic Republic there was no need to make amends. The East German communists refused as a matter of principle to accept responsibility for anything that happened before 1945; according to them only a tiny minority, not wide sections of the German people, had been involved in nazi crimes.

In a difficult period of German history Adenauer provided much needed stability and prudent leadership. One of his most important contributions was the reconciliation with France and the close collaboration that ensued after centuries of bitter enmity. Spaak, the Belgian Prime Minister, himself a great fighter for the European idea, wrote of Adenauer: 'Without him no Coal and Steel Pool, no Common Market, and no Euratom. Without him the dream of a United Europe would not have become a reality.' Yet with all this the effects of 15 years of Adenauer's rule were not all positive. The more ambitious plans for social reform were not carried out; there were strong conservative trends in German society, gravitating not towards nazism but more in the tradition of Wilhelmian Germany, which many still remembered with some nostalgia as the 'good old times'. Far too little attention was paid to the expansion of education, and the introduction of confessionalism in the schools created major problems. Adenauer's foreign policy was often criticised for its rigidity, sometimes unfairly, for until 1953 no opportunities existed to be missed in relations with Russia and the Eastern bloc. After Stalin's death a more elastic German policy towards the East would probably have done some good; at the very least it would have silenced the government's critics. Adenauer firmly believed that one day communism would crumble from within, or that at any rate the growing pressure of China on Russia would force the Soviet Union to modify its policy towards Europe. As a German patriot, he regretted the division of Germany and the loss of its eastern territories; as a Rhinelander and a Catholic he was orientated towards the West and showed less concern for reunification than many of his colleagues or critics. But was there ever a real chance that the two Germanies would be reunited? When the foreign ministers of the Big Four met in Berlin in January 1954, their points of view did not seem to differ widely; both sides professed to be, in principle, in favour of reunification. Molotov demanded the withdrawal of Allied troops even before the elections that would decide about Germany's future, and he insisted that the reunified Germany should remain neutral. Eden, on the other hand, suggested that the Allied troops should be withdrawn only after the elections, and that an independent German state should be free to enter (or to renounce) any international pacts and obligations. It has been maintained that the year 1955 was a turning point; with the gradual political and military integration of West Germany into the Atlantic alliance the door to German unity was closed. But there was even before that date no real prospect for reunification except on terms unacceptable to the great majority of Germans. Khrushchev clarified the Soviet attitude by his insistence on the 'political and social achievements' of East Germany, the DDR, which he said would have to be maintained in future, and by his opposition to any 'mechanical reunion' of the two parts of Germany which had developed in opposite directions. When Christian Pineau, the French Foreign Minister, enquired in Moscow in May 1956 about the chances of German reunification, he was told quite candidly that 'we prefer 17 million Germans under our influence to 70 million Germans even if they are neutral'.

The general European trend towards the right also affected Britain, for in 1951 the Conservatives returned to power. After the initial wave of reforms, the Labour Party showed signs of exhaustion; after 1948 it displayed little initiative or leadership. When the Labour lead over the Tories was whittled down to a mere 17 in the elections of 1950, the Attlee government preferred to eschew any controversial policies. The party was weakened by the resignation of some of its principal leaders: Bevin, seriously ill, retired in 1950, Aneurin Bevan and other spokesmen of the left wing resigned from the government the year after, following cuts in the social services. In 1951 Attlee called for new elections from which the Conservatives emerged with a majority of 26 over Labour; this majority increased to 67 in 1955 and to 107 in 1959. Churchill became Prime Minister for the second time in 1951; he was replaced in April 1955 by Anthony Eden, who after the Suez disaster gave way to Harold Macmillan. The Conservative Party was lucky to come to power at a time when the worst postwar shortages were over; the Labour Party had begun to abolish rationing and controls, which were so unpopular, and the Tories found themselves in the fortunate position of being able to finish the job. They denationalised the steel industry but were careful not to touch the structure of the welfare state which, within a very few years, had gained general approval. Any attempt to tamper with these services would have been to court political disaster. The Tories, in fact, spent more on social services than Labour; the Attlee government had built 200,000 houses a year, subsequent Tory governments provided 300,000. The country was able to afford these social policies, it was thought, in view of the small but steady economic growth which gathered further momentum during the late fifties and early sixties. By and large, however, economic expansion in Britain was slower than in any other major European country. 'Export or Die' had been the slogan after the war; exports did increase substantially, but imports grew even faster. As a result the balance of payments was negative every year (with the exception of 1958). Britain constantly needed fresh loans and there was a permanent danger of devaluation.

On the surface all seemed well. The fact that the country was living beyond its means was only slowly realised. The years of austerity were over, Britain seemed to be sharing in the general European boom. There was a great deal of new building and reconstruction, new suburbs sprang up, people were far better dressed and nourished than in the immediate postwar period. The capital regained its status and became 'swinging London'. The social services were a source of envy in most other European nations; they included free education at all levels. But despite the mild boom Britain did not keep pace with Europe; it spent much less on hospitals, roads, and reconstruction than most continental countries.

Britain still had a great many international obligations in the early fifties. The defence budget was a heavy burden on the impoverished nation, even though India, Ceylon, and Burma had become independent in 1948, and Ghana and Malaya in 1957. Eventually almost all former British colonies and protectorates attained independence; the emergence of a multi-racial Commonwealth was a source of pride. But it was not readily obvious whether the new Commonwealth would still be a major factor in world affairs. Goodwill alone was not sufficient to keep it a going concern: the economic interests of Britain and the former colonies frequently clashed. The underdeveloped countries of Asia and Africa needed economic assistance which the metropolis could not always provide. Immigration from Africa and Asia to Britain, not very substantial by world standards, gradually became a major problem, for Britain was already densely populated; unlike Canada or Australia, it could not easily absorb immigrants.

Britain was still compelled to allocate considerable sums to defence in view of the continued British presence in parts of Asia and Africa. Conscription ceased only in 1960; meanwhile an independent nuclear deterrent had been developed; an experimental A-bomb was exploded in 1953, an H-bomb four years later. The Commonwealth declined in importance from year to year, but both major parties were still far from enthusiastic about closer ties with Europe. Hugh Gaitskell, who had succeeded Clement Attlee as leader of the Labour Party in 1955, was as emphatic in this respect as the Tories. Gaitskell and the Labour Party opposed the Suez expedition in 1956 which came as the answer to the nationalisation of the Suez Canal Company by Colonel Nasser. Indifferently planned and badly executed, the operation encountered opposition all over the world. The Suez setback, though it caused the downfall of Anthony Eden, did not seriously weaken the position of the Conservative Party, but it did demonstrate that Britain had ceased to be a world power.

Britain in the nineteen-fifties presented a confusing picture to Englishmen and foreigners alike. There was full employment and a steady improvement in the standard of living. Harold Macmillan's slogan of 1957, that the British 'had never had it so good', was more than propaganda. And yet Britain was falling behind; partly this was an inevitable process, given the absence of natural resources and the need to import food and most raw materials. But few political leaders had sufficient courage to state bluntly that the country could not continue to live on borrowed money and that a greater national effort had to be made. Productivity was low, not much imagination and drive was shown by industrial managers or the trade unions, which often fought modernisation tooth and nail. There was 'inflation without expansion and inadequate investment in the wrong industries' (F.Paish). In some ways the malaise went even deeper: the welfare state had not brought real equality of opportunity, and there was less social mobility than in other industrialised countries; large sections of the intelligentsia were estranged; a sense of frustration and a narrowing of horizons was beginning to be felt at a time when most other European countries were in the middle of a great upsurge. It was a creeping malaise: Britain did not face a major, acute crisis, and yet there was nothing like the buoyancy, the confidence, and the excitement that was felt on the continent. The explanation that the loss of the Empire was the real cause of the decline is unconvincing; there was no direct relationship. France, Holland, and other European countries had overcome similar experiences without a major shock; their prosperity had not been affected by the loss of their overseas possessions. More difficult perhaps for Britain were the political and psychological consequences, the need to find a more modest place in the postwar world. To adjust itself to a new role in Europe was a painful process and there was a great deal of instinctive resistance among the left and right alike to facing unpleasant facts. This was to plague Britain for many years to come.

The Decline of Democratic Socialism

European socialism was in a state of decline in the nineteen-fifties: the Italian Socialist Party split, and the French party was in full retreat. The continental socialist parties were heirs to a proud tradition; founded in the last third of the nineteenth century they were all, in contrast to the British Labour Party, Marxist in inspiration, though for several decades there had been a growing discrepancy between their orthodox revolutionary theory and their revisionist practice. They did not reap lasting benefit from the great left-wing upsurge of 1945, which enhanced communist influence far more than theirs. The cold war was bound to damage the cause of socialism, for as far as public opinion was concerned socialism and communism were birds of the same feather. While communism in France and Italy succeeded in keeping its working-class basis, the growing opposition to communism among the rest of the population caused a swing to the right. Nor did it help that Stalin's crimes were committed, according to the official version, in the cause of 'peace and socialism'.

The Socialist Parties of France and Italy suffered from a lack of vitality. In 1945 the French party had polled almost a quarter of the vote (23 per cent); in 1946 its share had fallen to 18 per cent, in 1962 it was reduced to a mere 12.6 per cent. In 1946 it had 354,000 members but by 1960 only 60,000 were left. It became a party of aged officials, teachers, traditional laicists; left-of-centre in character, pro-European, but with no clear political or social programme. When Léon Blum, the prewar leader of the party, returned from his German prison he was aware that French socialism had to discard its more outdated elements; the emphasis was now to be on freedom and human rights, not on the class struggle. It was to be a popular radical party, not a proletarian one. But Blum was too old and tired to provide the necessary guidance and the younger party leaders were absorbed in quarrels about current political issues (such as French colonial policy, Vietnam and Algeria); no one had the time or the inclination to re-examine basic ideological issues. The left wing of 1945 (Guy Mollet) soon moved to the right, whereas the reformers of 1945 (André Philip and Daniel Meyer) found themselves on the left of the party or even outside it. The defection of the PSU (Unified Socialist Party) in 1960 further weakened the socialists, who had been discredited by their participation in so many shortlived and ineffectual governments of the Fourth Republic.

The Italian Socialist Party was perhaps the most radical and, in a Marxist sense, fundamentalist, of all European socialist movements: antimilitarism and anti-clericalism were central planks in its programme. Its general outlook had been shaped by the fascist experience and, after 1944, by the narrowly reactionary policy pursued by the Italian upper class. In the thirties and during the war the party had favoured a popular front with the communists. Pietro Nenni, its leader, was willing to continue to cooperate with his allies even after the outbreak of the cold war, but there was growing opposition from within; in January 1947 Saragat left the party and with him half its parliamentary deputies and a substantial number of the rank and file. The split drove Nenni into even closer collaboration with the communists, whereas the Saragat wing (the Social Democrats) took part in the government from 1948 to 1951, and again in 1958. Nenni was too clever a politician, and too much of a socialist and a democrat, to be entirely happy with his status as a fellow traveller. After Stalin's death, and in particular after the Hungarian rising, his party regained its independence and sought to re-establish its ties with the Saragat wing. It also began to accept the important changes that were taking place in Italy during the fifties; while not joining the government, it provided support for left-of-centre coalitions from the outside. Both wings of Italian socialism had better leadership than the French movement, and its decline was less pronounced during the fifties and sixties. But in both countries the communists were firmly entrenched as the main working-class party and neither socialist party could recapture its former position.

In the rest of Europe, as in Britain, socialism maintained its strength. Outside France and Italy communism was no serious rival, and the socialists retained their position as the main party of the left. This was their great strength, but being so closely identified with one specific social class they could not hope to appeal to others with much success. There were narrow limits to the growth of their influence: the Austrian Socialist Party, one of the strongest on the continent, with almost 700,000 members, polled 44 per cent of the total vote in the elections of 1945 – and exactly the same percentage in 1962. The Dutch party polled 28 per cent in 1946, and again 28 per cent in 1963. The figures for the Swiss Social Democrats were 26 per cent in 1947 and 26 per cent in 1963. Even in West Germany the Social Democrats did not succeed in making substantial inroads into the middle-class vote, and electoral fluctuations were therefore comparatively small. Since the numerical share of the working class in the general population did not grow, what hope was there for a decisive socialist advance in Europe? There was, of course, the example of the Labour Party, but it seemed doubtful whether its formula could be applied on the continent. The European socialist parties, trying to compromise between doctrinaire extremism and a 'sell out of basic principles', all too often fell between two stools. They neglected their socialist heritage: not a single socialist party in Europe managed to maintain an effective press and publishing house. There was little interest in politics beyond the current issues facing the parties, the general feeling being that in modern industrial society theory was no longer relevant.

In the late nineteen-fifties all continental socialist parties reached the conclusion that much of the old doctrinal ballast had to be jettisoned. The German Social Democrats in their Godesberg programme (1959) decided to transform themselves into a party of the whole people, with the emphasis on freedom, the rights of the individual, and social justice, rather than class interests; the class struggle was to be replaced by a progressive incomes policy. The party even expressed willingness to accept the principle of a free market economy, provided of course that there was real competition, not monopolistic rule. The Austrian party likewise stressed freedom and social justice in its new programme of 1958 and the Dutch Partie van de Arbeid which had modelled itself immediately after the war on the British Labour Party, noted in its 1959 programme the far-reaching changes that had taken place in capitalism and decided to concentrate on constructive efforts within the existing social framework. In the same year the Swiss Social Democrats, too, rejected many traditional Marxist principles. European socialism at last ceased to be revolutionary in theory as well as practice.

All these changes were clearly long overdue, for if capitalism had changed, so had the character of the working class. After the coming of the welfare state few workers were likely to respond to appeals to mount the barricades. But the implications of the changes had to be carefully considered. What exactly was the policy of a radical democratic party of the left going to be? If it accepted, broadly speaking, the existing economic and social set up, could it hope to persuade the electorate that it was able to run the country more efficiently than the advocates of free enterprise? If the stress was to be on economic and social planning, in contrast to the blind laws of supply and demand, what exactly were to be the social priorities? At the turn of the century many on the left had feared that the socialist leaders would be corrupted if they joined a bourgeois coalition government. Sixty years later, on the contrary, the main fear was that the socialist leaders would grow old and sour in opposition and that, as a result, they would lack experience to provide effective national leadership if their hour ever came. These assumptions were groundless, as later appeared. The German Social Democrats had acquired during the fifties a great deal of experience in ruling some of the *Länder*, including Lower Saxony, Hesse, Berlin, and Hamburg. The Social Democratic parties of Scandinavia were the governing parties and the Dutch and Belgian Social Democrats, too, participated in many coalition governments throughout the fifties. The Austrian party shared power with the Christian People's Party on the basis of a complicated agreement allocating all public offices according to a rigid proportional system. All these parties retained the support of the majority of the working class, and they tried, though not always with conspicuous success, to surmount in the elections the '40 per cent hurdle', which they regarded as a precondition for the extension of their influence beyond their traditional social basis.

European Communism

After Hitler's attack on Russia, European communism had taken a leading part in the resistance movement and had attracted many new followers. This, and the Soviet military victory, had made communism respectable all over the continent. In 1945 the communists faced little competition. Most of the prewar parties had been discredited because they had failed to resist the German occupation. Those with a resistance record equal to the communists were in a less favourable position because they were organisationally weaker; they had been less well prepared for conspiratorial work under the German occupation and, after 1945, they had difficulties in adapting themselves quickly to the new order that was emerging. Even in Holland, Belgium, and the Scandinavian countries, where communism had traditionally been weak, it was now a force to be reckoned with. The Dutch party's central newspaper had a circulation of a quarter of a million and the Danish and Swedish parties gained substantially in the elections of 1945. In Belgium the communists felt sufficiently strong to challenge the authority of the government shortly after it returned from London in November 1944; there were demonstrations and eventually a concerted attempt to overthrow the government. But the communists had overestimated their own strength and ignored in their calculations the presence of Allied troops; their insurrection was suppressed within two days.

Communist advances were most striking in France and Italy. The French party counted 800,000 members soon after the end of the war, while Italian communism emerged as the biggest political force in all the major cities except Milan, which remained for some years a socialist stronghold. At the time of the liberation large sections of southern France and northern Italy were in the hands of communist partisan units; these were reluctant to disband and to hand over to the representatives of the central government. But this was, on the whole, a rearguard action on the part of local chieftains; the party line did not envisage an armed insurrection while the war was still on. The exceptions were Belgium and Greece, but the challenge of the Belgian communists was easily defeated and the Greeks (EAM) feared that they could not hold out against the British troops stationed in the country. After the first round of the civil war was over they decided to sign an armistice agreement with the government.

In most countries the communists joined the national coalition governments that were formed after the liberation, while their partisan units (such as the French FFI) were absorbed into the regular armies. It was general communist policy in 1945 to press for close collaboration with the Social Democrats and other left-of-centre parties. Their programme was by no means particularly radical in character; they did not at first oppose the monarchy in Italy, even if this meant that the socialists appeared more radical; their aim was to extend their influence through the coalition. These moderate policies paid handsome dividends. In the elections of 1946 and 1947 they strengthened their position in France and Italy at the expense of the socialists. The turning point came in April and May 1947 for with the hardening of the Soviet line and the communist takeover in eastern Europe, the west European communists had to fall in line and, as a result, found themselves in growing isolation.

After 1948 communism was in opposition throughout Europe; the case of Iceland, where they remained part of the government coalition, was a mere curiosity. The 'hard course' of the Cominform excluded collaboration with non-communist forces, and in the circumstances the 'peace campaign', designed to attract non-communists, carried little conviction. The west European communists found it increasingly difficult to combine their continued presence in coalition governments with the more radical policies prescribed by Moscow. In France they decided to support a major strike in one of the chief nationalised industries. This left Ramadier, the socialist Prime Minister, with no alternative but to exclude them from his government. It is not certain that the action had been planned by the communists; the Renault strike had in fact been instigated by 'ultra left' elements, but once the majority of workers had joined it, the communists felt duty bound to support it. In Italy the communists decided in May 1947 that de Gasperi's new economic programme was unacceptable, and they, too, left the coalition. If the communist exodus had been unplanned, their subsequent actions were certainly coordinated. In October–November 1947 large-scale strikes broke out in France and Italy. French mines were occupied by strikers led by the communists, there were mass demonstrations and an open challenge was thrown out to the French and Italian governments. After some initial hesitation, Moch and Scelba, the respective ministers of the interior, were given full powers to deal with the emergency and they suppressed the disorders without undue difficulty. In Greece, the communist forces had decided even earlier (in March 1946) to renew the armed struggle. The situation was now more promising from their point of view, because the British troops had been withdrawn and the neighbouring communist countries were bound to give them full support. The first guerrilla activities were highly successful and in 1947 it was decided to proceed with the second stage of the insurrection. When large-scale fighting developed, Greece appealed for UN aid in view of the open assistance given to the communists from across the border. But the UN could do little but investigate the complaints and register them. Only in 1948 did the tide begin to turn against the communists. Support from Yugoslavia ceased. Under the Truman doctrine America extended help to the Greek army, and once America was involved, Stalin became sceptical about the prospects of the whole venture. A government offensive in the Grammos mountains in 1949 routed the communist forces and ended a civil war which had caused much loss of life, including 45,000 killed, enormous material damage, and had delayed the recovery of the country for many years.

The east European purges had their parallels in the west: old leaders of French communism such as André Marty, Charles Tillon, and Auguste Lecoeur were branded traitors overnight. After Tito's excommunication, Aksel Larsen, the Danish party chief, and Furubotn, the Norwegian leader, were expelled, and a similar fate befell prominent communists in West Germany and Greece (Siantos, General Markos, Zachariades), and the illegal Spanish party. Communist influence in Germany and in all the smaller European countries rapidly dwindled. The Belgian party, which had polled 14 per cent of the total vote in 1946, was left with less than a third that figure in the nineteen-sixties. Even in France and Italy, where communism on the whole managed to keep its position, the party press lost most of its readers, and party membership also declined.

In view of the shocks and convulsions in east Europe during Stalin's last years, the decline in communist influence in the West was less surprising than the fact that its eclipse was by no means total. Part of the reason was that the main trade union organisations were firmly under communist control, while the reports of the non-communist press about the Soviet Union and east Europe were *a priori* branded as lies and falsifications. When, after Stalin's death, it could no longer be denied that these accounts had been substantially correct, the communist leaders promised that, past mistakes having been corrected, there would be no recurrence of what was euphemistically called the 'cult of the individual'. Many intellectuals left the party after Khrushchev's revelations in 1956 and as a result of the events in Hungary; a few had already dissociated themselves at the time of the anti-Tito campaigns. But the rank and file was much less affected by events in distant countries. Communism in France and Italy was more than just a political party; it was a faith and a way of life. The prosperity of the fifties raised standards of living but it also made the injustices of the social system appear in an even more glaring light. The *condition prolétarienne* had by no means altogether disappeared in France; in Italy there was still massive tax evasion on the part of the rich, land was unequally distributed, and poverty in the south was disappearing only very slowly. Hundreds of thousands of Frenchmen and Italians belonged to communist social clubs and trade unions, read communist newspapers and literature, watched communist films; even their social life proceeded often within the framework of a closed system. Their dreams of a better social order did not conflict with the harsh realities of communism in practice, as it did in east Europe. By the end of the fifties there were no doubt more genuine believers in communism left in west than in east Europe. Western communism gradually dissociated itself from Stalinism, a process that began earlier and went further in Italy than in France. But the admission that mistakes had been committed induced the rank and file communist to leave the party as little as a religious believer would give up his faith because some church dignitaries had misbehaved. Communism in France and Italy had a far greater staying power than generally anticipated. Partly, no doubt, this was the force of inertia, the fact that political movements often continue to flourish for a long time after the conditions that produced them have disappeared. The Communist Parties of France and Italy at any rate maintained their influence on more than a quarter of the electorate in the two countries. The revolutionary *élan* lessened as the working class itself underwent important changes and became more 'bourgeois' in character. The communists could still count on a substantial vote in the elections and mobilise the masses for occasional mass demonstrations, though on a declining scale and less frequently. They still had powerful political machines at their disposal but not for revolutionary action. Was the history of social democracy to repeat itself? Gradually west European communism began to show 'revisionist' symptoms; the gulf between revolutionary theory and reformist practice grew steadily wider.

The End of the Stalin Era

The nineteenth congress of the Communist Party of the Soviet Union (CPSU) opened in Moscow in October 1952. According to the party statutes such a congress was to be convened every three years; in fact it had not met for 13 years, since 1939. This contravention of the statutes was not perhaps of great consequence, for the congress, far from being the supreme party instance, had long ceased to have any real influence on Soviet politics. But it was certainly indicative of the many anomalies in Soviet life, of the discrepancy between theory and practice. Stalin systematically ignored the rules he had himself helped to establish.

Great social changes had taken place since he had consolidated his power in the late nineteen-twenties; the working class now constituted more than a quarter of the population, and every fifth Russian belonged to what was somewhat sweepingly defined as the 'technical intelligentsia'. The country was run by a huge, centralised state apparatus, a giant bureaucracy which to all intents and purposes constituted a new class. All major decisions, and many that were not important, affecting all parts of the Soviet Union, however distant, were taken in Moscow. This lack of local initiative seriously impeded the country's development. Nor was there much stability at the centre: Stalin was apparently convinced that the party and government leadership needed a violent shake up from time to time. At the nineteenth congress Malenkov played the central role, and it was generally believed that he was now the heir apparent. Molotov and Mikoyan, though still members of the Presidium (as the politburo had been renamed), had in 1949 ceased to be Minister of Foreign Affairs and Foreign Trade respectively. They seemed to be the first candidates for a new purge. Voroshilov, another old associate, was thought by Stalin to be a British agent, and even Beria, head of the all-powerful secret police, was charged soon after the congress with gross neglect of duty. Stalin was firmly convinced that he was absolutely indispensable. We have it on the authority of one of his successors that he told his inner circle in 1952: 'You are as blind as kittens . . . What would you do without me? You do not know your enemies!'

The nineteenth party congress did not come to grips with the serious problems and imbalances facing the country. It changed the name of the party ('Bolshevik' was dropped) but did not provide new guidance. The discrepancy between heavy industry and the other branches of the national economy was to continue; the compulsory deliveries at nominal prices of agricultural products were to be maintained. Soviet foreign policy was to remain as rigid as before; it regarded the 'popular democracies' as satellites, not partners, and the rest of the world as one hostile reactionary bloc. In one of his last published tracts Stalin had written that a war was more likely to break out between capitalist countries than between them and the Soviet Union.

During the last year of Stalin's life there was a sense of approaching crisis; economic difficulties were becoming more acute and no more windfalls like the German reparations could be expected, while China's demands for economic assistance became more comprehensive and insistent. Official figures about production in heavy industry were most impressive but they exaggerated the real progress that had been made. The living standards of the bulk of the population had hardly risen. The cult of 'production' at any price had become an intolerable burden for the economy, with its exclusive stress on quantity and almost total neglect of quality and social need. Goods were often shoddy, could not be used, or had to be discarded after a short time. As planning became more and more rigid, commodities were produced without any regard for the laws of supply and demand. The question whether a factory (or a whole branch of industry or agriculture) was economically viable was hardly ever asked. Russia's industrial recovery since the war had made great strides, but there was so little coordination with other branches of the economy that the imbalances threatened the entire further progress of the country.

Immediately after the congress there was a further hardening in the political line and a number of indications that a new major purge on the scale of events in 1936–8 was being prepared. On 13 January 1953, the Soviet press announced that a conspiracy had been discovered: a group of prominent physicians (most of them of Jewish origin) had been responsible for the death of several Soviet leaders (such as Zhdanov and Scherbakov) and were now plotting, on behalf of foreign espionage agencies, to murder Soviet marshals and other leading figures of the régime. From that day on there was a crescendo of attacks on these poisoners, spies, vermin, animals in human shape, obviously directed not primarily against these underlings but their (as yet unnamed) sponsors inside the country. There were constant calls for more vigilance; denunciations of individuals and of entire categories of people became a daily occurrence. A great fear again spread throughout the Soviet Union, for everyone who remembered 1936 realised that the present accusations were merely the prelude to a much wider wave of repression which could ultimately affect millions of people. These purges were self-generating, as previous experience and the recent trials in the satellite countries had shown; each wave of arrests led to fresh accusations. Stalin's basic intention was to get rid of the party leaders and replace them by 'new and inexperienced people' as Khrushchev later asserted. But the incipient purge had also a strongly anti-semitic character; there was apparently a plan to deport all persons of Jewish origin to the Arctic region or some other remote area of the Soviet Union. Other nationalities, too, were suspect, and it was later said that Stalin did not envisage the deportation of the Ukrainians only because there were too many of them.

In the middle of this gathering storm, on the morning of 6 March 1953, Stalin's death was reported. The circumstances have given rise to much speculation; a great many people in the Soviet Union, including almost the entire party leadership, had every reason to feel threatened by the coming purge. There were rumours that certain Soviet leaders had in some way precipitated the demise of the ailing dictator, but no real evidence to this effect had come to light. Stalin's funeral was a great state occasion, but in comparison with the pomp and circumstance that had marked his seventieth birthday, the speeches and the articles in the press were restrained and sober. The new leaders were already preoccupied with the division of power among themselves. Certain important policy decisions had been taken even before the funeral; the Presidium, which with its 25 members was far too unwieldy to be the supreme decision-making body, was reduced to a membership of ten; Stalin's private secretariat was dissolved; it had been in practice the most important political institution in Soviet political life, though neither the Constitution nor the party programme had provided for its existence and it had hardly ever been mentioned in print. The purge was immediately stopped and the arrested doctors released. Two of them were no longer alive; their fate remains a matter of conjecture. A little later an amnesty was proclaimed: all prisoners serving sentences of less than five years were to be released. This effectively excluded political prisoners, whose turn came only during the next two years. There were the first admissions, albeit incidental and half-hearted, that 'individual officials had committed arbitrary and illegal acts'. Destalinisation, however modest, thus started even before the funeral orations had been held. A whole epoch in the history of the Soviet Union had come to an end with the death of the dictator.

The transition from one-man rule to government by a small committee (or 'collective leadership', as it was officially called) was not altogether smooth. Among the ten men who now shaped Soviet policy there were a great many conflicting ambitions, much mutual distrust, and also some real disagreements about the policies to be pursued. The tug-of-war between individuals and groups led to frequent changes in the Presidium until, four years after Stalin's death, collective leadership again gave way to one-man rule. Malenkov was both head of the Soviet government and general secretary of the CPSU for a few days after Stalin's death, but his colleagues, deeply apprehensive that one of them would concentrate too much power in his hands, soon forced him to resign his party job. Molotov and Mikoyan made a comeback as Minister of Foreign Affairs and Foreign Trade respectively; Bulganin became Minister of Defence, Beria was again in charge of the various police, secret police, and intelligence services; parts of his empire had been removed from his control under Stalin. Khrushchev became General Secretary of the party in September 1953; but since, under Stalin, the importance of the party had been substantially reduced, not much attention was paid to this appointment at the time.

Beria was the first member of the Presidium to fall victim to the bitter internal struggle. On 10 July 1953, it was announced that he had been unmasked as a capitalist agent; the name of this traitor was to be accursed forever. Six months later a brief report appeared in the Soviet press that he and six accomplices had recently been executed. Beria, the most powerful man in the Soviet Union, the 'faithful disciple and close associate' of his late countryman, one of the three orators at Stalin's funeral, thus overnight became an unperson. His political record was frightful; he had been responsible for the arrest and execution of hundreds of thousands of Soviet citizens between 1938 and 1953. It is unlikely however that his colleagues, all of them hardened Stalinists, decided to eliminate him in a sudden fit of moral indignation or because they were afraid that he would reintroduce orthodox

Stalinism. There were signs, on the contrary, that after Stalin's death Beria was one of the chief advocates of a liberal course; he seems to have suggested a compromise with the West concerning the future of Germany. His colleagues feared the concentration of too much power in his hands, and they decided, with the help of some army commanders, to nip this danger in the bud.

With Beria's fall the quarrels in the party leadership moved to a different plane. There were policy differences: Molotov, unbending, inflexible, Stalin's most faithful assistant, stood for the continuation of traditional policies, while Malenkov was more acutely aware that changes had become necessary. The current five-year plan which envisaged a rise in production of 50 per cent was going badly, and agricultural output per head was still little higher than in Tsarist times. Malenkov proposed to remedy the disproportion between investment in heavy industry and in the rest of the national economy, and to take urgent measures to raise the standard of living by spending more on light industry, housing, etc. He faced strong opposition on the part of his colleagues and after about a year his reforms were severely curtailed in scope. In foreign policy, too, he stood for a more conciliatory approach. In a speech in March 1954 he warned that a third world war would mean the end of world civilisation. Again he was disavowed and had to retreat; six weeks later he declared that a new world war would merely bring about the end of capitalism.

During the second half of 1954 it became evident that Malenkov's position was in jeopardy, and in February 1955 he had to resign as Chairman of the Council of Ministers, to be replaced by Nikolai Bulganin. There had been a heated policy debate in the Kremlin but it would be unwise to overrate the ideological element in this conflict. In both the economic field and foreign affairs, the policies of those who succeeded Malenkov differed little from those he had wanted to pursue. This was particularly evident in foreign policy. Feelers were again put out to the West suggesting discussion of some of the major outstanding problems in Europe. In July Bulganin met Eisenhower, Eden, and Mollet in Geneva, arousing great hopes for a general reconciliation and a speedy settlement of unresolved questions. The new 'spirit of Geneva' became something of a symbol. This general optimism proved to be unfounded. The new Soviet willingness to enter into discussions with the West did not necessarily imply a readiness to retreat from the old positions, and the talks were inconclusive. Agreement on the Austrian peace treaty in February remained the only positive achievement of the year 1955.

There were fresh initiatives in Soviet policy in other parts of the globe. The importance of the third world and the opportunity to enhance Soviet influence in these regions gradually dawned on the Kremlin, and measures were taken to establish closer links with the Afro-Asian countries. The arms

deal with Egypt in spring 1955 opened a new era in the relations between the
Soviet Union and the Arab world; the visit of Bulganin and Khrushchev to
New Delhi in November 1955 paved the way for closer ties with India. Efforts
were made to mend fences within the communist camp; attacks on the
'traitor and Judas' Tito and his 'fascist régime' ceased, and a high ranking
Soviet delegation, including Khrushchev, visited Belgrade in May 1955.
In a speech at Belgrade airport Khrushchev said that 'we sincerely regret
what happened and resolutely reject the things that occurred'. The accusations against the Yugoslav leaders had been fabricated by Beria, the 'enemy
of the people'. Molotov opposed the reconciliation with Tito but he was outvoted; the majority of the Soviet Presidium agreed that it was high time to
bury the hatchet. Yugoslavia continued to insist on its independence, whereas
Soviet criticism of the 'Yugoslav road to communism' by no means ceased in
1955. The most painful and embarrassing manifestations of the breach were
removed, even though this implied a vindication of Tito's policy and a loss of
face on the part of the Soviet leadership.

Nikita Sergeyevich Khrushchev had not been among the main contenders
for the succession while Stalin was alive, and he remained in the background
during the first months after his death. Gradually, however, the position of
the new General Secretary of the party increased in importance and strength
as the CPSU regained much of the influence it had lost in Stalin's last years.
Inside the party many key positions were filled with Khrushchev's personal
appointees. His name appeared more and more often in the press and on the
radio; after Malenkov's fall he was the most influential member of the Presidium. Not all his suggestions were accepted by his colleagues. Khrushchev,
who took a particular interest in agriculture, proposed to solve the permanent
crisis in the production of food and livestock by drastically expanding the
cultivated area, mainly in Kazakhstan and West Siberia (the 'virgin lands'
scheme) and by extending the area under maize. But these schemes were
criticised and partly rejected at the time, to be given top priority only several
years later, after Khrushchev had broken the opposition in the Presidium and
emerged as the undisputed leader.

There were dramatic changes in the intellectual climate after Stalin's
death: Pomerantsev's essay on the need for sincerity in literature appeared,
as did Ehrenburg's novel *The Thaw*, which gave its name to the whole period.
Not everyone welcomed these stirrings, and the first skirmishes between
'liberals' and 'conservatives' took place. It was not a clear, decisive break
with the legacy of Stalinism; the habits of the period of the 'cult of the individual' had become too deeply ingrained. Above all, those who succeeded
Stalin had without exception made their political career under him; they
were his nominees and close comrades-in-arms, and they could not dissociate
themselves entirely from him without committing political suicide. They tried

to eliminate some of the blatantly irrational and unnecessary features of the old régime, to rationalise and modernise it while keeping most of its essentials. This policy, which continued for many years, involved the Soviet leadership in many contradictions and inconsistencies. How much of the truth about the Stalin era could be safely divulged? Khrushchev at the twentieth party congress in 1956 made a first attempt to shed some light on the most recent period of Soviet history, but he did so in a report that was not published; soon the campaign of destalinisation was halted, and those who had gone too far in revealing the truth were sharply called to order. Nor was it easy to find a new political equilibrium after Stalin's death; collective leadership did not function too well; the principle itself was not yet firmly rooted, for one man rule (*edinonachalie*) had been the norm for a long time and had become deeply ingrained at every level of Soviet society. Those who had believed that Stalin's death would inaugurate a new era of real inner party democracy and the gradual liberalisation of the régime, came to realise before long that it would be, at best, a protracted and painful process, and that it would by no means follow a straight course.

Political developments in the people's democracies during Stalin's last years followed the Soviet pattern. Their policies were more and more closely coordinated with (and controlled by) the Kremlin. National deviations from the established norms, the 'national roads to communism', became anathema; the Soviet experience was to serve as the great example by which all these countries were to be guided. They all adopted five or six year plans to develop industrial production; collectivisation in agriculture was put on the agenda, the non-communist parties that had come into being after the war were dissolved or lost their independence. The armies, the secret police, architecture and literature, every aspect of life was closely modelled on the Soviet pattern. But despite the effort to attain uniformity there were still differences in the speed with which the process of Stalinisation proceeded. Bulgaria was quickest in emulating the Soviet Union and the most extreme; Poland and Rumania in some respects lagged behind; communism had even less mass support there than in the other east European countries. The Polish and Rumanian leaders were no doubt aware that the policies they were following were bound to promote disaffection among large sections of the population, and they tried to achieve their aims without arousing excessive antagonism. Thus, while 92 per cent of Bulgaria's agriculture had been collectivised by the end of the nineteen-fifties, the figure for Poland was only 15.

The political climate in the people's democracies during the late Stalin period was one of cynicism, servility, and moral corruption. In the Soviet Union indoctrination had already lasted for more than three decades and a great part of the population had gradually come to accept at least part of the official doctrine. East Europe, on the other hand, was more exposed to external influences and few people outside the middle and higher echelons of the party were well disposed towards communist policies. In the Soviet Union communism had a strong patriotic, even nationalistic appeal : the revolution had been carried out (partly at least) against outside enemies; it had made Russia a great industrial and military power. Communism in eastern Europe was a foreign importation, not an indigenous product. In the eyes of a Polish, a Hungarian, or a Rumanian patriot even the achievements of the native communist régimes were no reason for pride. The geographical proximity and the military predominance of the Soviet Union made for caution and obedience, but they did not make east Europeans sincere friends and loyal supporters of Russia.

The Czech coup and the break with Yugoslavia, both in 1948, were the most important milestones on the road to satellisation. The Czechoslovak Communist Party had emerged in the relatively free elections of 1946 as the country's strongest force. But communist domination was by no means total ; the police, for instance, were in communist hands, but the Minister of Justice, a non-communist, often refused to sanction their activities or even countermanded their orders. The non-communist parties which in 1945–6 had been satisfied with playing second fiddle, gradually asserted themselves. There was reason to doubt whether in new elections the communists would be able to repeat their 1946 victory. They had a small majority in parliament and shared the government with the Social Democrats led by Fierlinger. But among the socialists there was growing opposition to Fierlinger's policy which had made their party virtually indistinguishable from the communists. In November 1947, by a majority decision, Fierlinger was removed from the party executive. As a result the communists feared they would be outvoted and their position seriously weakened; even before this they had been criticised by Moscow and other communist parties for their lack of revolutionary zeal, their 'exaggerated willingness' to cooperate with bourgeois parties within the National Front coalition. A decision was taken to put an end to 'formal democracy' and to bring Czechoslovakia into line with the other east European countries. The party organised mass demonstrations and on 25 February 1948, took over completely. President Benes, ailing and unwilling to offend the Russians, felt in no position to resist the communist demand for full power. There were threats that the Soviet army units stationed in the country would be used unless the communist demands were accepted forthwith. The non-communist parties were dissolved or taken over by the communists and their leaders arrested ; Jan Masaryk, the Foreign Minister, was found dead on the pavement outside his office. There was no resistance; Gottwald, the communist leader who succeeded Benes in June 1948, is reported to have said that it was 'like cutting butter with a sharp knife'.

Soviet policies in Yugoslavia were far less successful. Of all the east

European communist leaders, Tito was the only one who had come to power by his own efforts, not through Soviet help, and his party had a broad popular basis. This from the very beginning put him in a special position, and made it possible for Yugoslavia to adopt a more independent policy *vis-à-vis* the Soviet Union. In 1945–6 the Yugoslavs represented the left, militant wing within the communist camp; they were disappointed at not getting stronger Soviet support for their territorial claims (Trieste); there were also complaints about Russian 'great power chauvinism' and Soviet sabotage of Yugoslavia's economic plans. After much friction between Yugoslav army leaders and the Soviet military mission in Belgrade, the Russian advisers were withdrawn in March 1948. A letter sent by the CPSU to the Yugoslav leadership contained threats and bitter complaints: Tito was compared with Trotsky and at the same time attacked as a nationalist; there was no democracy inside the Yugoslav party, and Tito was accused of trying to liquidate the CPY; Yugoslavia had been liberated and the Yugoslav party had come to power only following the advance of the Soviet army; Tito and his colleagues should therefore behave with greater propriety and modesty. The conflict between Moscow and Belgrade did not concern basic Marxist-Leninist principles, even though references to communist doctrine figured prominently in the correspondence. It was the direct result of the Soviet attempt to impose full control as in other east European countries. Stalin clearly misjudged the situation; according to Khrushchev he believed he had only to lift his little finger to overthrow Tito. But even a massive Soviet campaign lasting several years was not sufficient to dislodge Tito, who decided to fight once he realised that there was no room for compromise.

On 28 June 1948, the CPY was expelled from the Cominform and the quarrel became public. The Soviet Union brought every kind of pressure to bear except direct military intervention to overthrow Tito and the Yugoslav leadership. All the satellites attacked Belgrade, all economic agreements were broken, an attempt was made to starve Yugoslavia into submission. There was an unprecedented propaganda campaign against Tito and his colleagues, but only a handful of Yugoslav party leaders headed Stalin's appeal; the great majority rallied around Tito. The attacks helped to make the régime more popular inside the country, for Tito now appeared as the champion of Yugoslav national independence against foreign encroachments. During the following years Yugoslavia gradually developed its own brand of socialism: great emphasis was put on decentralisation, workers councils were established in 1950 to run the factories and attempts were made to limit the privileges of the new élite. The arrest of Djilas, one of Tito's closest associates in the early days, who maintained that democratisation in Yugoslavia had not gone far enough and that a new class had come into being, showed that there were limits to Tito's liberalism. But compared with the satellites, Yugoslavia was a shining example of democracy; it remained independent in its foreign and its domestic policy, and for many on the European left it was a beacon of hope during a dark period. From the Soviet point of view, the failure to overthrow the 'Tito clique' was a serious setback which boded ill for the future. In the global balance of power Yugoslavia hardly counted, but the self assertion of a small country against Soviet control was a matter of grave concern. Once one communist party had successfully defied the Soviet leadership there was the danger that insubordination would spread; it was the beginning of the end of the monolithic character of world communism.

The split between the Soviet Union and Yugoslavia precipitated mass purges and a series of show trials throughout eastern Europe, but it was certainly not the only reason; such trials were an inherent part of the Stalinist system. First came the trial of Laszlo Rajk, the Hungarian Minister of the Interior, and some other, less prominent Hungarian leaders in September 1949. Rajk was accused of having been an informer and police spy throughout his political career, an employee of Dulles and of Ranković, the Yugoslav Minister of the Interior. Rajk duly admitted all these charges as well as many others, equally fantastic, and was executed. Next was Traicho Kostov, the Bulgarian Deputy Prime Minister and a great hero of the party from the underground days. The charges were roughly the same as in the case of Rajk, but Kostov, hardened against torture in the prisons of prewar Bulgaria, in open court unexpectedly withdrew his confession, to the great consternation of those who stage-managed his trial. In Czechoslovakia the purge began in 1949–50 and reached its climax with the trial in November 1951 of Rudolf Slansky, former party secretary, Clementis, former Foreign Minister, and others. Slansky had been a faithful Stalinist, and his admission of guilt was even less convincing than that of the other communist leaders in east Europe. He and his colleagues were accused of being foreign intelligence agents, of engaging in financial speculation, and (an innovation) of being Zionists: there were openly anti-semitic overtones in this trial. It was common knowledge that Slansky, a Jew by origin, had been an implacable enemy of Zionism throughout his life. As the trials went on, the charges became more and more grotesque, but the accused continued to incriminate themselves; sometimes they were also denounced by their wives and children.

The outside world watched these proceedings with amazement and horror, unable to understand what pressure could have induced the accused to admit charges that were so manifestly absurd. In Rumania Anna Pauker and Vasile Luca, two of the most prominent party leaders, fell victim to the purge in May 1952; Patrascanu, a former party secretary, was executed in April 1954; in Poland Wladislav Gomulka, Marian Spychalski, and Zenon Kliszko were arrested in 1949. In East Germany Paul Merker was ousted from the leadership in 1950, and Wilhelm Zaisser and Rudolf Herrnstadt after the workers revolt of June 1953. These are just a few of the more outstanding among the many who were purged, arrested, or executed. Altogether some 550,000 party members were purged in Czechoslovakia, 300,000 in Poland and East Germany, and only slightly fewer in the other satellite countries. For a rank and file party member this usually meant no more than that he was likely to experience difficulties in daily life and perhaps to lose his job. But the more highly placed the victim, the more dangerous were the consequences. It is impossible to find a common denominator for the trials. In some cases internal intrigues and the struggle for power played a major role; there is little doubt that for Rakosi, Rajk was a dangerous rival, and Vulko Chervenkov, the Bulgarian leader, for similar reasons wanted to remove Kostov. It is more difficult to explain the particularly savage character of the Prague trial entirely with reference to dissension among the Czech leadership; Soviet pressure apparently played a major part. The Polish party leadership, while arresting Gomulka and his associates, resisted Soviet demands for a show trial. The trials and purges have been explained with reference to historical traditions, political and psychological mechanisms. It has been argued that the Stalinist system was based on the application of terror, and that recurrent trials and purges were needed to spread fear among the population. There is some truth in all these explanations, yet in the last resort motivation was irrational. There probably was no master plan and many events defy explanation to this day.

The last years of the Stalin era, in eastern Europe, as in the Soviet Union, were a period of remarkable industrial expansion, but the costs of production were inordinately high and living standards actually declined. Shortages in almost all fields of the national economy affected the consumer and imperilled future economic growth. Some countries were affected more than others: Hungary in 1953 was on the verge of an economic catastrophe, whereas the situation in neighbouring Czechoslovakia was less critical. Following the lead given by Malenkov after Stalin's death, all the 'people's democracies' adjusted their economic policy and there were also certain changes in the political field. In Hungary the 'New Course' went considerably beyond the limits set by Moscow: Rakosi had to give up the prime ministership and Imre Nagy, a 'Muscovite' like Rakosi but far more liberal and democratic in his outlook, introduced economic and political reforms. The development of heavy industry was no longer regarded as an end in itself; many political prisoners were freed, and the whole atmosphere became markedly freer. Nagy became very popular among the masses but for that very reason antagonised the old leadership. After Malenkov's fall, Nagy too had to go, and at the end of 1955 was excluded from the party. The Stalinist leaders made a comeback, even if they could not recover all the positions they had lost. The great and growing discontent among workers and peasants, and above all among the younger generation and the students, could no longer be contained and it led the year after to a major explosion.

There were signs of growing discontent in East Germany and Czechoslovakia, such as the revolt of 17 June 1953 in East Berlin and the big strike in the Czech town of Pilsen. Both governments took urgent measures to improve living conditions but opposed political reform. Klement Gottwald, the leader of Czech communism, died in 1953, but Zapotocki, and in particular Novotny, who subsequently emerged as the central figure in the régime, were typical products of the Stalinist era. Poland and Rumania were the last east European countries to introduce the 'New Course'. They had been slightly less affected than the other satellites by the trials and other tribulations of the late Stalin period. Bierut, the leader of the Polish party, had to give up the post of Prime Minister in 1954; in December of that year the Minister of Public Security had to step down after sensational revelations about the practices of the secret police had been made by a high Polish official who had defected to the West. The first reforms were purely economic in character, but the opposition movement soon gathered momentum. The Communist Party, whose membership had decreased over a number of years, found itself isolated from a population profoundly anti-communist, while inside the party there was growing opposition to the leadership. In Poland and Hungary a pre-revolutionary situation existed in 1955, and as events during the next year were to show, only minor impulses were needed to spark an explosion.

Stalin's policy in his east European empire had effected enormous political, social, and economic changes. With the exception of Yugoslavia, all the countries became part of a monolithic bloc. Their policy, their economy, their military forces were closely integrated under Soviet leadership and strict control. Comecon (The Council for Mutual Economic Aid) was established in Warsaw in January 1949 as an east European counterweight to the Marshall plan, and the Warsaw pact (signed in 1955) was the military answer to NATO. But this was only official recognition of the existing state of affairs. The Soviet Union under Stalin interfered in the internal affairs of its satellites without any hesitation, at every level and in every field. His successors showed more tact in their dealings with the east European capitals, though there were limits to their restraint, as events in Budapest in 1956 were to prove.

The Stalinist practice of centralisation and strict control contained the seeds of its own destruction. These policies were deeply offensive to intensely nationalist peoples and on occasion they antagonised even the communist leadership. While no communist leader wanted to reverse the social order, the idea of a national communism, free from outside interference, more democratic and humane in character, gained some open adherents and many more tacit sympathisers. National communism did not necessarily mean the gradual emergence of a more liberal régime, but it opened the door to the many changes that were to take place all over eastern Europe during the next decade.

PART II

ECONOMIC AND SOCIAL TRENDS

Ruin and Resurgence

Western Europe, occupying only three per cent of the world's land surface, contained in 1960 about nine per cent of the population of the globe. It produced one quarter of the world's industrial output, accounted for 40 per cent of the world's trade, and was thus the world's greatest market. Europe's postwar growth was spectacular; few observers had assumed at the end of the war that Europe would so quickly recover from its wounds. The prewar history of Europe did not augur well for the prospects of quick growth. Summarising Europe's position at the end of the nineteen-thirties, a Swedish economist wrote that it presented a picture of half-finished transformation in relation to technological change and the new developments in the international market. Many factors resisted change: obsolete equipment, restrictive practices by governments, management, and workers alike. Productivity in agriculture was low, many industries were stagnating, and widespread unemployment kept national output and income down: 'Europe was suffering from the arteriosclerosis of an old-established, heavily capitalised economic system, inflexible in relation to violent economic change' (Svennilson). The second world war caused enormous ravages and paralysed economic activity; it is estimated that nearly a year after liberation French and Belgian industries were running at only 20 per cent of their prewar level and that German production was even lower. Britain, which had suffered less direct damage than the continent, reached the prewar level of production in 1946, but in most European countries the situation seemed far less promising; in that year steel production in western Europe, to provide but one illustration, was only half what it had been in 1939. There were acute food shortages and high priority was given to means to avert the danger of starvation. Encouraging progress was made in 1945 and 1946, but then came the great setback of 1947 when disastrous climatic conditions caused havoc and destroyed much of the agricultural crop. After that catastrophic year the situation gradually improved as more fertilisers became available. Britain had been the first to mechanise its agriculture; the continent followed during the nineteen-fifties.

Industrial recovery, too, made rapid progress. In 1948 the industries of France and of most other European countries (except Germany) were already producing more than before the war. Recovery after the first world war, too, had been rapid, but many still remembered how this impetus had petered out after a few years and was followed by a long period of stagnation and decline. Would history repeat itself? The difficulties seemed overwhelming. As a result of the unsatisfied demand of the long years of war there was tremendous inflationary pressure. All European governments faced this danger, while the balance of trade with the United States grew steadily worse and resulted in a grave 'dollar gap'. More than ever before, Europe was dependent on exports, but it could restore its position as an industrial manufacturer only if it acquired new equipment and raw materials, and for these it was not able to pay. This balance of payments deficit was bridged only by very substantial American grants and, after 1947, by the Marshall plan. Marshall aid was the blood transfusion which 'sustained the weakening European economies and gave them the strength to work their own recovery' (OEEC: *Economic Progress and Problems of Western Europe*. June 1951). From the end of 1947 to June 1950 about 9.4 billion dollars were made available to the countries most in need. The effects in terms of economic progress were startling: total output of goods and services during those three years rose by 25 per cent, and during the second half of 1950 European output was already running 30 to 35 per cent above the prewar level. In certain key industries the advance was even more striking: steel production increased by 70 per cent between 1947 and 1950, cement by 80 per cent, vehicles by 150 per cent and refined oil products by 200 per cent. Exports rose by 91 per cent and Europe seemed well on the way to recovery when in the early summer of 1950 the Korean war broke out and put in jeopardy many of these achievements. It caused raw material shortages, rising prices, and new inflationary pressures. Devaluation had made European goods more competitive on the world's markets and helped to close the dollar gap, but with the outbreak of the war the prices of raw materials skyrocketed, profoundly affecting the terms of trade. At the same time it became necessary to strengthen Europe's defences; defence expenditure in 1950 absorbed a considerable part of the productive resources of Europe and the volume of goods available for civilian consumption had to be drastically reduced. Since some European countries such as Germany, Austria, and Greece, had made only a very imperfect recovery, and since a large part of Europe's imports was still financed by American loans, future prospects again seemed very bleak indeed. Yet the outbreak of the Korean war, it appears in retrospect, interrupted Europe's recovery only briefly. The re-equipment of industry and agriculture continued, structural unemployment and the dollar gap gradually disappeared. Each country had a separate national plan to speed up recovery; France's Monnet plan was the most famous of them. These plans had much to recommend them; they were all aimed at a rapid expansion of the national economy and of exports. But there was one fatal flaw:

there was no attempt to coordinate; on the contrary, there was a great deal of overlapping. It was soon realised that all European countries were bound to suffer unless customs barriers were broken down and trade liberalised, unless the European economy became far more integrated than it had been before the war. The Schuman plan was the precursor of the later and more ambitious plans for west European economic union. European planners regarded the recovery of the immediate postwar period merely as a first step towards a greater goal; it was gratifying that the European economy had so quickly reached prewar levels, but it was not forgotten that Europe in the nineteen-thirties had not exactly been a prosperous continent. Production in many countries had, in fact, been lower in 1938 than ten years earlier. With a growing population Europe needed a long period of continuous growth. *The Economic Survey for Europe* published in 1951 predicted a growth in industrial production of 40–60 per cent up to the end of the decade. But these targets were already reached by the middle of the decade, and the upward swing still continued to gather momentum. By 1964 Europe's industrial output was more than two and a half times as great as in 1938.

Economists agree that it is impossible to find a historical precedent for the extended period of prosperity enjoyed by Europe during the fifties and sixties: 'In continental Europe the decade of the 1950s was brilliant, with growth of output and consumption, investment and employment surpassing any recorded historical experience and the rhythm of development virtually uninterrupted by recession' (Angus Maddison). Andrew Shonfield has noted that the growth of production was extremely rapid, that there was no halt or reversal in the advance, and that the benefits of the new prosperity were very widely diffused. Michael Postan observed that the ever mounting affluence was the unique feature of the postwar economy; remarkable and unexpected also was the fact that the economic growth was so powerfully propelled by public sentiment and policies. The following table indicates the percentage average yearly growth of the Gross Domestic Product* of the main European countries between 1948 and 1963:

Austria	5.8	Italy	6.0
Belgium	3.2	Norway	3.5
Denmark	3.6	Sweden	3.4
France	4.6	Switzerland	3.4
Germany	7.6	United Kingdom	2.5
Holland	4.7		

At the beginning of the postwar period the rate of growth in Germany,

* The Gross National Product, GNP, is the total sum of goods and services produced, the finished goods delivered to final purchasers. The Gross Domestic Product, GDP, is the same minus the income received from abroad.

Austria and Greece was lagging behind the others because their economies had been more severely affected by the war. For the same reason, that is, starting from a lower point, their rate of development during the middle and late fifties was faster than that of the other countries. In Italy, too, after a sluggish start, the rate of development gathered momentum during the late fifties. In 1959 Italy was producing 64 per cent more than at the beginning of the decade; between 1959 and 1961 the annual rate of growth was 7.5 per cent. The expansion of production in France, the Netherlands, Switzerland, and Spain was near the European average, from 45 to 50 per cent, between the beginning and the end of the decade. In these countries growth accelerated towards the end of the decade and in the early sixties. Even the mature economies of Sweden and Switzerland, which had been least affected by the war, attained a rate of growth of 6 per cent or more in 1964. Production in Britain and Belgium rose more slowly; in Britain it was only 21 per cent higher at the end of the decade, in Belgium 26 per cent. But the rate of growth in Belgium quickened during the early sixties and in Britain too there was a belated, though still fitful advance. While Germany had topped the list of the fast growing economies during the fifties, a different picture emerged during the sixties:

GNP Annual Average Rate of Increase 1960–65

Italy	5.1	Britain	3.3
France	5.1	Japan	9.6
Germany	4.8	United States	4.5

The postwar growth of the European economy was first interrupted by the outbreak of the Korean war and then slowed down by the recession of 1957–8. The causes of the slump of 1957–8 were more complex than those of the earlier setback. Several European countries, notably France, Britain, Belgium, and Denmark, had adopted restrictive measures to lessen the pressure on their currencies, which had increased as the result of an adverse balance of payments. The slowing down of the rate of growth was deliberate and envisaged as a temporary measure. The recessions of the fifties were of short duration and had no lasting effects; even during the slump years 1952 and 1958 European production rose by approximately two per cent. The recessions of the nineteen-sixties were more serious in character: economic growth in France was slowed down in 1963–5, Italy went through a crisis in 1963–4, and the German economic miracle came to a halt in 1966–7. 1964 had been an excellent year in most European countries, with a rise in industrial output of 7 per cent; in some the advance was even more substantial but the poor showing of Italy (0.3 per cent) affected the general picture. 1967, on the other hand, was a year of crisis: in Britain, West Germany, and

Austria industrial production actually fell and the average European gain was only 1.2 per cent. During the following year the European economy recovered again but the planners did not expect that the record performance of the fifties and early sixties would continue.

The stormy development of Europe's economy during the two decades after the war has certain unique features. Never in its history, not even before the first world war, had industrial Europe made such striking advances. Even the sluggish performance of the British economy was in excess of Britain's development before 1914, let alone her economic record between the two wars. This performance provided economists with much food for thought. The Marxists among them (but not only they) had for a long time predicted the demise of capitalism, which they argued, had long exhausted its historical role. In their view, capitalist economy, as the crisis of 1929 and the slump of the demise of capitalism, which, they argued, had long exhausted its historical of economic development. The fact that the 'capitalist economies' of Europe had acquired a new lease of life and made greater progress than ever before seemed to belie these assumptions. American neo-Marxists maintained that the postwar boom was essentially military in character, with defence expenditure as the stabilising factor. Such arguments were hardly relevant to developments in Europe. There is no straightforward formula to explain the boom after the second world war. The European governments had on the whole digested the lesson of the great pre-war depression and were able to maintain high levels of purchasing power and thus to stimulate demand by the application of Keynesian techniques – manipulating taxation, monetary policy, spending, and borrowing. The customs barriers between the countries were reduced; the Common Market and EFTA, its rival organisation, provided large markets and thus stimulated economic activity. There was a much higher degree of collaboration between industries in various countries than before and Europe thus enjoyed some of the advantages from which America alone had benefited in the past. The great business concerns such as Unilever, ICI, the German chemical concerns and the German, Italian, and French car manufacturers (to name but a few) could plan and produce more cheaply and more rationally, and invest more in research. At the same time the European economy had become far more planned and less capitalist (in the *laissez-faire* sense) than in the past. The coal mines in Britain and France had been nationalised, the production of electricity was entirely in the hands of the state in Italy and Britain, and to a large extent also in France and Germany. So were air transport, the railways, and to a lesser extent sea transport (80 per cent in Italy, 37 per cent in France). About 40 per cent of the Italian and French banks were state-owned; 60 per cent of the Italian iron and steel industry, and the same percentage of the French aircraft industry (to give a few more examples) had been nationalised. The part played by the state in the national economy was thus infinitely more important than in the past, but these changes in ownership in themselves were not sufficient to explain the great postwar boom. West Germany, which adopted liberal economic policies, made as much progress as Italy and France, which put more emphasis on planning and state ownership. An influential school of economists (W. A. Lewis, Kindleberger) has argued that the rapid advance of Europe's economy was connected with the availability of a large supply of labour, stemming from a high rate of natural increase, from immigration, from the presence of unemployed workers, or from transfers from agriculture to industry; with the exhaustion of Europe's excess supply of labour, the rates of economic growth fell; instead of an annual increase of 6–8 per cent, a yearly growth of 2–4 per cent became more common. This was a plausible explanation: Europe had after the war large idle capacities both in manpower and equipment; once these resources were put to good use an unprecedented economic expansion ensued. Some of these factors were not likely to recur and hence the gradual decline in the rate of growth in the sixties. But other factors also contributed to the boom: greater productivity, technical innovation, the expansion of world trade, and even psychological considerations such as increased self-confidence on the part of industrialists, bankers, and economic planners.

Economic recovery in the Soviet Union also made rapid strides after the war.

INDUSTRIAL PRODUCTION IN EASTERN EUROPE
(*1958=100*)

	1938	*1948*	*1953*	*1959*	*1962*	*1965*
Bulgaria	11	22	55	121	170	238
Czechoslovakia	31	44	64	112	143	159
East Germany	38	27	66	112	137	159
Hungary	28	38	84	111	149	177
Poland	16	28	61	109	145	182
Rumania	25	22	63	110	168	243
Yugoslavia	29	43	53	113	150	217
USSR	23	40	58	111	146	184

The output of coal in 1952 was twice what it had been in 1945; the production of steel, oil, and electricity almost trebled during the same period. Stalin and his assistants were convinced that the performance of the Soviet economy was greatly superior to that of the 'capitalist world' because it was planned, because there was no unemployment, and because its resources would always be fully used. During the nineteen-thirties, at the time of the great recession in the West, the Soviet economy had indeed forged ahead and the country had become the second industrial power in the world. According to official statistics, the Soviet national income has grown since 1928 by a steady ten per cent per year; industrial output in 1963 was said to be 44 times as large as in the late nineteen-twenties. The aim of catching up with and overtaking America had first been announced in the early nineteen-thirties; Khrushchev declared in the nineteen-fifties that the target would be achieved in 1970. But the official figures of the Stalin era have always been, and justifiably, suspect, and there could be no doubt that Soviet standards of living were, even in the nineteen-sixties, substantially lower than those in the West. They were, in fact, inferior to the level reached by some of the countries of eastern Europe. The Soviet economy continued to advance but its rate of growth declined. Considerable progress was made during the nineteen-fifties: Soviet GNP was 36 per cent of the American in 1957, and reached the 50 per cent mark five years later. It seemed at that time it had a good chance of overtaking America within a decade or two if the same rate of growth continued. After 1962 progress became slower, whereas America, emerging from the recession of the early sixties, moved ahead faster. By 1968 the Soviet GNP was still only half that of America. In industrial production there was a similar pattern: in 1950 Soviet production was 32 per cent of America's; in 1961, after a great spurt, it had risen to 47 per cent, but in 1967 it was still only 48 per cent. The Soviet economic planners focused on the race with the United States, apparently ignoring the fact that economic growth in some west European countries, and particularly in Japan, was actually faster than in the United States.

The exaggerated claims made for Soviet economic performance did not have the desired propaganda effect in the West; on the contrary, Western observers, irritated by the glaring discrepancy between official statistics and the real situation, sometimes tended to belittle Soviet achievements. But even though the official claims were obviously inflated, the Soviet Union has made very substantial progress since the war. As in western Europe, it was progress at an unequal rate; the latter part of the nineteen-fifties were excellent years by economic standards; they were followed by a period of much slower growth and only after 1965 was there a new upswing. The Soviet economy like that of western Europe suffered from various imbalances, albeit of a different character. Under Stalin it had been the basic rule of economic policy to give priority to heavy industry at the expense of agriculture, light industry, and consumer goods in general. The stormy development of Soviet industry, with its strong emphasis on heavy industry and armaments, had spectacular results, but these were achieved at a high price, both from the political and the economic point of view. It entailed severe repression and a great deal of human suffering; it meant resisting the growing demand for a better standard of living. It also involved a great deal of waste. Since the emphasis was on quantity rather than quality, a high percentage of the goods produced were of such low quality as to be unusable. These imbalances became even more pronounced towards the last years of Stalin's rule, and his successors faced almost immediately the urgent necessity of reorganising Soviet industry and agriculture. Heavy industry continued to receive priority, but far larger resources were now devoted to agriculture, to housing, and to articles of mass consumption. Substantial progress was made in all these fields and there was a marked rise in the standard of living – not comparable with western Europe's but certainly impressive in comparison with the Stalin era. In the nineteen-sixties further economic reforms were carried out, mainly to decentralise the economy and to make individual industries and factories more profitable, and greater attention was paid to productivity. The new chemical and electronics industries were given particular encouragement.

Economic development in the communist countries of eastern Europe followed in broad outline the same course as in the Soviet Union. The rapid increase in industrial production in the fifties was followed by stagnation and decline in the early sixties, and a fresh upsurge in the late sixties. The emphasis in all these countries was on heavy industry; all faced considerable difficulties in the agricultural field. Between 1960 and 1963 agricultural production in East Germany, Hungary, and Czechoslovakia was actually lower than it had been before the war. The less industrialised countries, Bulgaria, Yugoslavia, and Rumania, developed the most rapidly, whereas Poland, East Germany, Czechoslovakia and Hungary, starting at a higher level, did not make equally striking progress. All these countries had a great many obstacles to overcome: the after-effects of the destruction of the war, reparations extracted by the Soviet Union, unfavourable trade agreements with their senior partner, and the severe dislocation caused by the collectivisation of agriculture. Considering all these adverse factors, their progress was impressive but it was not equal to west European economic growth, except for the slow-growing economies of Britain and Belgium. The following table indicates the percentage growth of the GNP of various European countries between 1938 and 1964:

West Germany	220	Rumania	118
Holland	152	Poland	115
Bulgaria	147	Greece	97
France	135	Hungary	84
Italy	132	Czechoslovakia	84

In absolute terms the Gross National Product of Poland was the largest in eastern Europe in 1964 (almost 28 billion dollars), followed by East Germany (24 billion dollars) and Czechoslovakia (21 billion dollars). The total GNP of all six east European communist countries was bigger than that of

France (97 billion dollars) but smaller than West Germany (115 billion dollars).

There were in broad outline similarities in the postwar development of western and eastern Europe: economic progress was quicker than at any previous period during the history of the continent; in both West and East there was a decline in the rate of growth towards the end of the second postwar decade. The most striking developments were the industrialisation of the less developed countries of eastern and southern Europe, and the all-round progress and consequent rise in living standards in the industrial countries. There were also enormous qualitative changes; housing conditions improved, working hours were reduced and educational facilities were spread more widely than ever before. The peoples of Europe were better fed and better clothed, unemployment had virtually disappeared by the middle fifties, and there was a great and growing demand for labour. Hundreds of thousands of workers from south and south-eastern Europe migrated to Germany, France, and Switzerland to find more-highly paid employment than in their native countries. Comprehensive social security schemes providing medical care, pensions for the aged, unemployment benefits, and many other grants and services were adopted almost everywhere. Great changes took place in technology, and with the growing specialisation a much higher degree of technical knowledge became necessary for industrial workers and farmers. The unskilled labourer gave way to the skilled or semi-skilled worker, the peasant to the agricultural specialist. The growing prosperity caused far-reaching social changes; many sociologists maintained that the manual workers were gradually absorbed into the middle classes. Marxists, on the other hand, argued that despite the improvements, social injustice and poverty continued to exist, and they rejected the findings of social scientists according to which the *embourgeoisement* of the worker was already an established fact. But no one was likely to dispute that 20 years after the second world war the European worker had more to lose than his chains.

DEMOGRAPHIC CHANGES

The population of western Europe (the OECD countries in Europe) was 264 million in 1940; it is now about 320 millions. In the nineteen-thirties no demographer had expected such a rapid increase. Population had grown steadily up to the first world war despite substantial emigration overseas, but had stagnated after 1918. Fertility declined by almost half between 1900 and 1940 in Britain, Germany, Scandinavia, and Switzerland, and the trend in other countries was only slightly less marked. Since the deathrate also fell substantially during this period, the age composition of the population became very different from what it had been in the past: Europe became preponderantly middle-aged. In the nineteen-thirties this trend became even more pronounced; in Belgium, Sweden, and Britain the number of births and deaths was about even, in France and Ireland there was an absolute decline because there were more deaths than births. Most demographers predicted that this decline would continue and even gather momentum throughout western and northern Europe; no one envisaged the increase of 12 per cent in western Europe that actually took place between 1940 and 1955. The postwar European baby boom was smaller than the American, and after 1955 the birthrate again fell. But the overall growth of population proceeded nevertheless at a higher rate than between the wars, as a result partly of the decline in infant mortality, partly of the fall in the deathrate. Particularly striking was the upward swing in France, once the most populous European country, where the population had hardly increased for almost a century. French postwar governments introduced generous family allowances, and the migration of several hundred thousand Frenchmen from North Africa further helped to change the outlook in a country which had been for a long time the classical example of 'race suicide'. Holland had always had one of the highest birthrates in west Europe; its population doubled between 1900 and 1958, and there was a similar striking increase in Switzerland, whereas in neighbouring Austria it remained as before – much below the European average.

Population (in thousands)

	1950	*1966*	*Natural Increase (1960–65) (annual average)*
Austria	6,900	7,300	+0.4
Belgium	8,600	9,500	+0.7
Czechoslovakia	12,300	14,200	+0.7
France	41,700	49,400	+1.2
West Germany	n.a.	59,600	+1.2
Hungary	9,300	10,100	+0.4
Italy	46,300	51,900	+0.7
Netherlands	10,100	12,400	+1.3
Poland	24,800	31,600	+1.3
Rumania	16,300	19,100	+0.8
Spain	27,800	31,800	+0.8
Sweden	7,000	7,800	+0.6
Switzerland	4,600	6,000	+1.8
United Kingdom	50,000	54,900	+0.6
Yugoslavia	16,300	19,700	+1.1
Soviet Union	180,000 (approx.)	227,000 (approx.)	+1.7

While the birthrate rose in almost all the developed European countries, there was a striking decline in south and east Europe as the result of industrialisation and urbanisation. The total population of east Europe, not counting the Soviet Union, increased between 1950 and 1964 from 106 to 120 million although the birthrate fell from 21 to 13 in Hungary, from 26 to 15 in Rumania, and from 30 to 17 in Poland. Significantly, the only country in which it remained as before the second world war was Albania (about 37–38), the least developed of all. The population of the Soviet Union grew to approximately 227 millions, while the birthrate fell from 26 to 19. The process of urbanisation in the Soviet Union was more marked than in any other major European country; the number of the city dwellers more than doubled between 1939 and 1964; in some of the larger cities it has trebled or quadrupled during the last 40 years.

POPULATION OF MAJOR SOVIET CITIES

	1926	1959
Baku	453,300	968,000
Dnepropetrovsk	236,700	658,000
Donetsk	174,200	701,000
Gorky	222,300	942,000
Kazan	179,000	643,000
Kharkov	417,300	930,000
Kiev	513,600	1,101,000
Kuibyshev	175,600	806,000
Leningrad	1,690,000	3,300,000
Minsk	134,800	509,000
Moscow	2,029,400	5,032,000
Odessa	420,800	667,000
Ufa	98,000	546,000
Perm (Molotov)	119,700	628,000
Rostov	308,100	597,000
Sverdlovsk	140,300	777,000
Tbilisi	294,000	694,000
Volgograd (Stalingrad)	151,400	591,000
Voronezh	121,600	454,000
Yerevan	64,600	509,000
Zaporozhe	55,700	435,000

The population growth and the emergence of huge conurbations posed a great many problems to the planners. The density of population in western Europe is four times as high as in the United States. The industrial and commercial heartland of Europe, Belgium and Britain, parts of West Germany, and Northern Italy, were gradually transformed into urban areas with hardly any agriculture, and it seemed likely that the congestion in these parts would become even greater as internal migration continued from the agricultural regions to areas offering greater economic opportunities. All over Europe the proportion of the population engaged in industry continued to rise, but the tertiary sector, the services, increased even more. Before 1914 almost half of west Europe's working population had been employed in agriculture, fishing, and forestry. By the nineteen-thirties it was only one third, and by 1955 the farming population represented only 24 per cent of the total. The trend continued during the fifties and sixties; by 1965 only 17 per cent of the Common Market population was engaged in agriculture (25 per cent in Italy, 18 per cent in France, 6 per cent in Belgium – in Britain it was no more than 3 per cent). In most south European countries agriculture was still the occupation of 40 per cent or more of the population, but there, too, the trend towards industry and the services was unmistakable. In Spain, two out of three workers had been employed in agriculture in 1910; but in the early nineteen-fifties the share of agriculture had fallen to less than 50 per cent, and by 1966 it was less than 33 per cent. In eastern Europe the process was equally marked; in all these parts agriculture had been dominant before the second world war. After 1945 the number of those engaged in industry rose rapidly, though agriculture continued to employ a relatively high percentage of the working population even in the industrialised countries of east Europe (Czechoslovakia, East Germany and the USSR). The degree of industrialisation was usually an indication of prosperity. There were exceptions: in Denmark, which boasts a highly developed and profitable agriculture, the percentage of those employed in agriculture is almost six times as high as in Britain, but its *per capita* income is higher. Among the major European nations the exodus from agriculture was most pronounced in Germany and France; between 1955 and the late sixties there was a further decline of about 20 per cent in the agricultural labour force of western Europe, but there was still over-employment in agriculture and the Common Market experts have demanded a further reduction of the agricultural labour force by five to eight million during the next decade. Political, economic, and cultural life had been concentrated in the big cities of Europe even at the time when the great majority of the population still lived and worked in the countryside. With the industrial revolution there was a constant stream to the towns which at times became a torrent; by the middle of the twentieth century Europe had become to all intents and purposes an urban continent.

The Recovery of European Industry

Europe had been the industrial centre of the world up to the end of the nineteenth century; the United States caught up with the old continent during the first world war and the Soviet Union reached the west European level of heavy industry output in the late nineteen-fifties. Europe, with 15 per cent of the world's population, continued however to be the world's greatest market; about 40 per cent of the world's GNP is still produced in the European continent including the USSR. The following table documents the steady rise of European industrial production since 1945:

INDEX OF INDUSTRIAL PRODUCTION
($1958 = 100$)

	1938	1948	1952	1959	1963	1967
USA	33	73	90	113	133	168
West Germany	53	27	61	107	137	158
France	52	55	70	101	129	155
Italy	43	44	64	112	166	212
Holland	47	53	72	110	141	182
Belgium	64	78	88	104	135	153
Britain	67	74	84	105	119	133
Austria	39	36	65	106	131	151
Spain	n.a.	n.a.	n.a.	102	149	215
Sweden	52	74	81	106	140	176
Japan	58	22	50	120	212	347

At the same time basic structural changes took place within industry. Coal and iron had been the traditional backbone of industrial development and their importance during the industrial revolution in the nineteenth and early twentieth centuries was paramount. Great political as well as economic influence was attributed to the giants of heavy industry: the names of Krupp, Mannesmann, Thyssen, Schneider-Creusot, Vickers and Skoda became symbols of the political-economic-military establishments, and their importance even if often exaggerated was, during that period, very substantial indeed. After 1945 the situation changed: coal was gradually displaced by oil and other fuels, the value of German steel production in the early nineteen-sixties was only two-thirds that of the chemical industry, Krupp fell to sixteenth place in the list of Europe's industrial giants. Of all the major industrial enterprises which had been family property only one (Thyssen) did not change hands and become a public company.

The eclipse of coal mining was felt all over Europe. Coal had been the fuel *par excellence* of the Industrial Revolution; it had no rival as a source of energy. Before the first world war Europe had exported considerable quantities of coal to other parts of the world, but after 1918, with growing domestic energy demands, a shortage developed. Europe's coal reserves are limited and coal mining became more expensive as deeper and less profitable seams had to be worked, and as a result Europe's supply pattern of sources of energy began to change rapidly. At first considerable quantities of coal were still imported, mainly from the United States, but from the early fifties the import of crude oil and refined petroleum products increased every year. Crude oil imports which had been a mere 17 million tons in 1929, rose to 450 million in 1967. As more and more unprofitable pits were closed down, the output of British coal mining, the most important in Europe, fell steadily; having reached its peak before 1914, when yearly output was about 300 million tons, it had fallen in 1964 to 196 million and in 1967 there was a further decline to 175 million. In 1966 oil supplied 51 per cent of the Common Market countries' energy demands. This spectacular rise became possible as the result of the discovery of vast oil resources, mainly in the Middle East, in the nineteen-forties and fifties; about 90 per cent of Europe's crude oil supplies now comes from the Persian Gulf area and North Africa. This dependence created new problems; while oil was very much cheaper than coal, it had usually to be paid for in foreign currency. There was also the danger that in a political crisis the supply would be stopped; this happened during the Suez crisis in 1956 and again during the Arab-Israeli war in 1967. The European countries tried to counteract the effects of these stoppages by storing several months' supply and by gradually developing other sources of energy, particularly natural gas and nuclear power; substantial quantities of natural gas were found in the Soviet Union but also in Holland and other west European countries. The development of nuclear power, mainly as a source of generating electricity, took longer than had originally been expected because of the high cost of technological progress, but there is little doubt that nuclear energy will play a major role in the seventies and eighties and will ultimately cover a large part of the increasing energy requirements, as forecasts for Britain demonstrate:

(*in millions of tons of coal equivalent*)

	1970	1975	1980
Coal	152	120	80
Oil	125	145	160
Nuclear and Hydroenergy	16	35	90
Natural gas	17	50	70

The coal mining industry had its defenders despite the high cost of production. While the critics argued that coal had ceased to be an industry and become a giant social insurance scheme requiring vast government subsidies, its advocates maintained that it was dangerous both from a political and an economic point of view to neglect coal mining altogether. The retraining of miners, too, presented major problems especially in West Germany and Britain. In West Germany about 15 per cent of the mining labour force changed their occupation between 1960 and 1963, but not everyone was able and willing to move to a new place and to look for a new job.

Industrial development in eastern Europe at first followed a somewhat different pattern. Coal production in the Soviet Union almost trebled between 1948 and 1965, increasing from 150 million tons to 427 million. It rose to 578 million tons in 1965 and remained at that figure. The production of oil increased tenfold to 309 million tons in 1968. Yet domestic demand rose even faster and the problem was most acutely felt in the communist countries of eastern Europe which, in contrast to the Soviet Union, had no sizable indigenous oil supplies. The Soviet Union, which had begun in the fifties to export considerable quantities of oil to western Europe and was also eastern Europe's sole supplier, might thus face a shortage in the nineteen-seventies. It therefore began to take an interest in the import of natural gas from Iran and Afghanistan. Fuel demand in eastern Europe was kept low in the nineteen-fifties, but with industrial expansion and the increase in road transport the relative importance of coal began to decline and the planners, aware that coal made for a high cost industry, were looking for alternative sources of energy. With some delay eastern Europe thus followed the example of the West.

Western Europe's share of world oil-refining capacity rose from four per cent before the war to over 20 per cent in 1960 with the erection of giant refineries in Rotterdam, Southampton, and Hamburg. The petrochemical industry made great strides, above all in France, and the network of pipelines was greatly expanded in the sixties. The German chemical industry had been traditionally strongest; I.G.Farben had monopolised the field to such an extent that the Allies thought it safer to dissolve it at the end of the war. Yet so rapid was the progress of the industry that by the sixties each one of the three successor firms (Hoechst, Bayer, and BASF) produced more than the old I.G.Farben. The output of the European chemical industry trebled between 1950 and 1960; Britain was again overtaken by Germany, while the French and Italian industries, which had started the race well behind these two leaders, developed at an even faster rate than Germany. In all these countries there was a tendency towards the amalgamation of enterprises, partly as the result of stiff competition, partly to meet the need to devote to research a larger share of capital than in any other industry. In Italy ENI joined forces with Montecatini and Edison and emerged as the largest single firm on the continent. Only the very largest units could survive the stiff competition unless, like the Belgian firm Solvay, they decided to limit their range of products; the biggest firms such as Bayer produced no fewer than 12,000 different items, most of which had not been known before the war;

and there were many new synthetic products which replaced natural fibres, metals, wood, and glass, and others in the petrochemical and pharmaceutical industries. In the Soviet Union the growing importance of the chemical industry was recognised with some delay, preference in investment had always been given to iron and steel. Under Khrushchev a determined effort was made to correct this disproportion, but it was not easy to catch up with the advance that had meanwhile been made in the West. By 1966 less than six per cent of the industrial production of the USSR originated in the chemical industry, whereas the percentage was twice as high in the developed industrial nations of the West.

The European chemical industries had to compete not only among themselves but also against the giant American concerns such as Du Pont which spearheaded the American economic invasion of Europe. The productivity of the American chemical industries was considerably higher; it outproduced the west European industry while employing only about 60 per cent of the labour force. The European industries lacked not know-how and labour but capital to finance their programmes of research, innovation, and expansion. American firms succeeded in gaining a foothold in the continental chemical industry above all owing to their greater financial strength. The European chemical industry had been centred in north-east England (ICI) and in the Rhineland and the Ruhr before the war, but in the fifties and sixties new locations were added: the Maas river where Shell and ICI established enormous plants, Lyons, and north and south Italy.

The postwar growth of the European automobile industry was comparable only to the development of the chemical industry. It had begun to establish itself before the first world war and reached maturity in the nineteen-twenties and thirties, but its early successes were dwarfed by the development after 1950. Germany emerged in the nineteen-sixties as the largest producer of motor vehicles, with a yearly output of slightly less than three million passenger cars, whereas Britain and France produced between 1.5 and 2 million cars each. The Italian industry, too, grew quickly from small beginnings, topping the one million mark in 1963. Germany was the biggest exporter; in 1961 one million German cars were sold abroad, more than 200,000 in the United States alone. Yet inside Europe the share of Volkswagen, the most successful postwar car, declined, whereas Fiat and the French cars advanced during the sixties. The American challenge to the European car industry was met by closer European collaboration. The invasion of the big American manufacturers had begun well before the second world war; Ford had long produced its own cars in England and Germany, and Chrysler bought itself into Simca in France and Rootes in Britain. This left only a handful of independent European producers – Volkswagen and Daimler-Benz in West Germany, the state-owned French Renault; Fiat tried to take over the ailing French Citroën, and the British Motor Corporation (BMC), a merger of Morris and Austin. The location of the European car industry has hardly changed. In Britain it is still concentrated in Birmingham and Coventry, Oxford, Luton, and Dagenham. Three of the four major French firms are located in and around Paris, and Fiat's two main factories are in Turin. The one major new development was the emergence of Volkswagen in Wolfsburg, a new town not far from Hanover which owes its existence entirely to the car industry.

The postwar history of the European aircraft industry is less happy. Britain and France developed their commercial jet liners such as the Caravelle and the Comet, but with the appearance of larger, faster, and above all far more expensive aircraft, neither the French industry, largely state-owned, nor the two British groups (Hawker and BAC), could go on competing with the great American firms. Europe's decision not to participate in the missile race was probably correct in the light of its economic priorities, but it also meant a further, perhaps fatal, setback to the development of its aircraft industry.

The European engineering industries had mixed fortunes during the two decades after 1945. The producers of textile, mining, and railway equipment did not fare too well on the whole. Britain, which had been the world's leading shipbuilder, lost out to Japan, which became the world's major producer accounting for nearly half the total new world tonnage by the end of the sixties, and was also overtaken by Germany. In the Soviet Union great stress was put on the production of machine tools, which became one of Russia's main articles of export. The fastest developing branch all over Europe was the electrical industry, and more particularly electronics. The main discoveries which paved the way for development of the electronics industry were made before 1914, and television was well established by the nineteen-thirties. But the techniques of automation were perfected only with the development of radar and of servomotors during the second world war. Big American firms like IBM took an immediate lead in the new field of computers, but the phenomenal growth of some European producers such as the Italian Olivetti and the French Machines Bull and Thomson-Brandt should also be registered. Some of them trebled their output within a few years. The biggest European electrical companies were, as before the war, German, British, and Dutch (AEG, Siemens, English Electric, AEI and Philips). Philips concentrated on radio, television, and domestic appliances, while the German firms put more stress on the production of heavy equipment (turbines, transformers, etc.). The 'American challenge' and the phenomenal growth of the Italian electrical industry were the two outstanding developments in this field during the sixties. By 1966 American firms had invested about 14 billion dollars in the industries of western Europe, with a heavy emphasis on electronics: 15 per cent of the production of radio and television in Europe, 50 per cent of semi-conductors and 80 per cent of computers were controlled by American concerns. These were the leading growth industries, and the investors felt certain that owing to superior American know-how further rapid progress could be anticipated in the factories controlled by US firms. The European industries countered by rationalising their production, spending more on research and development, and by closer collaboration among themselves, in particular among the French and the Italians. The progress of the Italian electrical industry, especially in the field of domestic appliances, was fastest of all in the decade after 1958; it advanced to third place in the world after the United States and Japan, and in some branches, such as the production of refrigerators, its products had no rival.

The overall picture of industrial development in Europe was thus one of intense development and, despite occasional crises and setbacks, of unprecedented prosperity. Western Europe made more rapid progress than the United States, and its living standards were far in advance of the Soviet Union and eastern Europe. But many observers maintained that western Europe's long-term industrial outlook gave cause for concern for a number of reasons, such as the failure to develop the use of nuclear energy for peaceful purposes on an adequate scale. In this respect there was a real technological gap between America and Europe and it was growing from year to year. Critics claimed that while Europe could not compete with America and Russia in the field of space travel and the most sophisticated types of aircraft, there was no good reason for the neglect of nuclear energy. Britain was leading in Europe, but even its efforts were comparatively feeble; the continental initiatives sponsored by Euratom did not receive sufficient priority. Some of these schemes, such as the Orgel reactor, were discontinued mid-way and the budgets allocated by France, Germany, and Italy for research and development were too small to tackle large-scale projects. Germany was the first country to appoint a minister for nuclear research and development, but there, too, progress was hampered by insufficient funds. The pessimists argued that within a decade or two it would no longer be possible to catch up with America and that as a result the whole industrial development of western Europe was bound to fall behind. Such criticism raised wider and more general questions, such as the problem of R. and D., basic research and development, the willingness of governments and private industries to allocate vast sums without any certainty that the investment would yield a commensurate return.

Changes in Agriculture

During the two decades after the second world war country life all over Europe changed out of recognition; technological innovation profoundly affected agriculture and the traditional peasant village all but disappeared. The number of tractors in use had been fairly negligible before 1945 except in the Soviet Union and Britain; between 1950 and 1962 it increased from 350,000 to 2.6 million in the Common Market countries alone. The use of fertilisers grew by over 85 per cent between the nineteen-thirties and 1959, and as a result of these and other improvements, productivity in agriculture doubled in France and West Germany between the early fifties and the middle sixties; a shrinking labour force produced far more food than in the prewar years.

The recovery from the ravages of war proceeded at first relatively slowly; it has been estimated that at the end of the war the level of agricultural production was only about two-thirds what it had been before, and in Germany, Austria, and Greece it was still lower. Agricultural yields surpassed the prewar level only in 1949–50 (again with the exception of Germany, Austria, and Greece) and the recovery in the output of livestock products took longer.

The land itself had not gone out of agricultural use during the war. During the war and for a period after it ended, however, the land was poorly farmed by a labour force which had suffered much dilution. Draft animals and tractors were scarce. The land was often sown with inferior seed, insufficiently supported by fertilisers. In many places humans were competing with animals for cereals, with a result that feed for livestock was inadequate and milk and meat yields fell. (Dewhurst *et al : Europe's Needs and Resources.*)

As the men returned to the farms and as investment in agriculture rose, the wartime shortages were overcome. By 1957 agricultural output in western Europe was about 35 per cent higher than 20 years earlier, and it continued to increase steadily. Livestock farming in Britain expanded, while in Denmark there were again more pigs, and in Ireland more cattle, than people. Great progress was made in animal breeding by the introduction of industrial methods, selective breeding, and artificial insemination; battery production increased the output of poultry and eggs. Agricultural education improved all over the continent; better strains of seed were used, and the widespread application of fertilisers and pesticides contributed to the rapid growth in agricultural output.

By the middle sixties the countries of western Europe, with the exception of Britain, produced over 95 per cent of their cereal requirements, almost all the meat they needed, more than their domestic consumption of potatoes, sugar, and vegetables. There was a glut of milk and butter, and the Common Market countries had to adopt emergency measures to cope with this surplus and to give subsidies to farmers to switch from milk to meat production. The Malthusians, who had predicted for so long that the growth of population would soon outstrip the production of food, were clearly proved wrong.

European agriculture is one of high yields but also of high cost; by and large it still is Europe's single biggest industry, contributing between 25–30 per cent of the national income in the countries of southern Europe, 10–20 per cent in Denmark and Italy, between 5–10 per cent in most other west European countries with the exception of Britain and Belgium, where it is less than five per cent. France is western Europe's leading agricultural exporter, the granary of the Common Market and also the chief supplier of meat and sugar, whereas Britain and West Germany are the chief importers of food. The agricultural labour force of Europe has steadily declined and is at present only about one-third of the prewar level. This decline would have proceeded even more rapidly but for the protectionist policies of most European governments. The progress made by European agriculture is impressive, but the general picture is less favourable when compared with the United States, where a farming population of seven million has attained a far higher level of output.

The main obstacle to rationalisation in European agriculture is the small size of farms. About half of western Europe's farms are under five hectares (12½ acres) and are not therefore economically viable, except for those growing specialised crops. In France the average size of the farm is bigger than in the rest of Europe (17.8 hectares in comparison with 10 in Holland and Germany and 7 in Italy), but even there a study made in the middle fifties reached the conclusion that almost half of the existing farms were too small to support their owners. In Germany and Italy the need for drastic reforms such as the merger of smallholdings is even more urgent.

The rising standards of life in the cities attracted a great many farmers, especially those of the younger generation. The problem facing most European governments was to speed up structural change and rationalisation in agriculture while preventing a mass exodus from the countryside which would have led to the total collapse of rural society. For a variety of reasons, such as balance of payments considerations, but also political expediency, it was necessary to offer the farmers prices high enough to give them incomes comparable to those obtained in the towns. At the same time it was counter-productive to give such support to backward farms, which puts a premium on inefficiency. The European governments have been only partly successful in striking the balance, and the attempts to coordinate the national agricultural systems have made only slow progress. By means of import tariffs and quotas, deficiency payments, export subsidies and many other devices, a high degree of protection has been extended to agriculture. Large farmers have benefited to a much greater extent than smallholders; the Poujade movement in France in the nineteen-fifties was a manifestation of the malaise affecting the small farmers.

Farming subsidies were the decisive factor in bringing about the dramatic increase in food production, but this progress was achieved at a high cost; it slowed down overall economic growth, caused inflationary increases in wages and prices, and the bill for the state subsidies had to be footed above all by the low-income consumer. The question posed to many European countries was: why produce locally what could be bought cheaper elsewhere? From a purely economic point of view there was no convincing case to justify the continuation of subsidies, but political considerations (as well as senti-mental reasons) played an important part in the decision to maintain them. The erosion of the peasant economy, the desertion of the countryside, depen-dence on the import of cheap food from outside, were feared, and it became the policy of most European governments to arrest the decline of peasant agriculture despite the high financial and social costs involved.

The liberalisation of agricultural trade and the adoption of a common European agricultural policy proved to be an uphill struggle, for there were conflicts of interest between the exporting countries eager to boost their sales and those with a less efficient or less competitive agriculture. It was official French policy to protect agriculture from American and Canadian imports, but at the same time to lower tariffs sufficiently inside Europe so that French agriculture could establish itself as the chief provider of agricultural produce for its neighbours. But other countries also followed a protectionist policy, even Denmark, which had the most competitive agriculture of all. Protec-tionism resulted in a larger volume of production than was needed, and pro-ductivity in agriculture remained substantially lower than in industry, with the exception of those countries (Denmark, Belgium) where it had almost reached it even before the introduction of protectionist measures.

The members of the European Community were committed to a common agricultural policy and to liberalising trade in agricultural products, yet the negotiations between the member states dragged on for many years and ran into untold difficulties and crises. The member states were willing to make a great many concessions on condition that the social and economic structure of their respective agricultural systems was not affected. But the whole point was that structural changes were inevitable to bring about a more rational division of labour in Europe and a common policy. Common Market agriculture was supported in 1961 to the tune of four billion dollars a year by the respective governments; while world market prices for food had fallen between 1950 and 1960 by 15 per cent, they rose in the EEC countries during the same period by 25 per cent. Despite these subventions and the high prices received, the productivity of European farmers was still only a little more than half that of American agriculture: European farmers earned less and European consumers had to pay more than the Americans.

After protracted negotiations agreement was reached, as the result of what was called a deal between German industry and French agriculture, on a common policy of fixing farm prices as from 1 July 1967. Reductions of agricultural prices were involved which led to violent demonstrations on the part of French, German, and Belgian farmers. Since the politicians could not ignore the pressure exerted by the powerful agricultural lobby, it was clear that the coordination and rationalisation of European agriculture would proceed only at a slow rate. There were other negative aspects: the new Common Market agricultural policy replaced national by European protectionism; while promoting trade between the countries of Europe it reduced world trade by excluding overseas producers such as the United States, Australia, Canada – not to mention the developing countries of the third world. Of all the aspects of European integration, agriculture proved the most complex and the one most difficult to tackle.

The Transport Revolution

Europe's spectacular industrial and agricultural recovery and its postwar boom would not have been possible without a corresponding expansion in transport. During the war communications all over Europe had been severely damaged, but the repair work was accomplished more quickly than anyone thought possible in 1945.

The railway network of the United Kingdom (30,000 km.) had hardly been affected by the war and those of France and Germany (40,000 and 35,000 km. respectively) were quickly restored. European railways now had to accommodate a far greater volume of traffic than before; both freight and passenger transport was 60 per cent higher in 1957 than in the last year before the war. During the next decade, between 1957 and 1966, progress was much slower, ranging from 15 to 20 per cent in western Europe, as railways met increasing competition from other means of transport (in Britain the volume of freight carried by rail actually declined during this period).

The total length of the railway network began to decrease as uneconomical lines were shut down. The loss caused by wartime destruction had delayed the modernisation of the European railway system. Even the countries that made most progress in the use of diesel locomotives and electrification (such as Switzerland) were often forced by their respective governments to operate at unremunerative rates so as to stimulate tourism and commerce. By the middle sixties the nationalised railways of Germany, France, and Britain had to be supported by their respective governments to the tune of 400–800 million dollars per year, and even the Swiss federal railways, which had operated during the fifties at a substantial profit, were running at a loss. But as the roads of Europe became more and more congested, it was clear that the railway age was by no means over and that, irrespective of financial considerations, no country could afford to neglect its railway system.

The merchant fleets of Europe, totalling 37 million registered tons (not counting oil tankers) in 1948, more than doubled in size during the subsequent two decades. The Greek fleet expanded from 1.2 million tons to 7 million, the Norwegian from 4 to 16 million, and the Soviet fleet from 2 to 9 million tons. The British fleet, 18 million tons in 1948, developed at a much slower rate; it counted 21 million tons in 1966. The increase in number of oil tankers, on the other hand, proceeded all over Europe very quickly, and with the growing import of Middle East oil mammoth tankers of over 100,000 (and even 200,000) tons entered service.

The most far-reaching advance revolutionising the whole transport system took place in the air and on the highroads of Europe. Between 1948 and 1965 the volume of airline business (passenger kilometres flown) increased roughly tenfold and it has continued to rise. Big shiny airports were built in the vicinity of all large cities, very much in contrast to the primitive, ramshackle constructions during the early, 'heroic' days of civil aviation. Almost all European airlines were nationalised and enjoyed a near monopoly, with the result that air fares in western Europe were considerably higher than in the United States (and, incidentally, the Soviet Union).

Transatlantic travel on the other hand was considerably cheaper. In 1958, for the first time, more people crossed the Atlantic by air than by sea, and after that sea travel gradually became the preserve of the wealthy tourist – more leisurely but also more expensive than the seven hour air route. Air transport on shorter routes inside Europe faced difficulties of a different character: congestion in the air and on the ground and the growing distance between airports and cities. The flying time between Paris and London airports was approximately 45 minutes in the nineteen-sixties, much faster than in the prewar days, but this was offset by congestion on the ground; it took as much time, if not more, to reach the centre of London or Paris from their respective airports despite all the technical progress. Delivery of mail, especially over short distances, to give another illustration, also became slower; 50 years earlier there had been several daily deliveries in most

European cities; this was reduced to one or two deliveries a day by the nineteen-sixties.

The motor vehicle had appeared on the inadequate roads of Europe before the first world war, but ownership of cars remained for a long time restricted to a relatively small section of the population owing to high prices and maintenance costs. During the war many cars and trucks had been destroyed and few new ones were built except for military use. In 1948 there were in western Europe five million cars in use, not counting 2.7 million trucks. By 1957 the number of trucks had doubled and the number of cars trebled. In 1965 the number of cars on the roads of Europe had again trebled, reaching a total of 44 million.

CAR OWNERSHIP IN EUROPE
(*in millions*)

	1948	1965
France	1.5	9.6
West Germany	0.2	9.0
Netherlands	0.08	1.2
Italy	0.2	5.4
United Kingdom	2.0	9.0

Road transport was far less developed in the communist countries. Poland, for example, had only about 250,000 cars in 1965, less than a tenth of the far less populous Benelux countries. In the sixties eastern Europe began to make efforts to catch up with the West; in 1966 the Soviet Union signed an agreement with Fiat for an annual production of 600,000 cars.

The motor car helped to solve some problems but it created many others. It made for much greater mobility; millions of blue and white collar workers streamed by car every day into London and Paris, Turin and Milan. In Germany and England it was not unknown for many thousands to travel 50 miles or more to their place of work, and in the Paris region more than two million had to make a journey lasting on the average one hour and twenty minutes. With millions more cars in use every year, it seemed that the total paralysis of the roads and cities of Europe, constructed in the pre-automobile age, was only a question of time. The Germans in the nazi era had been the first to build roads of a new type, the *Autobahnen*. This work was continued, but by 1967 there were less than 4,000 km. of these multi-lane motorways. Italy was second with less than half (including the famous *Autostrada del Sole* leading from Milan to Naples), followed by Britain, France, and Holland. There was an ambitious programme for the construction of further European super-highways across the borders, but the number of cars on the densely populated continent increased even faster, and the rush hour in the metropolitan area became a nightmare for drivers and planners alike.

The Expansion of European Trade

In 1960 western Europe's share of world trade was almost 40 per cent; the eastern bloc, including the USSR, accounted for another 12 per cent. These figures need to be amplified, for more than half of this trade was between the various European countries which were each other's best customers. Yet what remained was still impressive, exceeding the total foreign trade of the United States.

Before 1914 Europe had been the world's main banker, deriving substantial yearly revenues from its 30 billion dollars investments; these fell after the first world war, but Europe's dependence on world trade, its role as the workshop of the world, was not affected. It had to import food and raw materials and to pay for them by exporting capital goods. Britain, the leading trading nation in the nineteenth century, lost its position, regained it temporarily in the nineteen-thirties, but was again overtaken by America after the second world war, and also by West Germany in 1959. Germany led the postwar European expansion; its trade with foreign countries increased every year between 1948 and 1962 by an average 16 per cent. European trade increased faster than world trade, and this despite the fact that the continent's dependence on the import of food and raw materials (with the exception of crude oil) decreased as it became almost self-sufficient in agricultural produce, and as many raw materials were replaced by synthetic fibres and plastics.

Britain remained the leading European market for the import of food and raw materials, but its pattern of exports changed radically: before 1914 it had mainly exported coal and textiles; after 1945 their share decreased to about five per cent and the electrical and car industries became the main exporters. The expansion of British foreign trade was much less striking than that of the other European countries (about two per cent a year on average between 1948 and 1962), partly as the result of internal economic difficulties, partly because of Britain's exclusion from the Common Market, which during the nineteen-fifties became the biggest trading unit in the world.

In the early postwar period Britain showed marked reluctance to abandon its ties with the Commonwealth, its most important traditional export market. But the Commonwealth countries meanwhile pursued industrialisation programmes of their own, and Britain's share in their trade decreased throughout the fifties and sixties while its trade relations with the Common Market countries increased from year to year. Britain sought admission to EEC and, when this was vetoed by the French, EFTA, the European Free Trade Association, consisting of Britain, the Scandinavian countries, Portugal, Switzerland and Austria, was established in 1960 under British leadership.

Though EFTA made a contribution towards the further liberalization of trade in Europe, it was very much an ad hoc creation, lacking the political rationale, and the wider economic and social aims of the Common Market. Several EFTA members, Britain, Austria, and Switzerland, in fact traded more with the Common Market countries than with their own free trade associates. EFTA was generally regarded as a temporary stage on the road to a further merger of all European countries into one common market.

As Europe's economic recovery got under way, there were two major obstacles impeding the expansion of trade: the high tariffs imposed by many European countries during the inter-war period (and by some even before 1914), and the chronic shortage of dollars, which had become the main international payment medium. There was general agreement that trade should be expanded: GATT (the General Agreement on Tariffs and Trade), founded in 1947, pursued this aim; the Marshall plan and in the nineteen-sixties the Kennedy round were designed to achieve similar objectives. The Common Market envisaged in 1956 a 12–15 year period for the reduction of customs duties and quantitative restrictions. By 1965 customs were down to one-fifth of the 1957 level and total abolition was envisaged for 1970. These measures resulted within eight years in an increase of trade among the Common Market countries of about 240 per cent, whereas their trade with outside countries expanded by about 100 per cent.

The postwar dollar shortage was overcome mainly by Marshall aid, but European discrimination against American imports continued till 1956, and restrictions on capital movements remained in force in most European countries up to 1958. During the nineteen-fifties Europe's financial strength substantially increased; its dollar and gold reserves rose from 10 billion dollars in 1950 to about 30 billion in 1964. The 'dollar era' thus ended in the nineteen-sixties. American government aid to Europe had been discontinued in the late fifties and by 1963 more private European money was invested in the United States than vice versa. The emergence of a new currency unit, the Eurodollar, was regarded by many as a step towards the introduction of a common European currency, but the existence of different national monetary policies and taxation systems made it unlikely that this aim would be achieved in the near future.

Certain long-term trends emerge from an examination of the pattern of Europe's postwar trade. The liberalisation of trade had highly beneficial effects; it promoted economic growth and a rational division of labour between European countries, and, by pooling resources, made it possible to tackle major projects that would have been out of reach for any single country. Foreign trade was of paramount importance for nations such as Germany and Belgium, where domestic demand alone would not have been sufficient to sustain a high level of economic activity; every sixth worker in German industry was working for export.

The general trend was towards more trade between the various European countries and a lessening of economic ties with the rest of the world. Trade with the Soviet bloc increased but was not of great importance to either EEC or EFTA. Trade with America was on a much bigger scale and still expanding. This inward looking character of the Common Market (and of Europe in general) was widely criticised, mainly because of its impact on outside countries. As against this, Europeans have argued that the trend was a natural one, corresponding to local needs, and that heavy reliance on trade with non-Europeans made the continent too vulnerable to the effects and repercussions of political and economic crises in distant parts of the world.

VALUE OF EXPORTS
(*in billion dollars*)

	1960	1966
USA	20	30
West Germany	11	20
Britain	10	14
France	6	10
Japan	4	9
Canada	5	9
Soviet Union	5	8
Italy	3	8
Holland	4	6
Belgium	3	6
Sweden	2	4

The dominant feature of European retail trade before the second world war was the small, one family (or one man) business, of the type called in France BOF (*beurre, oeufs, fromage*). Some chain stores had existed for a long time and department stores had appeared on the scene following the American pattern; resistance to them had been part of the programme of the German Nazi Party. It was on the whole a wasteful system, with many middlemen, high prices, and an exceedingly low living standard for small traders with their diminutive turnover. This pattern persisted until well into the postwar period. Of the 550,000 shops in West Germany in the nineteen-fifties, only about half were thought to be viable; the rest yielded an income of less than 200 dollars per month.

The situation was worse in France and Belgium, where the fragmentation of the retail trade was even more pronounced. These one man or woman enterprises could not, of course, compete against the chains and department stores, such as Marks and Spencer and Great Universal Stores in Britain, Printemps in France, Rinascente in Italy, and Karstadt and Kaufhof in

West Germany, which greatly strengthened their position in the fifties. Even more important was the spread of self-service shops and supermarkets in the nineteen-fifties, first in Germany and Sweden, later in England, and ultimately, against much resistance, in France and Italy. Big mail order houses also began to flourish and discount shops and shopping centres appeared; the share of the super-markets grew from year to year, and more and more of the traditional shops went out of business or, correctly readings the signs of the times, joined forces in bigger and more efficient units.

France: Problems of Modernisation

Postwar economic developments in the various European countries were very similar in some respects and totally different in others. We must turn at this point, therefore, from a broad survey of the common trends to a discussion of specific conditions in the major European countries.

France experienced a boom which was totally unexpected. Not even the most optimistic would have predicted in 1945 an upsurge of this magnitude. France had been the museum of Europe, the country in which nothing ever changed; after 1934 the number of deaths exceeded the number of births. After the second world war this trend was suddenly reversed: between 1938 and 1967 the population grew by nine million, from 41 to 50 million, more than it had grown during the preceding 100 years. The country was unevenly populated; Paris and the north had most of the industry and in consequence a relatively high living standard; the south-west, on the other hand, had lost one-third of its population during the last 70 years. Brittany and the Massif Central were also underdeveloped regions.

Except for iron ore and bauxite, France had few natural resources favouring the development of its industry. It was less industrialised than Britain and West Germany; in 1936, 37 per cent of all Frenchmen were still employed in agriculture. Most of the farms in the south and west were too small to be economically viable. Even in industry the small or medium size family business was the most common; 60 per cent of all industrial enterprises and 90 per cent of the retail trade fell into this category as France entered the nineteen-sixties. The general mood during the postwar period was far from optimistic and new initiatives encountered much hostility. The mistaken economic policies of the early postwar French governments, especially their refusal to accept the Mendès-France plan (providing for currency reform and the taxation of war profits), resulted in inflation, the flight of French capital abroad, and a general climate of instability. In these unpromising circumstances Jean Monnet, the father of the plan, and a few of his colleagues maintained that the alternative facing France was modernisation or decline: there was no hope that the country could somehow muddle through by adopting half measures.

In January 1946 an office for overall economic planning was created under the first de Gaulle government which was to have a growing impact on the development of the French economy. In some respects there had always been more state intervention in the economy in France than in the other European countries because of its bureaucratic and highly centralised system of administration. But the idea of planning had won new adherents in the years of the Resistance, when many had pondered the deeper reasons for France's decline before 1940. The French plan, unlike the Soviet, did not prescribe detailed goals nor did the planners have the power to compel an enterprise to pursue a certain course of action. It simply provided an indication of the likely (and desirable) overall development during the years to come, but under a number of able directors (Jean Monnet 1946–52, Etienne Hirsch 1952–9, Pierre Massé 1959–65), the planners, with government help, did indirectly influence the course of economic development through the nationalised industries, and by directing credit investment and extending (or withdrawing) tax rebates. The French economy, it was said, had been ruled in the past by the proverbial 'two hundred families'; after the war there was no doubt that the balance of power had shifted, for the opinion of a few dozen high government officials mattered far more than the views of all the private captains of industry.

By 1954 a great deal of progress had been made; industrial production, to give but one indication, was 50 per cent higher than before the war. The French steel industry had been completely modernised and the electrical industry had doubled its output. Prototypes of modern cars and aircraft were developed and the French railway system was about to become the fastest and most efficient in Europe. But progress was limited to these sectors of the economy; the rest continued to stagnate. There was little new construction and Paris and the other major cities continued to decay. The peasants had no use for the 50,000 tractors offered by the plan; they wanted to stick to their traditional methods. Despite the stabilisation programme of the governments of Queuille and René Mayer, prices continued to rise and tax morale remained low. Yet with all this the Fourth Republic did increase its gross national product at an average rate of five per cent a year, a most creditable achievement, the fruits of which were to be reaped by de Gaulle's régime.

Contrary to popular belief, economic advance during the troubled years (1948–58) was greater than during the Gaullist decade (1958–68). Inflation continued in the Fifth Republic at a steady three to six per cent per year, whereas during the Fourth Republic there had been, on the whole, stability except for the increases (of 12–15 per cent) in 1951, 1952 and 1958. It was fortunate for France that the devaluation of 1958 just preceded the 1959 up-surge in world trade; devaluation made French exports more competitive, and they increased in volume by 30 per cent within one year. As a result France's gold reserves grew substantially; the percentage of its GNP that went to exports (16) was as high as that of Britain and Germany but the percentage of imports (11) was considerably lower, giving France greater self-sufficiency in food and raw materials.

The Gaullists (and many other circles inside France) had been at first strongly opposed to the Common Market; they realised only gradually that France would benefit more than any other country from European integra-tion: French sales to the other EEC countries accounted for 22 per cent of its total foreign sales in 1958, ten years later the percentage was 41. French agriculture, in a poor state before 1958, was saved by the Common Market; 18 per cent of French agricultural exports went to EEC countries in 1958, more than 50 per cent in 1968. Another factor which greatly contributed to French prosperity was, ironically enough, the influx of American capital, about which for obvious political reasons the Gaullist régime had mixed feelings.

Four years of economic progress followed after the Gaullists took power in 1959; the GNP grew between four and seven per cent per year and the investment rate was 22 per cent of the GNP. The index of *per capita* GNP showed a rise from 100 (in 1958) to 126 in 1964, compared to 136 in Italy, 131 in Germany, and 119 in Britain over the same period. Even if the achieve-ments were not equal to those made by Germany and Italy, the most ardent optimists would hardly have anticipated that the output of electrical current, 20 million kw. in 1937, would rise more than fivefold to 105 million in 1966, or that the output of steel would go up from 8 million to 19.6 million tons; 34,000 tons of aluminium had been produced in France in 1937, 363,000 in 1966; the production of cement increased from 4 million tons to 23 million tons. In 1937 ships of a total registered tonnage of 27,000 had been built in French docks, in 1966: 430,000.

A new spirit of optimism and confidence prevailed. New industries were established in the under-developed regions of the country and the modernisa-tion of agriculture made rapid strides. In view of its successes the French plan was widely studied abroad; French industrial management, the intellectual infrastructure of its economy, became a source of envy and French produce gained a high reputation for quality.

There were, admittedly, many shadows. In 1964 and 1965 the French economy stagnated, followed by a fitful upsurge in 1966–7. Total output in 1967 grew by more than four per cent but most of this was the result of good harvests, whereas industrial output increased by only two per cent. France was still the west European country in which industry absorbed the smallest proportion of total manpower, the only country in which the share of employment in manufacturing had actually declined. It was also the only European country which had not solved its housing problem; few new hospitals and schools were built despite the acute need and the great backlog; not one new school had been built in Paris between the wars. Rising land prices acted as a further brake on new construction and there was no clear central housing policy; old tenants benefited from low controlled rents, whereas for younger married couples and workers changing their jobs it was almost impossible to find new homes. French industrial development was held back by the absence of large units comparable to the great firms of Britain, Holland, or West Germany, and by the relatively small allocations to research and development. Many argued that the country was living beyond its means, and that the billions earmarked for de Gaulle's *force de frappe* would have been better employed for other purposes. The big traditional industries, now rationalised, such as coal, steel, and the railways, were overexpanded and showed large deficits. The performance of the new industries was more impressive, but the social climate was far from satisfactory, as the big strikes of May-June 1968 were to show. There were almost half a million unemployed in France in 1968, more than in any other European country with the exception of Italy, and the cost of living was rising faster than in any other major European country.

COST OF LIVING INDICES

	Germany	France	Italy	Britain	Holland
1958	100	100	100	100	100
1962	108	119	109	112	106
1965	118	132	130	125	122

Consumer prices were about 45 per cent higher in 1968 than in 1958 – the fastest increase in the Common Market countries. All this contributed to a feeling of malaise and it explains the dissatisfaction felt in France despite the great progress in industrial expansion and modernisation.

Germany: The Economic Miracle

The early phases of West Germany's postwar economic development up to the currency reform of 1948 have been described elsewhere in the present book. The first indication of what later became known as the economic miracle (the *Wirtschaftswunder*) appeared in 1949–50, when the volume of foreign trade doubled within one year. But the starting point had been so low that it was perhaps even more remarkable that it rose by 75 per cent the year after, and trebled between 1954 and 1964. Industrial production in West Germany increased sixfold between 1948 and 1964, while the level of unemployment fell from eight to nine per cent in 1949–52 to less than one per cent in 1961, and to an alltime low of 0.4 per cent in 1965. At that time there were six jobs for every person unemployed and hundreds of thousands of foreign workers (mainly from Italy, Spain, Greece, Turkey, and Yugoslavia) were needed to keep the rapidly expanding German economy going.

German economic policy differed greatly from that pursued in France. There was no overall plan; Erhard and the other neo-liberal architects of the miracle were firm believers in the free play of the market forces, of supply and demand. It was not a rigid, nineteenth-century style *laissez-faire* liberalism; they were well aware that state intervention was necessary from time to time, as in 1950, when building was encouraged at a time of slackness, or in 1951, when temporary import restrictions were imposed, and again after 1955, when the rediscount rate was raised to prevent the boom from getting out of hand. The success of Erhards' social market economy (*Soziale Marktwirtschaft*) was infectious; even the Social Democrats accepted the principle: competition as far as possible, planning as far as necessary.

German agriculture had been sheltered for generations behind a high protective tariff; it was backward and quite incapable of competing with the neighbouring countries, let alone overseas exporters. Subsidies were continued after the war and agriculture was relieved of direct taxation, with the intention of giving it a respite in which to modernise and become competitive. The wider use of fertilisers was promoted and the number of tractors in use increased from 138,000 in 1950 to 1,164,000 in 1965. As a result of those and other measures, productivity in agriculture in 1964 was two-and-a-half times that in 1950, while the number of those it employed fell from five to three million. The German village within a decade changed its face; it was barely recognisable to the visitor who had known it before the war; it had become virtually indistinguishable from a suburb of a big town; there were the same fashions and consumer goods, as many cars and television aerials. The idiocy of rural life of which Marx had written was a thing of the past.

The achievements of the German miracle are impressive but not unique. Italy and Austria made as much progress and the Japanese performance was even more spectacular. What surprised most observers was the fact that such striking progress was made within such a short time after total defeat. The restrictions imposed by the Allies on German economic development and the dismantling of factories continued well into the early fifties, but by 1958 Germany was already so prosperous that its currency could be made fully convertible. The problems arising from the influx of ten million expellees from the East were thought to be well nigh insoluble, yet within a few years the great majority had been absorbed. At the end of the war many German cities were in ruins, but between 1948 and 1964 eight million dwelling units were constructed and after 1953 half a million units annually, a higher rate *per capita* than in any other western country.

What were the mainsprings of the 'German miracle'? Above all, no doubt, German know-how, the presence of millions of skilled workers, and a great industrial tradition. The destruction during the war of so many factories made a radical new beginning possible, the newest machinery was used, and efforts were concentrated on the most promising branches of industry. Germany's success in expanding foreign trade has been mentioned; there was also a very substantial domestic demand for consumer goods that had been suppressed since the great depression. Germany had to spend much less on its defence than its neighbours, and up to the late fifties little if any development aid was extended to the Afro-Asian countries.

The postwar boom was unprecedented in German history. During the 17 years before the first world war, a period of continuous progress, a rate of growth of five per cent was exceeded only once; but during the first 17 years after the second world war such a rate was achieved no fewer than nine times, and in three years it exceeded ten per cent. Towards the end of the fifties the boom seemed to become uncontrollable; a great deal of foreign capital streamed into Germany and the government was seriously worried by a possible overheating of the economy. It tried to check the influx of capital by lowering the interest rate and altering (in 1961) the exchange rate of the German mark.

After 1962 the rate of growth slackened; demand slowed down and there were increased labour shortages. In the European growth league Germany was overtaken in the sixties by many other countries which had lagged behind during the nineteen-fifties, and in 1966 it was hit by a real economic recession. There had been some indications of this during the previous year, and under the impact of the crisis industrial production in 1966 rose only by one per cent over 1965. In February 1967 there were almost 700,000 unemployed, and many industrial enterprises, including Volkswagen, the symbol of the post-war boom, temporarily introduced a shorter working week. This in its turn had grave psychological effects: a public which had been accustomed to un-interrupted economic growth over a long period was totally unprepared for a recession and there were manifestations of near hysteria. According to a public opinion poll taken at the time, most citizens feared that a crisis of the magni-tude of 1929 was just around the corner. German self-confidence was not yet deeply rooted despite all the achievements of the miracle – the modernisation of industry, the fact that it had one of the most stable currencies in the world, and that of the major countries it was least affected by strikes.

In the event the German economy recovered quickly. While some branches of the economy had been hard hit, the economy as a whole continued to make progress, even during the year of recession, albeit at a slow rate, very much in contrast with what happened in the nineteen-thirties. Unemployment, which had risen to almost two per cent during the recession, fell again after a few months below the one per cent mark; under the impact of the shock most Germans had forgotten that unemployment had been very much higher even during the best years of the miracle.

The very rapid growth of the German economy was unlikely to continue for ever; the boom of the fifties had its roots in specific circumstances which were not likely to recur. The sixties were a decade of slower development and consolidation. The problems that West Germany was to face in future now appeared much clearer: the general prosperity had increased costs of production. Germany was so successful in the fifties because its industry had the most modern equipment and because it produced more cheaply than other nations. But meanwhile other European countries had also modernised their industries, and Italy, for example, could produce even more cheaply; it was perhaps symbolical that in the middle sixties Fiat began to outproduce Volkswagen. The Ruhr, once the backbone of German industrial development, became its main problem: with the transition to other sources of energy, less coal was needed every year, but there were hundreds of thousands of miners who could not easily be retrained.

Germany had made great advances in some of the new industries but the development of others, in the nuclear and space field and also in electronics, had been neglected. It spent only a fraction of what America did on research and development. Its educational system was not sufficiently geared to the needs of economic development; the universities turned out relatively few scientists and technologists. These were serious shortcomings which in the eyes of many observers imperilled further progress. There was a strong inclination among Germans to rest on their laurels. A fresh impetus was clearly needed if the country was not to fall behind in competition with others in the years to come.

Italy: Uncertain Beginnings and Stormy Growth

Postwar economic developments in Italy and in Germany were similar in some respects, although the 'Italian miracle' began later and lasted longer than the German. There were other important differences: Italy as a whole was not a highly developed industrial country; its output before the second world war had been only about one-third that of Germany. Up to 1956 more Italians were employed in agriculture than in industry.

Like Germany, Italy emerged from the war with an economy that had been severely damaged; industrial output was only one-fifth of what it had been in 1938 and agricultural production was slightly more than half. By 1948 Italian industry had again reached the prewar level, while the recovery of agriculture took a little longer. Inflation was the main problem during the early postwar years, but eventually Einaudi's policy was as successful as Erhard's in Germany. The situation began to ease after 1950, and in 1956 the Italian lira became partly convertible. Italian industry made tremendous strides during the nineteen-fifties and accelerated even further during the early sixties.

INDEX OF INDUSTRIAL PRODUCTION

1948	63	1961	200
1953	100	1963	241
1958	142	1966	285

In the early sixties Italy made more rapid progress than any other major country in the world, including the Soviet Union and even Japan. This advance was all the more striking in view of Italy's basic poverty; the country lacks raw materials for industrial development and is a major importer of food. The most impressive industrial progress was made in the production of cars, office machinery, and in the electrical industry; by 1967 every third refrigerator produced in Europe was of Italian origin. Existing factories expanded and new ones were established; the steel plant erected in Taranto in the backward south was among the most modern in the world. Italians belied their *dolce far niente* reputation and emerged as the most hardworking and inventive European people. Productivity rose steeply – between 1961 and 1963 alone it went up by about 30 per cent.

Tourism brought a growing stream of visitors into the country (27 million by 1966). Since they mostly came during certain periods and congregated in certain districts, the natives of Rome, Venice, and above all the coastal resorts found themselves at times outnumbered by the millions of tourists from the north.

Italian workers used to walk to their factories in the years after the war or get there by bicycle. In a famous postwar film the disaster that befell a family when the bicycle was stolen was given dramatic expression. In 1960 one out of 21 Italians was the owner of a car; by 1968, one out of seven.

Italians had about as many telephones and television sets per thousand inhabitants as the French. The standard of living in northern Italy approached in the sixties that of its most highly industrialised neighbours on the continent; there was hardly any difference between Milan or Turin and metropolitan centres in France or Germany. The backwardness of southern Italy continued to have a marked effect on the general picture; 36 per cent of the total population lived in the South, but they accounted for less than 25 per cent of the national income, despite years of effort to develop the Mezzogiorno, large-scale investment and development projects. The gulf between north and south widened further during the fifties and sixties, and there was a mass migration from southern Italy to the towns (and to Germany and France); entire villages were left without men, and in some places only the older generation remained. Not all were easily employable: in the 1951 census, five million Italians were found to be illiterate, and many more semi-literate. The effects of centuries of neglect could not be repaired in a few years.

Between 1959 and 1961 Italy's economy grew at such a fast rate (about 7.5 per cent per year) that the government, fearing inflation, took measures to curtail both domestic consumption and investment. The rate of growth fell to 4.8 per cent in 1963 and to about 3 in 1964–5, but rose again to 5.5 in 1965–7. While other European countries complained about stagnation, Italy forged ahead: its exports increased by a further 60 per cent between 1964 and 1967. As a late starter Italy could avoid many of the mistakes of the older industrial nations; unlike Britain and Germany, it was not burdened by outdated coal mines and steel plants. The textile industry was one of the weaker links in the Italian economy, but the situation was not dissimilar in other European countries.

Italy, some foreign critics have claimed, could outsell its rivals because wages there were for a long time considerably lower. There was also a substantial and apparently intractable residue of unemployment – almost seven per cent of the total labour force, 1.4 million, in 1961. Even during the boom years of the late sixties the number of unemployed hovered around the one million mark. There was however no deliberate policy to maintain an 'industrial reserve army' to keep wages down. On the contrary, wages went up substantially during the sixties and in northern Italy were nearly on a par with the neighbouring countries. Italian unemployment was largely a social problem; the migration of the agricultural labourers from the south into the cities of the north continued without interruption. During 1968 half a million such newcomers were counted and they all too often lacked the skills needed for industrial employment.

The Italian *miracolo economico* received less publicity than the German *Wirtschaftswunder* but in its overall effects it was even more impressive. As in

Germany and in France, the achievement tended to overshadow the short-comings: Italian agriculture, subdivided into diminutive holdings, had not shared equally in the general boom, not enough schools and new roads had been built, and not enough money was spent on higher education and research. Capital supply was exceedingly limited, and even the most substantial Italian firms (such as Olivetti) found themselves at one time or another on the brink of collapse and in need of state support. Fiat, Italy's largest enterprise, was an exception. It had developed in particularly favourable circumstances behind high protective tariffs in the fascist era. For many years it had a virtual monopoly on the domestic market. Fiat put the years of high protection to good use, and by the nineteen-fifties had become a very efficient and competitive producer. While many Italian industrialists were at first fearful of the implications of the Common Market, the owners and managers of Fiat had no such doubts and subsequent events justified their optimism.

By the middle sixties about 20–30 per cent of Italy's industry, including 60 per cent of its steel production, was controlled by the government. Of the nine biggest companies five were state owned (Montecatini-Edison, IRI ENI, Finsider, and Finmeccanica), and only four were in private hand, (Fiat, Pirelli, Olivetti, Suia Viscosa). Within the framework of the state corporations there was wide scope for empire builders like Mattei: ENI was established to produce hydrocarbons and exploit natural gas, but under Mattei's rule it became a giant holding company, owning, *inter alia*, the daily *Il Giorno* of Milan (Fiat owned *La Stampa* in Turin) and a corporation engaged in motel construction. Private enterprise has complained for many years about growing state interference and there has been a heated discussion about the desirable extent of economic planning since Fanfani's 'opening to the left' in 1962. But, given the many unsolved economic and social problems that have to be tackled in Italy during the years to come, it seems that the trend towards *dirigisme* is likely to become even more marked.

Britain: Stop-go

The postwar performance of Britain's economy has entered the annals of history as a tale of woe, of constant balance of payments crises, of overspending and living on credit. The US loan was exhausted in 1948 and in the following year the pound was devalued from 4.03 dollars to 2.80 dollars. The outbreak of the Korean war made a new rearmament programme necessary;

defence expenditure rose from six to ten per cent of the national income, and the building programme and other reconstruction projects had to be cut to meet the bill. There were further balance of payments crises in 1955, 1957, 1961, 1964, and 1967-8. In 1967 the pound was again under heavy pressure and only another devaluation and massive foreign intervention saved sterling from collapse.

The crises in the British balance of payments and the consequent fluctuations in the economy recurred so frequently and proved so difficult to overcome that in the end they came to be regarded 'not only as painful affliction but also as a symptom of an organic malaise of the British body economic' (Postan). Up to the nineteen-fifties both Germany and France had a living standard considerably lower than that of the United Kingdom, but in the sixties Britain was overtaken by its two rivals. This decline had begun well before 1945. In 1880 Britain, Germany and the United States were each producing about one million tons of steel; in 1913 Britain produced 8 million, Germany 17 million, and the United States 31 million. But it was only a relative decline: Britain's GNP grew between 1948 and 1962 by 2.5 per cent a year (3.5 per cent between 1947 and 1950, 3.3 per cent between 1960 and 1965), which compares favourably with any other period in modern British history (1.7 per cent between 1870 and 1913, 2.2 per cent between 1924 and 1937). The rise in the standard of living was on an unprecedented scale and Mr Macmillan's famous slogan of the 1959 election campaign, 'You've never had it so good', was strictly speaking quite correct. Britain did not stagnate, it simply advanced at a slower rate than the other major countries. Its share in world trade fell steadily during the postwar period – from 21.3 per cent in 1951 to 19 per cent in 1956. Two-and-a-half percentage points (as Andrew Shonfield has pointed out) may not seem very much, but it was, in fact, equivalent to one billion dollars of export earnings.

Various reasons have been adduced to explain Britain's relative decline after 1945. It has been argued that the welfare state became too expensive, that the state took too large a proportion of the national income, and that direct taxation was too high. But in France the state took an even larger proportion and taxation in both Germany and France was higher than in Britain and almost as high in the United States. It is also asserted that Britain did not spend enough on research and development, and as a result fell behind the other countries, but a comparison of the figures shows that Britain spent more on R & D. than any other European country, and, in proportion to the GNP, almost as much as the United States. Yet another school of thought has maintained that the poor British investment performance has been the root of the evil. The figures seem irrefutable in this respect; Britain was indeed at the bottom of the league:

	Investment Ratios 1955–64 %	Gross Savings as % of Disposable Income 1964
Japan	28.2	25.2
Germany	23.7	13.1
France	19.2	12.8
Sweden	22.8	10.2
USA	17.1	10.1
Britain	15.8	7.7

When confronted with a crisis during the postwar period, it seemed to be the policy of the British government to cut investment first. The decline of the British shipbuilding industry might serve as an illustration. Britain had many advantages at the end of the war to enable it to recover its leading position in this field – well-equipped yards, a highly-skilled labour force and a full book. But the owners were reluctant to invest in new productive capacity, with the result that tonnage built fell from 1.2 million tons in 1949 to 1 million in 1965, while tonnage built in Japan increased from 0.1 to 5 million during the same period.

A great deal of responsibility falls on British trade unions and management. Wages have consistently risen faster than output and productivity. There was a 20 per cent wage rise in real terms between 1951 and 1958, and a further 30 per cent rise between 1958 and 1964. Under Stafford Cripps the trade unions accepted a wage freeze on the understanding that the government would hold down the price level; ever since the union leaders have regarded such policies with great distrust and more often than not have refused to collaborate with the government. As a result many British products became so expensive as to be not competitive on world markets. Much damage to the economy was done by the antiquated structure of the trade union movement, (the existence of 600 unions compared with 16 in West Germany), with their guild and craft union mentality and their unending internecine fights about who should do what job. Frequently the work of many thousands of workers was paralysed by the action of a few hundred craftsmen striking for their own factional interest. There were wildcat strikes about whether the tea break should be at ten or eleven o'clock; nowhere did people go on strike on such frivolous grounds as in Britain. It was not so much the militancy of the trade unions that caused the disruption but their inability to think in modern terms, to adjust their outlook to the changes in technology and organisation.

Management bore an equal share of responsibility. Britain had been the pioneer of the industrial revolution, but the tradition of inventiveness and initiative seemed to have exhausted itself. The level of managerial know-how was low and there was not much interest in learning new methods; everyone talked about the need to export but the efforts were often amateurish and the after-sales service provided inferior to that of other trading nations. In an interesting study Professor Dunning has shown that within the British economy the section under American control has consistently yielded 50 per cent more return than British firms, due to lower administrative costs, better salesmanship, higher productivity, and greater capital intensity.

The economic malaise was partly due to wrong policy decisions taken at the top or, equally often, to indecision. By 1949 Labour had exhausted its ideas on how to run the economy; important branches had been nationalised but 80 per cent of the total was still in private hands, and to that sector the party had no lead to give. The Conservatives were at first luckier. When they came to power in 1951 it was possible to dismantle many of the wartime restrictions. Between 1952 and 1954 prices of raw materials went down by 25 per cent, which meant a substantial reduction in Britain's import bill. But after the boom of 1952-4 there were again several years of stagnation. Labour and Conservative alike were opposed to joining Europe; they 'knew in their bones' (as Anthony Eden said in 1952) that they could not join a European federation. Hugh Gaitskell, the new leader of the Labour Party, was hardly less emphatic. Meanwhile Germany and Italy increased their exports six times as fast as Britain, and Macmillan and Harold Wilson reluctantly reached the conclusion that the sterling area and EFTA were no real alternative to the Common Market.

It would be unfair (and unhistorical) to ignore the objective circumstances that aggravated the British malaise. Britain had lost as the result of the war most of its prewar income from overseas and found itself saddled with growing debts. Its financial and defence obligations overseas, and the remaining imperial commitments, constituted a heavy burden. It was clear that the country could not shoulder this burden indefinitely but it was not at all easy to find immediate solutions: Britain could not opt out of history and could not change basic geographical facts. It is more densely populated than France, Italy, or West Germany, and it needed to import more raw materials and foodstuffs than its continental neighbours and rivals.

No single factor, but a combination of circumstances, caused Britain's postwar difficulties. It was a constant vicious circle: the growth of the economy was held back by deflationary policies which were adopted to combat rising prices and inflation. Most other European countries, too, had recourse to a 'stop-go' policy, but much less often, and they made greater progress between the stops. Successive British governments applied various measures to combat the recurring crises: devaluation, cuts in defence spending, import controls and export incentives. But these were palliatives; the main problems remained: to increase efficiency, to improve organisation, to invest more wisely, and generally speaking to make the most of their resources.

Economic Development in Other European Countries

A striking feature of Europe after the war was the great similarity in the economic development of the small countries.

Between 1954 and 1964 industrial output doubled in Holland, Sweden, and Austria, countries that had little in common. On a different level, economic development took much the same course in Spain and Greece. These two countries faced similar problems, such as the need to find capital for investment in industry; their GNP grew in the sixties at about the same high rate (seven to eight per cent). In 1964 *per capita* income in the former was 570 dollars, in the latter 590 dollars. These were trends common to all European countries irrespective of their past history, geographical position, and economic structure.

Spain had stagnated for centuries. The consequences of the civil war of 1936–9 had paralysed its economy for two decades, but a change began to be felt in the late fifties, after Spain joined the United Nations and expanded its foreign trade. The rigid economic regulations were abolished and the country was exposed to the fresh wind of the free market; the government tried by trial and error to modernise the economic structure. There was also progress in Spanish agriculture; average output went up by one-third in the decade after 1956. Following substantial French, German, and American investment in Spanish industry, there was a marked upswing in industrial production after 1958, and the GNP grew at a faster rate than even the Italian. But since the starting point had been so low, there remained a great deal of leeway to be made up: even after a decade of boom, *per capita* income in Spain was only one-third that of the Scandinavian countries. Tourism was an important source of income; it developed rapidly in the late fifties and sixties as Spain overtook France, and with 17 million visitors in 1966 it took second place in Europe after Italy.

The boom in Greece had started a few years earlier than in Spain; the devaluation of the drachma had given a powerful stimulus to economic recovery. Between 1953 and 1963 the GNP grew at an average rate of 6.3 per cent; in 1966 it reached 8 per cent; but the country was still predominantly agrarian and the value of industrial output exceeded that of agriculture for the first time only in 1965. Inflation and political instability jeopardised the development in the sixties. The merchant fleet was a powerful economic asset and while the influx of tourists was not on the same scale as in Spain, the flow of visitors continued to grow from year to year and represented in 1964 about 13 per cent of the value of exports.

Both Holland and Belgium had suffered greatly during the war and their recovery was at first slow. The two countries were hit by a recession in 1958 but Holland recovered more quickly and, generally speaking, made quicker progress. Its GNP grew at an average rate of 5.4 per cent per year between 1958 and 1966; the Belgian advance had been among the most sluggish on the continent in the fifties (2.7 per cent), but it gathered speed in the early sixties (3.6 per cent). Belgium had always been more industrial in character and it was more heavily affected by the general European crisis in the coal industry and heavy metallurgy. Agriculture, however, provided more than 80 per cent of domestic consumption, thus reducing the import bill. Both countries lost their empires in Africa and South-East Asia after the war but this had surprisingly little effect on their economic development; on the contrary, Holland forged ahead more quickly than ever before, extending its chemical and electrical industries and improving its agriculture.

Switzerland was one of the few European countries that had been only indirectly affected by the war. No recovery schemes were necessary. Its postwar economic development proceeded at a slow and uneventful rate, but towards the late fifties, in the wake of the general European boom, its progress quickened, resulting in an average yearly increase of six per cent in the GNP between 1958 and 1964. This sudden spurt caused rising prices and inflation as in other parts of Europe, and the Swiss government adopted a stabilisation programme in 1964 to slow down the expansion.

The Austrian boom lasted even longer; there was a steady annual growth of almost six per cent in the GNP between 1953 and 1964, but Austria had started at a considerable lower level than Switzerland. The country suffered, moreover, from a lack of capital to promote industrialisation, and its exclusion from the Common Market had a detrimental effect on its economic development. Twenty-two per cent of Austria's industry had been nationalised, including 60 per cent of all big enterprises. There was a marked shift during the fifties from agriculture to industry; industrial output doubled between 1938 and 1954, and again between 1954 and 1965.

Sweden, like Switzerland, had emerged unscathed from the war. Like Switzerland its growth during the fifties was steady but unexciting; between 1958 and 1964 it gathered speed and reached an average yearly increase in the GNP of 5.1 per cent. Like Switzerland it faced a shortage of labour and had to adopt restrictive measures in 1964 to prevent the boom getting out of hand. Sweden's industry was high cost and highly specialised, but famous for its quality products; it exported about half of its industrial output and succeeded in doubling its exports between 1955 and 1965. Despite the lack of important natural resources, it attained the highest living standard in Europe, and one of the highest in the world.

Neighbouring Denmark and Norway are dissimilar in their economic structure. The former has a highly developed agriculture, whereas in the latter the merchant and fishing fleets are of paramount importance. Both participated in the general boom that lasted from 1958 to 1963 (in Denmark) and to 1964 (in Norway). Danish attempts to curb the inflationary pressures offer an interesting illustration of the effects of a stop-go policy; its GNP rose by 0.8 per cent in 1963, by 7.4 in 1964, by 4.7 in 1965. The country experienced difficulties in finding export markets for its agricultural produce because of its exclusion from the Common Market, and there was a deliberate shift towards investment in industry.

The pattern that emerges in all these smaller European countries is consistent: the postwar recovery was followed by years of comparatively slow growth in the nineteen-fifties, but towards the end of the decade the movement gathered momentum and there followed a boom of five to seven years duration. Since the middle sixties this development has again slowed down. Seen in a wider context, the postwar era was a period of unprecedented economic prosperity for all European countries, although considerable differences continued to prevail between them; the *per capita* GNP was still almost ten times higher in Sweden than in Turkey, and there were also great differences inside the various countries – the disparity between north and south Italy being one such example.

PER CAPITA GNP IN US $

	1965	1966
Austria	1,270	1,380
Belgium	1,780	1,910
Denmark	2,100	2,320
France	1,920	2,250 (1967)
W. Germany	1,900	2,400 (1967)
Greece	590 (1964)	690
Holland	1,550	1,670
Iceland	2,470	2,850
Ireland	920	1,010
Italy	1,100	1,350 (1967)
Norway	1,880	2,020
Portugal	420	430
Spain	570 (1964)	770
Sweden	2,500	2,730
Switzerland	2,330	2,480
Turkey	250	290
United Kingdom	1,810	2,050 (1967)
United States	3,560	3,840

The Soviet Economy

The Soviet economy recovered quickly from the destruction of war. Steel production, which had reached 18 million tons in 1940, was down to 12 million in 1945, but climbed to 34 million in 1952, the year before Stalin's death. The figures for coal are 166 million tons in 1940, 149 million at the end of the war, and 300 million in 1952. The recovery in the output of crude oil was even more spectacular: 31 million tons in 1940, 19 million in 1945, and 119 million in 1952. Progress in agriculture was much less impressive because of a number of adverse harvests, and especially as the result of the low priority accorded to agriculture in the Soviet economy.

Under Stalin the economic system was geared to the attainment of certain strategically important goals in certain key industries, to the detriment of everything else. It was to all intents and purposes a war economy even in days of peace. It imposed the tightest controls, concentrated all available resources on the development of heavy industry, and severely restricted occupational mobility. The political price that had to be paid was a ruthless dictatorship, constant purges, terrorism, and forced labour camps with millions of inmates, as an institutionalised part of the régime. It succeeded in keeping consumption low and maintaining a high rate of investment; the whole system was based on the exploitation of agriculture which provided the surplus for capital formation. From 1928 to 1955 gross investment grew twice as fast as the GNP, and three times as fast as consumption. Russia under Stalin provided (to quote Harry Schwartz) a classic case of forced rapid industrialisation. 'Tens of millions were transferred from agriculture to industrial and other non-farm occupations. A massive transfusion of scientific and technical knowledge from abroad was injected into Soviet society, producing a large cadre of skilled workers and a substantial technological élite of scientists.' Stalin expanded the range of Soviet industrial production and raised the physical volume enormously; under him Russia became the world's second industrial power. Measured in these terms his rule was no doubt a great success.

It is not at all certain, however, that this was the only road open to the Soviet Union; other countries made equal or even greater progress during the postwar period without paying such a terrible price in human suffering. For this reason the economic achievements of Stalinism, as distinct from the military gains, remain open to doubt. While Soviet heavy industry mushroomed and the armed forces were given the highest priority, the standard of living remained among the lowest in Europe. Stalinist economists argued that the concentration on heavy industry created the preconditions for all-round economic development and thus eventually for a general rise in the standard of living. But these predictions were only half fulfilled; the standard of life did rise, but less quickly than in most other western nations. In the major European nations real wages more than doubled between 1950 and 1966, in the Soviet Union they increased only by 83 per cent according to official figures which are open to some doubt; they should have risen much faster, since the starting point in the Soviet Union was so much lower.

Some observers have provided a historical justification for the Stalinist economic system, but even they conceded that by the time Stalin died it had outlived its usefulness. Those in authority in Moscow were aware that drastic changes were needed, above all in agriculture. Agriculture still contributed one third of the Soviet GNP but had been systematically starved by the government, receiving only 15 per cent of total investment. An intolerable housing shortage had existed for many years and the transport system, of vital importance for the further development of the national economy, was in a critical condition. The whole system of central allocation and distribution of materials had become more and more wasteful with the progressive growth and diversification of the economy – an army of bureaucrats continued to take decisions that were remote from realities and often inconsistent with each other. There were constant announcements of new achievements, but waste was growing even more rapidly: unfinished construction, stocks of unsold commodities, 'new machinery' that was in fact outdated and could not be used. The majority of Soviet economists and the leaders of the party had realised by 1953 that, to put it cautiously, the old régime had not made the best use of existing resources. Malenkov promised reforms and a better life for everyone. A new era in the Soviet economy seemed about to dawn.

Great demographic changes have taken place during the last 30 years. The population of the Soviet Union grew from 170 million in 1939 to 234 million in 1967. The growth was even quicker in the Asian regions of the country than in European Russia, the result partly of deportations or population transfers, partly of a higher birthrate. Russia was predominantly agrarian; even by the late nineteen-sixties about 36 per cent of the population was still employed on the land, but the percentage was falling. Urbanisation made steady progress, but in the year Stalin died the majority of Soviet citizens still lived in the countryside and only in 1961 did city dwellers for the first time outnumber the rural population. The birthrate declined from 26 per thousand in 1958 to 18 per thousand in 1966, and the natural increase fell in the same period from 18 to 14 per thousand.

Stalin's successors tackled with great energy the urgent problems facing them. They believed, like Stalin, that priority should be given to heavy industry, but they realised that the national economy as a whole was bound to suffer if the disproportion between heavy industry and agriculture remained too pronounced. The failure of agriculture under Stalin was concealed by spurious statistics; in 1952, for instance, the grain yield was officially stated to have been about 125 million tons, whereas the real harvest was only 90 million as Khrushchev revealed six years later. After Stalin's death a major effort was made to improve the food supply by cultivating the virgin lands of West Siberia and Kazakhstan, by paying higher prices to the *kolkhoz* farmers, and by lifting some of the restrictions affecting work on their private plots. The 1953 harvest was a disaster – 82 million tons, less than the yield in Tsarist Russia in 1913, and 1954 was not a much better year. After that the results of the new policy were increasingly felt: 127 million tons were harvested in 1956, 141 milion in 1958, and a record harvest, admittedly in very favourable climatic conditions, of 170 million in 1966–7. In between there were setbacks and the Soviet Union was forced to import wheat from Canada and other countries. But the general upward trend was unmistakable. In other fields achievements were less striking: the number of cattle in 1966 was 93 million compared with 60 million in Tsarist Russia; there were 137 million sheep and goats (as against 121 million before the first world war), while the number of pigs had almost trebled. Meat production consequently grew only at a slow rate from eight million tons (average 1946–50) to 10.8 million in 1966. This in turn affected the cost of living; in January 1962 the retail price of meat went up by 30 per cent.

Malenkov in a speech not long after Stalin's death had promised 'an abundance of food for the people and of raw materials for consumer goods industries in the next two or three years'. But this would have meant a radical shift in priorities, investing far more capital in consumer goods and agriculture. This policy, the 'new course', encountered stiff resistance from other Soviet leaders who demanded priority for heavy industry and for the requirements of the army. In the contest between guns (or, to be precise, rockets) and butter, most of the old leaders opted for continuity in economic policy and Malenkov's proposals were defeated. Nevertheless his initiative had not been altogether in vain, for some of his suggestions were adopted by his successors; important reforms continued in both industry and agriculture after his downfall. The virgin lands programme got under way, the Machine-Tractor Stations were disbanded, minimum wages were raised, and there were changes in industrial organisation: 25 ministries were abolished as part of a drive to combat over-centralisation. More attention was paid to urban housing: construction completed in 1958 was twice as high as in 1955. Altogether the output of Soviet industry and agriculture in 1958 was thought to be more than a third above that of 1954. Economic growth during this period was impressive, but towards the end of the fifties there was growing evidence of a slowdown; in 1957 the sixth five-year plan had to be scrapped as a new dispute over the allocation of resources developed. The Soviet leadership was over-committed; it tried to accomplish too much in too many directions at the same time. It attempted to match the military-space programme of the United States despite the fact that the resources at its disposal were much more limited; it had opted for large-scale investment in new industrial plant and equipment; and the returns from farming in the virgin lands proved to be disappointing after the first successful harvests. The rate of growth fell as defence spending increased by one-third between 1959 and 1963. In absolute terms the key industries continued to make great progress even after 1958. Steel output rose from 54 million tons in 1958 to 84 million in 1964, oil production doubled (113 million tons to 225 million), so did the output of electricity and cement (33 million tons – 63 million). Soviet steel production in 1963 was greater than that of Britain, France, and West Germany combined, and was 80 per cent of American production; in 1968 it was 85 per cent of the United States. But industrial growth as a whole was less impressive and the Soviet leaders were troubled by the declining rate of development. It fell from 13 per cent in 1954, to 10 per cent in 1958, and to 7.5 per cent in 1964. The decline in the rate of growth of the Gross National Product was even more marked. It had been 10 per cent in 1958 when the Soviet GNP was about 44 per cent of the American. This was a considerable advance over 1950 (32 per cent) and 1955 (36 per cent), but in 1961 it fell to 6.5 per cent, in 1962 and 1963 it did not exceed 3 per cent, and while there was a recovery in 1964 (7–8 per cent), progress during the years following was again less striking. In the race to overtake the United States little headway was made between 1961 and 1967; the Soviet Union was marking time. At the twenty-first congress of the Communist Party Khrushchev had declared that by 1970 the Soviet Union would outproduce the United States not merely in absolute terms but also on a *per capita* basis. These boasts were soon forgotten; two days after Khrushchev's fall in 1964, *Pravda* editorially denounced the style of the deposed leader, his 'hare-brained scheming, immature conclusions, hasty decisions and actions divorced from reality.' The Soviet workers and peasants had been promised lower prices, a shorter working week and, generally speaking, a much higher standard of living, but the price index of food was actually higher in 1964 than at the beginning of the Khrushchev period, and the production of textiles (to give another example) had increased only slightly. The goals of the seven-year plan (1959–65) had to be revised in view of continuing imbalances – steel and machinery construction made faster progress than anticipated, but other industries, and above all agriculture, were again lagging behind. The virgin lands had produced a good harvest in 1958 but failed to equal, let alone exceed, their performance thereafter. The economy was suffering from an acute capital shortage and the somewhat half-hearted attempts to obtain loans from the West bore little fruit. Fulfilment of the seven-year plan was further impeded by additional increases in military spending between 1961 and 1963, which in a critical period withdrew important resources in manpower and materials from the national economy. In 1957 the country was subdivided into a number of large economic units (the *Sovnarkhozy*) to make for more effective economic planning and to lessen the effects of the dead hand of a centralised bureaucracy. This new emphasis on regionalism was not, however, successful, for within the framework of the Soviet economic system the coordination of the overall plan was possible only on the basis of information available nowhere but in Moscow. Khrushchev's successors therefore returned to the centralised ministerial planning system. These gropings for a new form of organisation reflected the general feeling that the existing planning and control techniques were unsuited for an economic system that was becoming year by year more diverse and sophisticated. A new school of mathematical economics emerged; in the past this approach had been considered alien to the spirit of Soviet ideology, but gradually these techniques were adopted because they promised a better system of information and control. Slowly the debate about reorganisation began to affect vital issues, such as pricing, the autonomy of industrial enterprises, and the wider use of profitability as a guideline for planners and managers. Professor Libermann, one of the main spokesmen of the reformers, argued that it was the main criterion of efficiency; this led to the demand for greater managerial freedom. This, of course, was anathema to the traditionalists who had grown up in the belief that profitability was not the correct criterion to apply in a socialist society. The innovators were given some scope for experimentation but the reforms did not go very deep. A great many unsolved questions remained, above all the problem of striking a viable balance between plan and market: 'What should be the role of the political leadership and of the central planners? Should prices be allowed to fluctuate in response to supply and demand? If they are so allowed, then how would the state exercise control over the economy?' (Alec Nove). Western observers sometimes tended to overrate the political effect of the economic reforms; it remains to be noted that some east European countries were less cautious than the Soviet Union in applying the new ideas: in 1967 about 30 per cent of all prices in Hungary were determined by market forces rather than by the plan; in the Soviet Union the percentage was probably nearer five.

Khrushchev's downfall was partly connected with the setbacks of the Soviet economy in 1962–3. In one of his last speeches before that event he argued in a spirit of self-criticism that even large allocations of capital would fail to have the desired effect if the investments were spread over an enormous number of projects. His successors faced the same dilemma. They said they regarded the development of heavy industry as of foremost importance, but they also demanded an instant improvement in agriculture. They promised higher living standards but at the same time announced higher military spending. Agriculture was initially given high priority, but after the good harvests of 1966–7 investment in agriculture was again reduced. Money incomes were increased and the rate of consumer goods production, which had steadily decreased during the last two decades, went up again in 1966–7.

	Capital Goods Industries	Non-Durable Consumer Goods
	Percentage	
1951–55	12.4	10
1956–60	13	6.9
1961–65	11.3	4.8

But consumer demand was not even remotely satisfied; while retail sales went up by 37 per cent between 1961 and 1966, personal savings rose during the same period almost six times as fast. The burden of defence expenditure became heavier from year to year; it rose from about nine billion rubles in 1960 to almost 17 billion in 1968. These were the official figures; the real cost of the competition with America in the field of rocketry and nuclear weapons was probably even higher. At the same time the rate of investment in the national economy fell sharply; in the nineteen-sixties it was little more than half of what it had been in the previous decade. As far as quantity was concerned, achievements were still impressive; according to the official statistics the Soviet Union had a higher GNP per head than Italy and Japan. But hardly anyone familiar with conditions in these countries would maintain that the standard of living of the average Soviet citizen was equal (let alone superior) to that of the average Italian or Japanese. There was a technological and quality gap which escaped the official statistics, a whole economic and social dimension that was missing in the Soviet economic performance and which had to be overcome in order to catch up with the West.

Western appraisals of the Soviet economic performance have been subject to frequent changes. After the massive advance of the late fifties many Western observers were inclined to accept Khrushchev's boasts almost at face value. After the setback of 1962–3, on the other hand, there was a tendency to belittle both past Soviet achievements and future prospects. A realistic appraisal must take into account both the impressive growth of heavy industry since the second world war, and the weaknesses of the Soviet economy that have been revealed. In the quarter century between 1940 and 1965, the consumption of electricity in the Soviet Union grew elevenfold, the production of oil eightfold, of steel fivefold, and the output of coal more than trebled. The production of consumer goods was much less impressive; in general the rate of growth has shown a steady decline as the Soviet economy emerged from its early industrialisation period. After Stalin's death there were important changes and a more sophisticated system of planning was adopted, but there was no radical shift in priorities and the managers did not take over from the political commissars. The party machine, the planning and administrative bureaucracy, still issued commands, and with all the streamlining of the economy, most of the basic questions about its future direction were still open 15 years after Stalin's death.

The Industrialisation of Eastern Europe

For the first decade after the second world war the economic development of the communist countries of eastern Europe closely followed the Soviet pattern, but there was greater diversity after 1955. During the immediate postwar period, following the communist takeover, industry was nationalised and the first measures to collectivise agriculture were carried out. The economies of eastern Europe were exploited to speed up the recovery of the Soviet economy; Moscow exacted its tribute from some of its satellites in the form of reparations; elsewhere joint companies were set up, giving the Soviet Union a dominating position. Russia insisted on the People's Democracies directing their foreign trade towards Moscow; the establishment of the Council of Mutual Economic Assistance (CMEA or Comecon) in January 1949 was one of the instruments for coordinating the economic activities of the Soviet Union and its allies. It was not an alliance between equals: the Soviet exports of raw materials and machinery were well above world market prices, whereas the People's Democracies were forced to sell their goods to Russia cheaply. Industrial progress was nevertheless made in eastern Europe, though at an appalling price. The industrial output in East Germany and Czechoslovakia almost doubled between 1948 and 1955, and in the less industrialised countries, starting from a lower level, it rose even faster. According to official figures the national income in Bulgaria and Rumania rose between 1950 and 1955 at the rate of 12 and 14 per cent a year respectively, and in Yugoslavia even faster, a performance never again repeated by any other east European country in later years. How meaningful these and similar figures really are no one can say; there is no doubt that the foundations of industrialisation were laid during that period in the less developed countries, but the imbalances of Stalinism were even more palpable there than in the Soviet Union, particularly the dislocation in agriculture following collectivisation and the effects of heavy spending on defence. After Stalin's death Malenkov's new course was adopted for a little while in eastern Europe as well as in the Soviet Union. Wages were increased, prices and taxes cut, investment in heavy industry temporarily reduced, agricultural production boosted. An attempt was made to reduce the dangerous economic tensions that had developed, but in some countries these reforms did not come in time. There was unrest in East Germany and Czechoslovakia, and on a far more dangerous scale in Poland and Hungary. The Soviet Union was forced to reconsider its whole relationship with the Popular Democracies and the grosser forms of exploitation ceased. In some instances Moscow had to come to the help of its allies by extending credits, cancelling debts, and other emergency measures.

Under Khrushchev the policy of economic integration of the Soviet bloc was pursued, and the east European countries became even more dependent on Moscow for deliveries of raw materials required for their industrialisation programmes. There was more diversity: Poland was in no hurry to collectivise its agriculture and in Hungary in 1958 there were only half as many collective farms as in 1956. All over the Soviet bloc the rate of growth was lower during the second half of the fifties than before; in Rumania and East Germany it was only half the rate of the early fifties. During 1960–5, again following the Soviet pattern, it fell even further, except in Rumania. In Czechoslovakia and Hungary these were years of virtual standstill. The average yearly growth of the GNP in Czechoslovakia during 1961–5 was 1.3 per cent, nowhere in the Eastern bloc did it exceed five per cent. After 1965 most east European countries recovered from the crisis and economic progress quickened again.

	Index of Industrial Production 1938 = 100 (1964)	Index of Agricultural Production 1938 = 100 (1960–63 average)	Per capital GNP 1964 $
Bulgaria	625	111	690
Rumania	498	129	680
Poland	370	132	890
Hungary	314	98	1,020
Czechoslovakia	242	92	1,470
East Germany	208	80	1,400

The industrially backward countries of eastern Europe made much faster progress than East Germany and Czechoslovakia. The disparity in their rates of growth became significant in particular during the second decade, after they had overcome initial difficulties (such as balance of payments problems).

Agricultural production, on the other hand, was lagging behind in all of them; the situation was most favourable in Rumania and Poland, but in Czechoslovakia, East Germany, and Hungary average output was below the prewar yield. (The index of agricultural production in France and Italy, for example, was 151 and 147 respectively, compared with the last prewar year.) Since most east European countries were still predominantly agrarian in structure, the stagnation in agriculture depressed the economic performance as a whole. Despite all the industrialisation efforts, per capita income in Bulgaria and Rumania in the middle sixties was not substantially higher than in Greece. Twenty years after the end of the war *per capita* income in the more developed Comecon countries was still twice as high as in Bulgaria and Rumania, and *per capita* income in the industrialised countries of western Europe was still almost twice as high as in Czechoslovakia and East Germany, and more than twice that of Hungary. Two bumper harvests in succession and a speed-up in the production of consumer goods in 1966–8 accounted for a marked rise in income per head in most east European countries, but it is too early to say whether this recovery constitutes the beginning of a long-term trend.

Comecon was the arena of much dissension between the Soviet Union and its junior partners. With the secession of China from the bloc, which incidentally also had economic consequences, and the spread of polycentrism, political and economic nationalism asserted itself. There were few difficulties with East Germany and Bulgaria in view of their political dependence on the Soviet Union; three-quarters of Bulgarian trade was with Russia and the other bloc countries, and East Germany remained not only Russia's most faithful ally but also its most important trading partner. But among the others there were many complaints; Rumania was in open rebellion, maintaining that the internal division of labour decided by Comecon was detrimental to its economic interest and impeded its industrial development. Czechoslovakia, Hungary, and Poland argued that they had to pay prices considerably above world market prices for Soviet raw materials, while for their part the Russians contended that the products they bought from eastern Europe were not up to world market quality, and that in any case, world market prices were not appropriate as a yardstick in trade relations between socialist countries; Moscow was firmly opposed to any attempts by its allies to attract Western capital and technological expertise. On the other hand, it insisted that eastern Europe together with the Soviet Union provide military and industrial equipment, sometimes free of charge and always on special terms, to Egypt, India, and other Asian and African countries, usually in the pursuit of Soviet foreign policy objectives. Such Soviet demands were not necessarily in the best interests of the east European countries and a great deal of ideological, political, and even military pressure was needed to overcome their lack of enthusiasm. Certain concessions had to be made by the Soviet Union; Hungary and Czechoslovakia were permitted to introduce economic reforms (less emphasis on heavy industry, increased incentives, more stress on market forces) that went beyond those adopted in the Soviet Union. Rumania as well as Poland, Hungary and Czechoslovakia expanded their trade with the non-communist world up to 40–45 per cent. Comecon, unlike the Common Market, was not based primarily on a community of economic interests; the Soviet Union had a far more vital interest in close collaboration with the bloc than most of its partners. It kept its reluctant allies in line less by stressing common economic interests than by ideological pressure and above all by reminding them from time to time of the harsh realities of political and military power.

Social Changes in Postwar Europe

Profound changes have affected almost all aspects of European social life since the end of the second world war. This was a new age of social reforms, and although some of them had been initiated well before the first world war, their full impact was felt only after 1945 when the social security services expanded in new directions and became far more comprehensive. The welfare state removed some of the most oppressive features of early industrial society, but it could not, as some had apparently hoped, effect a radical transformation of the human condition. Poverty was not stamped out except in the most advanced countries of northern Europe; the hardships and pains of sickness and old age were alleviated but did not disappear. The welfare state made people healthier but it did not necessarily make them happier. On the contrary, once material deprivation became less acute, other forms of suffering were more intensely felt: the boredom and anonymity of life in the big cities, or, to use the catchword of the sixties, alienation. The figures for drug addiction, suicide, and juvenile crime climbed steadily higher. But if the impact of the welfare state on the human condition was not as deep as some had expected, there was no doubt about the material benefits. The terrible insecurity which had for so long haunted so many all over Europe disappeared as it became generally accepted that no one should starve, that everyone had a right to shelter, and that lack of money should not stand in the way of health. True, not everyone benefited from these reforms in equal measure; some of the provisions were inadequate (such as old age pensions in many countries) and some categories of people were unaccountably left out altogether. Measured by the standards of an ideal society, the postwar changes were highly inadequate, at best a few steps in the right direction; but compared with conditions in the past and with the present state of affairs in other parts of the world, it was a tremendous achievement, probably the greatest social advance made in many centuries.

There was a marked increase in mobility between the classes; the old élites in some countries were still firmly entrenched in strongholds such as the foreign service and the officer corps. But a new meritocracy gained most of the key positions in the higher civil service and in business; the *haute bourgeoisie* was no longer secure even in its control of the conservative parties of western Europe. Progressive taxation narrowed the gap between the highest and lowest incomes but businessmen still succeeded in amassing great fortunes and sometimes even in evading the increasingly stiff death duties. But with growing prosperity and more equal opportunity in education, the marks distinguishing the classes from one another became much less pronounced; the old proverb, 'clothes maketh man', lost significance as it became more and more difficult to 'place' a man or woman according to his or her attire; even the car they were driving was no longer a reliable guide to their class status.

The postwar world produced the mixed economy and the welfare state; it also witnessed the emergence of the 'permissive society'. The war 1914–18 had seen the first great break with the morals and manners of the nineteenth century, and the new freedom had been widely celebrated in the early twenties in the capitals of western Europe. But this movement had affected only a relatively small layer of society; the moral code of the nineteenth century had been severely shaken; though often tacitly ignored, outwardly it was still very much in evidence. The changes that took place after the second world war were deeper and more far-reaching than those after 1918: church attendance dropped all over Europe; all authority was questioned; sexual freedom spread to an extent unknown before, and by the late sixties the academic youth of Europe was everywhere up in arms against the 'establishment'. Even before the revolt of the students a great deal of restlessness had been felt among working class youth; European newspapers during the fifties were full of the exploits of the *teddy boys* (in England), the *Halbstarke* (in Germany), the *blousons noirs* (in France), the *gamberros* (in Spain), not to mention the *Khooligans* of communist Europe. Youth movements, both inchoate and organised, had been part of the European scene in one form or another almost without interruption since the Romantic age; the idea of a youth culture, the concept of the revolt of the younger generation, of the class struggle in school and university, had been widely discussed in central Europe even before the first world war. But at that time parents, teachers, and other authorities had not considered even for a moment abdicating what they regarded as their natural responsibilities towards the young generation; law and order was then not a slogan, it was the self-evident foundation of society. After the second world war the self-confidence of the older generation had been severely shaken and as a result there was much greater readiness to take the ideas of young people seriously and to accept their demands. But this did not necessarily satisfy a movement often devoid of rational and clearly formulated programmes; protest was above all a biological necessity (as it had been throughout history), the urge to self-assertion was stronger than the desire to carry out any specific reform.

The student power movement was certainly more spectacular than the struggle for the full emancipation of the weaker sex. By 1945 women had attained almost complete legal equality, even if in Switzerland they did not have the right to vote, and although certain discriminatory provisions with regard to property rights still persisted in many countries. Women entered many professions that had been virtually closed to them before and many more of them now received a higher education. But the limits of social, as distinct from legal, emancipation also became more obvious. The principle of equal pay for equal work was not accepted in practice in most European countries, and many leading positions in the economy and in public life remained as before closed to them. The situation in eastern Europe was basically the same. True, woman had made great progress in various professions; there were, to give one illustration, more women than men physicians in the Soviet Union. But no women rose to key positions in the Communist Party or the state apparatus. A few women-politicians, such as Anna Pauker in Rumania, had played a prominent part in the first years after the war, but they did not last long. The politburos of the various east European communist parties were as much a male preserve as the traditional London clubs. The social emancipation of women had made more progress in Scandinavia than in any other part of Europe and it was these countries that were also the pioneers of the new sexual freedom. Legislation in this respect became more liberal, sex education in schools was no longer opposed, and as far as public opinion was concerned premarital sexual intercourse was accepted in theory as well as in practice. Books, plays, and movies faced more lenient censors than in any other period in modern history; subjects that had formerly been taboo were now freely discussed; the underground presses of Europe went out of business for hard-core pornography was widely published and in some places openly traded. The contraceptive pill was freely obtainable by the middle sixties in many countries (not, however, in the Soviet Union) and this too, contributed towards a profound change in sexual mores. In Britain in 1966 there were six times as many divorces as in 1938; the divorce rate was very high in the immediate postwar period, fell during the fifties, but increased again in the nineteen-sixties. It was higher in most east European countries

(Hungary, Rumania, and the Soviet Union) than in the West and higher in Denmark and Sweden than in Britain and Benelux. Couples married at an earlier age and with increasing longevity they could look forward to married life lasting almost twice as long as fifty years earlier.

The permissive society modified its attitude towards crime and punishment. Juvenile crime and acts of violence against persons increased, but in some other respects there was a fall in the crime rate: 1,200 adults out of 100,000 had been sentenced by German courts in 1900, 1,190 in 1930, but only 780 (not counting traffic offenders) in 1960. As the social roots of crime were better understood and as new theories about the possible influence of genetic factors were discussed, there was more emphasis on rehabilitation than on punishment. The prison régime became more liberal and capital punishment had been abolished by the middle sixties by all countries except those of eastern Europe, France, Greece, and Spain. This liberal trend was however by no means undisputed; it was usually advocated by a relatively small section of intellectuals whereas society as a whole was less inclined to initiate progressive social experiments. As the negative features of the new liberalism were more palpably felt, many claimed that too much in this direction had been done too fast. The police forces and the courts usually took a more conservative attitude towards the treatment of criminals than the reformers who were dealing with the problems from a distance.

In the Soviet Union the repressive effects of the Stalin era were all-pervasive; social services were far less comprehensive than in any developed capitalist country; the principle of free education was no longer adhered to as tuition fees were reintroduced in the universities and the upper forms of secondary schools. Divorce was made difficult and abortion was virtually abolished. While the Soviet Union enjoyed the reputation among Western progressives as the country with the most highly developed social services, and while Western conservatives were convinced that sexual licence in communist society was without precedent or parallel, the real situation was very different indeed. After 1956 more liberal attitudes prevailed; old age pensions and other benefits were increased, school and university fees were abolished, and the restrictions on divorce and abortion partly rescinded. But this liberalism had narrow limits: there was no permissiveness about drug taking and other such abominations as practised in the 'decaying West'. The manifestations of the new sexual freedom in the capitalist world were emphatically rejected and Soviet literature, cinema, and plays remained the cleanest (in the Victorian sense) on the continent; the official Soviet attitude towards psychoanalysis was no more lenient than that of the Vatican.

Many postwar fashions were ephemeral and two decades are too brief a period to assess which of them are likely to last. But there was no doubt that a great deal of qualitative change had taken place in European social life, that the social policies pursued had resulted in a society that was in many respects totally different from any previous one. The welfare state was something essentially new, and it is to this concept and its practical aspects that we shall turn next.

Reforms in Social Welfare

Germany in the age of Bismarck had been the pioneer of social legislation such as compulsory insurance, old age pensions, and sickness insurance. Other European countries, following the German example, had also introduced similar legislation for the protection of industrial workers well before the first world war. France and Belgium had been the first to grant family allowances; Russia, and Germany under Hitler, gave special assistance to mothers bearing more than the average number of children. But most of these prewar schemes were rudimentary and selective; they were designed to give a minimum of security to the very poorest, but the concept of public assistance at the time was not far removed from the charity schemes of the Victorian era. The principle of equality of opportunity was not yet generally accepted, nor was the idea that society had certain duties towards all of its members.

The social reforms carried out all over Europe after the second world war seemed at first to be only an extension of the legislation of earlier years, even though their character was much more systematic and they went much further than all previous schemes. Western European expenditure on social services quadrupled between 1930 and 1957; in Sweden it was six times higher in the latter year, in France seven, in Italy 14 times. Taken separately, the new measures were merely a continuation of a policy inaugurated decades before, but they also had a profound cumulative effect, gradually giving birth to the welfare state.

Social welfare schemes varied greatly from country to country in scope, in their priorities, and in the way they were financed and administered. The highly industrialised countries had more comprehensive services, the poor countries of south Europe (except Italy) introduced social legislation only later, and the services they offered were much inferior to those of Britain and Sweden which were the most comprehensive. West Germany and Belgium now provide old age pensions which are among the most liberal and France offers the highest family allowance and sizable sickness benefits. Social security in Britain is operated by the state while many services in Scandinavia, such as unemployment insurance and the health service (except in Sweden) are run by non-governmental bodies. In Germany, France, and Italy, co-operative insurance agencies play an important role and some of the insurance programmes were until recently financed almost entirely by contributions by employers and employees; state contributions have only recently become a factor of importance. In the communist states of eastern Europe the trade unions have traditionally played the central role in administering the social services.

The various insurance schemes had originally been sponsored to assist the industrial working class and were extended only much later to the self-employed. By 1960 almost the whole population of Britain and Sweden was covered by the health service, and the great majority of citizens in France, Germany, and Italy (85, 87 and 88 per cent respectively). In the Soviet Union, too, most social services were extended after 1965 to cover the peasants, hitherto excluded from most of these benefits. Free medical care was provided in the nineteen-fifties to all insured persons in Britain, Italy, Germany, Spain, and a number of smaller countries, whereas in France, the Scandinavian countries, Belgium, and Switzerland, sick persons had to make a contribution, usually ranging from 10 to 25 per cent of the cost. In France and Belgium it was customary to pay directly but to claim a refund later. Sickness benefits varied greatly; they were about 20 per cent (for the first six weeks) in West Germany. Old age pensions were paid to men in most countries at the age of 65 (60 for women); in France and Italy the retirement age was 60 (55 for women in Italy), whereas in Sweden it was 67 and in Norway 70. Old age pensions in France and Britain were low, approximately 40 dollars per month for a man over 65 after 40 years of work; they were twice as high in Italy where, however, fewer people qualified for these benefits. Family allowances also varied greatly from country to country. In Scandinavia the scheme extended to all residents: elsewhere it was restricted mainly to wage earners. In many places the rate per child increased up to the third or fourth child, in some it was constant irrespective of the size of the family. Those allowances were paid in some European countries up to the age of 14, in others up to 21, and there were striking differences in the level of allowances: a family with three children received almost 60 dollars per month in France (in 1964), but only 24 dollars in Italy, and only about 10 dollars in Britain. All European countries with the exception of Portugal also had maternity allowances, and a few provided additional benefits ranging from marriage grants (Belgium, Spain, Switzerland), to home furnishing loans for young couples and low cost holidays for housewives (Sweden).

Equality in educational opportunity has been one of the basic features of the welfare state concept; higher education is now free or available at nominal charges in all west and north European countries. In 1953 more than 70 per cent of the students in Britain received state grants; subsequently grants were extended to all students without exception. In France, too, public education is free at all levels; some German *Länder* demand a fee of about 150 dollars per year while others (such as Hesse) have abolished tuition fees altogether. In Scandinavia and Holland tuition is either free or financed by state loans to be repaid over a period of five to ten years. These reforms involved growing state expenditure on education; while national income rose quickly, the proportion of the GNP spent on education increased even faster: from 2.7 to 4.2 per cent in Sweden between 1938 and 1956, and at approximately the same rate in Britain.

Friedrich Engels, writing on the housing question, maintained that there were already enough houses in existence to provide the working class with room and healthy living accommodation. Later advocates of the welfare state underrated in a similar way the cost of the services they envisaged: costs invariably outran the original estimates. In 1967 almost 17 per cent of the German GNP was spent on social services, 14–15 per cent in France, Sweden, Belgium, Italy, and Holland, 11 per cent in Britain and Denmark, 10 per cent in Switzerland and the Soviet Union. In the Scandinavian countries expenditure on the social services now accounts for about one-third of the net expenditure in the state budget. Different means were used to raise this money. In Scandinavia, as in Britain, the state contributes the main share of welfare and pension funds, in contrast to 18 per cent of the total cost in West Germany (in 1963), 11 per cent in Italy and 6 per cent in France and the Netherlands. In Britain employers contribute less than 20 per cent of the cost, whereas in France and Italy they contributed about two-thirds of the social security bill. Before the second world war Germany and Britain had been leading the rest of Europe by a great margin in per capita expenditure on social security; after 1945 the picture began to change.

PER CAPITA SOCIAL SECURITY EXPENDITURE IN DOLLARS
AT 1954 PRICES

	1930	1957
Belgium	12	148
France	17	136
Germany	54	132
Holland	10	56
Italy	5	54
Sweden	22	135
Switzerland	24	96
United Kingdom	59	93

As public outlays continued to rise year by year, there was growing criticism in some circles of some of the provisions of the welfare state. According to their argument reforms had gone too far, making the individual utterly dependent on the state and destroying every urge towards self help. Critics in Britain suggested that those who wanted to contract out of the national health service should be encouraged to do so, and that more scope should be given to private initiative in education. They argued that the burden on the state was too heavy, that growing expenditure for social services had raised taxation to such an extent that there was little incentive for the individual to exert himself for his own good and that of society. But these critics were a minority; most citizens enjoyed the benefits of the welfare state and took them for granted. A radical reduction in the social services was politically impossible as the great majority would have resisted it tooth and nail. Minor changes apart (such as for instance the reintroduction of a nominal charge for drugs), successive British governments, however hard pressed financially, did not dare to touch the provisions for social welfare, and the situation on the continent was similar.

Social services extended by the communist countries of eastern Europe are broadly speaking similar in scope to those enjoyed by citizens of western Europe. Social insurance, introduced in Tsarist Russia, was expanded after the 1917 revolution. Under Stalin's rule, however, full social benefits were restricted to workers who had been employed at their place of work for at least eight consecutive years; the law of 1948 was designed to combat labour turnover and to introduce stricter labour discipline. The whole social insurance system was reformed in 1956, when some of the higher pensions were reduced, while the benefits of the lower income groups were increased. The minimum old age pension was fixed at 300 roubles a year, the maximum at 1,200 according to the average earnings of the last twelve months or the best five years of the last ten. Hospitalisation, treatment in hospitals and out-patient clinics, is free in the Soviet Union; sick benefit rates are 90 per cent of wages after 12 years of continuous employment at one place of work, falling to 50 per cent after three years or less.

Health

Advances in medical knowledge and the greater availability of health services to entire populations have resulted in a significant improvement in the state of health of the peoples of Europe. The average life expectancy in Switzerland around the turn of the century was 50 years, it is now 70; in Spain during the same period it has risen from 34 to 60 years. Infant mortality, 27 out of a thousand in 1900, fell to 20 in Austria 50 years later and decreased from 13 to 1.4 in the Netherlands. There was a dramatic decline in epidemic diseases following the discovery of new powerful drugs; tuberculosis ceased to be one of the main killers. While little progress was made in curing mental diseases, a whole arsenal of new medicines made it much easier to control these illnesses and to reduce the number of those permanently hospitalised. Cancer, on the other hand, was on the increase; and with rising life expectancy there was also a higher incidence of diseases of the heart and the nervous system.

There was also a steady rise in deaths from traffic accidents; between 1948 and 1956 their number doubled in Germany, Norway, and the Netherlands; in France, Italy, and Spain they more than trebled.

Greater attention than before was paid to preventive medicine, to health in school and industry, to the purification of water and air. The number of practising physicians doubled, roughly speaking, between the late twenties and 1960; there was one physician for every 700 residents of Switzerland, but only one for 1,700 Finns, with other European countries somewhere in between these extremes. The number of dentists increased even faster during this period, while 80 per cent more hospital beds were available. Western European expenditure on medical care was almost four times as high in the nineteen-fifties as during the decade before the war, but a higher share of the total was devoted to the ancillary medical services. The British example tended to show that while the initial outlay was high, a national health service, once established, could be run without yearly increases in allocations that were disproportionate with economic growth. Expenditure on the health services in Britain remained fairly stable at four per cent of the GNP between 1950 and 1960. The improvement in the state of public health during the postwar period was striking throughout Europe, but, as in most other fields, expectations rose even faster than achievements. There were still serious shortcomings and few medical experts would have agreed even after two decades of continuous progress that the situation in this respect was really satisfactory.

Housing

Whole stretches of Europe were in ruins as the second world war ended. Some countries had been more affected by the destruction than others: 20–25 per cent of all houses in Germany and Greece had been totally destroyed by military action, but only six to seven per cent in France and Britain; big cities naturally fared worse than the countryside in this respect. Europe's housing situation had been far from satisfactory even before the war; urban building had been interrupted during the first world war and had again come to a standstill during the great depression. The prewar cities of Europe were essentially a product of the nineteenth-century, houses of brick and stone solidly built, meant to last at least a hundred years. With the rapid growth of the urban population many of them had become overcrowded and most of them were ugly, with large tracts of monotonous rows of buildings that had degenerated into slums within a decade or two. In France and Belgium at the end of the war only every other house had running water, only every third in Italy, Spain and Austria. Only one house in ten in these countries had a fixed bath, one out of three in highly developed countries such as Germany and Sweden. The housing situation in Britain and the Scandinavian countries, in Belgium and Switzerland, was on the whole better than in the rest of the continent, certainly as far as space was concerned, but it did not meet minimum standards of safety and health, let alone of comfort; 20–30 per cent of the buildings in many British cities had been declared unfit even before 1939. The state of affairs had further deteriorated during the war when no major repairs could be undertaken.

In this critical situation all European governments had to give priority to housing construction, allocating on the average three to five per cent of their GNP for this purpose. By 1950 the number of houses in western Europe was already higher than before the war. In eastern Europe, on the other hand, where the shortage was even more acute, little new building was carried out during the first postwar decade. During the nineteen-fifties there was further substantial progress in western Europe; the number of houses, roughly speaking, doubled. Construction in a good year in the sixties was more than half a million units in West Germany, 400,000 in France and Italy, almost 400,000 in Britain, almost 300,000 in Spain. There were also extensive programmes of slum clearance, so that the real increase in accommodation was smaller than indicated by these impressive figures. The quality of building was low during the immediate postwar period when utility standards prevailed; later on, during the late fifties, the new flats and houses became more spacious and more pleasing to the eye. Greater attention was paid to layout and individual design, to landscaping and community amenities. It was by no means easy to achieve the goals that had been set; the building industry was on the whole inefficient and conservative in outlook, consisting mostly of small firms. The methods of building had changed little since the nineteenth century, and in view of the seasonal fluctuations in building activity it was difficult to attract and keep a sufficient labour force. During the second postwar decade rationalisation and mechanisation of building processes made considerable progress and with it the production of prefabricated houses, concrete panel construction and the standardisation of materials, components and fixtures. To boost housing Britain had established a Ministry of Town and Country Planning even before the end of the war; ministers of housing were also appointed in Spain and several other countries. Modern technology and a more imaginative approach made for comfortable and aesthetically pleasing living, but not necessarily for cheaper houses and flats. The rising cost of building was another problem that could be solved only by massive state subsidies. Generalisations are difficult, for standards of housing differ greatly between countries (and between town and country) in accordance with social and climatic conditions. Tradition also played its part; in Britain and Holland city dwellers have a preference for houses, whereas elsewhere on the continent there has been for a long time a preference for flats. Owner occupancy is everywhere greater in the rural than in the urban areas. The price of land had gone up in all European cities; if the cost of an average size house was not much less than 3,000 dollars in southern Europe in the late 1950s it was likely to be almost three times as high in central and northern Europe. Such prices put new houses out of reach of the great majority of the population and made state assistance imperative. There was little speculative building during the first years after the war; rents were controlled in most European countries, and with the progress of inflation the landlord's outlay on repairs was usually higher than his income from rent. There was little incentive for private initiative in building and most of Europe's new postwar housing was state supported by means of tax reliefs (West Germany), loans at low interest rates (Switzerland, France, and other countries), direct initiative by the local authorities (Britain), or special benefits accorded to housing cooperatives (Scandinavia, Holland, Austria). Later on, with growing prosperity, the share of private building increased; mortgages in most countries were available at five to eight per cent interest for a period of 10–25 years. Switzerland was an exception; money there was available on more favourable terms and as a result 90 per cent of new buildings was privately financed. State support and rent control made for cheap housing and most people spent a smaller proportion of their income on housing after the second world war than before. In 1938 10–14 per cent of expenditure on private consumption in the major European countries went on housing; 20 years later it was only eight per cent in Britain, five per cent in France, three per cent in Italy. By 1963 it had again risen to an average of eight to ten per cent in these countries. Rent control was necessary to protect the low income groups and it was also supported as an anti-inflationary measure. At the same time the system gave rise to many injustices: those who lived in old, controlled buildings paid only a fraction of the rent demanded of those in new houses or flats, even if these were subsidised. Young people in particular were affected, they found it difficult to make the substantial down payment and obtain mortgages for a house or a flat of their own. During the late fifties housing was decontrolled in some European countries; elsewhere rents increased in accordance with the rise in the cost of living.

Sweden, Switzerland, and West Germany were among the countries that made most progress in housing, but Britain was still in the lead in the average number of rooms per person; around 1960 it was 1.5 in Britain, 1.1 in West Germany, 1.0 in France, 0.9 in Italy. There are no comparable statistics for the Soviet Union, but it is known that only after 1956 was a major effort made to alleviate the acute housing shortage; construction almost trebled between 1953 and 1960 and more than two million units were built in 1965. Housing conditions had been abysmally bad during the Stalin era; there is reason to believe that even a decade after Stalin's death, after a major building effort, the urban population in the Soviet Union had only just as much space per capita at its disposal as before the revolution. The average Soviet family lived in a single room, and it had to share kitchen and other amenities with its neighbours; it spent a lower percentage of its budget (less than four per cent) on rent, fuel and light than in the West, but given the inferior standard of housing such comparisons are not very meaningful. To combat overcrowding strict regulations were introduced in the Stalin era to restrict the influx of new residents into Moscow and other cities. The decrees of 1957 which stressed the gravity of the situation and accorded higher priority to urban housing brought a substantial improvement. During the sixties most Soviet families in urban areas were able to move into two or three roomed flats, according to the size of the family. Even so, the targets of the plan for 1957–65 were not reached, the quality of the new buildings was inferior, and the standard of Soviet housing is still much below that in Western countries. It is declared Soviet policy to abolish rent altogether in the not-too-distant future; meanwhile private initiative through cooperative housing is encouraged, and the share of owner-occupied houses and flats is as high as in many west European countries. The housing situation in eastern Europe was on the whole slightly better than in the Soviet Union, but still much below west European standards. There were 1,572 rooms per thousand inhabitants in Belgium in 1961, compared with 832 in East Germany, 666 in Hungary, 580 in Poland, and 545 in Bulgaria. While there has been an improvement since 1956 there has not been as much new building as in Russia. Building cooperatives have been encouraged, following the Soviet example; prospective buyers have to make down payments of between 15 per cent (Poland) and 40 per cent (Russia) of the price and borrow the rest of the money needed from the banks, loans being granted for 10–15 years. In the more prosperous east European countries, notably East Germany and Czechoslovakia, the quality of building has markedly improved since the middle fifties.

The design of new housing has also greatly improved of late throughout Europe; there has been a general orientation towards sunlight, space between high blocks, and efforts are made to avoid monotony and uniformity. The idea of new garden cities first appeared in Germany and England towards the end of the nineteenth century. These concepts received fresh impetus with the Abercrombie plan adopted in Britain during the second world war which provided for several new cities to be established within a radius of 60 miles from London in order to disperse the population in the most heavily congested areas. There were similar plans for satellite towns around Paris, and five new cities have been built in the Ruhr. Near Stockholm two new cities, Vallingby and Hoegernaestaden, have developed since 1945; these have been in most ways the most successful of Europe's new towns. Speculative building has been instrumental in building near Paris a new middle-class suburb (Paris II) promising to 'introduce a new quality into urban life'. Interesting and on the whole successful experiments were undertaken in Berlin; the Hansa Viertel represents a unique but not unharmonious mixture of styles, each house being designed by a different architect. Walter Gropius has been in charge of the building of new residential areas in the north and the south-east of the city.

In comparison with the state of affairs before the war, the housing situation in Europe has greatly improved. Nowhere has the problem been entirely solved, partly as the result of rising costs, but also in consequence of higher standards and expectations. What was considered adequate housing in 1918 is now no longer acceptable. At the earlier date only a tiny percentage of houses and flats in Britain had central heating; now it is considered essential by most house buyers. Rents in the centre and 'desirable areas' of European cities (Paris, London, Rome, Geneva, and Zurich being the most flagrant cases) have skyrocketed; much cheaper housing is usually available in the outlying suburbs but the growing distance between these new residential districts and the places of employment now presents an increasingly difficult problem.

Prosperity and Changing Consumption Patterns

Throughout the nineteenth century Britain had enjoyed far higher living standards than the continent; it has been estimated that around 1870 *per capita* GNP in Germany, France, Denmark, Sweden, and Belgium was only two-thirds that of the United Kingdom, and in the other European countries even less. Between 1870 and 1913 *per capita* GNP in Britain rose by more than 80 per cent, between 1913 and 1955 by almost 70 per cent, and in the subsequent decade by about 50 per cent. But in the other countries just mentioned it rose even faster; all but Belgium had overtaken Britain by 1965. With growing prosperity important changes took place in consumption patterns; Europeans were not just consuming more of almost everything; there were far-reaching qualitative changes.

Food has been traditionally the largest single factor in private consumption; it is estimated that one hundred years ago about 65 per cent of private expenditure in Germany went on food, drink, and tobacco, but that by 1965 this had fallen to 36 per cent. A similar trend could be observed throughout Europe; the corresponding figures for the developed countries of western and northern Europe were in the range of 32–42 per cent, but considerably higher in the south of the continent. The more prosperous a country the smaller the proportion of the budget spent on food and drink, and the same applies to higher and lower income groups within each society. Eating habits have always varied according to national (and local) traditions; many of these have remained unchanged, but the consumption of cereals has declined all over Europe in comparison with the prewar period, and so has the consumption of potatoes everywhere except in Italy, where they have never been a major item. The consumption of meat and fish, or sugar, milk, and eggs, on the other hand, has risen rapidly and so has the calory intake in general, from 2,800 in France in 1950 to 2,940 by the end of the decade, and from 2,300 in Italy to 2,750. The main nutritional problem of western Europe in the nineteen-sixties was the fact that people ate too much rather than too little, and in most prosperous countries a slight decline in the calory intake could already be detected. Italians and Belgians were still the greatest bread eaters in Europe (122 kg. *per capita* per year), the Belgians and the French ate more meat than the others (56–58 kg.), whereas the Dutch were drinking more milk than anyone else (153 litres) and the Italians came first in the consumption of fresh fruit (54 kg.). The consumption of wine in Italy rose from 84 litres a year before the war to 95 in the sixties, but fell in France (where mortality from alcoholism had been fairly high) from 138 to 116 litres within one decade. Expenditure on alcohol was roughly the same in the various European countries, accounting for five to seven per cent of the total, but there were marked variations in prices. The same amount of money bought more than three times the quantity of alcohol in France and southern Europe as in Britain. *Per capita* expenditure on tobacco was roughly four per cent of personal consumption throughout western Europe, the Dutch, Danish, Swiss, Belgians, and British being the heaviest smokers. The discovery of the connection between lung cancer and cigarette smoking caused a slight drop in cigarette smoking in the sixties and higher taxation also acted as a brake; the share of taxes in the retail price of a packet of cigarettes was 75 per cent in Britain in 1955, and it has increased since.

That northern Europe spends more on fuel and light than the south is self-explanatory; more significant is the general postwar rise in spending on household durables. The number of telephones, television sets and radios, like that of refrigerators and cars, has become the usual yardstick of the statistician for measuring the standard of living. It is not always a reliable one: Denmark (to give but one example) with a standard of living roughly equal to that of West Germany, has twice as many telephones per head, and France with a higher standard of living than most, has even fewer telephones per head than Germany. Middle-income families have as many, if not more, television and radio sets as those in the high income brackets. Broadly speaking, expenditure on household appliances has risen faster than on any other item in the household budget; the use of washing machines, refrigerators, vacuum cleaners, which before the second world war was restricted to a small section of the population, spread during the fifties and sixties to the low income groups: European kitchens became mechanised as more women went out to work and as domestic help was no longer freely available. The price of many of these appliances remained fairly high but the widespread availability of hire purchase schemes brought these commodities within the range of the great majority of the population. Canned, tinned, deep frozen and pre-cooked foods increased in both volume and variety, ranging from frozen orange juice to instant coffee. 'Do it yourself' operations became of growing importance; for some it was a hobby, for others a necessity, since there were now so few artisans who could be called upon to undertake repair work. Europeans were better dressed in the postwar period despite the fact that they spent relatively less on clothing; the share of this item in the personal budget fell in France from 14.5 per cent in the late twenties to 11 per cent in the middle sixties, from 14 to 12 per cent in Belgium, and from 13 to 11 per cent in Britain. The most important new feature in this field was the growing use of synthetic fibres, the production of which quadrupled between 1960 and 1966.

The new design for living, especially the new products, had a marked egalitarian effect; the same type of furniture and appliances was often found in flats and housing estates all over western and northern Europe, especially among the younger generation, regardless of their class status. The deproletarisation of the working class made rapid strides in both western and eastern Europe despite the great differences in income, and middle-class attitudes gradually extended far beyond the traditional confines of this class.

Leisure

Leisure, idleness, activities undertaken as an end in themselves, have usually been the preserve of a happy few, the aristocracy and those with great inherited wealth. As the working week contracted and as physical work became less strenuous, leisure in the developed industrial societies became for the first time an inherent part of the new way of life. It is true that the change came slowly; there was no dramatic and sudden decrease in the time spent at work. The working week had been 48 hours in most European countries before the second world war and fell to 42–44 hours in the nineteen-fifties. France, which had introduced a 40 hour week in the nineteen-thirties, was the one major exception, but this was more apparent than real, for it represented the legal minimum and most French employees were only too eager to work overtime. But there was more time at the disposal of the individual with the increasing number of paid holidays and as vacations became longer. By 1955 there were 29 days paid holidays a year in Sweden, including vacation and paid statutory holidays, 28 in Germany and Italy; in the sixties their number had risen to 32–35 in these countries. Rising productivity and the introduction of more sophisticated machinery reduced the physical effort needed at work and increased output. This made it possible to get both more pay (and hence more goods) and more leisure. With the introduction of still more modern equipment and with automatic methods especially in the growth industries, it was predicted that the working week would shrink in the not-too-distant future to four days and ultimately to less.

By upbringing and education men and women have been prepared over the ages to be useful members of society, but very few knew other than by instinct how to spend their free time in the most enjoyable way; they needed to relearn, what previous generations had mastered to a high degree, how to transform free time into genuine leisure. Greater leisure offered many opportunities; some took up or further developed hobbies ranging from stamp collecting to bird watching, from sailing and camping to cultivating small gardens. A minority preferred strenuous activities such as mountaineering; the majority stuck to less exacting pastimes like watching television, bingo, or attending ball games. The do-it-yourself industry prospered, car and photography fans devoted much time and frequently invested a great deal of money in the pursuit of their hobbies. Others joined adult education courses ranging in scope from the study of languages to folk dancing, the collection of antiques or the emulation of Grandma Moses. The number of radio hams, of members of rifle clubs, and of many other associations and *verein* increased; the news-stands offered an almost unlimited variety of periodicals devoted to every hobby and pastime. There was a steady increase in the attendance of concerts, plays, operas, the ballet, and exhibitions, and the number of amateur artists and those making music at home also went up substantially.

More leisure did not by itself contribute to greater happiness and the full development of the faculties of individual members of society; there was also growing boredom and a feeling of emptiness. Leisure, like work, had its discontents, and men and women had to be retrained to seek fulfilment in their free time. Authoritarian régimes tried to provide organised leisure activities, as fascist Italy had done with its *dopo lavoro* schemes and nazi Germany with *Kraft durch Freude*. In the West the negative aspects of mass culture, propagated and magnified by advertising, induced many to spend their time in activities which, while certainly an end in themselves, were neither enjoyable nor profitable.

These were the birthpangs of the new *civilisation de loisir*. With all its problems, few doubted its tremendous advantages and possibilities. On the benefits of tourism there was little dispute. It was almost always rewarding, it helped to broaden the horizon of millions of people, and in some ways contributed to better undertanding between men and women of different nations.

Tourism

Mass tourism was virtually unknown before the second world war. Biarritz, Baden Baden, and a few other watering places and some Italian and Swiss resorts, had had their influx of visitors of over a century, some thousands of wandering scholars and artisans had ventured outside their native countries, but the great majority of Europeans had no more thought of travelling abroad than of visiting another planet. The great change in this respect came with growing prosperity, and above all with the greater mobility provided by the motor car, chartered flights and package tours. By the middle fifties 30 million tourists were crossing European frontiers every year, and in 1966 their number exceeded 100 million. Domestic tourism, needless to say, was even more extensive; it is estimated that in any year during the sixties three out of four Swedes and almost every other German and Frenchman took a holiday outside his usual place of residence; Europeans spent some 45 billion dollars in the process. But most of the glamour attached to foreign tourism and its economic importance for many countries was of the highest order. During the months of July and August the highroads of Europe, the railway stations and airports, were scenes of mass migration the like of which had never been witnessed in human history. Governments promoted the stream of tourists by making it much easier to cross frontiers; visas between most European countries were gradually abolished, and by 1960 there was only the most perfunctory border control. Enterprising businessmen cashed in on the tourist boom, organising group travel at a fraction of the price individual travellers would have to pay. Hotels, motels, and camping sites mushroomed all over Europe, catering for all tastes and purses. 1967 was declared International Tourist Year and the travel agencies' prospectuses grew in size and scope with every season; they covered international congresses of every possible description, festivals, exhibitions, *son et lumière*, pilgrimages, safaris in Africa, cheap excursions for music lovers, bachelors, senior citizens and children. Within a few years the stream of foreign visitors to Spain reached the 17 million mark and 27 million tourists were counted in Italy in 1966. Six to seven million visitors went to Switzerland, Austria, and Germany every year, and almost 12 million toured France, where rising prices acted as a brake on the rapid expansion of mass tourism. Spain and Italy were so much cheaper and for this reason, if for no other, tapped a larger share of this ever growing stream. The number of visitors from other continents was relatively small, but that too increased steeply: half a million Americans had come to Europe in 1955; by 1966 their number had trebled and there was a growing stream of visitors from Japan, Australia, and other distant places. Few Europeans, other than immigrants, went to the United States before the second world war; in 1966, 562,000 took the trip across the Atlantic.

The average European tourist spent less on his foreign holiday in this age of mass tourism than the well-to-do traveller in earlier periods; many of the visits that appeared in the statistics were day trips with no economic benefit for the host country but for the occasional cup of tea or coffee and the purchase of some souvenirs. At one stage or another Britain and France were forced to introduce severe currency restrictions on money spent on holidays abroad, and President Johnson called on his countrymen to spend their holidays in their native country to combat a persistent adverse payments balance. Despite these restrictions, foreign tourism became an economic factor of ever growing importance; the earnings from tourism in Austria rose from 2.6 per cent of the GNP in 1956 to 6.2 per cent in 1965, from 1.3 to 5.3 per cent in Spain during the same period and from 1.0 to 4.2 in Portugal. In absolute terms Italy had the highest surplus on tourism in 1966, with more than 2 billion dollars, followed by Spain with 1.5 billion. Tourists accounted for about 40 per cent of the visible and invisible foreign currency income of Spain, for roughly 10–20 per cent in Italy, Switzerland, and Austria. Germany was the biggest spender, leaving 1.5 billion dollars abroad, followed by France with 1 billion and the United Kingdom with 800 million dollars per year. Altogether total receipts from international tourism were estimated at about eight billion dollars in 1966, increasing at the average rate of about ten per cent per year.

Eastern Europe, which had been hermetically sealed off to foreign tourists during the Stalin era, gradually opened its borders during the late fifties. Czechoslovakia had 2.7 million foreign visitors, Hungary 1.6 million in 1966, and Rumania attracted hundreds of thousands of tourists to the Black Sea shores. Few Western visitors went to the Soviet Union, although the Black Sea coast and the Caucasus were great tourist attractions. Russia was still a far away country for most Europeans, and there were still too many restrictions on free movement; tourist facilities had been greatly expanded but they were, all other considerations apart, not remotely sufficient to absorb a mass invasion as in Spain, Italy, or even Yugoslavia.

The New Social Structures

The political and economic changes that have taken place in Europe since 1939 have deeply affected the nature of European society. There is however no unanimity about the significance of these developments, for long-term social trends are usually more difficult to assess and interpret than economic developments. Orthodox Marxists, with their traditional emphasis on the (relative) pauperisation of the working class, on the capitalists' rising profits, and on the sharpening class struggle, question whether there has been qualitative change. They had predicted the impending demise of the capitalist system and were unprepared for a long period of accelerated economic growth and visibly rising living standards. They had always put their hopes on the industrial working class as the main agent of social revolution, but with rapid technological change this class ceased to expand in the most developed countries. There were more jobs each year but not necessarily for manual workers; the decline in the number of coal miners has already been noted. Insufficient militancy among the workers had previously been explained as the result of general ideological backwardness, an inadequate class consciousness and the presence of a 'labour aristocracy'. These traditional explanations were found wanting in the postwar world; the changes in the vocabulary of the critics of society betrayed an awareness of social change as the 'establishment' and the 'military-industrial complex' replaced the 'ruling class', and the stress on the proletarian character of the revolutionary movement gradually diminished. The non-Marxists, on the other hand, emphasised that the character of the ownership of the means of production had radically changed since the heyday of *laissez-faire* capitalism, that economies were now mixed, that a new class of managers had emerged, that the tertiary (service) sector of the economy had grown much faster as an employer of labour than industry, that class differences had become blurred, and that everywhere the state engaged in the redistribution of the national income by means of progressive taxation and the welfare state. In between the two extremes, the total rejection of the established order and its more or less unqualified acceptance, there was a whole gamut of opinions.

About the statistical facts there was little dispute. Fewer Europeans were employed in agriculture every year; the industrial labour force was not expanding in the most developed countries; in Britain, Belgium, and Switzerland 46–47 per cent of the labour force was engaged in industrial production in 1910 and since then there have been only insignificant changes. In West Germany its share (including mining, construction, etc.) was 48 per cent in 1950 and remained at that level during the fifties and sixties. In the modern industries, such as engineering and chemicals, about one quarter of the industrial labour force is salaried, i.e. technical and administrative staff. In the industrially less developed countries such as Italy and Spain, on the other hand, the number of wage-earners in industry continues to rise. The percentage of women in the labour force rose in most European countries between 1945 and the middle sixties; it was the highest in the Soviet Union, Sweden, and Austria (50–60 per cent), much lower, but increasing, in the Mediterranean countries (20–35 per cent), and decreasing in Norway and France. The percentage of the self-employed declined in most countries, from 32 per cent in West Germany in 1950 to less than 20 per cent in 1964. The tertiary sector, the service industries, increased at the most rapid rate; the number of white-collar workers, including government employees, rose in West Germany in 1950–64 from 20 to 33 per cent. International comparisons are difficult as statistical definitions vary from country to country. In the more advanced European countries one third or more of the total labour force is now engaged in providing various services and the proportion is still rising. With technological progress there was a growing demand for skilled and semi-skilled workers, and the number of salaried employees in industry rose twice as fast as that of wage earners.

A consistently high rate of employment has been one of the main features of European postwar economic development. There was unemployment in the early postwar period; more than 1.5 million unemployed were counted in Germany and Italy in 1950. Italy, and to a lesser extent Belgium, were plagued during the fifties by a persistent unemployment problem, but almost all other European countries had by 1955 reached full or overfull employment. In 1964 Ireland still had an unemployment quota exceeding three per cent, but in Italy it had fallen to 2.4 per cent, and in Germany that year there were 16 unemployed for every 100 vacancies. There were fluctuations: the recession of 1966 caused a temporary increase in unemployment but within a few months it fell again and by late 1967 it was well below the full employment rate of two per cent in France and West Germany.

Another category of employees, the guest workers, became a factor of vital importance in the national economy of many European countries. There had been such migrants even before the first world war: Polish agricultural labourers, for instance, went for the harvest to East Germany, and thousands of Polish miners went temporarily or permanently to work in the coal mines of northern France. But the migration of the fifties and sixties was of a different magnitude. In Switzerland entire branches of the national economy, such as the building industry were taken over by the Italians; in 1958 about 17 per cent of the labour force was thought to be of foreign origin; ten years later their share had doubled, and this despite the efforts of the Swiss government to combat the danger of *Überfremdung* and to reduce the number of foreign workers by ten per cent. West Germany attracted about 1.3 million foreign workers (1965), there were 1.8 million in France, many of them semi-permanent, and hundreds of thousands of immigrants from the Commonwealth had settled in Britain. The guest workers in Germany came mainly from south Europe; Italians were the strongest contingent but there were also many Turks, Greeks, Yugoslavs, and Spaniards. Few of them intended to settle permanently in Germany. The guest workers in France came above all from North Africa and those in England from the Caribbean, India and Pakistan, many of them British citizens who could claim to be in England of right, not on sufferance. The presence of the guest workers was an economic necessity, but socially and politically it created major problems. There were language difficulties, they did not always enjoy equal social benefits, and during a recession they were likely to be the first to be dismissed. They took over entire quarters and suburbs in European cities, and there was friction with the local population. When Enoch Powell, a British Conservative leader, asked for voluntary repatriation in 1968, he had the leadership of the political parties and the whole establishment against him, but public opinion in the areas affected were largely on his side. The government of the day adopted stringent measures to restrict further immigration, which meant in some cases that holders of British passports were prevented from entering Britain.

The outward manifestations of rising living standards were all too obvious, but not all classes and groups of people benefited from the general prosperity to the same extent. Average living standards do not indicate the contrast between rich and poor, or between the urban and the rural population. The following figures are indicative of the general trend but leave a great many questions unanswered: real wages increased between 1953 and 1965 by approximately 36 per cent in the United Kingdom, by 58 per cent in France, 80 per cent in Italy, and 100 per cent in West Germany. In absolute terms wages were highest in 1964 in the Scandinavian countries (1.25–1.40 dollars per hour as compared with 2.00 dollars in the United States). In West Germany, the Netherlands and Switzerland the hourly wage was at the time roughly one dollar, but in France only 75 cents and in Italy 60 cents. Real hourly wages in West Germany in 1948 had been about as high as in 1914, 35 cents, but they trebled during the next 15 years. Since then the wage level has tended to become more uniform in the major European countries. Wages in light industries (textiles, food, shoes) have been consistently below the average, whereas printers, miners, and those employed in the growth industries were paid the highest wages. The wages of unskilled workers increased faster than those of their skilled and semi-skilled colleagues. Wages rose faster than prices which were relatively stable in the fifties; between 1955 and 1960 they rose by a mere seven to nine per cent in West Germany and Italy, whereas in France they increased by 35 per cent in the same period. During the next five years the general trend was much more uniform; West European prices rose by 20 per cent, with Germany and France slightly below the average, and the Italian figure up to 24 per cent.

This constant rise in real wages was the result of a steady increase in productivity. Productivity in Germany and Britain before the war was, roughly speaking, equal, but in the United States it was more than twice as high. Within Europe there were substantial differences, with the most developed industrial countries in the lead. Europe suffered from certain obvious disadvantages in comparison with America: a low level of investment, a limited market with its corollary of small-scale production and insufficient allocations for scientific and technological research. Nevertheless all European countries witnessed an unprecedented rise in labour productivity in the nineteen-fifties, partly as a result of technological improvement but mainly because of more efficient use of machinery and of the labour force.

GROWTH OF LABOUR PRODUCTIVITY 1949–59
(*compound annual percentage of growth*)

West Germany	5.7	Holland	3.6
Italy	4.8	Sweden	2.9
Austria	4.8	Belgium	2.7
France	4.3	United States	2.0
Spain	4.3	United Kingdom	1.8
Switzerland	3.7		

Despite this remarkable progress, the feeling grew in Europe in the sixties that there was a dangerous technology gap and that the old continent was falling behind the United States. While European productivity was approaching the American level in some traditional industries, the gap was clearly noticeable in the most modern (and most promising) fields of advanced technology such as automation, electronics, rocket research, etc. It manifested itself in the increasingly favourable American technological balance of payments (the royalties paid by Europeans for American patents), the expanding activities of leading American firms (such as IBM) in Europe, and, of course, the brain drain. America spent more than any European country on research and development (between 3 and 3.5 per cent of its GNP) in the nineteen-sixties, compared with 2.2 in Britain, roughly 1.3–1.6 in France and Germany, and less than one per cent in Italy. There are no reliable figures for Russia, but Soviet expenditure was believed to be between two and three per cent. In absolute terms the discrepancy was even more striking: American expenditure in 1962 was more than four times as big as that of Britain, France, and Germany combined. True, research in America is more expensive than in Europe, salaries there are higher, and a comparison of the manpower engaged in research and development was less unfavourable for Europe. The total personnel engaged in these operations in the USA in 1962 (1,580,000) was only about twice as high as in western Europe. In the Soviet Union it was almost as high as in the United States: over two-thirds of all the world's research and development scientists and engineers were concentrated in the sixties in these two countries. Superior working conditions and substantially higher salaries attracted many European scientists and technologists to the United States; during the late fifties it was only a small flow, about 1,300 persons between 1956 and 1961, but these included some of the most promising young graduates who had decided to join MIT, Caltech, or private industry. Their number increased in the sixties and eventually affected between 10–20 per cent of the science and technology graduates in Switzerland, Holland, the Scandinavian countries, and in certain critical fields also in Britain.

Trade Unions, Their Power and Their Problems

European trade unions have for over a century played an important role in defending the rights of the working class; after protracted struggles they gained universal recognition. By 1945 the struggle had been won and they became a powerful force on the social scene, whether supporting the government or in opposition although at times public opinion was antagonised. In the eyes of revolutionaries the trade union leaders were reformists, defenders of the establishment who had given up the struggle for a radical transformation of society; all they wanted were better conditions for their members within the present social order. In the view of the non-socialist critics, the ossified trade union bureaucracy, with its shortsighted, bigoted approach, constituted the major obstacle to modernisation, invariably putting the factional interests of their members above that of society as a whole.

In the European trade union movement the communists had two strong bases, the French CGT (which before 1940 had been close to the socialists) with 1.5 million members, and the Italian CGIL with 3.5 million members. These two were the strongest trade union movements in France and Italy. They had however to compete with sizeable minority groups (CFTD and CGT/FO in France and CISL and UIL in Italy) which were under socialist and Christian Democratic influences respectively. The British Trade Union Congress (TUC), close to the Labour Party, had about eight million members and was thus the strongest union movement in Europe; the German DGB followed with about 6.5 million members (1967). The communist trade union movements belonged to the Soviet controlled WFTU (International Confederation of Free Trade Unions). But these parent bodies exerted only a limited degree of control; the communist unions, for instance, did not approve the Soviet invasion of Czechoslovakia in 1968, much to the chagrin of the Soviet sponsors of the WFTU. The communist unions of western Europe displayed a great deal of militancy but were not really preparing for social revolution, as shown by the stabilising role played by the French CGT in the dramatic events of May-June 1968. France and Italy had a high incidence of strikes (higher in Italy than in France) but this had its roots in the general social climate of these countries, not in the beliefs and activities of union leaders. Strikes in England, which were only slightly less frequent than in France, had a more disruptive effect on the economy because so many of them were unofficial in character. In the British union movement the archaic concept of the craft union still prevailed and there were still hundreds of small unions, whereas in the United States, in West Germany, and in many other countries, workers were organised in big industrial units, such as the I.G. Metall in West Germany, uniting all workers in a given industry regardless of their job in the factory. British trade unionism was plagued by demarcation disputes and frequently a minor quarrel between two small unions paralysed a whole industry. There were some mass strikes in other European countries (for instance in Denmark in 1965, in Belgium and Sweden in 1966), but on the whole there was not much social unrest in the small European countries and even less in West Germany, where strikes were virtually unknown – though strike threats were not. The German union leaders were not less tough than their colleagues in France,

Italy, and Britain, and they were more successful in getting higher wages and better working conditions for their members; they were more aware that modernisation was inevitable and took a more positive attitude towards the introduction of automation in industry. Some of their colleagues in Britain and France, on the other hand, fought tooth and nail for the survival of crafts and methods of work that were antiquated and clearly wasteful. The Germans realised earlier that they had to adapt themselves to technological progress, and decided to run their own retraining schemes for their members.

Trade union leaders attained a much higher status than ever before; in Britain they were knighted, in Germany even the radicals among them became members of the supervisory councils of leading enterprises, in France and Italy their views were listened to with attention by the leaders of the state. But at the same time the limits of trade union power had become much clearer. The membership was not on the whole interested in political demonstrations; their attitude towards the unions was utilitarian; they needed them to defend their interests and to improve their conditions, but not as the chosen instrument to carry out their political demands.

The Managers

James Burnham in a book widely read during the second world war had drawn attention to the political implications of the emergence of a new class, the managers, who, he predicted, would gradually gain control over politics and the economy in both the communist and the Western world. In their extreme form these predictions have not materialised; the technocrats' influence has certainly grown but they are running neither the Soviet Union nor the leading Western countries. Economic decision-taking in France as in Britain, in Germany and in Italy, has passed from the traditional nineteenth-century *patron* or *Unternehmer* to the high civil servants in collaboration with the managers controlling all but a few big companies. These managers are employees; they do not own the companies they represent, but ownership itself has become far more complex, with the family business giving way to the anonymous company.

This was one of the new trends cutting across existing class divisions; whether it had a basic effect on the social structure, except for providing greater mobility, is still open to doubt. The managers are not strictly speaking a 'new class', certainly not in the classic Marxist concept of class, but since so much power has been concentrated in their hands, it seemed that a re-examination of the whole issue of the legal ownership of the means of production and its political significance was overdue. In a similar way the higher ranks of the civil service have gained a great deal of power, independent of class interests and pressure groups, however influential. This trend became even more pronounced as socialist governments came to power and whole industries were nationalised. No one in his right mind was likely to argue that class interests no longer mattered, but the whole issue had become far more complex. This applied not only to the new breed of managers and civil servants, but equally to a Churchill and de Gaulle, primarily concerned with the greatness of their native country; they subordinated economic and social considerations to this overriding concern.

In the Soviet Union, as in the West, important changes took place in the social structure, but not always in the direction foreseen by the founding fathers of the régime. The Soviet Union remains committed to the ideal of a classless society, the means of production are not privately owned, and capitalism has not been restored even though left-wing critics of Russian communism have for long predicted it. There still is a great deal of social mobility and the favoured social groups have no firm tenure or security. At the same time there are enormous differences in status, income, and above all in political power. Various theories, such as the concept of 'bureaucratic collectivism', have been applied to interpret the growing divergence between theory and reality. For in reality, while everyone was equal, some were clearly far more equal than others, with a spread of 20:1 in the range of salaries, an income tax maximum of 13 per cent, virtually no death duty and with growing emphasis on rank, insignia, hierarchy, and social differentiation. Political power is in the hands of a small ruling élite consisting of high party, government, and military officials; in the selection of these officials and in the shaping of the policies they pursue, the average Soviet citizen has little if any say. Under Stalin the trend towards social stratification was particularly marked; the old Tsarist system of uniforms and ranks returned with a vengeance. After Stalin's death Khrushchev tried to do away with the extremes of inequality. The high rate of economic growth has worked strongly in favour of upward mobility. As far as the goal of social equality is concerned, the Soviet Union ranks somewhere in the middle of the European scale; differences in income and status are clearly more pronounced there than in the Scandinavian countries, while the welfare services are less developed. On the other hand, Soviet society is obviously more egalitarian than the societies of south Europe with their extremes of incomes and property. Some observers have argued that with growing prosperity the distortions of the communist ideal would gradually disappear and the ruling élite would fade away. Such determinism, even in its most sophisticated version, ignores both the innate anti-democratic trends of modern industrial society and the desire of the ruling group to perpetuate its rule. More than any other European country, the Soviet Union seems to be subject to Michel's 'iron law of oligarchy'; instead of 'withering away', the state has become omnipresent and omnipotent, very much in contrast to Lenin's expectations; he wrote that so long as the state existed, a Marxist had no right to speak of freedom.

In western Europe the general development has been towards greater equality; wages and salaries have risen everywhere whereas income from property (interest, profits, rents) has fallen in Britain from 33 per cent before the war to 26 per cent of the national income, in France from 47 to 33 per cent, in Germany from 39 in 1950 to 30 per cent in 1963. These figures are only roughly approximate; millionaires, too, earn salaries, and workers and peasants on the other hand also have incomes from savings and rents. (It has been estimated that in Britain the working class accounts for two-thirds of all personal savings.) All industrialised European countries have introduced income policies to ensure a fairer distribution of income and property. These measures have however been more successful in achieving a more equitable distribution of earned income than property. It was estimated that in Britain in 1960 five per cent of the population still owned about 75 per cent of the total personal wealth, and there were still many ways and means of accumulating great wealth and loopholes for evading death duties. The concentration of personal property is decreasing, though slowly, as taxation gradually takes its toll. The redistribution of the national product of Europe in favour of the lower income groups has been more marked since 1945 than during any other period since the nineteenth century, but the continuing existence of so much unearned income and property has been a source of much resentment. Trade unionists have not as a rule taken kindly to the suggestion that they should pursue a policy of wage restraint while other (unearned) income was not affected by such restrictions.

Social goals in Europe after the second world war differed from those in America; there has been less public squalor in the midst of less private affluence. The welfare state has softened class divisions in European society but it has not done away with them; so far it has achieved only a modest redistribution of income. Social services have brought greater economic and social equality but there has been an inclination to belittle their effect; social reform came not in the wake of a great revolution but as the result of blueprints and administrative decisions. It came without sound and fury, there was no bloodshed and no great passions were aroused. There was no great wave of idealism and anti-climax such as usually happens in a revolution. For these reasons the postwar social reforms have not gripped the imagination of the masses; they were welcomed, taken for granted, but they did not arouse much enthusiasm. In the long run, however, it is not the commotion that counts but the enduring results and in this perspective the European welfare state with all its imperfections and limitations does not compare at all badly with the more spectacular and radical attempts to transform society in the twentieth century.

PART III

THE CULTURAL SCENE

The Postwar Climate

Philosophers and poets had pondered the idea of Europe during the darkest hours of the war and nazi oppression. By 1945 little was left of intellectual Europe; many universities were in ruins, leading scientists, writers, and artists had perished. After Hitler's rise to power there had been a large-scale exodus from Germany, and later on, to a lesser extent, from France and Italy, Austria and Hungary: writers and physicists, sociologists and art historians, painters and composers settled in the New World and made important contributions to the development of their disciplines and of intellectual life in general in the United States. In some nazi-occupied countries such as Poland the intelligentsia had been systematically exterminated. In the German universities entire disciplines such as sociology and psychology had been suppressed, while others had been reduced to a mere shadow existence. In Italy the hand of the dictatorship had been less heavy on cultural life; it had not invariably opposed modern art, and an intellectual opponent of the règime like Croce had been left more or less in peace. But not one outstanding Italian novel or film, musical or artistic creation had emerged: the climate of the dictatorship had not been congenial to the muses. Germany, Italy, and the occupied countries had been cut off for years from current trends in the outside world; a new generation had grown up in cultural isolation. Soviet Russia under Stalin had become a cultural wasteland and the worst was yet to come.

No one doubted that it would take a long time to overcome the cultural ravages of fascism, Stalinism, and war. The terror and the war had been an experience that had profoundly affected all those who had lived through them. Perhaps that would act as a powerful stimulus to a new cultural revival. But the experience had been too negative, the destruction too extensive. What inspiration could satirists draw from Auschwitz? As the war ended the shadow of mass destruction hung heavily over mankind. As one of the characters in Max Frisch's *The Chinese Wall* said: 'A slight whim on the part of the man on the throne, a nervous breakdown, a touch of neurosis, a flame struck by his madness, a moment of impatience on account of indigestion – and the jig is up. Everything! A cloud of yellow or brown ashes boiling up towards the heavens in the shape of a mushroom, a dirty cauliflower – and the rest is silence, radio-active silence.'

The prevailing mood as the last gun fell silent was one of anguish and helplessness. Human nature had been revealed in its basest aspects, and there was no certainty that there would not be an even more murderous repeat performance. But the hangover was not equally strongly felt in all countries; it did not hit them at exactly the same time and it did not manifest itself everywhere in the same way. How valid is it then to generalise about European intellectual life in the postwar period? There had always been common European currents and fashions transcending national borders, but no country was quite like another, and alongside similarities there were profound differences.

The economic, social, and moral climate of France after the liberation was one of impotence and despair: 'Everything seemed destined for failure in a country torn and disoriented, convinced that its future did not depend on itself' (Michel Crozier). But within this general prostration there was an intense and enthusiastic intellectual life whose exponents enjoyed a very wide audience; their dramatic differences of opinion were treated as events of national importance: 'They were prepared to involve themselves in politics, or at least in social criticism; they felt they were endowed with a mission and they sought by all available means to take part in action.'

Fifteen years later a totally different situation prevailed. Optimism had returned following the great economic advance, and the people as a whole had regained confidence in a society which no longer seemed doomed. But intellectual life had lost its fervour and distinction:

Labour leaders and politicians, and with them the scientists and the social scientists, talk of nothing but rates of growth and the necessity of planning, while the literary intelligentsia is immersed in problems of a very different kind, intellectual fashions around 1960 favour formalism and detachment. The intellectuals stand aside deliberately and refuse to interest themselves in the profound changes that are revolutionising social relations. At the same time they seem to have lost both their power to fascinate and their wide audience. Intellectual life continues to be active and passionate, but it is no longer in the foreground in anything like the way it once was (Crozier).

This description of the moral and intellectual climate of France after the war does not at all fit the British scene. The mood after 1945 was optimistic on that side of the channel, but there were few outstanding intellectual leaders, and they certainly did not have a wide audience. The wave of protest in England came only ten years later; it was not born of cosmic despair, nor of Orwell's dire forebodings. Orwell had written after the war that 'since about 1930 the world had given no reason for optimism whatsoever. Nothing in sight except a welter of lies, cruelty, hatred and ignorance. . . .' The protest of the angry young men had its roots in the boredom of the welfare state, the dissatisfaction with a far too rigid class structure, the disgust with the 'shiny barbarism' of mass culture.

In West Germany, following the experience of nazi rule and the postwar dislocation and uncertainties, it took a long time for any intellectual movement to develop. The literary avant-garde and some of the students constituted themselves a protest movement, but this became an event of national importance only in the middle sixties when student demonstrations hit the headlines. Some of the sources of this movement were specifically German, such as the protest against the conservative tendencies in German society, the complacency about the economic miracle. Others were part of the general European mood of boredom and the feeling of impotence; whatever the literary intelligentsia said or did, however shocking or revolutionary, it somehow seemed not to matter.

In Italy the intellectual climate resembled that of France in some respects but not in others, and the situation in countries that had been spared the ravages of war was again quite different. There was no common spiritual European denominator in 1945, and subsequent developments were not always on parallel lines. Sociologists noted a progressive Americanisation of European mass culture, but on a higher level of intellectual endeavour differences between Europe and America, and also often between the various European countries, became on the contrary more marked.

All over Europe the distance between the 'two cultures' widened. In science tremendous advances had been made during the war years which were now applied to civilian use: atomic energy, jet propulsion, radar, antibiotics. In medicine whole groups of new drugs for dealing with infectious and mental diseases came on the market; tuberculosis, once a dreaded killer, was all but stamped out. This was the beginning of a new era of organ transplantations, cardiac pacemakers, and cryosurgery. The bio-chemists established new fields such as molecular biology in their search for the secrets of the genetic code (DNA). Biological manipulation, for so long the preserve of science fiction, seemed now a distinct possibility. In other fields, such as space travel, science fiction was overtaken by the rapid advance of science: the invention of semi-conductors in 1948, of integrated circuits and lasers, the development of guidance and control systems and of data processing generated a new technological revolution. The role of the computer was compared to that of the steam engine in the nineteenth century; it was likely moreover to match or simulate many of man's intellectual capacities. Many of these new discoveries were made in Europe. It was a time of tremendous excitement among scientists and technologists; entirely new vistas opened up and they found themselves out of step with the mood of the literary intelligentsia. National frontiers mattered so much less to the physicist than to the writer or poet; he was less addicted to pessimism and *Weltschmerz* and, incidentally, less to anti-Americanism.

Economists, sociologists and political scientists, were in demand as advisers and consultants to government commissions, travelling abroad on behalf of national and international organisations, providing guidance to private business and public bodies. In various ways the critics of society were integrated, drawn into 'the system'. Many of them felt that with the old passions spent, the end of ideology was in sight. This left the literary intelligentsia, the writers and poets, the theologians and philosophers, as the only ones to fulfil what they thought of as the real mission of the intellectual; to be an outsider, to undertake a comprehensive critique of society, radically to reject existing conditions and to appeal to the conscience of mankind. This function they fulfilled with all the verve they could muster, but also all the traditional fondness for broad generalisations and the same contempt for hard facts which Tocqueville had noted a century earlier when writing about the *hommes de lettres* in the age of the French Revolution.

The story of the postwar-European *Zeitgeist* is largely the story of the moods and frustrations of the literary intelligentsia. The decay of prewar Europe as they saw it was now even more advanced; everything had become, as Moravia said, an imbroglio of lies. In the new philosophy being was without reason, without cause, without necessity. If human existence was unintelligible, so, very often, was the new art: the new drama concentrated on the more painful aspects of life, and conversation became often altogether unintelligible, an 'absurd noise'. Anxieties and obsessions, crime and guilt, sickness and insanity, torture and the collapse of morals, became the central topics of the contemporary novel, the avant-garde play and film. To describe them was thought to have a cathartic effect, to be the best cure. In this general reaction against nineteenth-century optimism even theologians preached that religion was torment, not peace; malady, not health; it did not mark the road to salvation but revealed the whole problematic character of existence. It was not a comforting picture, and the politics of the men of letters were not surprisingly those of radical protest. The protest did not always follow from their philosophy, for despair does not necessarily breed activism. The protest was the expression of a mood, not a logical conclusion.

How deep was this postwar despair? In part no doubt it was a fashionable and highly marketable *Weltschmerz*. As material conditions improved and the economic miracle got under way, the public seemed positively to relish the joyless plays, novels, and films. In part it was genuine, especially during the early postwar years. There is a world of difference between the stark horror and pessimism of that time and the fashionable *ennui*, and *noia* of the late fifties. But the despair of the man of letters had more specific origins: he realised with bewilderment that his universe had become an unsolvable mystery; the separation of culture and scientific knowledge had become almost complete in a world of progressive specialisation. The scientists had made tremendous progress and gained great prestige as a class. To what comparable achievements could poets and composers point, or philosophers and theologians? It was only too tempting in this situation to question the value of scientific advance; what good was it to mankind if so much of it was devoted to inventing and perfecting means to destroy civilisation and human life? The man of letters and the artist felt isolated in this absurd world. The radical departures from tradition in modern art were rejected by a public which preferred the Beatles to stochastic music, *My Fair Lady* to both the theatre of the absurd and kitchen sink drama, and Brigitte Bardot to Ingmar Bergman. The marital affairs of Queen Soraya and Queen Fabiola, not to mention Aly Khan, continued to preoccupy the millions, the ideas of Lukacs and Ernst Bloch only a few thousand. The revolutionaries were now talking in a language which only the avant-garde could understand. Alienation became the favourite and often misused catchword of the literary intelligentsia, which refused to look for a place in a world that seemed both hopeless and senseless. A great many prophets of doom raised their voices and found an enthusiastic public.

With all this the literary intelligentsia had by no means altogether lost their importance as opinion makers and moulders of the *Zeitgeist*. New media of mass communication developed, above all television, brash, vulgar, and all-pervasive. After initial violent opposition to this most recent and, many thought, most pernicious form of mass culture, the literary intelligentsia was drawn in and through it reached a much wider public than ever before for their works and ideas.

The widening of the gulf between the intellectuals and the rest of society, the radical protest against the 'establishment', the increasing distance between the man of letters and the artistic avant-garde on the one hand, and the social and natural scientists on the other, were phenomena common to many countries as the capitals of Europe moved nearer to each other. Before the second world war a trip abroad was considered a luxury, a preserve of the affluent. By the early sixties it became almost the exception to find high school graduates who had not visited one or more foreign countries, often for a lengthy period. National frontiers mattered less than at any time. German philosophy triumphed in France after the war, Kafka and Brecht were discovered in Paris and London, Italian films had a profound impact on the cinema throughout the continent. Music and theatre festivals at Salzburg, Bayreuth, or Edinburgh brought leading composers and critics together each year. Boulez found more congenial surroundings for his work in West Germany, Stockhausen was equally at home in France or Germany. The Italian composers Berio and Nono, were fêted in England as much as in their native country. Among the pioneers of the new style in French painting Hartung and Wols were German by origin, de Stael and Lanskoy Russian; Zak was Polish, Vasarely Hungarian, Michaux Belgian. Cross currents and cross fertilisation could be observed in every field: successful novels were translated into foreign languages within a few weeks; hit songs spread within days to the farthest corner of Europe. Movies and TV programmes steeped in local colour were shown all over the continent; millions of Czech citizens watched with bated breath the incredible adventures of that improbable German hero of the Wild West, Old Shatterhand; millions of Poles followed with breathless tension the successes and failures of Dr Finlay, the Scots country physician. The impact of American civilisation was felt even in France, jealously guarding its cultural independence. It is impossible to explain French postwar literature without reference to Faulkner and Hemingway, and by 1960 the French language itself had been so corrupted that there was an out-cry against that new bastard lingo, 'Franglais'. It was not, of course, a one-way traffic, for every European intellectual current and fashion, from Existentialism to the mini-skirt, was eagerly absorbed in the United States.

Some of these currents were mere seven-day wonders, others had a lasting effect. Psychoanalysis profoundly influenced European thought. The significance of the work of Sigmund Freud, who died in 1939, had been realised before the war by a small circle of devoted followers in Germany; in his native Austria he was virtually ignored. There was a handful of disciples in other European countries, but academic psychiatry had rejected psychoanalysis and few others had anything but a vague notion about the super ego, transference and the Oedipus complex. During the nazi era, psychoanalysis was banned as a ferment of decomposition; in the Soviet Union and postwar eastern Europe it was considered a counter-revolutionary trend, and the catholic church, too, vehemently denounced it. The prospects of psychoanalysis at the time seemed very dim indeed, yet after the war, having become firmly rooted in the United States, it was rediscovered in Europe and enjoyed a great revival. Its impact in the medical field was not so strong as its indirect influence on education, literature, and the arts.

More pervasive still was the impact of Marxism. There had been Marxist parties in Europe for almost a century, some of them fairly strong; but amongst the intelligentsia Marxism had not made great strides before 1945, except perhaps in Weimar Germany and among some east European and Viennese intellectuals. This changed after the war: many French and Italian intellectuals were attracted by Marxist ideas; the prewar polemics between little groups of *cognoscenti* about class consciousness, imperialism and dialectics of nature, were rediscovered and eagerly refought. Even among the British, the traditional empiricists and enemies of philosophical speculation, Marxism found some fervent advocates. As a rule it was not Marxism in its simplified Russian form, which in the European context seemed too crude and unsophisticated; nor was it the traditional orthodox Marxism of Karl Kautsky, which was too pedantic and uninspiring. European intellectuals were more interested in the ideas of the young Marx on alienation than in his economic doctrines. Lenin and Stalin were less eagerly studied than the intellectual deviationists such as the Italian Gramsci or the German Karl Korsch. Lukacs, the Hungarian communist who had quarrelled with the Russians in the nineteen-twenties about the function of class consciousness, had a remarkable revival after the war; so, within more modest limits, did Ernst Bloch, who on a Marxist basis had developed an unmaterialist philosophy of hope. In France and Italy native schools of Marxist thought developed; much of this was devoted to the exegesis of the master rather than to innovation. Even nonconformist Marxists such as Lucien Goldmann or Althusser did not venture far beyond the ideas that had their origins in Germany, Holland, and Austria between the two world wars. At the end of the fifties the interest in Marxism abated somewhat; the new radicalism of the sixties had different sources. The war in Vietnam acted as a catalyst for a protest movement which was more often anarchist, pacifist or utopian-socialist than Marxist in character. The new rebels had few illusions about the role of the proletariat as an agent of revolution; the workers, they maintained, had been corrupted by the welfare state and absorbed into neo-capitalist society; fresh impulses towards radical change could emanate only from among the young, especially the students, and their natural allies, the 'damned of the earth', the down-trodden, exploited masses of the under-developed countries. The new revolutionary movement of the sixties was élitist and anti-liberal in character, and while it did not reject the Marxist heritage altogether, its real roots were not dissimilar to those of earlier youth movements in Europe before and after the first world war – romantic protest against society and its conventions, in which cultural pessimism and boredom were mixed with an awakened social conscience. In part the new youth movement was rational and political in character, in part it was an irrational manifestation of a new malaise of post-industrial society, a rebellion without a cause, rejection without an alternative programme, and a repudiation of what was without a vision of what should be.

The Great Confrontation

The great confrontation among intellectuals in the late forties and fifties was between communism and its critics. It is not easy in retrospect to understand its intensity or the passion that went into it. The popularity of communism was mainly due, as Georges Bernanos said, to the shortcomings of western societies and the moral default of those who should have stood for spiritual values; young intellectuals became communists in the same way as young priests and young nobles in the eighteenth century had been enraptured by by the Social Contract and Jean Jacques Rousseau. They were disturbed by the injustices of western society; the direct impact of the Soviet Union (of which hardly anyone had first hand knowledge) was relatively slight. In France and Italy communism appeared as the legitimate heir of the resistance movement, the one most likely to realise its dreams and aspirations. Guilt feelings played an important role; of those in Italy who had been fascist fellow travellers as young men or those in France who had refrained from active involvement in the resistance, many now became zealous converts to communism. Their position was not enviable as the cold war unfolded: the communist intellectuals had to defend the policies of Stalinism which became progressively more irrational and indefensible. Communism was then in its most belligerent mood and became more and more isolated. At one stage or another every single communist intellectual was bound to have doubts about the infallibility of the party, but many hesitated for a long time to express any critical view, for they felt that by voicing doubts they would not merely put themselves outside the party but in fact join the class enemy, reaction and fascism. Robert Debreuilh in Simone de Beauvoir's *Mandarins* knew about the existence of forced labour camps in the Soviet Union but refused to talk or write about them; it would be 'tantamount to working against mankind'. This then was the typical dilemma of the fellow-travelling intellectual of the late nineteen-forties; whatever its current difficulties, communism was not only basically true, it was also the wave of the future.

There was a great deal of confusion and fear among all classes of the population after the Prague coup and the outbreak of the Korean war, when Soviet occupation of western Europe seemed a distinct possibility. Communists in France and Italy at that time dominated the writers and artists associations, calling on fellow artists and writers not merely to protest against American agression in Korea, or to sign manifestos for world peace, but to condemn 'Judas' Tito and the many other wreckers and criminals who were so suddenly and implausibly uncovered in the socialist countries of the East. This was the age of the big cultural congresses (Wroclaw 1948, Paris and Prague in 1949); Fadeyev, addressing the Wroclaw Congress of Intellectuals, declared that 'if hyenas could use fountain pens and jackals could use typewriters they would write like T.S.Eliot'. The World Peace Council claimed 550 million signatures to its appeal – not all, admittedly, intellectuals; Picasso and Joliot-Curie, Neruda and Laxness, Yves Montand, Gerard Philippe, Simone Signoret, and the Dean of Canterbury were among the many enthusiastic supporters.

The communist campaign was bound to provoke resistance among some sections of the intelligentsia. It was not likely to clash with believing Christians for with them it had no common language. Right-wing intellectuals, with a few exceptions, had been discredited during the war. The counter movement originated among left-wing intellectuals, not a few of them ex-communists. David Rousset,who with Sartre and Camus had helped to found a new left-wing party in Paris, appealed in November 1949 to all former fellow deportees to nazi Germany to support an investigation into conditions in Soviet con-centration camps. The communist reaction was predictable, but Sartre and many other fellow travellers also turned against Rousset: 'With whom are you – with the people of the Soviet Union, building a new society, or with their enemies?' But more and more intellectuals began to raise their voices in defence of freedom of culture and rival cultural congresses were arranged. The communist leadership in the writers' and artists' associations was challenged, new literary magazines came into being. Each fresh wave of repression in the East caused new defections among the pro-communist intellectuals. The Soviet campaign against Tito, the trials and death sentences in eastern Europe, the increasing repression during Stalin's last years, made it more and more difficult for an intellectual to defend communism with an untroubled conscience. After Hungary, and especially after Khrushchev's famous 'secret speech', it became obvious who had been right, in the quarrels between communist and anti-communist intellectuals during the first decade after the war, about the real situation in the Soviet Union.

There has been a temptation to belittle in retrospect the part of those who had defended cultural freedom when it was under attack. By accepting American help they exposed themselves to criticism once the cold war abated ; by concentrating on the confrontation with communism they were bound to lose sight of other injustices and causes of support. There were apocalyptic visionaries among them who ignored the possibility that communism, too, might one day change. But, in the last resort, Stalinism was a greater threat to the cultural values of the West than Franco or Salazar, and it demanded both more foresight and courage to stand up and be counted at that time of peril than to stay neutral. In later years critics claimed that the Stalinist danger had been mythical and that the cold war had been largely the crea-tion of the intellectual cold warriors who had strayed from the real vocation of the intellectual, which was to be a critic of his own society and an enemy of his government; by betraying their true mission the intellectuals defending cultural freedom had committed a new *trahison des clercs*. The anti-Stalinist intellectuals were not easily forgiven for being right.

After 1956 the thaw set in and within narrow limits cultural exchanges between West and East got under way. Some Western films were shown in Moscow, a few musicians and orchestras were exchanged, Soviet and Western scientists met at international congresses. These meetings were friendly, often cordial, but they had no great effect, for Soviet policy did not envisage coexistence in the ideological field. Moscow continued to oppose the free circulation of ideas in the East; it welcomed books on science and technology, Shakespeare, Cervantes, Balzac, and Goethe, but, as before, banned most modern writings. Western modern art, history, sociology, philosophy, economics and psychology were incompatible with Soviet ideology and therefore harmful. The cultural exchanges had nevertheless a considerable indirect impact on the younger generation in the Soviet Union, and even more in the Popular Democracies, which were more receptive to European ideas. Beyond the official condemnations, Soviet intellectuals remained acutely aware of their European heritage; they wanted to be part of Europe and to be accepted in the West as well as in their own country. The intelligentsia in the Soviet Union and east Europe fostered revolutionary ideas and thus came into conflict with the conservative elements in communist society, above all in the party leadership which, correctly from their point of view, regarded the criticism of the intellectuals as a menace undermining their authority.

Modernism and the Church

Far-reaching changes took place in the Catholic church in the late nineteen-fifties. The first stirrings of the reform movement came immediately after the war when a group of left-wing French Catholics tried to win the working class back to the faith. The worker-priests had decided to share the proletarian existence of their flock; they took jobs involving heavy manual labour, joined communist-sponsored trade unions, took part in communist demonstrations. It was their deep conviction that the place of the church was with the masses; it was not for the church to defend the propertied classes and the status quo. In their endeavour to be 'with the proletarian masses' they provoked the ire of their clerical superiors and sometimes went too far for their own good; better trained in theology than in political doctrine, and anxious to be totally identified with the masses, they accepted ideological tenets that could not be reconciled with the teachings of the church, however liberally interpreted. On instructions from above, the recruitment of worker-priests was stopped in 1951, and in 1959 their activities ceased altogether. It was a small movement embracing at its height not more than a hundred priests, but it attracted attention far beyond France as a genuine attempt to liberalise the church, to open it to fresh influences, to change its official character as a pillar of society.

Protestant theological reform preceded the Catholic movement. There was a liturgical movement trying to clarify and simplify prayer and the meaning of religious rites. Theologians such as the German Rudolf Bultmann advocated a de-mythologisation of the world of the New Testament; the belief in demons or in Assumption could no longer be accepted. It was not an easy undertaking and not free of danger, for what would remain of the Kerygma and of the church itself after the demolition of primitive myth? Among British churchmen even more radical changes were suggested and discussed, though not generally accepted. The Catholic church was traditionally more unbending than the Protestant churches in doctrine, though not always in practice. Among Catholics there was a great deal of uneasiness, a feeling of crisis; the attacks on Pope Pius xi for his silence and inactivity during the war had probably harmed the church less than the feeling that it lacked orientation and that its message was no longer heard because it had become irrelevant to the problems of the modern world. When Angelo Roncalli became Pope John xxiii in 1958 he adopted a policy of *aggiornamento*, introducing sweeping reforms that almost amounted to a revolution. A man of humble origin, he had known poverty in his childhood; during his diplomatic missions in the Balkans and as Papal Nuncio in France he had become far more aware than most of his conservative colleagues in the Italian Curia that the church needed to adapt itself to modern social and political developments. Unlike them, he was not afraid of change; during his relatively short term of office more changes were introduced than in preceding centuries. The encyclical *Mater et Magistra* revolutionised the social teachings of the church; *Pacem in Terris* was the first Papal message addressed not only to Catholics but to all men of goodwill, and it opened a new era of dialogue. Above all, after only three months in office, John xxiii announced his intention of convoking an Ecumenical Council, the third in the history of the church since the Council of Trent in the sixteenth century. After several years of preparation the Council opened in October 1962, and in its four sessions which lasted till December 1965 ranged over a wide field of church doctrine and organisation, covering relations with other religions, the function of bishops and priests and the place of the laity in the work of the church. During the first session of Vatican ii (as the Council was called) the progressives with their strongholds in western Europe and America realised, somewhat to their surprise, that they constituted a majority. During the interval between the sessions the Roman Curia with its conservative supporters in Spain and some other countries staged a counter offensive. John xxiii died in 1963, and it was generally assumed that his successor, Paul vi, formerly Cardinal Montini, would follow a more conservative line and leave less freedom to the Council than his predecessor. Paul vi had been Archbishop of Milan, one of Italy's main working-class centres. Although less of a reformer than John, he seemed intellectually aware that the changes initiated by his predecessor had been overdue. Part of the legacy of John he made his own, telling the Curia that it had to adapt to its new functions and calling for a removal of the barriers separating the Christian churches. Paul's visit to Constantinople and Jerusalem, where he met the leaders of the Eastern churches, was an unprecedented step towards ecumenism, the realization of Christian unity. Many bones of contention remained: Protestants argued that there could be no meaningful dialogue until the Vatican retreated on such basic issues as Papal infallibility and its attitude towards mixed marriages. Meanwhile the conservatives under Cardinal Ottaviani succeeded in slowing down the movement for reform; the declarations on religious liberty and the Jews (absolving them of deicide) were watered down. But at the same time the powers of the Supreme Congregation of the Holy Office (the Curia) were limited; they could no longer condemn a heterodox author without giving him the right to defend himself. The guardians of theological orthodoxy found themselves in a minority, and if one of their leaders was asked to formulate a new church policy on birth control, this was interpreted not as a victory for them but as a stroke of diplomatic genius on the part of the Pope, casting the orthodox in the role of midwives presiding over the labour of reform (Xavier Rynne). This prediction failed to come true, for in the end the Pope himself came out unambiguously against birth control. Despite this grave setback to the liberal forces the movement for reform continued. In the words of Cardinal Bea, Vatican II marked the end of the Counter Reformation. The Pope in an interview after the end of the Council added: '. . . will everything go back to what it was before? Appearances and customs say Yes, but the spirit of the Council says No.' The church would move slowly and cautiously as it always did, but the door that had been opened would never be closed again. Above all, the *aggiornamento* had extended the limits of Catholic 'polycentrism', making it possible for the bolder spirits within the church to follow their own policy without constant fear of official rebuke and disavowal. The decision in 1966 to renew (under close supervision) the worker-priest experiment in France was one such straw in the wind.

The Knowledge Revolution

The qualitative changes in European intellectual life after the second world war are not easy to measure; the confrontations and polemics of the nineteenth century had not been dissimilar, but the exchanges after the war certainly affected many more people than ever before. European intellectual life up to the nineteenth century had been the preserve of a small section of the population where, figuratively speaking, everyone knew everyone else. It had been almost entirely confined to the main cultural centres such as Paris, London, Rome and a few other places. These were still the main centres of European intellectual life, but by 1960 there were in addition a great many people all over the continent who were interested and took an active part.

After the war came the paperback revolution and the long-playing record, highbrow radio channels and educational television. The beginnings of the paperback can be traced further back: Penguin in England began to publish in the thirties; Reclam in Germany had already been functioning for many decades. But after 1945 the sales figures of books and records shot up as never before. Nor was it all a consumers' culture; more people wrote, painted, composed, and performed music than ever before. The number of scientists alive in 1960 exceeded that of all scientists that had ever lived over the centuries. New universities came into being – Nanterre in France, Bochum and Konstanz in Germany, Sussex, Essex, East Anglia, Surrey and Kent in England. Many more were planned, but the universities, too, had become big business and there was not sufficient money to carry out all projects. University enrolment almost trebled in France, Italy, and Britain between 1938 and 1960, and went up by more than half in West Germany. In the smaller European countries the rise was even more spectacular: the number of students in Sweden and Belgium quadrupled in comparison with the years before the war, in Holland there were more than a 100,000 students in 1960 compared with fewer than 10,000 before 1940. Since the establishment of new universities did not keep pace with the growing enrolment, most of the students had to be absorbed in the existing institutions of higher learning; the average number of students at European universities increased considerably during these years and the largest, such as the Sorbonne, counted almost 100,000, and more than 60,000 students were registered at Rome. Classes swelled to enormous size, teachers hardly came into personal contact with their students and there were no lecture halls big enough to accommodate crowds of this magnitude. The student protests in the nineteen-sixties were partly the outcome of this hypertrophy of the university and the resulting shortcomings in higher education. Around 1960 university study became virtually free in both Britain and Scandinavia, while the fees that had to be paid in most other European countries were small. The percentage of students of working-class origin increased but was still relatively low; everywhere in western Europe there was a preponderance of male students; only in Sweden was the numerical relation between the sexes (by 1960) very nearly even. There was a great influx of foreign students, above all from other European countries, but also from Asia and Africa. They constituted about

10 per cent of the student body in England and France, almost 30 per cent in Switzerland and, surprisingly, also in Austria. (In a few universities such as Geneva the majority of students consisted of foreigners.) More European students than ever before went to the United States for their post-graduate work. But it was not a one way traffic, for thousands of American students came to Europe, and several American universities established permanent campuses on the old continent.

All this was indicative of the general expansion in higher education, but the percentage of students was still small in comparison with both the United States and the Soviet Union; it was lowest in England among the major European countries. The results were felt in science and technology: western Europe, with a population larger than the United States or the Soviet Union, produced in the nineteen-sixties 47,000 science and technology graduates in comparison with 88,000 in the United States and 140,000 in the USSR.

Educational Reform

Changes took place in the university curriculum: the importance of classical studies declined as new disciplines were introduced, but it was not easy to change the basic structure of university education. Jealously guarding traditions and privileges, the universities were slow to adapt themselves to social and economic change. The Europeanisation of higher education made little progress, although a convention about the equivalence of diplomas leading to university admission was adopted. School reform was equally urgent and was given greater priority after 1945. Before the war selection for secondary education had taken place very early, usually before the age of 11, and the majority of school children had no chance of a secondary education. During the postwar period all European countries adopted new laws providing for the extension of compulsory education up to the age of 16 in France, parts of Germany and Switzerland, 14–15 in most other countries, with Spain, Greece, and Turkey lagging behind. At the same time most countries decided to extend comprehensive education and delay selection and differentiation. Sweden established a nine-year comprehensive school; in France, following the recommendations of the Langevin-Wallon committee, a post-primary *école unique* covering the ages from 11 to 15 was introduced. About specialisation this committee said in its report that the training of the specialist must not jeopardise the development of the man. The general tendency in European educational policies was towards democratisation but the good intentions of the planners were frequently defeated by demographic and economic facts. The number of school-age children increased rapidly as a result of the postwar baby boom. Secondary school enrolment in France, Holland, and Belgium was twice as high in 1960 as ten years previously; in Italy the increase was probably even higher; it quadrupled in Turkey, and in England and West Germany it grew by more than 50 per cent. These pressures frequently delayed the reforms; in Britain, where legislation had already been passed raising the school leaving age to 16, the realisation of the scheme had to be postponed indefinitely for lack of funds. In many European countries there was an acute shortage of school buildings and equipment; teaching was in two, sometimes three shifts.

Beyond the harassing problems of absorption there remained the basic question of 'education for what'. There was all over Europe a distinct trend away from the arts and the German tradition of liberal education (the Humboldt model), which had aimed at promoting an all-round culture. Vocational, in particular scientific studies, became more attractive to a growing number of students, but in the opinion of many scientists the science teaching in schools was still woefully insufficient as a preparation for the universities and the gap continued to grow. At the same time there was the danger that progressive specialisation would perpetuate and widen the gulf between the 'two cultures'; science and vocational training would produce specialists, not men with a sound, well-rounded general education. The importance of education continued to grow, and by 1960 it was commonly accepted that it was everywhere part of the productive forces of the country, and a very essential part at that.

Science and Technology

During the two decades from 1945 to 1965 immense progress was made in science and technology. In the nineteenth century, and indeed well into the twentieth, the great discoveries had often been the result of the sudden inspiration of lonely geniuses. But after the first world war, and to an even greater extent after the second, science and technology became more and more complex, costly, and institutionalised, and teamwork spread widely. European governments fully recognised the importance of scientific and technological organisation: in France a minister-delegate for scientific research was appointed in 1958, in West Germany a federal Ministry of

Scientific Research was established in 1962, and Britain set up a Ministry of Technology in 1964 in addition to the existing Ministry of Education and Science. In Sweden and Belgium science policy councils were set up directly under the Prime Minister. Britain and West Germany spent about two per cent of their Gross National Product on scientific research. These were decisions of vital importance, since private institutions in Europe, such as big firms and foundations, could not support research to the same extent as in the United States. Without massive state support there was the danger that the scientific and technological gap between America and Europe which had opened in the thirties and forties would grow wider. A divided Europe could not support the massive and specialised scientific activities that were becoming an essential precondition of progress in certain fields, first on a modest basis: CERN, the European Centre for Nuclear Research, was founded in 1953, and also Euratom, which set up reactors in Norway and Britain and coordinated national research programmes. ESRO (the European Space Research Organisation) was founded in 1964; ELDO specialised in space vehicles, working on a three-stage rocket called Europe I. There were joint ventures in the development of new types of aircraft (France and Britain cooperated on the Concorde); and mergers in the chemical industry (Agfa–Gevaert) created bigger units and thus a broader basis for technological development. But a divided Europe still found it difficult to compete with America. While important progress continued to be made in Europe (such as the advances in bio-chemistry and molecular biology in France and England), the American lead in space and aircraft research, in computers and other components of the second industrial revolution, became almost unassailable. Many European scientists and technologists (and often the best among them) migrated to the United States. Of those who joined the brain drain some were attracted by better laboratories and research conditions, others by higher salaries; often it was a combination of these and other factors.

The Soviet Union gave high priority to nuclear research; the first Soviet A bomb was exploded in 1949, a thermonuclear device in 1953. Equal attention was paid to the development of missiles: Sputnik I on October 1957 inaugurated a new age of space exploration; it was followed by Sputnik II in which Laika, a dog, circled the earth. Major Gagarin's flight in Vostok I (12 April 1961) heralded the progress from two to three dimensional geography. After Luna 9 and the American Surveyor I had soft-landed on the moon in 1966, it took the Americans just three more years to land their cosmonauts on the moon. That these advances had direct military implications goes without saying; the fact that since 1957 the Soviet Union had a global delivery system and intercontinental ballistic missiles (ICBM) revolutionised the world balance of power. Britain, it should be added, carried out its first nuclear test in 1952, and France in 1960.

These scientific and technological achievements were not isolated break-throughs; there was progress along the whole front. Among scientists the conviction grew that within a few decades they had contributed more to the development and wellbeing of mankind than all the arts and literatures over many centuries. For scientific and technological progress had immediate consequences; it lessened the domination of nature over man and made it possible for man to develop his own environment; manual work was gradually replaced in industry and agriculture as automation continued to progress, and a shorter working week left more time for leisure than ever before. Science and technology made life easier and improved man's physical health. It did not necessarily create a paradise on earth nor did it add to his content-ment. Science, it was said, was neutral; it merely opened up new doors but did not compel man to pass through them. In practice this fine distinction between scientific discoveries on the one hand and their social application and consequences on the other was not very meaningful, for mankind was irres-istibly drawn to adopt new inventions and techniques. Automation dis-placed workers who had to be retrained. Cybernetics necessitated state supervision and planning to a far greater degree than ever before in a democratic society; decision making became more and more complicated and thus raised vital questions: how could democracy survive if so many important decisions depended on specialised information which only a few could have? Advances in the life sciences, such as the transplantation of vital organs and genetic manipulation, raised basic moral issues for which medical ethics were ill-prepared.

Science and technology had always transcended national frontiers; in the twentieth century they became truly international in character. The 'German' mathematics and physics produced by some overzealous scientists in the Third Reich and similar efforts in Stalinist Russia were of short duration and subsequently became the occasion for much hilarity. Most German and Russian scientists had never believed that there was or could be a specifically national scientific discipline. In literature and the arts on the other hand, in the social sciences and the humanities, national traditions and character continued to play a far more important role despite all the inter-national cross currents and the greater mobility. There were still great differences between the quality of life in the countries of Europe; the con-tinuing division into nation-states was reflected in the differences in intellec-tual climate. From a European overview we shall have to turn next therefore to a review of cultural developments inside the major countries.

French Existentialism

Intellectually France was the most exciting country in Europe after the war; there existentialism emerged as the philosophy of the day. Jean-Paul Sartre, its high priest, was 40; he had studied German philosophy and been profoundly influenced by Husserl and Heidegger. A philosophy at the same time pessimistic and activist, existentialism maintained that man was essentially what he made of himself, and that his existence preceded his essence. The world was not by itself intelligible; it was up to man (and man alone) to choose a meaning for his life, and for the world in general. There was no room for religion or any other metaphysical scheme in this philosophy; in Sartre's view God and Reason had disappeared from the world in the twentieth century. His philosophy was one of freedom and choice, leading man beyond despair; it was to save mankind from the basic absurdity of life and the lack of purpose by *engagement* and the cult of action. Under the impact of the war and the influence of Marxism, existentialism, originally a highly individualistic philosophy, stood for the radical transformation of bourgeois society. Sartre had described the moral decay of this society in his first novels, but he was then still a passive onlooker. During the war existentialism became activist, politically engaged on the extreme left and quite influential much to the surprise of contemporary observers. For existentialist philosophy had been held and discussed in Germany for many years, but had not assumed a political character. The political engagement of the French existentialists did not necessarily follow from their philosophy. Their great success has to be explained largely by extraneous factors, such as the style of the new movement, the charm exerted by Sartre, its chief spokesman, the literary grace of its exponents, the combination of a non-Marxist philosophy and a revolutionary programme. The existentialists were obviously on better terms with the *Zeitgeist* than any other philosophical school.

In October 1945 the first issue of Sartre's journal *Les Temps Modernes* appeared; soon after the RDR, a political action group, was founded by Sartre and his friends. The RDR disintegrated after a short while, when one of its leading members raised the issue of Soviet concentration camps. Sartre did not deny their existence but refused to be drawn into adopting a 'counter-revolutionary position'. One of his colleagues, Maurice Merleau-Ponty, even justified the Moscow trials; he admitted that the charges had been false, but this was of no consequence since Stalin's justice was the justice of the future; the accusers were talking in the name of a universal history not yet achieved. Reasoning in a similar way, Sartre argued that the Communist party of France ought to be judged not by its actions but by its prospects. He criticised the working class, once the chosen instrument of Marxism; if the working class occasionally refused to follow the communist lead, this did not imply that the party was wrong; it meant that the proletariat was confused and corrupted by bourgeois influences. Sartre was in some ways more communist than the communists themselves; in his long and chequered relationship with the party he often found himself closest to them when the communists were isolated from the masses, as during Stalin's last years.

The political philosophy of existentialism was both uncertain and inconsistent. Sartre had not been personally involved in the resistance movement and his plays were produced under the German occupation; yet after the war the mystique of the Resistance pervaded all his writings. He gave political support to communism but rejected its philosophy until 1960, when he recognised that existentialism was no more than an ideology, whereas Marxism was the most advanced and comprehensive philosophy of the age. But the communists could still not accept his insistence that being was without reason, without cause, and without necessity. Existentialist humanism, the thesis that man's relationship to others was essential to him (with sex as the main proof) was not compatible with communism, however liberally interpreted. Sartre sincerely believed that Russia under Stalin was moving towards full freedom of criticism, but later he supported the Hungarian revolution in 1956 against its opponents. He expected America to go fascist and launch a nuclear war, and de Gaulle was for him for many years a symbol of the most reactionary trends in a decaying bourgeois society.

The basic weakness of these manifestations of political protest was their abstract character. Sartre and his friends were usually less interested in the real facts and merits of a case than in the correct position to be taken by the intellectuals. The correct intellectual position being one of protest, it was absolutely essential never to criticise communism from the outside. Sartre's literary brilliance could not cover the inherent weakness of such a position in which facts hardly mattered, which was detached from life and became more and more romantic and indeed, metaphysical. The existentialists expressed growing contempt for the French working class which under the impact of the welfare state and the mass society was beginning to shed its proletarian character. With the widening of the gap in the West between 'revolutionary intellectuals' and 'passive masses', the existentialists felt far more enthusiastic about the revolutionary potential of the third world. Following his disciple Frantz Fanon, Sartre expected that Algeria after its liberation would establish a revolutionary socialist régime that would be a beacon of hope for all mankind. When these hopes faded too he transferred his expectations to Castro's Cuba, a country in which he found that his dreams about the coexistence of Marxism-Leninism, spontaneity, and avant-garde art and literature, had at last come true.

By the early nineteen-sixties most of the original impetus of existentialism had petered out. Merleau-Ponty and Sartre had parted company at the time of the Korean war; Sartre wrote that while the North Koreans had started the war, the South Korean feudalists and the American imperialists had provoked it and it was therefore immaterial who had actually fired the first shot. Merleau-Ponty found this difficult to swallow; he had genuinely believed that communism was never aggressive in the military sense, and found his theories refuted by events. In a book on the *Misadventures of the Dialectic* he admitted that the existentialist philosophy of the revolution as absolute action was based not on scientific theory but on *a priori* moralising. He retreated into left-wing liberalism, non-revolutionary in character, preaching (as Sartre saw it) reformism in the guise of gradual progress towards social equality at home and ideological coexistence abroad. Several years later came the open break with Camus. With the publication of *The Plague* Albert Camus, born in Algeria, had become one of the leading writers of the young generation. He shared the existentialist conception of the intellectual as a rebel, but found himself unable to follow Sartre into the jungle of dialectics, partly no doubt because he was above all a writer, only incidentally a political philosopher. Unlike Sartre he regarded political commitment as a necessary evil, not a virtue in itself. While Sartre became more militant, Camus came to appreciate more the freedom and tolerance prevailing in Western society. He found it impossible to explain away Stalin's crimes by reference to the 'wave of the future', as Sartre did. Nihilism and extreme violence could give birth only to new injustice; this was not the only way to manifest protest, for moderation, too, could be a form of rebellion. Towards the end of his life (he was killed in a car accident at the age of 46) Camus became deeply preoccupied with the 'harmonious Mediterranean spirit' – shades of his Algerian youth? – which could perhaps guide mankind towards an escape from the anxieties of life.

The debate between Sartre and Camus, like most left-bank controversies, proceeded on a high level of abstraction. The mandarins were, as one observer put it, in search less of facts and knowledge than of an attitude befitting the traditional role of the intellectuals – their 'correct pose':

In the postwar world one needed to make carefully balanced protests against tyranny in Spain and tyranny in Czechoslovakia, race discrimination in America and forced labour in Russia, executions in Persia and executions in Budapest, in order to preserve a clear conscience and one's own intellectual equilibrium which was constantly subjected to new threats. In the end the only theme of the *littérature engagée* became itself and the engagement ended in solipsism. Jean-Paul Sartre above all, even in his polemical writing and in his plays, never dealt with any other subject and never had any other conversational partner than himself; among his followers a whole literature has grown up by intellectuals for intellectuals about 'the intellectual', in which every ripple in the pond of this literary-political-philosophical debating club becomes a monument of the history of thought. (Herbert Luethy).

The left-wing Catholics who published the influential monthly *Esprit* were neither existentialists nor believers in the materialist conception of history; their philosophy was personalism as developed before the war by Emanuel Mounier. Yet their politics were remarkably similar to those of Sartre's circle; they bitterly opposed the established order and thought little of Western civilisation in its present state. They tried hard never to oppose the Communist Party, because it represented the *demiurge du monde*, meaning the working class; it was the progressive force *par excellence*, and the motor of history.

For a few years after the war the position of the communists among the intellectuals was very strong, almost unassailable. They dominated CNEC, the association of writers and were second to none in stressing their patriotism: 'My party has given me back the colours of France,' Aragon, the leading communist poet, wrote. They were *le parti des fusillés*, the heirs of *toute grandeur humaine*'. Above all they were the party of hope, hope for a better world without exploitation and war. The right-wing intellectuals, many of whom had been very influential before the war, had lost much of their audience; some were reduced to near silence because of their record during the occupation. The Catholic establishment was oddly out of tune with the *Zeitgeist*. Malraux, always a lone wolf, published little and his influence asserted itself only in later years. The Catholic philosophers Gabriel Marcel and Jacques Maritain seemed to have no immediate message for the troubled postwar world. The reaction which set in around 1950 against *littérature engagée* was anti-ideological and anti-metaphysical in character; political and social messages were ignored, the problems of the 'human condition' dismissed. The new literature wanted to please and to entertain; it did not intend to be modern at any cost. This apolitical trend also manifested itself in the reappearance of some of the traditional prewar literary journals. With the emergence of the *nouveau roman* and the Theatre of the Absurd towards the end of the decade, the anti-ideological trend became even stronger. In the novels of Robbe-Grillet, Butor, and Nathalie Sarraute there was neither psychological analysis nor ideological argument, but a kaleidoscopic, enigmatic catalogue of things and facts; immediate sensations were described but the whole remained puzzling. In the plays of Ionesco, Beckett and Adamov there was no psychology; the characters were automata, caricatures of human existence; there was no coherence or logic. Sometimes it was effective theatre, but like the new novel it had little substance and was therefore basically uninteresting. As Roland Barthes saw it, writing had reached its zero, literature had become counter-communication. These trends and fashions continued to preoccupy a small group of writers and critics. The general public's curiosity had been satisfied; it followed their debates with declining interest.

Both the existentialists and many of their adversaries, immersed in abstract and often highly abstruse debate, were oblivious of the fact that the society around them was rapidly changing: 'The mandarin, like the revolutionary (Stuart Hughes wrote), was succumbing to irrelevance. In the new France of optimism and confidence about the future, the apocalyptic rhetoric of the immediate post-liberation era rang hollow; intellectual life had lost both its fervour and its special prestige.' The liberation had been the intellectual's great moment and the mandarinate had enjoyed unprecedented public eminence:

> Yet it never succeeded in defining a content for its doctrine of universal responsibility; it had oscillated erratically between the total liberty of the individual revolutionary and the total constraint of Stalinism. By the nineteen-sixties such preachments had lost their vertiginous appeal. The younger French social scientists were denouncing their 'excessive ambitions'; their research was becoming more positive and cumulative; no longer claiming 'to deal with everything at once', they were far more conscious than before of the relation of their work to social action.

The change in the social climate deeply affected the intellectual world; manifesting itself both in a general uneasiness, in esoteric trends in literature and the cinema, and also in a new rationality and a cautious optimism. Existentialism had not changed French politics; on the contrary the naïveté of the late forties caused many a hangover and a great deal of disenchantment in the fifties. The new revolutionary wave of the late sixties owed little to existentialism. But in personal relations a new freedom developed with the gradual passing of traditional bourgeois society, its morality and vision of the world, and to this existentialism had made a notable contribution. The generation of intellectuals which grew up in postwar France took this new freedom for granted while it was deeply suspicious of the high flown, abstract rhetoric of its elders, their contempt for practical experience and their disdain for facts. The vicious circle of 'impotence and revolutionary verbiage was broken, the intellectual alienation and the practical sterilisation of the intellectual left persisted, but it was a defensive and declining position' (Michel Crozier). Structuralism began to take over the positions in which existentialism had reigned supreme. Structuralism was preoccupied not with the content of human thought and action but with its basic categories, the structure of its different elements, the way they were combined. Claude Lévi-Strauss' research among the Nambikwara Indians had first made him question many accepted categories of thought: were not magic and science two different ways of acquiring knowledge? He differentiated between 'cold' and 'hot' societies, the former 'backward' and unchanging, the latter in a state of perpetual motion. If Ranke had thought that each nation was *unmittelbar zu Gott*, Lévi-Strauss put in doubt the cultural superiority of the West, believing that each society had its intrinsic values, that the importance of history should not be exaggerated. From anthropology and linguistics the new trend spread to psychology (Lacan), Marxism (Althusser), history (Foucault and Dumézil), and the study of literature (Barthes). It was at one and the same time a new positivist attempt to broaden the borders of knowledge, to regain for the intellect a field that had been abandoned to the absurd, and a powerful on-slaught against traditional humanism. Many questions remained: the fact that magic had a logic of its own did not necessarily mean that it was equivalent to science, the near-absolute relativism of structuralism was bound to lead it into indefensible intellectual positions, and its neglect of content into sterility and irrelevance. There was a basic inconsistency between the politics of the structuralists and their anti-historicism as well as their reservations with regard to human progress.

French intellectual life has been moving from extreme to extreme: after the war there was an intense debate on general philosophical principles more radical in spirit and less optimistic, but basically in the tradition of the eighteenth and nineteenth centuries. Twenty years later France experienced something akin to a wave of logical positivism. One could predict with reasonable confidence that after the re-examination of language and concepts the pendulum would again swing back – not to 1945, but to a renewed preoccupation with the enduring and unsolved questions, both of France and of humanity.

Britain: The Angry Young Men

The richness of Europe's intellectual history in our time makes it imperative to concentrate on certain trends and movements to the neglect of others. This selective method is the only possible one but it is also highly arbitrary and unjust, putting a premium on fashions and currents. It entails preoccupation with the intellectual climate, however changeable and ephemeral, not with lasting individual achievements. Existentialism and structuralism for all one knows may be a mere footnote in the history books of the twenty-first century, whereas postwar French painting, the poetry of René Char of Yves Bonnefoy, the discoveries of the French biologists or biochemists, may be of lasting value. The intellectual history of postwar Britain presents even greater difficulties. In France, Italy, and Germany there were distinct groups and schools of thought but there were no such movements in Britain and generalisations about the intellectual climate there are next to impossible. The mood after 1945 was very different from that on the continent; there was little cosmic despair or abstract activism. The intelligentsia, even more heterogeneous as a group than intellectuals elsewhere, had become more politically conscious during the war, but communism was not a powerful magnet and did not play a predominant role as in France and Italy. The Spanish Civil War had marked the high tide of the left-wing current among the intellectuals; after 1945 there were outlets other than the Communist Party. Labour had come to power, and there was great hope for far-reaching changes under the new government, which included many young intellectuals such as the future party leaders Gaitskell and Wilson, both former Oxford dons, Strachey, Crossman and Crosland. There seemed to be much less reason for pessimism in postwar Britain than on the continent despite the deprivations and the austerity. Nor did ideological controversies dominate the scene. Discussions like those between Sartre, Camus, and Merleau-Ponty were unthinkable in England because there was an instinctive dislike of abstract controversies, high flown oratory, and political moralising. The British tradition was to discuss liberty, reform, and revolution empirically and in concrete terms, in their political, social, and economic context, on the basis of facts and figures. England in the postwar years was less open to foreign influences than the continent; existentialism hardly caused a ripple, Marxism was discovered by the New Left only in the late fifties; until then it had been the preserve of a few specialists. What cultural magazines there were paid scant attention to developments outside Britain, less perhaps from ignorance than from the conviction that they did not matter, or at any rate had no relevance for Britain. This deeply rooted insularity began to change only in the fifties, when Brecht was discovered in London, when *Encounter* was launched as a joint Anglo-American magazine (but significantly on American inspiration and with American funds), when London became very much part of the European artistic and musical scene. It is impossible to point to any outstanding group, trend, or movement in Britain during the first postwar decade: T.S.Eliot and E.M.Forster the most respected writers among the older generation, were not the centre of a circle, and there was nothing in common between men like Siegfried Sassoon and Evelyn Waugh, George Orwell and Graham Greene but their individualism; they were certainly not part of any school.

The younger generation just back from the war failed to make a distinctive mark; the transition to civilian life absorbed most of their energies. After the immediate hopes connected with the Labour victory had faded, there was a strong trend towards apathy. (One of the latter day cultural manifestos was significantly entitled 'Out of Apathy'!). The break came with the advent of a

new generation, the angry young men, to use a common if somewhat sweeping and misleading description. Kingsley Amis's *Lucky Jim* was published in
1954, *Look back in Anger* opened in 1956. These were followed within a very
short time by several novels and films, some of them very successful (such as
John Braine's *Room at the Top*) in a broadly similar vein. They constituted a
clear break with tradition; the children of the welfare state were not merely
revolting against upper-class arrogance and imposture, against the hypocrisy
of a genteel middle-class way of life; they were equally unhappy about the
new, brave Socialist Britain, bored above all by the tedium of the welfare
state. Rootless and classless men, they had been educated, as one critic said,
to discontent and they were cheerfully biting the hand that was feeding them.
Political factors played a certain role: this was the first generation that had
grown up in the shadow of the atomic bomb; 1956 was not only the year of
Look back in Anger and *The Outsider*, but also of Suez and Hungary. But with
all their resentment against antiquated class distinctions and their contempt
for mass culture, these young men of lower middle-class or working-class
origin were anything but rebels with a clear, well-defined political programme: Jimmy Porter, the hero of *Look back in Anger*, thought that there
were no good, brave causes left to adopt. Joe Lampton (in *Room at the Top*)
went for the big money, not for socialist ideals.

What were the young men angry about? Were they fighting straw dum-
mies, was their protest anything more than (as one of them put it) an existentialist statement put in sophomoric terms? Was there any reason to see
anything more in Colin Wilson's reflections on a dying culture and his
search for superman than a tract of the times by a young man of some
imagination but not very familiar with philosophical and political thought?
The common features of the Angry Young Men of the fifties were their youth
and vitality, their delight in breaking certain taboos, the freshness of their
approach and the originality of their topics, not the philosophical content of
their works. Their contribution to literature was not equal to that of older
writers like William Golding or Angus Wilson, certainly not to the Angry
Young Men of 1920 such as Robert Graves, whose work in the forties continued to be influential. But Amis and John Osborne were pace-setters,
paving the way for what unkind critics called the kitchen-sink school of
literature. Arnold Wesker's *Chicken Soup* trilogy, Alan Sillitoe's *Saturday night
and Sunday morning, A Taste of Honey*, and others. Naturalism was not the only
offshoot; there was also the English equivalent of the Theatre of the Absurd,
above all Pinter's plays, interesting in their use of new dramatic forms and
techniques, but lacking plot and depth of character, and thus in the last
resort devoid of real interest. Frustration, poverty, and the less pleasant
aspects of human relations in general found expression in scores of plays,
movies, and novels. Poverty gradually ceased to be a central topic, as the

workers moved from slums into council houses and acquired cars, refrigerators, and television sets; Britain, too, had its modest prosperity during the fifties. There remained the intangible frustration of soul and body, the boredom, the feeling of being stifled in a small and shrinking country, the general dissatisfaction of writers with their own private surroundings and the world at large.

Most of the angry young men subsequently made their peace with the world but the still younger generation, those who appeared on the scene after them, adopted radicalism with a vengeance. They put themselves into deliberate opposition to the unpolitical fifties; for them the 'end of ideology' was over. They were unhappy about Britain's internal crisis, shocked by the nuclear threat, by Rhodesia, Greece and Vietnam. Their protest manifested itself in demonstrations against the government of the day, and, on a different level, in a flowering of satire in the theatre, television, and the press. Some of it was genuinely funny, some a curious combination of social snobbery and political radicalism. The ideologists of the New Left discovered Lukacs and Gramsci, Adorno and Ernst Bloch; Isaac Deutscher with his unflinching optimism became their mentor for things Soviet and Frantz Fanon their guide to the third world. These influences were limited to a relatively small circle; far more widespread was an emotional leftism, which supported extreme positions without necessarily subscribing to any ideological rationale. The English left shared with the upper class a missionary feeling: Britain had come down in the world but it could still provide much-needed leadership. The Campaign for Nuclear Disarmament and the Committee of 100 (supported by Earl Russell) were born in Britain and served as prototypes for similar groups all over western Europe. Anti-Americanism became almost *de rigueur* after 1960, but the number of young people who emigrated to America exceeded those who demonstrated in front of the American Embassy.

In Britain, as in other European countries, the new mass media had the unfortunate effect of magnifying and giving great publicity to everything that was new and far out. In this way the new politics were boosted as well as the image of 'swinging London' (high life cum Maoism) with its fashions, discothèques, and other trendy phenomena, even though only a tiny part of the young generation shared or cared for the Chelsea way of life. Television put a premium on the shortest mini-skirts and the silliest political opinions. The real England, the significant positive achievements, remained in the shade. Beyond the intellectual and sartorial fashions, there was the real cultural revolution of the nineteen-fifties and sixties. Theatre, the opera, concerts, and art exhibitions flourished, attracting vast audiences. For the first time in its history Britain became one of the world's art and music centres; much of the art trade moved from Paris to London. The many thousands queuing for the opera, the ballet, and the promenade concerts were a more reliable and a more encouraging guide to the interests of the young generation than the declarations of the fashionable gurus of politics, religion, and culture. The taste of the public improved immensely and cultural provincialism diminished. The triumph of Brecht was followed by the discovery of other continental influences in the theatre, the avant-garde cinema, the concert hall, and many other aspects of cultural life. The London cultural scene in the early sixties resembled somewhat Weimar Germany in its vitality, experimentation, and irresponsibility; the Brecht fashion was, so to speak, no accident. Much of this gave rise to apprehension, but the era of boredom was certainly over. In the academic world important changes took place; the glamour of Oxford and Cambridge faded with the emergence of the new 'plateglass' universities. Sociology, formerly the Cinderella of academic life became highly fashionable and was given official recognition. The study of social psychology, of contemporary history, and other relatively new disciplines received a fresh impetus. In scientific research, despite insufficient means, individual and group work of the highest importance was undertaken. The new Elizabethan age was not just a period of horror comics and the birth of the teenage industry, of *Private Eye* and the Beatles, of pop art and pop politics. It also witnessed, more significantly, a new wave of intellectual activity, and within limits, a cultural renaissance.

Germany: The Lean Years

German cultural life had suffered such setbacks under nazism that even a partial recovery was not expected for a long time. Before 1933 Berlin had been one of the world's cultural centres, in some respects perhaps the most important. Germany shared with France the lead in modern art; in the sciences, in philosophy, in political and social thought, its position was pre-eminent. Its cinema and its press were of the highest quality; German literature in the twenties had few outstanding achievements to its credit, but its general level was second to none; it was certainly among the most lively, interesting and cosmopolitan in the world. Nazism eliminated the Jews who had played a prominent part in German intellectual life; it was profoundly anti-intellectual, cut down university attendances, fought a relentless battle against all manifestations of modern art, which it defined as 'Cultural Bolshevism'. This anti-cultural policy, even more than the destruction of the war was the cause of the decline. The German universities were reopened soon after the end of the war, but in most respects they had become second rate; newspapers reappeared and movies were released, but their level was far inferior to that of the Weimar period and could not stand comparison with France, Italy, and other European countries. Within a decade Germany's economic reconstruction was virtually completed, but there was no German *Kulturwunder*. Owing to the nature of their medium, it was easier for the musicians, the painters, sculptors, and architects to rejoin the mainstreams of Western culture; within a relatively short period they absorbed the forms and the content of modernism. By 1960 West Germany had become one of the centres of contemporary music and had the most attentive audiences for experimental music; the works of Stockhausen and Hans Werner Henze (who had moved to Italy) were performed all over the world. Efforts were made to continue the great architectural tradition of the twenties (Gropius, Mendelsohn, Mies van der Rohe) and the work done by painters and sculptors in that period. Most difficult was the task of the playwrights, writers, and poets. The idea that the writers were the conscience of the nation had been less deeply rooted in Germany than among its eastern neighbours, yet after the nazi experience the general feeling was that the past had to be overcome, to be mastered, individually as well as collectively, before a return to 'normal' literary life with its preoccupation with private concerns could be envisaged. This recent past, *die unbewaeltigte Vergangenheit*, the question of how it could have happened, was the central theme in the works of many of the representatives of the middle generation, such as Albrecht Goes and Heinrich Böll, of H.W. Richter and Alfred Andersch; their books focused on the question of personal responsibility.

Some of the leading writers of the older generation were still alive, but Thomas Mann did not return to Germany for any length of time; Gottfried Benn still practised medicine in Berlin and Ernst Jünger collected beetles; neither produced any major work after the war and they had no substantial impact on postwar cultural development. Several leading writers of the pre-nazi era congregated in East Berlin after 1945: Arnold Zweig, Anna Seghers, Theodor Plievier, and above all Bertolt Brecht. For a little while it seemed that powerful new impulses would emanate from this circle which provided the link with the Weimar left-wing tradition, but the hope soon faded. All these writers were past their prime and as intellectual life in East Germany became progressively more regimented, a few escaped to the West, while those remaining were reduced to silence or to the production of a literature of 'social command', about which the less said the better. Brecht was the exception, a maverick who flourished even in the worst days of Stalinist repression; but even he did not produce any major plays after 1945 and his chief influence was that of mentor to the younger generation. After Stalin's death intellectual controls were relaxed but there was nothing comparable in East Germany to the Polish or Hungarian 'thaw' of 1956, or the Czech cultural renaissance.

Sensitive to the subversive political effects of the demand for cultural freedom, the East German government took stern measures against its critics; some (such as the young philosopher Wolfgang Harich) were jailed, others cowed into submission or reduced to silence. Some of the leading intellectuals, such as the philosopher Ernst Bloch and the literary historian Hans Mayer, escaped to West Germany. Bloch was a Marxist, but it appeared that West Germany was a more congenial place in which to live and work not only for Western liberals but also for their severest critics. The East German régime did much to promote higher education, but like the other communist countries it faced in doing so an insoluble dilemma. It needed highly-qualified experts, but there was always the danger that students would ask awkward questions to which those in charge of political education had no satisfactory answer. The young intellectuals could be intimidated but not persuaded; below the surface a permanent conflict developed between the régime and the intelligentsia.

West Germany faced problems of a very different character. Up to the late nineteen-fifties it was difficult to define the distinctive features of the new intelligentsia; the work of individual writers, poets, and artists did not constitute a trend or a school of thought. There was 'group 47', a body of writers of protest, but their political commitment, with a few notable exceptions such as Günter Grass, author of *The Tin Drum* and *Dog Years*, was vague. The polarisation between intelligentsia and society became more pronounced during the late fifties as the intellectuals became more rebellious. During the sixties the feeling of alienation (to use the fashionable term) among the literary intelligentsia was in fact more acute in West Germany than in any other European country. The intellectuals declared that society was conservative, smug, dishonest, devoid of cultural values, while 'society' reacted by declaring the litterateurs irresponsible, purely destructive in their criticism, and uninformed about the basic facts of social, economic, and political life. While the writers went on castigating the 'lies of bourgeois society', their critics claimed that many of the new plays and novels on political subjects were a travesty, a deliberate falsification of history.

The influence of the left-wing avant-garde was limited; in the universities it had its main support in disciplines such as philosophy, theology and German studies, fields that were afflicted by much frustration and heart searching. With the spread of a new activism in the universities in the middle sixties, the confrontation became a matter of national concern. In some ways it was a repeat performance, the re-emergence of the youth movement of the early twentieth century in a new disguise – the revolt against society, the underlying cultural pessimism, the élitist sense of mission, the rejection of democracy. They, the few, were called to redeem the many who, befuddled and manipulated by the impact of the new mass media, had no real will of their own.

To a large extent this was part of a general European and, indeed, world phenomenon. In Germany it assumed certain specific characteristics with its esoteric philosophical language, its overweening intellectual ambitions, its intransigence, self-importance, and lack of humour. It not only provoked the hostility of the establishment, which was to be expected; it was rejected by many on the left including its early mentors such as Günter Grass and the philosopher Jürgen Habermas. These men followed with concern the development which with all its radical left-wing verbiage contained dangerous reactionary and authoritarian elements. The conviction gained ground that tomfoolery had its limits and that even a permissive society had occasionally to defend itself.

The demonstrations of the sixties made the headlines; more significant, if less sensational, was the gradual improvement in the general intellectual level. The German film industry raised its sights, television became more ambitious and enterprising than that of most other European countries, the leading newspapers caught up with the rest of the world. Avant-garde art and music found not only individual supporters but enthusiastic audiences. More foreign books were translated, more plays by foreign authors performed in Germany than in other European countries. True, there was nothing left of the erstwhile German hegemony in philosophy and sociology, and in the natural sciences one could at best point to individual achievements. But in other fields the balance sheet was more encouraging. In history for instance a genuine attempt was made to study the country's recent, most painful period. There were occasional attempts to embellish and to find excuses, but on the whole there was an honest confrontation with the past, a genuine attempt to understand and to draw the necessary lessons. Contemporary history had been almost unknown as a discipline in Germany; it developed rapidly after the war and became a respected subject of study, assisted no doubt by the interest of the public. There was widespread awareness of the great damage done by Germany's cultural isolation in the past, and a genuine effort to overcome provincialism. The churches showed an unprecedented interest and activity in cultural and social affairs and encouraged in their communities active political involvement. Catholic and Protestant conferences discussed the problems of mass society, Germany's eastern borders, and often played a positive role in encouraging democratic discussion. Adult education expanded and there was great emphasis on the study of civic subjects. The German cultural balance sheet 20 years after the end of the war was still disappointing if compared with the achievements of the nineteenth and the early twentieth century, when Germany had been the *Kulturnation par excellence*. But those days were gone for ever; if measured by more modest yardsticks, and viewed against the background of the German catastrophe under Hitler, postwar developments were not unpromising.

Postwar Moods in Italy

Italy, like Germany, was in the throes of a deep crisis in 1945, but the hang-over from fascism was different in character. The question of personal responsibility hardly ever arose, since the people's identification with the régime that had been overthrown had been much looser, there was no purge of Italian intellectual life after 1945. Many leading figures in the literary world and the cinema had published their books and produced their first films under fascism. Quite a few had been members of the Fascist party at one stage or another, though most of them had fallen out of favour and some had joined an opposition group. The cultural policy of fascism had been more liberal than that of nazism and for that reason it had been easier for the intellectual to accommodate himself to the régime; only those actively involved in anti-fascist politics had emigrated. By and large they had not been deeply troubled; Mussolini was a great misfortune but then the individual intellectual had to survive, with honour if possible, without, if his existence was at stake.

The moral hangover came with the end of the war, when the conviction grew that many of them had squandered their time and talent by compromising, that there had been a massive *trahison des clercs*, and that as a result Italy was in a state of disarray. Most intellectuals agreed that it was their vocation in future to describe the world as it was without embellishment or mercy. The Italian film industry had been equipped with the largest and most modern studios in Europe; there was an excellent cinema school and a host of good producers and actors. But the opportunities offered could not be used under fascism; Italian films had dealt mainly with historical subjects and fables. According to official fascist doctrine the Italian people was always to be depicted as a people of heroes, fearless and honest, virile and dynamic. The reaction after the defeat was not surprisingly in the opposite direction, one of rejection and brutal honesty. The early postwar movies which were so successful, such as *Rome – Open City* and *Bicycle Thieves* portrayed the fear, the poverty, and the weakness of Italy during the last year of war and immediately after the liberation. The actors were not always professionals but they gave eloquent expression to the torment and hopelessness so characteristic of those years.

Neo-realism permeated the work of the novelists: Italian society as they saw it was sick and corrupt; there had been a general moral collapse culminating in fascism and its defeat. The novel showed in graphic detail the corruption of the upper classes; it was preoccupied with anxiety, brutality, and vice. Many prominent Italian writers and producers turned to the extreme left after 1945; this too, was a delayed reaction against fascism. But there were also other undercurrents such as the old anti-clerical tradition;

every country has its unsolved social questions, but Italy had more serious problems than most. There was a general feeling that the upper classes, having cooperated with fascism, had failed dismally and this helped to enhance the prestige of the communists and the left-wing socialists, after the Action party had failed to gain mass support. The former emigrés, on the whole, were less prone to be attracted by communism. Silone, to give an obvious example, had written *Fontamara*, the best anti-fascist novel, 15 years earlier; he had opposed Mussolini from the beginning, he did not need to prove his anti-fascism after the defeat. But he had no illusions about communism either, and about the efficacy of political ideologies in general, and found himself therefore out of step with the prevailing mood among his fellow intellectuals.

The postwar Italian novel was concerned not only with politics. In Moravia's work sexual problems played an even greater role than the critique of bourgeois society, and he had few illusions about human society in general. Nino, the revolutionary hero in one of his novels, says shortly before committing suicide: 'Rich people are terrible, but the poor are not much better, though for different reasons. The history of mankind is one long yawn of boredom.' There was heavy emphasis on the class struggle in the work of such writers as Vasco Pratolini and Elio Vittorini; Sandrino, Vittorini's *Hero of our Time*, a perfect specimen of fascist education, ends up by murdering his mistress, an act that is made to appear perfectly natural both in view of his politics and in the context of his social background. But the underlying libertarian-humanist convictions of the writer sometimes raise this kind of literature well above the level of mere propaganda. Pratolini's *A Tale of Poor Lovers* is the chronicle of the inhabitants of one small street, the Via del Corno, in a working-class quarter of Florence. Corrado, better known as Maciste, the blacksmith and proletarian hero, decides at great personal risk to save a liberal deputy who is about to be arrested and is liable to be killed by the fascists. Corrado is a communist militant, and from the party's point of view such sentimentality is misplaced, for the liberal is an enemy of the working class and there is no reason for Corrado to endanger himself and his comrades by trying to help a man who is an anti-fascist 'by pure accident'. The blacksmith is arrested by the fascists and executed. But Pratolini does not accept the party's reasoning: 'You, Corrado,' he says, 'have a great heart, and the party will accuse you of having erred by listening to the call of your heart. But if you had not listened to your heart you would not have joined the party in the first place.' Vittorini later admitted that he had not read a line of Marx, Lenin, or Stalin before he became a communist; for him it was simply choosing the side of the angels in the struggle for a better world. The literature of social conscience was the prevailing trend in the immediate postwar period; Italian writers discovered the working class of

Italy's north, and that large section of their country, the desperately poor and backward Mezzogiorno which hardly seemed to belong to Europe. 'No one has come to this land,' Carlo Levi wrote in *Christ stopped at Eboli*, 'except as an enemy, a conqueror, or a visitor devoid of understanding.'

After 1950 subtle changes took place; the partisan leader as hero disappeared, and though there was still revulsion against upper-class moral corruption (*La Dolce Vita*), despair with the lower middle class way of life (*I Vitelloni*), and the emptiness of human existence in the small town was equally often the main theme. Much of Italian writing was deliberately regional in character; there is not one cultural centre, as in France and England. But there were other reasons as well; resistance to fascism, to name but one, had first arisen outside the big cities. Literature became less political and more 'literary', there was a growing preoccupation with individual rather than social problems and the cruelty of society in general. The positive heroes became more contemplative, even passive.

During the fifties Italy underwent great changes and became more prosperous; the theft of a bicycle was no longer a major disaster. Even the South experienced a boom; the working class preserved its political loyalties but became more bourgeois in its way of life; small town life became more modern though not necessarily more attractive. These social and economic changes were reflected in the writing and the films of the late fifties and sixties. The Italian communists, never quite Stalinist in inspiration, became more critical of 'socialist realism' and doctrinaire Soviet cultural policy. Even under Zhdanov, the Italian communist painters of the 'New Front' had tried to combine Marxism, formalism, and avant-garde aesthetic theory. Italian film makers realised that their movies were shown all over the globe with the exception of the communist world. At a film festival in Moscow the Soviet judges most reluctantly accorded the first award to a movie by a pro-communist Italian director (Fellini for his $8\frac{1}{2}$), commenting nevertheless that a film permeated by such an unhealthy outlook could not be shown to the Soviet public. The left-wing intelligentsia protested against the Soviet intervention in Hungary, against the persecution of Pasternak which even Togliatti said had been a mistake and against the writers' trials in Moscow. The humanist tradition in the Italian intelligentsia proved stronger than party discipline; among the intellectuals the heretical view gained ground that communism as practised in the Soviet Union was not a guide for western Europe. Tradition and the negative features in Italian society still made a reconciliation between left-wing intellectuals and the establishment unlikely. Pope John's *aggiornamento* had its main impact outside Italy, and for that reason, if for no other, a rapprochement with the church seemed equally unlikely. Tension continued in the universities; there was deep discontent with the unchanged, conservative structure of academic life.

Italian cultural life in the fifties and early sixties thus presented a contradictory picture of somnolence and hyper-activity, of provincialism and openness to outside influences. The postwar historians showed great vitality not only in tackling the fascist period with great frankness and in abundant detail, but also in reopening vital discussions on such questions as the character of the Risorgimento and the plight of the South. But few dealt with Italian history after the liberation and there was little interest in historical developments outside the country. The tradition of the great Italian films of the immediate postwar period was continued by Antonioni, technically no doubt on a higher level; but the specifically Italian character of this new school became difficult to define. The latest avant-garde French novels and Soviet poems became known in Italy earlier than in other countries, but the creative tension of the postwar period had faded. No new Pavese came to the fore, Vittorini died in 1965, and the response aroused by leading writers of the younger generation such as Pasolini or Calvino was not comparable to that which marked the literary scene during the years after the war and which had radiated far beyond the borders of Italy.

The Humanities and Social Sciences

There were no sensational, epoch making new developments in European postwar philosophy. The academic philosophers continued their traditional exercises, but hardly anyone outside the profession took much notice; existentialism was the only exception, no doubt because it was more literary than philosophical in character. It claimed that ideas were objects of consciousness, to be ascertained and described but not problems to be solved and contradicted. Those outside this school vehemently rejected this; they interpreted existentialism as a reaction against nineteenth-century optimism, a specific French effort to overstep the narrow confines of Cartesianism. They did not accept the concept that being was nothingness and that there was no essence in man.

The various philosophical schools had little in common with each other; usually they did not even share a common language. For a logical positivist the pronouncements of Sartre (and indeed of most other traditional philosophers) were anathema. They were preoccupied with the analysis of the nature of language; traditional philosophy was senseless because it asked the wrong questions and produced meaningless answers. As for the ultimate questions, Wittgenstein in a famous aphorism had noted that one should be silent about what one could not talk. The analytical school had been strongly influenced by the work of the Vienna circle between the two wars; it now had its main bastion in Britain (Ryle, Wisdom, Austin, Ayer, Weissman). It gained enthusiastic adherents, but not many outside England or America. For the continental philosopher this was not a new beginning but abdication, the end of philosophy. For him man still was the central question of all philosophy, and logical positivism was interested in anything but the human condition. Catholic and Protestant philosophers continued their work; some of the Catholics had also been influenced by existentialism, but not in the same way as Sartre. Gabriel Marcel and Jacques Maritain (both converts to Catholicism) were the most famous among them. They belonged to an older generation but their work (as that of Karl Jaspers and Martin Buber) extended well into the postwar period and exerted considerable influence.

There was an infinite variety of philosophical schools in western Europe, whereas in eastern Europe there was but one, Marxism. The philosophical impact of orthodox Marxism in the West was strictly limited; only a very few westerners had embraced communism as the result of studying the philosophical works of Karl Marx, or Lenin's *Empiriocriticism*. Those who were most fascinated by Marxism were the theologians – German Protestants and German and French Thomists, who discovered a certain affinity with it, despite the atheistic character of Marx's teachings. After Stalin's death the revisionists provided a new interpretation of Marxism. They rejected the mechanical application of dialectics to nature, and, in contrast to the element of inevitability in Leninism-Stalinism, stressed, sometimes with reference to Kant, the element of individual moral responsibility in socialism. The rediscovery in the nineteen-thirties of certain hitherto unknown philosophical manuscripts written by the young Marx had wide repercussions; the concept of alienation as expressed in these writings was adopted by the revisionists, who found the philosophical reflections of the young Marx more interesting than his later economic work. Bloch and Lukacs have already been mentioned in this context; there were others such as Henri Lefebvre, Leszek Kolakowski, and Kozyk in Czechoslovakia, and a whole school of Yugoslav philosophers who throughout the fifties and early sixties developed their views, much to the chagrin of the guardians of Leninist orthodoxy.

Sociology and political science expanded after the war, but it is difficult to point to any major European contribution after 1945 to the development of these disciplines. Europe had been the cradle of modern sociology; before the nineteen-thirties all the significant writings had been produced in western Europe, but after the war the scene shifted in large measure to the United States. Many of the new theories and approaches which blossomed there were seven-day wonders, but there was also much vitality and some interesting and important work. Sociology spread in France and England, and regained some of the influence it had lost in Germany; individual Frenchmen or Englishmen produced work equal or superior to that of their colleagues in the United States, but one can hardly point to a breakthrough even remotely equal in importance to the work that had been produced in Europe during the years before and after the first world war.

Under Stalin sociology had not existed as a separate field of study in the Soviet bloc, for Marxism-Leninism fulfilled among many other things the function of sociology. In the late fifties a freer hand was given to those who wanted to study Soviet society and while a great many subjects remained taboo it was now possible for the first time to pursue research into some of the politically less sensitive aspects of social society.

The war had given a powerful stimulus to the study of history in Europe. New institutes for the study of the second world war, the nazi era, and the resistance movements came into being in Germany, Holland, France, and Austria; new periodicals were devoted to the same topics (the German *Vierteljahreshefte fuer Zeitgeschichte*, the French *Revue d'Histoire de la Deuxième Guerre Mondiale*). Contemporary history had long been neglected by professional historians on the continent and abandoned to journalism and political science, but there was a change after the war and from then on its position was firmly established. The development in Britain followed a similar pattern which manifested itself, *inter alia*, in the establishment of an association of contemporary historians and the publication of the *Journal of Contemporary History*. Modern and contemporary history had suffered in Britain from a prolonged eclipse; the class of modern history at London University in 1897 and 1898 consisted of one student, and in 1899 there was none. The prevailing attitude (as in many other European countries) was that recent history was not a fit subject for scholars because there were no documents from which to study it. The historian moreover was thought to lack the detachment and objectivity needed to examine controversial topics in a truly scientific spirit. These arguments lost much of their force as abundant source material about the recent past became available; the danger after 1950 was not of a drought, but of being drowned. There were fewer illusions about the scientific character of historiography; not many members of the profession shared any longer the view that the study of distant times was necessarily more scientific and objective in character than that of more recent periods. All history, in Croce's much quoted words, was contemporary history; each generation recreated history in its own image. The experience of Hitler and Stalin had a direct effect on the interpretation even of the ancient world and the Middle Ages.

The expansion of the study of contemporary history was merely one of the many new developments in historiography. Historians all over Europe followed with interest the work of their colleagues in the social sciences; there was more cross-fertilisation than ever before between the disciplines. In France Lucien Febvre and Marc Bloch and their friends, the editors of *Annales*, had been engaged since the nineteen-twenties in an ambitious attempt to create an integrated school of history, applying among other things the insights and methods of natural science, geography, statistics, and social psychology. Under their influence the study of social and economic history prospered in France; Braudel's school gave a powerful impetus to geo-history. The French school was a reaction against over-specialisation and the danger of antiquarianism. For Febvre and Bloch history was above all a living discipline; they were not at all certain whether it had any concrete, cut-and-dried lessons to offer, but they maintained that the historian had to act as if history was a science and to extend the borders of knowledge to the utmost limit.

Diplomatic history was least of all affected by these new approaches, but cultural history drew some fresh inspiration from psychology (as in Dumézil's reinterpretations of myths). Above all economic and social history began to change its character under the impact of cliometrics (the application of econometry) and quantitative history (the study of national accounts, demographic processes, etc.). In Paris the Foundation Nationale des Sciences Politiques (better known as Sciencespo) was founded in 1945 and served, among many other things, as a centre for the study of political parties. German historians were on the whole more conservative, less open to the application of new techniques; their main achievement was the reinterpretation of German history in the light of its most recent, disastrous phase: Meinecke devoted his last book to the lessons of the catastrophe, Dehio reflected on the mistakes of German foreign policy, and Gerhard Ritter wrote about the army and politics in modern German history. A great controversy ensued after the publication of Fritz Fischer's book on German war aims in the first world war; his thesis that Germany was far more to blame for unleashing the war, and its drive towards world power both more planned and more ambitious than previously believed, was criticised by most of his colleagues. Valuable work was done by historians and political scientists on the Weimar period and the advent of the Third Reich, the parties, and the interest groups.

The postwar era in the Soviet Union and eastern Europe was not a happy one for historians even though the situation improved somewhat with the thaw after Stalin's death. The party line made any radical re-examination of the last century of Russian history impossible; there was more scope in the less sensitive fields, especially those not directly affected by current politics. Outside Russia the relaxation of controls went further: Polish and Czech, Hungarian and Rumanian historians were able to study the history of their countries with a greater measure of freedom than before. They realised, albeit belatedly, the danger of provincialism; most of these countries had been part of larger states before 1918; the end of the first world war had brought them national independence but also cultural isolation. They were no longer in the mainstream of European culture, and historians, like other intellectuals, felt that a special effort had to be made to counteract the effects of isolation. A meeting of historians from the successor states of the Austro-Hungarian monarchy in the sixties, and the heated discussions that ensued was an interesting new departure. International conferences and seminars helped European historians to overcome the parochial attitudes that had often marred even the best historical writing during the nineteenth and early twentieth centuries.

Economics

In economics as in sociology the centre of gravity moved after 1945 from Europe to the United States, but the basic ideas on which postwar economic thought came to rest had emerged in Europe during the previous decades and those who developed it further were often European emigrés. This refers to the doctrine of individual liberalism (Hajek, von Mises) as well as to neo-Marxism. It applied above all to the work of John Maynard Keynes, who in his *General Theory of Employment, Interest and Money* had enunciated a number of basic ideas that were later on widely accepted. Keynes maintained that the era of pure individualism had passed and that a growing measure of state initiative and control was inevitable. He further argued that the main purpose of a national economy was to provide full employment, that inflation and rising prices were not (as orthodox economists had believed) an un-mitigated disaster, and that in any case a crisis could be regulated by means of monetary manipulation. Keynesianism was a revolutionary breakthrough because it showed how to overcome the recurrent crises which had plagued western economies for more than a hundred years. In England Keynes's friends and pupils, including Roy Harrod and R.F.Kahn, continued their work on multipliers and the acceleration factor, but there was also progress in other directions such as the economics of growth (Colin Clark and his studies of national income). In the fifties there was a shift away from economic theory to the application of new techniques such as econometrics and input-output analysis. Again America led the way, but most of the spade-work had been done by Europeans (John von Neumann and Oscar Morgenstern in games theory, Wasily Leontieff in input-output analysis). These new tech-niques were of considerable practical importance for they made it possible to estimate fairly accurately future demand and the dependence of one sector of the economy on another, thus enabling the output of goods to be maximised. At the same time they were also of theoretical interest, for they provided answers to some of the questions that had preoccupied economists for a long time, such as problems of monopoly and of economic coalition.

Partly as the consequences of these advances in western economic thought, partly as the result of their own practical experience, Soviet economists too began to modify their concepts and methods. In their discussions during the late fifties and early sixties they accepted essential features of Western economic thought such as the role of demand in pricing and the basic function of profits in the national economy. Though they claimed that profit and a charge on capital were consistent with Marxist-Leninism, this was in fact a far cry from the Marxist-labour theory of value. It meant in practice a new orientation towards market socialism, linear programming (as developed by Kantorovich), and other mathematical devices which had previously been rejected as capitalist in character. There was unanimity in the idea that market criteria should be used, but some economists advocated that this should be done within a general scheme for the improvement of central planning by means of computers. It soon appeared, however, that the existing information system was inadequate for this purpose and those who advocated the other alternative, namely decentralisation, carried the day. The question left unsolved was the degree to which the market mechanism would replace central planning in the Soviet Union and the other east European countries.

Interesting work in economics was not confined to the major European countries; the great Swedish economic tradition was continued in the postwar work of Bertl Ohlin, Eric Lindahl, and Gunnar Myrdal, to mention only the outstanding figures among the older, internationally known generation. Jan Tinbergen and other Scandinavian economists made important contributions to the study of mixed economies, economic backwardness, and the economics of planning. Some of the most interesting new departures in socialist economic thought were made in Hungary and Czechoslovakia (Ota Sik). It appeared that even in a discipline in which for obvious reasons all the odds seemed to favour the theorists and practitioners living in the political and economic centres of the world, these had, in fact, no oligopoly of wisdom, knowledge, and creativity.

The Avant-garde

In the scientific field the lead passed after the war to the United States, and the Soviet Union too made great strides. A divided Europe could not compete with the massive investment in scientific research made by the two super powers, even though important discoveries continued to be made by individual Frenchmen, Germans, and Englishmen. But Europe's position in literature, music and the arts remained almost unchallenged. Even in its crisis, its weakness, its unfulfilled promise, Europe remained the world's cultural centre. The growing estrangement between the 'two cultures', and the breakdown in communication between the avant-garde and the general public, were not specific European phenomena but affected all modern civilisation; if Europe could not overcome it, no one else could. The work of the avant-garde had become more and more esoteric, remote not just from tradition but often also from quality and sanity; too often it betrayed a spurious preciosity, loss of balance and of standards. The argument that novel forms of great art had always been rejected at first was unconvincing; not all art that was rejected had been great.

The public realised that there had been a radical break, that contemporary music and painting were essentially different in character from all that had gone before; the distance between Monteverdi and Richard Strauss was far smaller than that between Richard Strauss and Stockhausen. The limited appeal of modern art has been explained with reference to the public's insufficient sophistication. The public, to be sure, was not greatly interested in the discussions on 'formal' and 'informal' music and the advantage of 'aleatory techniques'; it looked with disbelief and occasional amusement at the 'fabulous objects', the collages which had been pioneered by Schwitters and others, and it did not enjoy electronic music. Its feeling was that the avant-garde was not out to find new forms of art but to destroy it, as some of the more enterprising young composers put it. Much of modern art had reached a dead end and a major effort was needed to rescue it from the quagmire of unlimited experimentation, and the expansion beyond the limits of art towards incoherence and absurdity.

A survey of modern art written in terms of the changing fashions and shifting fortunes of small avant-garde groups tells only part of the story; it is as relevant as political history which concentrates on a succession of kings and emperors. On the public at large, these curiosities did not have a great impact; they were forgotten within a very short time. If contemporary art found itself isolated it was not for want of a public willing and able to appreciate art. With the spread of education the number of people who genuinely cared about art had greatly increased during the last few generations. The artist, it seemed, was isolated not because he was ahead of his age but because he had lost touch with his fellow human beings. In past ages cultural styles and movements had always been part of the *Zeitgeist*, the general intellectual climate. Much of the output of contemporary musicians, painters, and writers moved in an intellectual and artistic vacuum, and although they still maintained that they were socially and politically committed, it was exceedingly difficult to discern the nature of this commitment from, say, Picasso's pictures or the films of Italian producers or the music of H.W.Henze. Adamov declared himself a communist while Ionesco opposed not merely communism but political engagement in general. No one would have guessed it on the basis of the study of their works alone.

The break with tradition was most pronounced in painting and music. When the war ended many of the great French painters of the older generation were still alive: Picasso and Matisse, Braque and Léger continued to be active; Chagall received more acclaim than ever before. The leaders of the next generation, those who were distilling nature into abstract forms, Soulages, de Stael and the rest, shared no common language with them. For the general movement was towards an art 'non figuratif, non objectif', and even a Picasso who showed remarkable adaptability did not qualify by the exacting standards of the pure abstractionists who insisted on a geometric, two dimensional approach, emphatically rejecting anything even vaguely resembling figurative patterns. Their work was greatly influenced by modern science and technology.

In Germany the break with the past was similarly complete; some of the leading German painters of the twenties who had been banned during the Third Reich, such as Beckmann, Höfer, Pechstein, Heckel, and Schmitt Rottluff, had a great revival: their exhibitions were well attended, their pictures in considerable demand. But neither they, nor emigrés like Kokoschka, had any significant influence on the younger artists, who took their inspiration from Kandinsky and Mondrian, who had died in 1944, and Paul Klee, who died the year after. Abstractionism dominated in Germany as in France, sometimes in the form of abstract expressionism. There was no specific British tradition in painting and sculpture on which to fall back. Henry Moore studied Mexican and Sumerian art in the British Museum; Pasmore (who was converted from Impressionism to Constructivism after the war) and Ben Nicholson were influenced by Mondrian like so many of their contemporaries on the continent. The visions of Graham Sutherland and the work of Francis Bacon showed an individual style of their own; there was no 'School of London' comparable to the 'Ecole de Paris', but there was a great flowering of the arts in Britain.

Abstractionism was the dominant trend, but it did not by any means have the field to itself. Impressionism was not quite dead, surrealism had a brief renaissance, so had expressionism, albeit in a form very different from that of the twenties. Abstractionism came into being as a revolt against the traditional forms and media, which restricted the artists in their quest for expression. But abstract art created new problems, above all of communication. Since the advent of Cubism during the first decade of the century, there has been a feeling of malaise among artists and the public alike. The militant opposition of totalitarian régimes to modern art ('cultural Bolshevism', 'rotten and decadent bourgeois liberalism') was profoundly reactionary and philistine. But such attitudes quite apart, there was a great deal of uneasiness, a growing feeling among many painters that they should again become *témoins de leur époque*. Many of them realised that the unconscious and the natural sciences, if given free rein, would lead painting into a dead end, that personal idiosyncrasies had been carried too far. Kandinsky had proclaimed that a mental state could be directly transmuted into forms and colours, but even his admirers realised that there was no short cut from a mental state to the act of painting. Sections of the public came to regard certain fashions as little better than a joke; the advent of pop art, an American discovery in 1960, did not strengthen the prestige of contemporary art. Some critics claimed that modern art could not be judged by objective standards. If so, others argued, the differences between one of Giacometti's spindly sculptures and the work of a child or a mental defective could only be asserted, not proven. The argument that an artist always expressed the spirit of his times, and that a chaotic age necessarily produced an art reflecting disorder, fear, and mental confusion, was not universally accepted; other periods had been equally or even more chaotic, but in less permissive ages fear had been suppressed and confusion had not been made a virtue. Modern painting and sculpture came under fire not so much because of daring experimentation, but because of its sterility, its solipsism, its neglect of any effort to communicate with the viewer. This explained the lack of enthusiasm for modern art in comparison with the enormous interest in the works created in other periods. Visitors to museums and galleries preferred the old masters even if they did not express the spirit of the age; the price of Impressionist paintings soared to dizzy heights, the public voted with its feet and its cheque book.

The postwar revolution in architecture was less sweeping; the medium imposed obvious restrictions and the governments and municipalities commissioning public buildings were not willing to put up with an unlimited amount of experimentation. The general trend was towards a new, comprehensive kind of town planning, new garden cities and the improvement of the total environment. Some of the rebuilding after the war was done in a haphazard way; there was not enough time to plan and, during the first decade, usually not enough money. Some of Germany's leading architects had emigrated in 1933, and little remained of the tradition of the *Bauhaus*; nevertheless West Germany showed as much enterprise in this field as the other

European countries. France had a great master in Le Corbusier and many of the younger French architects modelled themselves on him, but his most interesting buildings were erected outside his native country. The Scandinavian countries played a pioneering role in architecture as well as in interior decorating and the styling of furniture; in this respect the break with nineteenth century taste was complete. Some distinguished new buildings went up in Rome and Milan, and, as an antithesis to the monumental-heroic tradition, in eastern Europe. The postwar development in architecture did not constitute a break with the past; the general trend towards good, elegant, but simple design, and the idea that not single buildings but the whole environment should be built (or rebuilt) were not new but had originated in the first three decades of the twentieth century.

The origins of the revolution in modern music likewise went back to the first decade of the century; it gathered momentum after the first world war and modernism became the dominant school after 1945. Even famous composers of the older generation, such as Stravinsky, were converted to serialism; Hindemith, who had been rejected in the twenties as ultra-revolutionary by large sections of the public, had hardly any influence on a new generation in whose eyes he was almost a conservative. The main formative influence on the young was Schönberg, and even more, Webern, as classic dodecaphony turned into 'total serialism' and neo-serialism. Electronic music appeared and Pierre Schaeffer's 'musique concrète'; the total 'dismantling of music' became a frequent topic of conversation among the more enterprising members of the younger generation. Immediately after the war musical Europe looked to Paris for its inspiration, above all in the works and teaching of Oliver Messiaen and his star pupil Pierre Boulez. During the fifties West Germany became the most important centre, and the leaders of the contemporary movement in many European countries gathered in Cologne and Baden Baden, Darmstadt and Kronichstein to discuss 'music of chance' and stochastic asymptotes, 'music in space', 'sound structures' and similar topics of common interest. Violins were burned in public performance and there was music for amplified rubber bands and glass plates. There were symphonies without an orchestra and 'silent sonatas' such as John Cage's '4.33', in which the pianist sits at the piano for precisely this time, poised to play but never playing. In Theodor Adorno they had the influential contemporary European philosopher of music. There were music festivals entirely devoted to *musica viva*; events like the first performance of Stockhausen's *Gesang der Jünglinge* were widely discussed in press and radio. But while there was enthusiasm and great activity there also was almost total isolation. The contemporary movement remained a hothouse plant which existed only owing to the continuing support given by a few Maecenas, above all some gullible foundations and radio networks. Restricted to its own resources, the movement would have collapsed. There was a great upsurge in musical interest, but contemporary composers hardly benefited from it. The sales of long playing records reached new heights every year, bigger and more appreciative audiences than ever flocked to concerts and operas. In England, a country without a rich and developed musical tradition, it became the custom to queue for days and nights to get tickets for an interesting first performance. The surviving conductors of the older generation such as Toscanini, Bruno Walter and Klemperer, were given a tremendous welcome on their European tours. New names appeared such as Herbert von Karajan, new singers such as Maria Callas and Dietrich Fischer-Dieskau, and a plethora of gifted young soloists. Music festivals in Bayreuth and Edinburgh, Warsaw and Salzburg, Glyndebourne and Lucerne, attracted thousands of enthusiasts from all over Europe. The works of the contemporary composers were by-passed; beyond Mahler and Debussy few conductors and orchestras wanted to venture, nor was there any strong demand for them from the public. In opera the situation was not dissimilar. Few contemporary composers cared for the medium; Nono with his *Sul ponte di Hiroshima* and *Intolleranca 1960* was one of the exceptions. Henze's *König Hirsch* (1956) was well received, so were Shaporin's and Khrennikov's new operas; Benjamin Britten's *War Requiem* even became a popular success. But these composers were usually far from avant-gardist; the very medium compelled them to adhere to certain traditional forms. No opera composed after 1945 gained a firm foothold in the repertory; the public voted for Mozart and Verdi and occasionally Wagner, as it had done in the past. The golden age of the operetta ended in 1914; there was a renaissance in the twenties (Lehar, Kalman, Paul Abraham) but it did not last. After the second world war the operetta virtually ceased to exist; it was replaced by the musical, an importation from the United States which was immensely successful both on the stage and the screen: *My Fair Lady*, *Annie Get Your Gun*, *West Side Story*, were performed for years in all European capitals. The operetta, from *Die Fledermaus* to *White Horse Inn*, had been a product of central Europe; Vienna had been its principal home, and it had branches in Paris and Budapest. The attempts to create a European musical failed – there was no Offenbach, nor even a Paul Lincke to compete with the slicker, better produced, artistically more appealing American musicals. Light music in general remained very much influenced by the Americans, jazz progressed from 'cool' to 'modern' and rock 'n roll replaced the boogie-woogie. In the field of pop music American dominance was less firmly established; the Beatles conquered the United States as well as Europe. A whole galaxy of singers from Edith Piaf to Charles Aznavour continued the Paris tradition of the chanson, and local jazz, pop, and folksong groups emerged and became popular all over Europe.

Reviewing the European musical scene in the sixties one observer wrote that 'the public everywhere turns away from the new music. Although it is possible to maintain here and there with the support of a present-day Maecenas (helped by tax exemption) ivory towers as a last bastion for contemporary composers, true contact between the general public and modern music does not exist. A real genius will be needed to find the narrow path between experimentation and tradition that may lead to a revival' (R. Klein). But with the growth of an appreciative and enthusiastic audience, with the improvement in musical taste and culture among the public, such a revival was perhaps closer at hand than the pessimists suspected.

The postwar European theatre showed astonishing vitality and at the same time signs of retrogression and decay. Unlike modern music, it retained much of its audience; even the theatre of the absurd had a certain fascination for people from all walks of life. Martin Esslin describes how much the inmates of San Quentin penitentiary enjoyed a performance of Samuel Beckett's *Waiting for Godot*, and how they did not find it at all difficult to grasp the meaning of the play. Playwrights are more dependent on the public than other artists; they need more than canvas, brush, and easel for self-expression, and theatres all over the world cannot function without financial support. Even among enlightened state and municipal legislators enthusiasm for experimentation in modern drama was not unbounded.

Among the new trends which emerged in the early postwar drama were Sartre's plays, unequal in interest and artistic accomplishment, full of philosophical messages; the more effective theatre of Anouilh and Christopher Fry, not without intellectual ambitions but lacking in depth, in force, and in conviction, and, most influential of all, Brecht's epic theatre (*Zeitstücke*). This tradition continued in Germany well into the sixties (Peter Weiss, Hochhuth, Heiner Kipphardt) and with the innovations in its *mise-en-scène* profoundly influenced playwrights all over Europe. Brecht's plays were of great, sometimes deceptive simplicity; his political beliefs were a mixture of sincerity, naïveté, and cynicism, and he was, to put it cautiously, not always original in the choice of his subjects. With all this he was a producer of genius, and his was no doubt the most effective theatre of the period. In the hands of his pupils the epic theatre lost much of its appeal though little of its actuality. They claimed poetic (or dramatic) licence for their running comments on current history, refashioning, often distorting, and sometimes falsifying it. Brecht was a communist of sorts, but in eastern Europe his plays were performed only belatedly, and while he was acclaimed (not always without misgivings) for the political content of his work, young dramatists were discouraged from following in his footsteps. With all his praiseworthy intentions, Brecht was too much of a pacifist, too bourgeois, ultimately too sceptical to be a wholesome influence in a communist society.

The fifties and early sixties were dominated by the theatre of the absurd, which for a number of years enjoyed an enormous success. The plays of Adamov and Ionesco, of Beckett and Genêt, and of their followers in Britain and elsewhere, were widely performed and provoked many discussions and a considerable interpretative literature. The origins of this school were traced back to Dada, to 'Ubu Roi', and even further. There was usually no action in these plays; they presented a succession of meaningless events; the figures who trod the stage were automata, caricatures of human existence, the dialogue usually deliberate gibberish. Human conversation, as Ionesco said, became an absurd noise; no one knew why a certain character appeared, no one understood what he was saying or what would follow; his actions and motives were incomprehensible. There was not meant to be any inner logic, for the new theatre was intended to reflect the whole meaninglessness of human existence, the private nightmares of the author. They created poetic images and situations that were absurd, not necessarily ridiculous (though this was a frequent side effect) but devoid of purpose. It was, in brief, anti-theatre.

The pretensions of the theatre of the absurd provoked criticism and hostility. Forty five years earlier Dadaism had been an entertaining joke, but no one, not even its main protagonists, had made any far-reaching claims for it. The theatre of the absurd on the other hand was intellectually ambitious; the unconscious was brought in, aesthetic theory and contemporary philosophy; a major effort was directed at making nonsense intellectually respectable. The theatre of the absurd was said to be not merely profoundly sincere, springing from deep-seated fears and obsessions, but also to express the madness of the times and the perplexity of the authors, the despair that ensued from realising that human existence was shrouded in darkness. There was a world of difference (as one of its historians wrote) between artistically and dramatically valid nonsense, and just nonsense. With all this it was bound to be a passing fashion, for not all authors were equally confused and perplexed; the theatre of the absurd was an act of regression, in psychoanalytical terms, a victory of the id over the ego. It lacked both content and psychological depth, resembling a Rorschach test into which different people could read different meanings, but such a test, however useful in other contexts, was not art.

There seemed to be a premium on insanity and crime in modern drama. Many contemporary plays and movies were based on the assumption that (as one critic put it), a prostitute and a criminal were *a priori* more honest and more interesting than other people. A student of human nature basing his observations on the insights of the avant-garde modern theatre and cinema was bound to reach the conclusion that life was not merely senseless, but had no redeeming features at all. Love, ideals, honesty, heroism, kindness, the spirit of sacrifice, optimism, were left to mass culture and thus became 'kitsch'. The public reacted to avant-garde plays by queueing for *The Mousetrap*, Agatha

Christie's thriller which ran in London for more than sixteen years, by showing a clear preference for boulevard plays on the Paris stage and for revivals of
the prewar drama, and also by turning from the theatre to the cinema and
television. Europe's leading theatres, such as the Burg Theater in Vienna,
the Schiller Theater in Berlin, Zürich's Schauspielhaus, the Théâtre de
France and the Comédie Française, Milan's 'Piccolo', Dublin's Abbey
Theatre, and Britain's National Theatre, showed a bias in favour of a conservative repertory, and not just because their directors lacked enterprise and
interest in contemporary drama. They depended on subsidies which meant
that they could not ignore the wishes of their sponsors and of the public.
State grants for the theatre had only recently been introduced in Britain,
France, and Italy; in Germany and Austria there was a longer tradition
of public support and audience organisations had helped to keep theatres
afloat. Good theatre could not simply depend on the law of supply and
demand, but neither could it ignore public taste altogether. The problem
was partly solved by the emergence of theatre workshops and small experimental groups. The state, however tolerant, could not be expected to spend
public funds financing the performance of plays which were rejected by the
public. It was up to the directors of the theatres to strike a judicious balance
between the popular and the esoteric, the generally accepted and the new
and unfamiliar – not an easy or enviable task.

The Mass Media

Even at a time of crisis the European theatre maintained its pre-eminence;
Brecht and the leading French and British playwrights invaded America and
were staged all over the world in the fifties and sixties. In the cinema, on
the other hand, America had dominated the scene from the beginnings of the
movie industry; Germany and Russia had produced interesting films in the
twenties, and the masters of the French cinema of the nineteen-thirties (such
as René Clair and Jean Renoir) were artistically more accomplished than
even the best American films; Marcel Carné's *Quai des Brumes* and *Le Jour se
lève* had been among the most powerful films of all times. But the public still
flocked to see the products of Hollywood which catered for almost every
taste and behind which there were far greater resources than the European
film industry could command. With the end of the war a new contender
appeared on the scene; the Italian neo-realist school was the most interesting
phenomenon in the history of films during the postwar period and had a great

influence all over Europe. *Bicycle Thieves* and *Rome–Open City*, were setting the trend, Vittorio de Sica and Roberto Rossellini became the most revered names in the field of movie-making. But the average European cinema-goer (30 million of them each week in Britain alone) still wanted to be entertained; a diet consisting mainly of *Umberto D.* or *Miracle in Milan* would not have brought prosperity to the industry. The French and the British cinema (David Lean and Carol Reed) rallied in the fifties as new stars appeared in the firmament: Martine Carol, Gérard Philippe, and Simone Signoret – later on Brigitte Bardot, Jean Pierre Belmondo and Jeanne Moreau, Sofia Loren and Mastroianni, Richard Burton and Elizabeth Taylor. But the films with the greatest popular success were still produced in the United States; monster productions with a religious background (*The Robe, The Ten Commandments*), musicals which had been adapted to the cinema (*South Pacific, My Fair Lady, West Side Story*), adventure stories (*Around the World in Eighty Days*) or quasi-documentaries (*The Longest Day*). These films each cost many millions of dollars; European film-makers, even the biggest among them like the Rank organisation in Britain, could not afford to take such risks. The Russian state industry could, but only with *War and Peace* in 1967 did it produce a film comparable in scope to the American spectaculars.

In the nineteen-thirties the position of the theatre had been threatened by the cinema; after the war cinema felt the pinch as the result of the rapid progress of television. Around 1950 there were the first signs of a decline; in the United States in 1955 cinema attendance was only about half what it had been at the end of the war. In Europe the full impact of television was felt several years later but the results were not less severe; between 1957 and 1963 one third of all British cinemas went out of business and were converted into bowling alleys or bingo halls. The same trend was visible in other European countries; the number of films produced in France fell from 110 in 1951 to 80 in 1962. The prospects for individual producers lessened as investors pondered the advisability of putting money into what seemed a declining industry. Innovations were introduced to compete more successfully with television, screens became curved and wider. After Cinerama (1953), there came 3 D (for which Polaroid spectacles had to be worn), still later Cinemascope and other wide-screen processes. Colour techniques were improved and television with its insatiable demand appeared not only as a rival but also as a consumer of the film industry.

The competition for the mass audience made for more concentration in the film industry; co-production between companies became more frequent. The avant-garde cinema benefited indirectly; European film-makers enjoyed a greater freedom than most Americans for, as they could not aspire to produce 'blockbusters' anyway, they were less constricted by the Hollywood formulas for success. The Italian cinema had a revival in the late fifties;

films of Antonioni, Visconti, and Fellini were admired by some and widely discussed, so was the new cinema of Jean Luc Godard, Truffaut, and Alain Resnais. At their very best the *nouveau vague* films such as *Hiroshima mon Amour* or *Last Year in Marienbad* had a freshness and a poetry that had not been seen in the cinema for a long time. The films of Ingmar Bergman were full of mystery and allegories and often a stark mental torment, impressing viewers with their power and strange beauty. But many of them resembled nothing so much as a maze; replete with stylistic fancy work, they did not try to tell a story and for that reason were rejected by many viewers as something beyond the realm of art. The 'art house cinema' was criticised for the same reason that much of modern drama came under attack – the heavy emphasis on pessimism, crime, and perversion, the deliberate subjectivism and the lack of purpose bordering on madness. A work of art that offered nothing but *Weltschmerz*, cosmic despair, carefully constructed perversions, seemed as much a distortion of life as the sugary, happy-end products in which Hollywood excelled, or the obligatory heroic optimism of the Soviet movies. The art house cinema had its enthusiastic audience but the great bulk of European cinemagoers, working class in character, wanted a very different kind of film on Saturday night – thrillers, light comedy, or a story with a clear message. The great success of a film such as *War and Peace* showed that the old-fashioned cinema was likely to outlast the precious symbolism of the art house.

The full impact of television was not felt at once; in its early years many thought of the new medium above all as an extension of the press and radio. But gradually it was realised that it had modes of expression, techniques, and above all a tremendous appeal of its own that made it a most dangerous competitor for radio, press and the cinema. Television was launched in England in June 1946 with 1,750 subscribers (after a brief first start before the war); in France it started in December 1944, a few months after the liberation; West Germany joined them in 1952 (with 1,500 subscribers); Italy and other European countries followed in 1953–4. By 1965 there were thirteen million sets in England, almost ten million in West Germany, five million each in France and Italy, almost two million each in Sweden and Holland, and the number was nowhere near saturation point but still growing rapidly. Ownership and organisation differed from country to country; in east Europe television was a state monopoly, as it was in France, Spain, Belgium, and Denmark. In Ireland and Luxembourg it was in private hands, while in Italy, Sweden, Holland, and Switzerland mixed companies were established. In West Germany the television networks were financed by the *Lander*, while Britain opted for a pluralist scheme; commercial and public television existed side by side. These networks began by televising only a few hours a day; by 1960 they were on the air for most of the 24.

Television drew audiences far larger than the other mass media and had therefore an even greater impact on the public. Controlled by the state, it presented a potential grave danger to freedom of information, and thus ultimately to democracy. But what were the alternatives? Commercially sponsored television was an adman's paradise, but a nightmare for a great many other people; there was every likelihood that it would cater for the lowest cultural denominator. The qualitative superiority of European to American television, once the diseases of infancy had been overcome, had much to do with its independence of private sponsors, the absence of constant interruptions by commercial plugs. State censorship did not usually weigh more heavily in a democratic society than the control by commercial interests. Television made and unmade political careers; it helped de Gaulle, it was the undoing of Senator Joe McCarthy; it made it more and more difficult for minority groups to reach a wider public unless they deliberately stressed their extremism and so became newsworthy. The question whether the sessions of parliament should be televised was discussed in several countries; there was strong opposition, based on the fear that it would put a premium on playing to the gallery instead of bringing about greater involvement in politics on the part of the people. Both the strengths and the weaknesses of television in relation to the press appeared clearly during the fifties; the new medium provided a much fuller and more impressive coverage of spectacular events than the newspaper; it excelled in social reportage and other documentaries, adding (to use a current cliché) a new dimension to the coverage of current affairs. It could not provide an analysis in depth of any complicated subject; at best its brief comments and interviews whetted the appetite of the public. Television opened new vistas to millions of people though its tremendous educational potential was only beginning to be realised and used. But it did not merely reflect life, it also had a growing influence on politics, culture, social life and manners. Its effects were often unfortunate. In the television scale of values and priorities entertainment counted for far more than seriousness and solidity; frequently it put a premium on flippancy, exhibitionism, and stupidity, provided only that it was not boring.

The early aversion of the intellectuals to the 'idiot box' was overcome as television began to cater for the highbrow on special channels. But television had its greatest successes in the field of light entertainment; as far as mass audiences were concerned it beat all records, became a way of life, and a fascinating topic of study for sociologists, psychologists, and all students of mass culture. There were prepacked television dinners and at peak hours, whenever one of the more popular shows was being broadcast, the deserted streets of Europe's cities were living proof that there had never been anything like television. New stars were born: Gilbert Harding and David Frost in Britain, Werner Höfer and Kulenkampf in West Germany, Léon Citrone in

France, far more popular than even the most famous film stars, half masters of ceremony, half commentators – neither professional actors nor newspapermen. It was difficult to define what had made them such enormous successes but it was clear that the new medium had produced its own type of hero.

The cinema and the press became gradually reconciled to the idea that television was to expand even further. The movie industry sold its old films to the television networks and various schemes of pay television were mooted. These were to supply a link up by special cable which for an extra payment would provide new films and other special programmes. The popular press suffered more from the inroads made by television than the quality newspapers. In some countries major newspaper chains bought stations or acquired shares in television companies, but the future of the popular press was left wide open. The quality newspapers on the continent had a small but secure and growing market: *Le Monde, Neue Zürcher Zeitung, Frankfurter Allgemeine Zeitung*, carried news coverage and analysis unrivalled anywhere. They were at the same time eminently successful from a financial point of view. The British quality press, including *The Times*, the *Guardian*, and the *Observer* faced financial problems even though their circulation was equal to, or bigger than that of the continental papers. Such were the crazy economics of the press that the position of a popular newspaper in England was thought to be precarious if its circulation fell below the two million mark. The position of weeklies and monthlies was even more precarious; only a handful of weeklies of general political or cultural interest prospered. Most of them belonged to the new type of news magazine such as *Der Spiegel* in Germany, *L'Express* in France, *Elseviers* in Holland, which, based on the *Time-Newsweek* formula, found a ready market in the fifties and sixties. None of the highbrow cultural periodicals was self supporting; they were all financed by publishing houses or foundations. The weakness of these periodicals is an interesting sociological phenomenon; they had to compete with paperbacks, the Sunday newspapers, and the highbrow programmes on radio and television. They had a much bigger potential readership than 60 or 80 years earlier, but there were also many new distractions.

Britain had some of the best and some of the worst newspapers in Europe; the level in France, Italy, and Germany was more even. New press lords emerged in the postwar period, such as Roy Thomson in Britain and Axel Springer in West Germany, and the dangers of oligopoly were widely discussed. Political parties needed mouthpieces but they were not very successful in launching mass circulation newspapers: the public preferred its newspapers not to express a party line. The failure of European socialism in this respect is particularly striking but other movements did not fare much better. The dullness of the Soviet and east European press also acted as a deterrent; official pronouncements do not as a rule make interesting reading. The east

European press was freely sold in western Europe but it had no revolutionary appeal whatsoever. Citizens of eastern Europe, on the other hand, did not usually have access to Western newspapers, but the Western radio, even if jammed, was for them an important source of information. East Europeans, cut off from western Europe, lacked a real understanding of the quality of life in the West, but, avid radio listeners, they were often well informed about current affairs on the other side of the curtain.

Cultural Crosscurrents

The intellectual fashions that received most publicity in postwar Europe were not necessarily those likely to have a lasting impact. In the world of ideas Europe maintained its role as *arbiter elegantiarum*; it confounded the prophets of doom who had predicted nothing but ruin and decay, though it did lose its scientific monopoly; both American and eastern Europe experienced a cultural explosion as a new intelligentsia emerged, counted, for the first time in history, in millions rather than thousands. But this new intelligentsia still lived on the substance created by previous generations in west and central Europe.

Even in the postwar period European cultural life was unrivalled in its vitality and richness. It had something to offer to everyone, avant-garde and conservative, progressive and reactionary, high aesthete and unrepentant middlebrow. Many schools of thought coexisted, not always happily, and if it is difficult to point to outstanding individual achievements comparable to the loftiest peaks in the past, the general cultural level was higher than ever, the number of those who cared about cultural traditions and values much bigger. Figures are not necessarily the best yardstick to measure the greatness of a civilisation, but neither can they be ignored: many more people than ever before went to concerts and the opera, attended exhibitions, read serious literature. The intense intellectual life of the immediate postwar years was followed by a quieter, less eventful period. The cold war claimed a high toll in eastern Europe and left its mark in the West, too. But even the strongest controls and the almost total suppression of free thought in the Soviet Union and its satellites did not completely obliterate cultural impulses; with the emergence of a new generation of intellectuals, less beset by fears and suspicion, there was new hope for a cultural revival. Thought control still persisted, indoctrination continued, and adherence to the party line remained obligatory; but if the quest for cultural freedom had survived

Stalin there was every reason to assume that it would outlast the autocratic cultural policies of the post-Stalinist régime.

The advent of a new generation in the West put an end to the quiet (and quiescent) fifties; it manifested itself in various trends and fashions such as the New Wave in the cinema after 1956, the success of the theatre of the absurd, the emergence of structuralism. Above all, there was a renewed emphasis on ideology, often in the form of a self-styled neo-Marxism. But this was not a mere rehash of the twenties; orthodox Marxists commented with disdain on the 'utopian' and 'anarchist' character of the New Left. As the cold war abated, intellectuals felt under less constraint to take up defensive positions, many of them reverted to what they regarded as their main vocation, the revolt against their own society. The sixties also witnessed the onslaught on the 'establishment' of a youth movement unprecedented in modern European history in its scale and intensity. There had been similar movements in the past – mostly apolitical or orientated towards the extreme right. The youth movement of the sixties, originating in the universities, gravitated towards the left and spilt over into the political arena, much to the surprise of the professional politicians who had traditionally belittled the role of intellectuals in politics. The politicians had failed to realise that by its function in society and by sheer numbers the intelligentsia had become a force to reckon with. Radical student groups proved strong enough to spark off widespread revolt. These movements of protest were not motivated by any specific class interest, but by a general dissatisfaction with society, by boredom and a longing for change.

With all its vitality, postwar European culture faced grave problems. The stultifying effects of mass culture, the standardisation of the mass media, the commercial production of cultural goods, constituted an insidious danger which in this form had never existed before. At the other extreme there were the futilities of an esoteric, precious, often sterile 'high culture', divorced from real life and from people, a dead end rather than a narrow pass on the road to new cultural peaks. Culture had become less spontaneous and far more costly; true, there was much more time for leisure pursuits, far more amateurs were writing, painting, and making music than ever before. But only a handful of serious writers in each country could make a living from their books. Professional actors and musicians, other than those at the very top of their profession, were badly paid and their number, as a result, was dwindling. The maintenance of theatres, orchestras and museums became far more expensive, beyond the pocket of even the wealthiest individual patrons. Since there were no cultural foundations on the American scale, the state had reluctantly to provide support. But state support for the arts created new problems. No one doubted that science had to be financed by the state, but the benefits of modern art were less readily obvious. There were many contenders with conflicting claims, and who was to decide about preferences and priorities?

Closer cultural contacts than ever before were established between the various countries, but these did not necessarily mean cultural integration and uniformity. Despite Hemingway, jazz, and pop art, Europe was not really Americanised, just as America retained its own specific cultural character despite all the European influences. West European literature, music, and the arts had an enormous impact on eastern Europe, and strengthened the consciousness of its cultural heritage and the desire to maintain earlier connections despite the difference in social systems. The contacts and cross-currents promoted understanding and in certain fields something akin to a European style developed. In others, particularly literature, national peculiarities reasserted themselves and the distance between Europe and America and even between European countries was as wide as ever.

The imminence of cultural ruin has been debated at short intervals since time immemorial, and cultural pessimism is as old as human civilisation. Yet a period of crisis is also often a period of fruitful creative tension; there is no foregone conclusion that the crisis of European culture which dates back to the beginning of the century will necessarily be fatal. It was an age of transition from the certainties of the nineteenth century, from a solid and stable society to a new post-industrial civilisation, to caverns as yet unmeasured by man. It may enter history as an interesting period of transition rather than as a golden age, a period replete with uncertainty, fear, anxiety, the disintegration of established values, but full of challenge and new impulses and not devoid of hope and promise.

Russification in Eastern Europe

Eastern Europe's intellectual life had been concentrated before the second world war in a few major cities; in Rumania and Poland it had gravitated towards Paris, in Hungary and Czechoslovakia towards Vienna and Berlin. Fascist and right-wing influences were stronger than the left during that period among the numerically small intelligentsia and nationalism and the churches dominated the intellectual establishment. Left-wing tendencies manifested themselves usually in a vague populism or national socialism. On occasion military dictatorships helped to make communists out of liberals. Incipient fascist movements had a strong following in the universities. There was an even wider gap than in the West between the intellectual avant-garde, familiar with current trends and fashions in Paris, Berlin, and London, and the great majority of the people, indifferent to intellectual matters. Czechoslovakia, or at any rate its western part, was an exception; it had been thoroughly westernised over the centuries, so was Budapest and to a lesser extent other Hungarian cities. Culturally they did not belong to eastern Europe but were still part of the mainstream of European intellectual life.

With the establishment of communist dictatorships after 1945 a radical cultural reorientation took place. The influence of the church decreased greatly as the result of the pressure exerted by the new rulers, even though in Poland two decades of constant attacks did not suffice to break it entirely. The Soviet Union became the great example to be imitated: Soviet curricula were adopted in schools and universities, the style of Soviet art and literature was copied in all east European countries. Cultural connections with the West were severed; Polish, Hungarian, and Rumanian artists and writers had to burn all their former gods. These policies created great psychological difficulties for the east European intelligentsia who found it even more difficult than the Russian intellectuals to accept the 'cultural revolution' wholeheartedly. For in the Soviet Union Stalinist-Zhdanovist cultural policies aroused certain sympathies at least among some sections because of their strong nationalist undertone, whereas in eastern Europe these Russian importations could not evoke a similar response. The intellectuals were not just expected to become communists; they had in addition to embrace its specific Russian elements, which caused great resentment. Whoever refused to comply with the new commandments was likely, at the very least, to lose his job. Since few intellectuals wanted to starve or to go to prison for their beliefs, they decided to conform: Czeslaw Milosz in his essay *Murti Bing* has described the complicated process of accepting Stalinist cultural policies in postwar eastern Europe. The intellectuals could not of course believe wholeheartedly in 'socialist realism', in Russian scientific superiority to the West, or rejoice in giving up their own national traditions. But neither could they pay lip service to the official line without absorbing at least part of it, and moral corruption claimed its toll. The dilemmas facing the liberal or left-wing intellectual were often more painful and acute than the problems confronting the erstwhile supporters of the right. The left-wing intelligentsia had been attracted to the communist cause by, among other things, the revolutionary character of Soviet culture, the experimentation in form and content. By 1945 this early 'heroic' period had long passed and been replaced by a new orthodoxy which could satisfy none but the most primitive minds, not necessarily among the left. For the new order was conservative rather than revolutionary, and it ran against the grain of the left-wing intelligentsia with its inbuilt rebellious streak. The rightists, on the other hand, found the atmosphere somewhat more congenial; for them it was easier to adopt an apolitical attitude, to stress in their work the traditional national themes, which became fashionable again once the worst excesses of cultural Stalinism were over. They had never believed in the great civilising mission of the Soviet Union anyway and for that reason their idols, unlike those of the left, had not been shattered.

These were, broadly speaking, the two main currents in eastern European intellectual life. The majority of the intelligentsia took a position somewhere in between; they had learned from bitter experience that it was unwise to expose themselves to repression by straying too far from the official line. The intellectuals rallied and took political action only at the time of a general national upsurge, as in Hungary and Poland in 1956 and in Czechoslovakia in 1967–8. The rulers distrusted the intelligentsia, and not without reason; they were a ferment of decomposition, their demands seemed utopian; if given free rein they would in no time undermine the communist order. The party leadership assumed that this rebellious mood was a transient phenomenon; once the old 'bourgeois' intelligentsia had disappeared and been replaced by a new socialist intelligentsia recruited from among the working people, they would become loyal supporters of the régime. The new régimes did a great deal to spread education; illiteracy in its grosser forms was stamped out, secondary school and university enrolment grew by leaps and bounds. But their assumptions about the future of the intelligentsia were based on a miscalculation; the new generation of intellectuals proved to be no more trustworthy from the régime's point of view than the old; higher education involved as before exposure to subversive ideas. But for the fact that most east European régimes underwent a process of liberalisation and de-Russification after 1956, the conflict between intelligentsia and party leadership would have become even more acute than in the Soviet Union.

East Germany, Bulgaria and Albania were least affected by intellectual turbulence. Bulgaria and Albania had been cultural backwaters, very much in contrast to Germany. The German intelligentsia in their majority had traditionally tended towards order and discipline rather than rebellion. Once the East German régime had made it clear that it would suppress with an iron hand all demands for intellectual freedom, the intelligentsia quickly fell into line. Such *Gleichschaltung* meant a great cultural impoverishment, but this was not how the authorities saw it; in their scale of priorities, intellectual problems did not figure very high; there were more vital political and economic problems to be solved. With the scientists they found it easier to get along; a scientist was far more likely to be an exemplary citizen, and to mind his own business provided he received the money needed for his work and provided also the authorities did not bother him unduly in his research.

Before 1955 conditions did not differ essentially from one country to another, but the second post war decade brought in its wake a movement towards more intellectual freedom, albeit interrupted by many setbacks, and the differences between the various countries became far more pronounced. Polish and Yugoslav painting (Jarema, Kantor, Wledarski, Stupica, Pregelj – to name a few artists at random) in the late fifties had more in common with the work being done in Paris than in Moscow or East Berlin. Music had suffered less than the other arts even in the Zhdanov era and a major revival took place after 1955. There existed a real national tradition: Kodaly, Martinu, Enesco and the other patron saints of modern east European music had used popular themes widely in their work, which helped to make their music acceptable to the authorities. Patriotic considerations played an important role; Bartok's music was far out by prevailing Hungarian standards and Ionesco's plays could not be described as socialist-realist, but the very fact that Bartok and Ionesco had been highly successful abroad facilitated their acceptance in their native countries. Cultural relations between eastern Europe and the West (except for Bulgaria and East Germany) were renewed after 1956; while lip service continued to be paid to Soviet culture, there was a general reorientation towards the West coupled with a reawakening of national themes. After 1956 the intellectual climate in eastern Europe (again excepting East Germany and, later on, also Poland) was much freer than in the Soviet Union, but the demand for more of the same was even more intense.

POLAND

There were dramatic changes in the intellectual climate in Poland during the postwar period. The first years after the war were relatively free from interference; the turning point came in 1949 when cultural life was reorganised on Soviet lines. The writers' and artists' unions and all cultural periodicals were taken over by the communists. According to the new Polish histories written in Moscow, the partition of Poland in the eighteenth and nineteenth centuries had been the work of France, not Russia. After Stalin's death changes set in, slowly at first, gathering speed in 1955. A few daring spirits, such as the poet Adam Wazyk, took the initiative; in his 'Poem for Adults' (on life in Nova Huta, one of the new industrial regions) he described without embellishment the social ills of the country. The fact that someone had given a truthful account of the situation created a sensation; others followed in his steps. Jan Kot attacked 'socialist realism', noting that the decline in communist culture had begun already in the nineteen-thirties. Lipinski, Kotarbinski and Infeld, distinguished academics of the older generation, noted the decline in economics, philosophy, and science respectively that had resulted from the imposition of strict guidance and control. The philosopher Leszek Kolakowski, a prominent representative of the younger generation, questioned the doctrines of Marxist-Leninism itself: the theory of revolution had to be re-examined, the monopoly of the party had to be reconsidered; the capitalist system had not broken down as Marx had predicted, and the 'socialist, democratic régimes' that had been set up in eastern Europe were neither socialist nor democratic. Historians began to dismantle the straitjackets of the Stalin era, some of them even acknowledged the role of the *Armia Kraiova* (the Home Army), anti-communist, and patriotic in character which had been the leading force in resistance to the Germans.

The old Stalinist leadership was replaced in October 1956 by Gomulka and his friends, but the intellectuals, much as they welcomed these changes, could not unreservedly rejoice in them. The disappointment was shattering, especially among those intellectuals who had supported Stalinism and who were now among the most deeply affected. The spirit of despair and cynicism spread among old and young alike; the defection of Mareck Hlasko, the *enfant terrible* of Polish literature, was symptomatic of the disillusionment of a whole generation. The Stalinists were eased out of the leadership of them writers' unions; in music and the arts the 'modernists' received an almost free run, much to the consternation of observers in the Soviet Union. In 1958 the university regulations were rescinded; higher education was no longer to be modelled on the Soviet pattern and the *numerus clausus* for children from non-proletarian homes was dropped. The literary magazines such as *Nowa Kultura* published translations from contemporary western writers regardless of their political outlook. In a polemic against Isaac Deutscher, the Marxist-Leninist living in London but of Polish origin, who had claimed that the young Polish revisionists had gone too far in their revisionist ardour, one of the Polish writers quoted the story of the Jew who had consulted the wise old Rabbi: 'Rabbi, can one build socialism in one country?' 'Yes,' replied the sage after pondering the question for a little while, 'One can build socialism in one country, but one should live in another.'

Gomulka welcomed the support of the intellectuals against diehard Stalinism, but once he was firmly in the saddle he made it clear that there were limits to liberalisation and the demand for cultural autonomy. In October 1957 *Po Prostu*, run by the leading group among the young intellectuals, which had played such an important part in the revolutionary movement the year before, was banned. The year after a new minister of culture was appointed who did not sympathise with the revisionists and further limited their freedom of action. *Nowa Kultura* was taken away from the liberals, *Europa*, another new magazine, never got off the ground; leading intellectuals such as Wazyk, Jastrun, Hertz, Andrzejewski, left the party in protest as 'socialist realism', the official artistic doctrine of the Stalin era, was partly restored to favour and as 'revisionism' was again denounced as the main danger. For its gradual retreat in the cultural field the party leadership found however only few supporters among the intellectuals and it had therefore to make certain compromises which resulted in an uneasy period of coexistence. For a number of years after 1956 there was still more freedom in Poland than in the rest of eastern Europe. Polish film makers had a free hand to produce such remarkable films as Andrzei Wajda's trilogy (including *Kanal* and *Ashes and Diamonds*), the avant-garde painters and composers, though officially discouraged, were not banned or arrested. After the twenty-second Soviet Party Congress and the second wave of disclosures about the 'cult of personality', the intellectuals made fresh demands for greater cultural freedom; among their chief spokesmen were again some of the most respected Polish scientists of the older generation such as Infeld, Kotarbinski and Chalasinsky. Adam Schaff, the party philosopher and a liberal Marxist of sorts, announced that party control should be restricted to the social sciences. Polish intellectuals were occasionally permitted to travel to the West, and could engage in cultural experimentation and criticism provided they did not make sweeping political demands. Western books and newspapers could be obtained in Polish cities. Any form of organised opposition was, however, squashed; the 'Crooked Circle', an intellectual group which had succeeded *Po Prostu*, was banned in 1961. Schaff himself ran into trouble with his colleagues in the party central committee.

October 1956 had raised high hopes in Poland as well as outside its borders, but with the gradual retreat elation gave way to despondency. Within a decade Gomulka, who had come to power as a freedom fighter, the symbol of liberalisation and reform, turned into a hidebound conservative. He was outflanked on the right by a powerful group of authoritarian bureaucrats with many supporters in the army and the police. These 'Partisans' were no more pro-Russian or pro-communist than Gomulka, but anti-liberal, anti-Jewish and anti-intellectual in orientation; they advocated a return to 'order', curbing the unruly intellectuals. These nationalist and antisemitic policies bore an uncanny resemblance to the attitudes of the Polish right between the two world wars. Open conflict between the intellectuals and the party leadership reached its climax in early 1968, when students demonstrated against the banning of a play by Mickiewicz, the national Polish poet, which contained some highly critical remarks about Tsarist Russia. The government took stern measures against the students and professors who had supported these demonstrations, and subsequently launched a major purge of all liberal and left-wing elements. Within a few weeks the clock was put back by almost 20 years. In some ways this purge was unprecedented in communist history; no secret was made of its openly antisemitic character; almost all Jews were removed from cultural and political life. The Church, on the other hand, traditionally not very friendly towards the 'liberals', gave them cautious support, realising that the fight for freedom of conscience was indivisible.

The return to extreme forms of cultural repression may well have seemed inevitable from the authorities' point of view, but it was bound to have fateful consequences for the culture and the prestige of the country. A whole generation of students and young intellectuals was antagonised and the régime compromised itself from an ideological point of view by jettisoning the principle of 'proletarian internationalism'. The freedom of which generations of Polish intellectuals had dreamed and for which they had fought in their country and all over Europe seemed more remote than ever.

CZECHOSLOVAKIA

The years between 1948 and 1953 were among the darkest in Czech history; regimentation was more severe, the purges more extensive, and the trials more savage than in any other east European country. Since western influences had been traditionally strong in Czechoslovakia, a special effort was needed to uproot them. Leading party functionaries such as Zdenek Nejedly (a history professor) and Kopecky slavishly followed Zhdanov's directives; after their death the regimentation of Czech cultural life passed into the hands of minor functionaries like Ladislav Stoll. The universities were reorganised in 1950; children of non-working class origin were admitted only in exceptional cases, a policy which resulted in a marked drop in university enrolment. Novotny warned the writers to be on guard against 'liberalism and sentimentality'; writers of the older generation such as Maria Pujmanova and Nezval abjectly obeyed the authorities, however absurd and grotesque the demands put to them.

After 1956 controls were relaxed all over eastern Europe; in Czechoslovakia Ivan Svitak reminded writers that there was a difference between science and propaganda, and the change could be seen in the poems of Jaroslav Seifert and in Josef Skvorecki's novel *Cowards*, a truthful account of life in a small Czech town during the last weeks before liberation in 1945. But on the whole the thaw was less evident in Czechoslovakia than in most other communist countries; the party leadership reacted almost immediately against what it regarded as an unwarranted and dangerous attempt by the writers to regard themselves as the conscience of the nation. While the Polish and Hungarian intelligentsia were in the forefront of the struggle for freedom in 1956, there was not much stirring among the Czech intellectuals and not a few outside observers commented that Czechoslovakia was behaving according to a time-honoured historical pattern. The 'good soldier Schwejk' seemed again to have become an unofficial national symbol. But such pessimism was misplaced, for whereas in Poland and Hungary 1956 was the high tide of liberalisation, followed by a long retreat, the Czech thaw, albeit belatedly, resulted in a remarkable revival of the cinema, painting, and music. Czech cultural magazines suddenly became the most interesting in eastern Europe; the writers were still warned by Ivan Skala, the head of their official union, against western influence, but no one heeded his advice. The party leadership under Novotny tried to suppress the movement by applying the traditional 'administrative' measures; several magazines were banned, writers were arrested and given stiff prison sentences, demonstrating students were savagely beaten up by the police. Ladislav Mnacko, a leading Slovak writer who had chosen to stay in Israel in protest against Czechoslovak policy in the Middle-east conflict, was deprived of his citizenship. But the demonstrations did not cease, and the students did not find themselves in isolation, as Polish students did, when the showdown came in 1968; they had the support of the liberals among the party leaders such as Dubcek, who succeeded Novotny in March 1968. The changes that took place in the spring of that year were more far-reaching than those in other east European countries; there was a sudden upsurge of optimism and confidence among the intelligentsia whose spokesmen on radio, in the press, and above all on television, had played a leading part in the restoration of freedom. The limits of the new freedom became painfully obvious after the Soviet invasion, but the Czech intellectuals would not easily surrender their newly won gains.

HUNGARY

In Hungary, as in Poland, the communist leaders faced a native intelligentsia that in its majority was opposed to communism, and there was a strong populist tradition, combining admiration of the peasant and commiseration with his difficult lot with a mystic belief in the mission of the Hungarian nation. Of this group of populist writers many had sympathised in the nineteen-thirties with fascism; others, such as Gyula Illes and Aron Tamasi, became fellow travellers after 1945. Most key positions in Hungarian cultural life were occupied after 1948 by emigrés who had returned from the Soviet Union, or in some cases from the West. The party bureaucrats in charge of ideological affairs (such as Josef Dervas) followed an uncompromising Stalinist line, whereas the communist intellectuals such as the philosopher Georg Lukacs and the dramatist Gyula Hay were inclined to interpret the party line more liberally. With the end of the Stalin era and the beginning of the thaw, intellectuals began to play a leading role in the fight for cultural, as for political, freedom. The writers joined forces in the Petöfi circle in 1955, and they and the students played a decisive part in the overthrow of the Rakosi régime. Soviet military intervention put an end to the dreams of a free Hungary; the imposition of the Kadar régime was followed by severe repressive measures against the intelligentsia, including the arrest of leading writers such as Tibor Dery and Gyula Hay; but with all its loyalty towards Moscow the new leadership was aware that old style regimentation would sooner or later cause a new explosion; repression gradually gave way to a milder intellectual climate as the party leaders accepted the need for more freedom in the cultural field. Gradually those who had been arrested after the Soviet intervention were released from prison and their books were again published.

The government accepted that the intellectuals in their majority were 'petty bourgeois' in their outlook, i.e. not sympathetic towards communism; they did not want to embrace 'socialist realism', and cultural contacts with the West attracted them far more than exchanges with the East. An uneasy compromise was reached between the government and the intellectuals: the government reduced its interference in cultural affairs to a minimum on the understanding that the intellectuals for their part refrained from openly anti-Soviet or anti-communist manifestations. The compromise worked better, on the whole, than in Poland, for the intellectuals, too, had learned their lesson; 1956 had shown that the Soviet Union, which considered Hungary part of its sphere of influence, would not tolerate a régime more liberal than Kadar's. It was up to them to accommodate themselves as well as they could.

EAST GERMANY

Hungary was a far from happy country, but in comparison with East Germany it was a haven of cultural freedom. In 1945 the Soviet zone of occupation seemed off to an excellent start; many famous emigré intellectuals had returned to East Berlin, and their situation appeared at first equal, if not superior, to that of the West Germans. The names of Brecht, Arnold Zweig, Johannes R.Becher, Anna Seghers, Plievier, were known all over Europe. Brecht's theatre at the Schiffbauerdamm, Felsenstein's operatic productions, the German academic tradition and the Gewandhaus orchestras, attracted interest far beyond the borders of Germany. The intelligentsia were given preferential treatment even during the most difficult postwar years, and received greater food rations than the rest of the population. Much was done to keep them happy, if only because the régime feared that if many of them took refuge in the West its own prestige would suffer. But while the intellectuals accepted with thanks bigger rations and better living quarters, they also demanded that party interference in cultural affairs should be kept to a minimum. This the party would not concede; a policy of relentless indoctrination and strict control made life very difficult despite the material incentives. Thousands of intellectuals opted for West Germany; of those who stayed behind many withdrew into an 'inner emigration'. After the failure of the 1953 revolt, most intellectuals realised that no basic change in the character of the régime was to be expected in the near future. But they found an accommodation with Ulbricht and the SED not at all easy because the government and the party in East Germany were less willing to make ideological concessions than the rulers elsewhere in eastern Europe. The need to compete with West Germany, with its far greater resources, made East Germany more vulnerable. As a result the régime became more militant than the other 'Popular Democracies' and demanded total identification on the part of the intellectuals. A dialogue with the West was ruled out, a retreat into 'aestheticism' as practised in the literary magazine *Sinn und Form*, was unacceptable. Everyone had to contribute his share in the struggle against 'West German imperialism'; the scientists usually got away with paying ritual lip service or signing a manifesto, but the writers and artists, not to mention the historians and philosophers, could not escape so lightly. While Polish, Czech, and Hungarian intellectuals were given, albeit without enthusiasm, a certain measure of freedom to experiment, to search for new forms and styles, few such concessions were made to the East Germans. There was no room for an East German *chansonnier* (Wolf Biermann) as there was for the Georgian Bulat Okudjava, and if Professor Havemann only lost his job and was not jailed for his unorthodox lectures about Marxist-Leninist philosophy, it was mainly because of his European reputation and the fact that he was one of the very few East German intellectuals with a distinguished resistance record.

The attempt to infuse new blood into the intelligentsia and make them politically more reliable by encouraging a specific working-class literature (the Bitterfeld experiment) was a failure. The older writers continued to write but their best work had been done before 1945, and that could hardly be regarded as a product of the German Democratic Republic. On the credit side there were the early postwar DEFA films which had a certain freshness, a moving novel on life in a Nazi concentration camp by Bruno Apitz, *The Divided Sky* by Christa Wolff, an unusually honest book about the motives that were driving citizens of the DDR to escape to the West, and the writings of 'internal emigrés' like Peter Huchel and Johannes Bobrowski. East German architecture, following the Soviet example, moved from the monumentalism of the Stalin Allee to a more functional and rational style. But on the whole the demolition of the personality cult was more hesitant and less far-reaching in the DDR than in the Soviet Union itself; it was regarded by the party leaders as an embarrassing necessity, not a liberating act; their chief concern was to avoid any lessening of the party's authority and power.

The party could legitimately point to certain practical achievements:

secondary education was now free and university enrolment had risen considerably. The East German intelligentsia, despite their opposition to Ulbricht and his policy, came to identify themselves to some extent with the new state, partly because they were critical of the negative features of life in West Germany, but mainly because they were proud of their own achievements: East Germany had recovered from the ravages of war and become the most prosperous country of the east European bloc. Whatever the political régime, the German worker was still proud of a job well done; there still was something of the Prussian ethos of duty and service among the intelligentsia. All this explains why the régime functioned relatively smoothly. But a heavy price had to be paid, for culturally East Germany became a near desert with only a few oases. Its achievements had to be compared, after all, not with Bulgaria or Albania, but with the great cultural tradition that had existed not so long before. Once part of one of the world's cultural centres, East Germany became an east European backwater.

YUGOSLAVIA

After 1949 writers, artists, and scientists were granted more freedom in Yugoslavia than in any other east European country. The role of the writer as critic of society was acknowledged by the party, the acceptance of 'socialist realism' was no longer mandatory. The party continued to oppose 'reactionary' trends and 'abstract artistic principles', but it did not instigate a witch hunt, nor did it claim to be the supreme judge in cultural affairs; the intellectuals themselves were asked to work out a formula acceptable to both sides. The Djilas case highlighted the limits of permissible criticism. The former party leader had severely criticised in his *New Class* some of the most basic tenets of communist society in both Russia and east Europe, advocating a return to democratic and humanitarian socialism. Djilas was arrested and kept in prison for many years; also arrested was Mihailo Mihailov, a Zagreb university lecturer who had gone too far in his criticism of the Soviet cultural scene. The Croat theoretical journal *Praksis*, having served as a platform for various revisionists, was under constant attack in 1967–8 as the patience of the authorities began to run out. Fanatics of truth like Djilas and Mihailov were bound to run into trouble even in an enlightened communist régime; by more modest standards life in Yugoslavia was tolerable for the intellectuals, nor did the government obstruct cultural links with the West. A writer of the old school, the prewar diplomat Ivo Andric who wrote on anything but contemporary topics, was, unlike Pasternak, not compelled to reject the Nobel prize; on the contrary, he was fêted in his homeland.

RUMANIA

Rumania moved towards national communism more than a decade after Yugoslavia. Tension between Rumania and the Soviet Union had been building up for years, but came to the surface only in 1963, and then in an economic context. Unlike Poland and Hungary, Rumania witnessed no dramatic cultural upsurge; controls were relaxed only in 1964, in particular after the writers' congress of February 1965. Rumanian history was rewritten in a patriotic spirit; Mihail Beniuc, President of the Writers' Union, who had been identified with Stalinist cultural policies, was removed. The leading writers of previous generations such as Rebreanu and Goga were rehabilitated, though their political outlook had been remote indeed from communism; they now joined in the Rumanian Parnassus Tudor Arghezi and Mihail Sadoveanu, who had already been accepted as the great masters of Rumanian literature. The national policy of Gheorgiu Dej, and later on Ceausescu, had mass support, but the intellectuals unlike those in Poland and Hungary in 1956, or Czechoslovakia in 1968, did not play a leading part in this movement and there was no corresponding pressure for cultural freedom.

SOME GENERAL CONCLUSIONS

Intellectual life in eastern Europe after 1955 thus followed a pattern that differed from country to country. Intellectuals played a leading role in the movement towards greater political independence, but their efforts were not always crowned with success. Their failure in Poland was followed by a deliberate anti-intellectual crusade instigated by a government fearful of its survival. There, as in the Soviet Union and East Germany, the intelligentsia were found to be ideologically weak and in need of constant control. The work of some intellectuals, especially the scientists, was clearly vital; others were thought to be expendable. As the party leadership saw it, intellectuals all over the eastern bloc indulged in unnecessary and usually harmful ideological deviations. Instead of popularising the official doctrine and strengthening cultural ties with the Soviet Union they had almost everywhere been whoring after false gods; they had few achievements to their credit, they were still politically unstable and had to be closely watched and guided in their endeavours. The hope that a new generation of intellectuals of working-class origin would be different was not fulfilled; the inclination towards opposition and deviation seemed to be inherent in intellectual activity. This, in brief outline, was the official Soviet view and it had many supporters in leading places in eastern Europe.

The more liberal among the communist party leaders in eastern Europe were inclined to give freer rein to the intelligentsia, partly because they were convinced that the intellectuals (provided one did not deliberately antagonise them) were basically harmless, partly because they realised better than their more obtuse colleagues that strict cultural controls were counterproductive and that culture could not flourish unless it had a minimum of freedom. Some of them genuinely cared about culture and were more willing to turn a blind eye when faced with what seemed to them extravagant behaviour or excessive demands on the part of intellectuals.

The chief merit of the party leadership was that it had helped to spread education: new schools, universities, libraries and museums were built. With the transformation of backward agrarian into industrial societies, tens of thousands of new teachers and physicians, economists and technicians of every description were needed in every field. With this spectacular growth in numbers, the social composition of the intelligentsia changed radically. In Poland, Hungary, and to a lesser extent Rumania and Czechoslovakia, Jews and members of national minorities had formerly been heavily represented; their share decreased drastically during the fifties and sixties, as it had in the Soviet Union in earlier decades. Most members of the new intelligentsia were not intellectuals in the customary sense of the word, i.e. thinkers and artists, 'free floating' critics of society predominantly interested in ideas. These new men and women were largely members of the 'technical intelligentsia' with narrow professional horizons, firmly rooted in society. But many of them were nevertheless bound to stray outside their field of specialisation; interest in literature, the arts and music grew by leaps and bounds. No major cultural impulse emanated from eastern Europe during the decades that have passed since the end of the second world war, but the groundwork was laid for a richer cultural life for many more people than in the past. Given favourable political conditions, it promised a flowering of intellectual life unprecedented in this part of the world in modern times.

The Zhdanov Years

During the grim years of war the Soviet intelligentsia had dreamed of greater cultural freedom and a relaxation of controls. While the fighting lasted a more liberal cultural policy had been pursued by the authorities; the individual scientist, writer, painter, or composer who made his contributions to the war effort was usually forgiven both past ideological deviations and present 'doctrinal weaknesses'. Millions of Russian soldiers were exposed to western influences as they advanced into Europe. Like the Decemberists in the early nineteenth century, they were to act as agents of reform. Many Russians believed that the authorities, in recognition of this and of their greater strength and confidence, would not insist on a return to the stringent forms of thought control that had been in force since Stalin came to power. These expectations were bitterly disappointed; with the hardening of the political line, thought control was reintroduced with a vengeance.

In the early months of 1946 a new era began in Soviet cultural history: in a series of decrees affecting literature, music, the cinema, and eventually every aspect of cultural life, the intellectuals were told that with the passing of the immediate military crisis, the authorities regarded political indoctrination as a matter of top priority, and far stricter discipline would from now on be demanded. These early decrees were sponsored by Andrei Zhdanov, one of the leading members of the politburo. But it was by no means an individual, partisan initiative; Zhdanov died in 1948 but the policy which came to bear his name gathered even greater momentum after his death. Russian intellectuals were told that their approach had to be partisan (*partiiny*) and popular-Russian (*narodny*); works of art had to be typical (*typichny*), they had to deal with personal problems only in so far as these were of general interest and concerned the country as a whole. These general prescriptions seemed vague enough, but their rigorous application in the harsh climate of Stalinist Russia virtually paralysed creative activity in some fields and did serious harm in all. To be partisan meant more than to be politically tendentious; writers and painters had slavishly to adhere to the current party line in every little detail; there was no room for individual digressions or initiatives. It did not just mean that Soviet painters had to adopt socialist realism as their style; the very choice of their subjects was narrowly circumscribed: pictures of Stalin in various poses during the different stages of his career, machine tractor stations, the portraits of model workers or peasants – assignments that could have been carried out much more successfully by colour photography. Socialist realism meant that painters and sculptors had to embellish reality, not to depict it truthfully. Soviet historians, philosophers, and economists had not just to express the party line in their work; they had to quote Marx, Lenin, and above all Stalin, as often as possible. Many books and essays written during that period are little more than a series of quotations from the 'classics' loosely strung together. *Partiinost* in literature meant that both recent and distant Soviet history could not be truthfully described; it also implied the almost complete exclusion of lyricism, and of course of satire. Every novel, every play and poem, had to deliver a constructive message; its heroes had to be positive, larger than life; real conflicts were taboo, for according to official doctrine conflicts had disappeared from Soviet society; the only conflicts that persisted were those between the good and the better. Some leading Soviet poets and writers were silenced by decree or by denunciations in the press; Anna Akhmatova, a gifted poet who had been widely published during the war, was now again ostracised as a 'museum piece'; even Alexander Fadeyev, the head of the Writers' Union and a faithful party stalwart, was forced to rewrite a war novel describing anti-German resistance by young people in a small Russian town. No one had found any flaw in it when it was first published, but after the war it seemed out of keeping with the new and stricter ideological controls.

Narodnost meant that books, paintings, movies and symphonies had to be easily digestible by the masses; avant-gardism or innovation in general, was ruled out. Writers, painters and composers had to serve the people; their job was to make a contribution to socialist reconstruction. Any work of art that did not conform to this pattern was at best irrelevant; more likely it was considered positively harmful. Writers and artists had not only to be committed but to produce according to social command; their own moods were of no interest to the public. It was their business to bring joy to the hearts of the masses, to help in making them better workers and peasants, and above all better communists. *Narodnost* also implied that intellectuals had to put great emphasis on the individuality of Russian culture, its greatness, its superiority to all other cultures, both past and present. After 1948 there was a concerted attack on 'rootless cosmopolitans', 'passportless wanderers in humanity', on anyone found deficient in patriotic enthusiasm. This was directed largely against Soviet Jewish intellectuals, many of whom lost their jobs and some also their lives in the new purge. But other non-Russian nationalities were also affected, for the theory of Russian superiority both past and present involved, *inter alia*, the wholesale rewriting of history textbooks. No one could feel secure in an atmosphere in which any deviation from the party line, real or imaginary, was likely to be branded as high treason.

The principle of Russian exclusivity and superiority conflicted with the concept of internationalism, traditionally one of the fundamental tenets of communism. But the growing disparity between ideological declarations and the real state of affairs did not unduly bother the Soviet leaders. Ideology seemed to have become a convenient cloak for all kinds of strange developments, elastic enough to explain everything. The 'cult of the individual', the totalitarian dictatorship and many other features of the régime were in clear contrast to traditional socialist ideals. The new Soviet ideology that replaced them did not develop according to a preconceived master plan; Stalin and his assistants seemed oblivious to its inherent dangers. They realised only belatedly that the emphasis on Russian nationalism was a double-edged weapon. While making the régime more popular among Russians it created serious problems in relation both to the non-Russian nationalities and to the communist régimes that had been established in east Europe and east Asia. It was unlikely that Poles, to give but one example, would take kindly to the idea that the history of their country was to be written in Moscow, not Warsaw. If the Russification of the Soviet régime was inevitable so was, after Stalin's death, the spread of polycentrism, the seeds having been sown many years before.

The concept of *typichnost* created additional difficulties for Soviet writers, painters, and film-makers, for it did not mean that their works had to deal with typical people and situations, just as 'socialist realism' was not a synonym for a realistic style. 'Typical' referred always to the future, whether a man was concerned, or a factory, or an apartment; not present day squalor but future splendour was to be described; existing realities had to be viewed through rose-coloured glasses. The basic insincerity of this system was clear to Soviet intellectuals; it humiliated them and caused profound cynicism among both producers and consumers of this kind of culture. Everyone knew the real state of affairs, yet no one could describe it truthfully.

The Soviet cultural scene in 1950 was gloomy, but not everyone was equally affected by official policies. Writers, painters, film-makers, historians economists, and philosophers were most severely affected, both because their work was widely exposed to outside criticism, and because their subject matter was closest to the very core of official ideology. Everyone in authority felt entitled to judge a picture or a novel, whereas the appraisal of a new theory in astronomy by laymen, however highly placed, presented obvious difficulties. Historians dealing with the recent past were more vulnerable than those dealing with Byzantium. Scientists on the whole were in a more fortunate position, even though guidance from above was given to every one of them; often it was irrelevant, sometimes, as in genetics, it had ruinous consequences. But a geologist was not likely to be bothered, provided he paid lip service to Stalin as the greatest authority in his field and made some passing references to the warmongering activities and the reactionary-imperialist character of the work of his Western colleagues.

The general public reacted by taking refuge in the classics of Russian literature and music; if no work of similar stature could be expected at the present time, there was always Pushkin ('Pushkin, help us in the silent struggle', Alexander Blok had written in 1919) and Tolstoy; most of Dostoevsky's works were unobtainable during those years. The leading composers of the day, Prokofiev and Shostakovich, Khachaturian, Shebalin, and Myaskovsky, came under fire and virtually ceased to publish, but there was the great heritage of nineteenth-century Russian music to fall back on. Great are the powers of human resilience: even if cultural standards suffered heavily during these years, even though the self esteem and moral authority of many was fatally affected, the traditions and values of Russian culture as a whole were too deeply rooted to be totally destroyed in the years of darkness.

Thaw and refreeze

A gradual improvement took place after Stalin's death. Slow at first, the thaw gathered momentum after 1956, to be followed by a refreeze in the sixties. This became the recurring pattern in the post-Stalin period; a few daring spirits probing the limits of cultural control tried every now and then to extend the borders of cultural freedom. These forays were usually followed by a fresh wave of repression, not nearly so harsh as under Stalin but sufficiently menacing to deter all but the most courageous spirits. During the first decade after Stalin's death two steps forward were almost invariably followed by one backward step; by the end of the decade the outer limits of the new freedom seemed to have been reached and any further progress was sternly repulsed. The literature of the thaw aimed at reducing the gulf between official slogans and realities; blatant propaganda was discouraged and 'sincerity' became the new watchword. Dudintsev's *Not by Bread alone* was the most famous novel of the period, describing the struggle of the technologist-inventor against the party bureaucrats trying to stifle new ideas and opposed to any change. The same topic was featured in several novels, films, and plays (by Granin, Alexander Bek and others). Dudintsev was fiercely attacked for calumniating the whole Communist Party in the person of the reactionary local secretary, but he was not arrested, and several years later it was made known on the highest authority that he was not an enemy of the people after all, and his persecution ceased.

The liberals included Soviet writers and artists whose reputation was long established such as Ilya Ehrenburg (whose multi-volume autobiography helped to 'open a window to Europe'), Konstantin Paustovsky and Alexander Tvardovsky, editor of *Novy Mir*, who tried hard to convince the authorities that there were no major risks involved in relaxing cultural controls. But the main support for the liberals came from among the younger generation of writers, who began to publish only in the post-Stalin period: Evgeny Yevtushenko and Andrei Voznesensky were the poets best known in the West; others in this group included Kazakov, Tandryakov, Aksyonov, Yuri Nagibin, as well as Viktor Nekrasov and Vera Panova who were already in their forties. In their works there was both a new lyricism, a rehabilitation of the individual sphere, and social criticism which, tame by Western standards, was almost revolutionary in the Soviet context. Some of their novels, *horribile dictu*, had no political message at all; Kazakov's *Arcturus* was the story of the death of a blind old hunting dog. Dudintsev's *New Year's Tale* introduced fantasy into a literature in which socialist realism had reigned supreme. Many members of the older generation had been identified with Stalinist cultural policies; some of them were not devoid of talent, but they had no moral prestige in the eyes of the younger generation and they did not find it easy to adjust to a new climate. Alexander Fadeyev who had been secretary of the Writers' Union under Stalin, committed suicide during the thaw; his death was in some ways symptomatic of the fate of a whole generation.

With the advent of the thaw efforts were made to circumvent censorship; public and semi-public gatherings were arranged in which the younger writers read their poems and short stories; these happenings often attracted thousands of listeners though they had not been publicised in advance. The new spirit in the cinema was reflected in films such as *The Cranes are Flying, Clear Skies* and *Ballad of a Soldier* and there were many new plays on similar lines. Dealing with subjects that had hitherto been taboo, they castigated the inhumanities of the Stalinist period; their positive political message, if any, was not too obtrusive. In a passage in a novel by the writer Kochetov he describes the success of one of the anti-Stalinist plays:

> They saw the new play by an untalented but clever new playwright. He knew how to titillate the audience. In every single act all through the play a good man was being done down. Everyone was doing him down: the party organization, the trade union, the factory management, some despicable individuals. He struggled through a flood of tribulations, rousing the audience's pity and even drawing tears from many female spectators.

Kochetov was the chief spokesman of a small but influential group of die-hards who deeply resented the changes that had taken place after 1953. They were convinced that on balance the Stalin era had been positive and that it was suicidal to introduce too much democracy and liberalism: 'Party members will be hung from the lamp posts if the relaxation of controls goes too far,' Kochetov wrote in a novel after the Hungarian events of 1956. Writers in this group were authoritarian by temperament and Russian nationalists by conviction; Marxism did not play a major part in their mental make up; their interest in European culture was minimal and they did not hide their dislike of Jews. The heroes of their works were trustworthy working-class stalwarts, their villains shifty intellectuals of doubtful provenance and loyalty. This new brand of national socialism was much closer to the post-Stalinist leadership; it expressed the ideas of the party bureaucracy and had official support. But there was no writer of real talent among the Kochetovs, the Gribachevs and the Sofronovs; they held influential positions but had only a small audience in the Soviet Union and no international standing.

Mikhail Sholokhov was the most substantial supporter of the bureaucracy; a natural and genuinely talented writer, he managed to be on good terms with Stalin, Khrushchev, and Khrushchev's successors. In his younger days he had taken great pride in being a maverick; after the war he became more and more conservative. His best novels had been writen in the twenties; his later work did not remotely compare with *And Quiet Flows the Don*. In the late sixties Sholokhov too ran into trouble with the censors for having written a novel on the early years of the second world war that was too realistic in tone. Khrushchev had strongly admonished the writers in 1957 to keep within the bounds set by the party; he made it known that his hand would not tremble if transgressors had to be shot; there would be no Hungarian style revolt in the Soviet Union. Khrushchev's warning was followed by a general attack on the dissemination of 'rubbish', i.e. ideologically harmful and obsolete literature. Literature and works of art should be *ideiny*, it was announced; they should have a message which conformed with the party line. But what were the standards by which *ideinost* was to be judged, Ehrenburg asked in one of his essays. 'Sometimes a work the idea of which conflicts with the ideology of the critics is branded as idea-less (*bezideiny*).'

The narrow limits of the new freedom were shown in the case of Boris Pasternak. A great master of the Russian language, deeply imbued with a mystical belief in Russia's past, its soil, its people, he was awarded the Nobel prize in 1958 for his novel *Dr Zhivago*, published in Italy the year before. This was the story of a 'superfluous man', a physician deeply perturbed by the sufferings of his country but incapable of deciding between the camp of the revolution and its enemies, an anachronism, a hero very much in the tradition of the great nineteenth-century Russian novel. Zhivago was not an enemy of the Soviet order; he simply did not belong to it. Pasternak was forced to reject the Nobel prize, and was attacked in the Soviet press in the most violent terms as a degenerate and traitor to his country. He was ostracised, but neither arrested nor exiled whereas younger writers who had evaded Soviet literary censorship fared much worse: some were sent to lunatic asylums (such as Esenin-Volpin), others were exiled or given stiff prison sentences. The case of Sinyavsky (Abraham Tertz) and Yuli Daniel attracted attention and aroused a protest campaign all over the world. These two had written novels and essays for publication in the West, an act of high treason for which they were sent to a forced labour camp. In 1967 a similar fate befell a group of even younger writers (Dobrovolsky, Ginsburg, and others). Under Stalin these writers would have disappeared without trace; in the trials of the sixties not even an admission of guilt was obligatory and there was always the chance that after an interval of five or seven years the writers, if still alive, would be permitted to rejoin society though probably not in their professional capacity. The trials did not pass without protest inside the Soviet Union either: leading scientists, writers, and artists denounced the sentences despite the risks involved in incurring the displeasure of the régime. But there was less fear than before: those who had survived the Stalin era were unlikely to be overawed by his successors; the younger men and women who had reached maturity after 1953 were even less easily intimidated.

The Solzhenitsyn case is of great symptomatic interest in this context: a former army officer who had been interned for eight years in a forced labour camp described conditions there in a powerful autobiographical novel. The publication of *One Day in the Life of Ivan Denisovich* was not merely a literary event but a political sensation; the very existence of these camps had never been mentioned in print. The author was almost immediately attacked for distorting reality, for a pathological preoccupation with marginal and utterly insignificant aspects of Soviet life. The censorship refused to pass his next major novel (*The First Circle*) which was published eventually outside Russia. But Solzhenitsyn was not easily silenced; he circulated letters of protest to members of the Writers' Union, and his stand was a source of inspiration to many others. *Novy Mir*, the leading literary monthly and the main bulwark of the 'liberals', continued to appear despite constant threats and chicanery, sticking to its convictions within the limits of elementary caution.

The painters had come in for heavy attack in 1962 when Khrushchev, visiting their yearly exhibition, had been appalled by what he had seen. The same year the film makers ran into trouble for denigrating the achievements of the older generation and for showing ideological weakness in general. But despite these setbacks the rehabilitation continued of Soviet writers who had been purged in the thirties and forties; not only disgraced Soviet writers such as Isaac Babel or Michael Bulgakov were again published, but even some of the emigrés like Ivan Bunin and Konstantin Balmont. Western 'modernist' writing remained anathema, but the attacks became less strident; a few novels by Kafka and some plays by Ionesco were translated into Russian. The artistic merits of the decadent western writers were not denied, but it was maintained that works reflecting bourgeois decay and cultural disintegration could hardly be of relevance in a communist society. Interesting nonconformist literary and artistic work was done in outlying centres such as Tashkent and Alma Ata, Erevan and Tiflis, whereas in the past almost all such activity had been confined to Moscow and Leningrad; 'far from Moscow' had been synonymous with backwardness and reaction.

Soviet literature ceased to be monolithic; there were a great many internal conflicts, not to mention the usual literary feuds; in addition to the published

books there was a great deal of 'submerged' literature, privately circulated or
kept for posterity. 'Socialist realism' with its corollaries *partiinost* and
narodnost continued to be the official party line binding every writer, artist,
and composer, but it was so ill defined, had been undermined by so many
changing interpretations, that the invocation of the term had become fairly
meaningless; it meant that censorship was to continue, that no book critical
of the party line could appear, and that works of art should not be too
'modernistic' in character. Within these limits writers and artists had to
accommodate themselves. The older generation was on the whole thankful
for the progress that had been achieved since Stalin, but the younger one was
not easily satisfied with half measures. The very idea that a semi-educated
bureaucrat should prescribe to them what and what not to write seemed
intolerable.

Soviet intellectuals had been contemptuous of Khrushchev, the *muzhik*
whose bark had however been worse than his bite, they were unwilling to obey
his successors blindly. A generational conflict developed; the intellectuals of
the younger generation were certainly not anti-communist and their patriotism was certainly above suspicion. They did not question Marx, and Lenin
in their eyes was a mythical figure, beyond criticism. But for the problems of
the nineteen-sixties they failed to find answers in the writings of the fathers.
They saw nothing inconsistent between Marxism-Leninism (as they understood it) and the search for truth; they wanted to know all the facts about
the Stalin era and demanded guarantees to prevent a recurrence. They stood
for greater cultural freedom; the ban on writers such as Proust and Joyce
seemed indefensible as a matter of principle, and the restrictions on travel
abroad they resented as unacceptable police interference. Not all young
intellectuals belonged to the camp of the rebels; there were careerists and
conformists among them as among other age groups. The leaders of the
Komsomol (communist youth organisation) were in fact among the most
conservative elements in Soviet cultural life.

The great majority chose a compromise between the two extremes of open
rebellion and conformism; the poet Yevtushenko, one of the early rebels,
having been called to order by the authorities, continued to maintain an
independent pose while accepting, no doubt with reservations, the limitations
imposed on him. Within this area of licence, Yevtushenko and many of his
contemporaries adjusted themselves, hoping for further relaxation of controls
at some future date. Some of them dreamt about a moral rejuvenation of
communism, but it was not quite clear who would initiate such a movement.
Others rediscovered religion, while a few found a source of inspiration in Cuba
or similar far away countries, a modern version of the concept of the Noble
Savage. The official writers and artists organisations which had been of paramount importance up to the middle fifties lost their leading role and were

often bypassed. Public readings and exhibitions were arranged in the late fifties and early sixties, attracting sometimes thousands of people though they had no official sanction and there were certain risks involved.

The party leaders were firmly resolved not to give up control of literature and the arts. They viewed student activities with great misgivings; events in Poland and Hungary in 1956, and in Czechoslovakia in 1968, strengthened their belief that the most dangerous political consequences would ensue if the intellectuals and especially the intellectual youth were not kept on the leash. Intellectuals were always potential troublemakers; if their claim to be the conscience of the nation was not checked in time they were liable to spark off a real revolution. But the party authorities were also aware that some latitude had to be conceded to the intelligentsia, that control by the political police as blatant as in Stalin's days would cause much harm, that extreme measures had to be avoided, if only because they antagonised so many people inside the country and harmed Soviet prestige abroad. Since it was impossible to reach agreement on the extent of freedom to be granted to intellectuals, this became a permanent bone of contention between the intelligentsia and the authorities.

Mention has been made so far mainly of Soviet literature because it reflected so faithfully the vicissitudes of the party line in the post-Stalin era. Certain arts fared better than others; Soviet composers were more fortunate than painters and sculptors, for there was less government interference. The turning point in music came in 1957 with the second congress of Soviet composers. There was a real revival of Soviet music, especially in the symphonic field. Myaskovsky's last three symphonies, Prokofiev's sixth and seventh symphonies, Tikhon Khrennikov's violin concerto, and Shostakovich's symphonies nine to thirteen belong to that period. True, Shostakovich's thirteenth symphony had to be withdrawn, not for any musical reason but because it was based on Evtushenko's poem 'Baby Yar', describing the mass murder of Jews in Kiev under the nazi occupation, a subject that was looked upon with extreme disfavour by the party authorities, for it suggested that Soviet citizens had not done their utmost to save their fellow Jews. But his opera *Katerina Ismailovna* (Lady Macbeth of Mstensk), which had provoked such scandal in the thirties, was again performed and became the great musical event of 1962. Modern Western composers such as Hindemith, Poulenc, Milhaud, Orff, Britten and Honegger were again performed in the Soviet Union; even Stravinsky visited Moscow and was fêted like a prodigal son. All this was in stark contrast to the Stalin era, and if serial music re-remained beyond the pale, this did not prevent individual composers of the younger generation from employing the new idiom in their work, for private experimentation or enjoyment if not for publication. Western critics of the Soviet musical scene were in two minds as to the balance sheet of the fifties and sixties. The advance that had been made since Stalin's death was tremendous, the standards of performance were high and Soviet composers had brought musical enjoyment and literacy to millions of people. At the same time candour forced them to admit that (as in Soviet literature) there was less excellence and novelty in the sixties than in the twenties; that, to put it bluntly, no great composer and no interesting new theme or medium had emerged since Prokofiev and the young Shostakovich, i.e. since about 1930.

Soviet painters and sculptors were more in the public eye and fared on the whole less well. The monumental architectural style of the Stalin period went out of favour, the portraits of the Generalissimo disappeared, and the heroic-patriotic school of Gerassimov and other academicians no longer had the field all to itself. Foreign residents in Moscow as well as the literary avant-garde and many scientists patronised Neizvestny, Ilya Glazunov and other unorthodox painters. Like some members of the elder generation, such as Zaryan, Grabar, and Konchalovsky, they did not have to depend on state patronage. Occasionally attempts were made to bring the works of the more daring spirits to the knowledge of the general public. This seemed not too risky, for by Western standards their paintings and sculptures were certainly not avant-garde. Some had been influenced by expressionism, there were touches of surrealism, but also specific Russian motifs (as in the case of Glazunov). Yet since Russia had not shared in the post-impressionist development of painting these new works created a great furore and came under heavy attack, culminating in Khrushchev's explosion during his visit to the Manège exhibition in 1962. Bilyutin's pictures and Neizvestny's sculptures were more than the then party chief could stomach. But it was not a permanent setback as many had feared at the time; the clock was put back, but not to 1952. Little by little, forays continued to be made by courageous artists into the twilight zone between the officially approved and the officially forbidden.

The Soviet cinema moved away after Stalin from monumentality, stilted pathos, and black and white portraits; Chukhrai's *Ballad of a Soldier* and *Clear Skies*, Bondarchuk's *Destiny of a Man* and Kalatozov's *The Cranes are Flying*, were to the Soviet cinema what Ehrenburg's *Thaw* had been to literature. The human tragedy of the second world war was described with a great deal of feeling and truthfulness. Later on, in the late fifties and early sixties several films gave a realistic account of some of the real problems of Soviet citizens, without necessarily containing a clear positive message. There were successful adaptations of novels and plays (*Hamlet*, Yutkevich's *Othello*, Heifitz's *Lady with a little Dog*), which aroused much admiration in the West. In some important aspects the Soviet cinema continued to differ from contemporary Western films; its pathos, for instance, was a constant cause of bewilderment to Western viewers. That the Soviet cinema did not follow all the Western fads and fashions was not necessarily a great loss, but neither did it produce a style of its own that seemed of lasting interest and value. There were many competent and some interesting films, but no new Eisenstein or Pudovkin appeared on the scene. It was almost impossible to point to a specific Soviet school of the cinema, to fresh motifs and new approaches. The Soviet films of the twenties had been in the forefront of cinematic art and won great acclaim all over the world because they had something new to say. With a few exceptions, the films of the sixties clung to a well-established routine; they did not create much excitement inside Russia and did not evoke much interest outside.

The social sciences did not remain unaffected by the thaw: history and philosophy, economics, and psychology received a fresh impetus after 1953. Topics that had been taboo previously could now be discussed, many more books and new periodicals were published; historians, philosophers, and economists became, on the whole, much better informed about the work done by their colleagues in the West. The grosser forms of interference of the Stalin era (as in genetics and linguistics) ceased. The basic outlook, however, changed little; philosophy, economics, and history could be approached only on the basis of dialectical and historical materialism, and Marxist economics respectively. The assumption still prevailed that all fundamental issues had already been settled in the works of Marx, Engels, and Lenin, and that the only assignment of present-day philosophers, historians, and economists was to apply their methods to current problems. Any real advance beyond Marxism-Leninism was *a priori* impossible. True, according to the official doctrine Marxism-Leninism was a creative method that could and should be 'developed' further; but in practice it was treated not as a method but as a very detailed set of rules. Individual philosophers or historians were no more entitled to develop Marxism-Leninism than a medieval scholar would have been able to propound heterodox views on Christian theology. To have to conform with a dogma was bad enough, but historians, philosophers, and social scientists had to cope in addition with the recurrent changes in the party line and the reshuffles in the party leadership. This involved, to give but one example, the periodical rewriting of textbooks on recent Soviet history. There was less emphasis on Pavlovian psychology than in the Stalin period, but psychoanalysis and related schools still remained beyond the pale; philosophers and natural scientists had the difficult task of bringing Lenin's *Empiriocriticism*, written before the first world war, into line with revolutionary insight gained by modern science subsequently. Lenin's book officially remained the basic source of inspiration for the philosophers; the scientists usually bypassed it as irrelevant to their work. This became in many ways the general practice; wherever practical exigencies, as in the natural sciences, demanded it, outdated aspects of official doctrine were ignored; the scientific and technological development of the Soviet Union was not to be retarded, its economic and military power not to be impaired, because Engels in the *Dialectics of Nature* or Lenin in his writings had failed to foresee certain developments. There was much less elasticity in philosophy and history, in economic and social sciences. Basic changes in these fields would have undermined the ideological cohesion and thus ultimately the monolithic character of the Communist Party. Philosophy, history, and related disciplines were not independent sciences in the eyes of the party authorities but part and parcel of the official doctrine, and for that reason it seemed only logical that its practitioners had to act within a strictly defined frame of reference and under close supervision.

These, in broad outline, were the general principles of Soviet cultural policy. Fortunately, there was in practice often more latitude for the individual than might be expected. Provided lip service was paid to official doctrine and the ritual references made to the patristic texts, individuals could get away with a great deal of unorthodox, sometimes even heretical, ideas. While the body of doctrinal tenets did not change, the intensity of ideological belief lessened over the years. The intellectuals knew that official doctrine could not be frontally challenged, but there were many opportunities to circumvent and bypass it.

The position of the intelligentsia improved after the death of Stalin; their living conditions compared favourably with other sections of the population, ideological interference lessened outside the most sensitive areas. But intellectual ferment continued; far from being satisfied with the progress made, many intellectuals pressed for more far-reaching changes. They found it intolerable to be excluded from any effective say in basic decision making; they resented being prevented from freely travelling abroad, and having to suffer supervision and control by officials of little education and overbearing manner. Some observers of the scene had predicted that the gradual spread of cultural freedom was inevitable simply because the number of people with higher education was growing so rapidly over the years; in the long run it would be impossible to satisfy their demands with half measures. But the course of events has not so far given much support to these optimistic predictions; the aspirations of the intelligentsia cannot apparently be satisfied while the leadership insists on the ideological monopoly of the party, and the demand for more cultural freedom seems to be too intimately connected with the explosive issue of political liberty. Occasionally there has been willingness to grant a certain measure of freedom to intellectuals within the confines of their professional sphere on the understanding that they would refrain from expecting similar concessions in the political field. But such compromises were bound to be brittle, for the rebellious younger generation was always likely to ask for more than the party could concede.

The party leadership needed the intelligentsia and did not want to antagonise them, but it could even less afford to accept their more extreme demands. It was a basic conflict and it is likely to become even more acute. From time to time the more backward sections of the population with their latent anti-intellectual resentment had to be mobilised against the obstreperous intellectuals. The hopes that had been nurtured after the war, and again after Stalin's death, were thus not fulfilled. Cultural life in the fifties and sixties was still largely cut off from the rest of the world, and this at a time when the feeling of being part of the mainstream of European culture by both tradition and current aspirations was as acutely felt as ever among Soviet intellectuals. Much creative endeavour was frustrated and stifled, but there was also a great intensity in Soviet cultural life precisely because it evolved in an atmosphere of real tension. Russians have had to suffer in their recent history more than other European peoples and for that reason the longing for freedom was perhaps deeper and more genuine. They seemed to care more for these values because they had a better understanding of what it meant to be deprived of them. Soviet writers, artists, or scientists were in no way inferior to their colleagues in the West, even if they often lacked the opportunity to display their talent. A great creative potential existed, much of it submerged under official controls and restrictions. Sporadically some of this appeared on the surface and there was great promise for the day when the shackles would at last be broken.

PART IV

EUROPEAN POLITICS: 1955–1969

Introduction

Stalin's death and the gradual disappearance of the worst features of his régime gave rise to high hopes in the West: the end of the cold war was believed to be at hand, a new era of détente and peaceful coexistence seemed to have dawned over a continent torn by bitter strife. Such optimism was only natural; the international climate was bound to improve after having reached its nadir in 1951–2. But the optimism prevailing at the time in the western capitals was not altogether warranted; to a certain extent it was based on a misjudgment of the motives of Soviet policy, on the mistaken belief that 'cold war' and 'peaceful coexistence' were mutually exclusive policies, whereas in fact they were only different aspects of Soviet foreign policy. The new rulers of Russia resented many of Stalin's methods; they wanted, within limits, an improvement in relations with the West, and above all with the third world. They had a more realistic understanding than Stalin of the consequences of a nuclear war, and wanted therefore to reach an agreement on the banning of the use of nuclear weapons. But they were still Stalin's disciples, good communists and Soviet patriots, feeling in their bones that their régime was not secure so long as communism had not prevailed all over the world. They felt acutely threatened by the spread of western ideas to the 'Popular Democracies' and ultimately to the Soviet Union. It was not at all clear whether they could afford to pursue a policy of peaceful coexistence without jeopardising their whole system. Militarily the Soviet Union had little to fear and even though its economic performance was lagging behind western Europe's, there was steady improvement. Since only a handful of Soviet and east European citizens had the opportunity to compare western and communist living standards at first hand, economic discontent did not constitute a major problem. The demand for more political freedom presented a more serious challenge. To resist this with any effect the Soviet rulers had constantly to stress (and to exaggerate) the dangers allegedly facing the socialist camp from outside. Such an approach, however necessary for the survival of the régime, limited from the very beginning the scope of a *rapprochement* with the West. There was room for agreement on specific topics, but there could be no peaceful coexistence in the realm of ideas, as Soviet leaders frequently emphasised, and this in the last resort made a real détente impossible.

It is unlikely that the concept of world revolution has played a central role in Soviet political and strategic thought since the early nineteen-twenties. Under Stalin Soviet foreign policy was directed to the acquisition and consolidation of spheres of interest, and his successors pursued basically the same line. This at first sight seemed a reassuring development from the western point of view, for it created the precondition for a détente based on a division of spheres of influences as practised at Yalta and Potsdam. But the Soviet Union was still the leader of the communist camp; it could not simply abdicate from this role and the growing conflict with China made it altogether impossible for Russia to follow a policy based only on national interest. The West based its policy on 'status quo' thinking; the Soviet leaders could not do so, for it would have fatally undermined the legitimacy of their rule. Soviet communism had little appeal in Europe beyond the borders of the Soviet state, but this did not make the Soviet leaders lose interest in the outside world. The Soviet positions in Poland, East Germany, Czechoslovakia, and Hungary were, they argued, necessary guarantees for the security of the Soviet state. But were the achievements of socialism in the 'Popular Democracies' safe without yet another *cordon sanitaire* beyond the Iron Curtain – a neutral Germany, for instance? These aspirations clashed head-on with the desire of the European peoples to remain independent. Soviet troops had advanced into the heart of Europe; they were now stationed 150 miles from the French border, 300 from the English Channel. Any further advance would have given them total domination of the continent. It is unlikely that Soviet leaders actively contemplated at any time after the war a march on the Channel, but it is not so certain that they would have missed the opportunity, had it arisen, to acquire a dominating position in western Europe.

The Military Balance

Military considerations played a central role in the political negotiations of the fifties and sixties and they ought to be at least briefly discussed. 'Massive retaliation' was the official American strategy during the middle fifties, the threat to use the American nuclear arsenal to repel even a local Soviet attack. Russia could not at the time threaten the American continent, but western Europe was to all intents and purposes a Soviet hostage. In October 1957 the first sputnik was launched and at about the same time the Soviet Union began to develop its first intercontinental ballistic missiles (ICBM). In Europe there was growing scepticism about the massive retaliation doctrine; would America in a real crisis be willing to sacrifice American cities for the sake of Berlin or even Paris and London? Would not undue reliance on nuclear bombs eventually lead to defeatism? For while a general war was ruled out, local military action by the Soviet Union was certainly not, and there was no known way to counter it but by matching it in conventional strength. France and Britain had their own modest nuclear programmes, but their conventional forces were inadequate, and western Europe could not be defended without American help. France and Britain, Germany and Italy had mobilised millions of soldiers in the first and second world wars, but in the postwar world they found it increasingly difficult to make even the modest military effort needed to contribute their share to the defence of Europe. Britain and France had imperial commitments, but even after these had been liquidated the military position of the West in Europe did not substantially improve and NATO was permanently under strength. There was a striking incongruence between western Europe's economic performance and its military impotence which restricted its freedom of action and ultimately its political influence. It had, for instance, a much greater stake in the Middle East than the United States in view of its dependence on oil supplies from the Persian Gulf and North Africa, but because of its military weakness and the absence of a common policy, it was incapable of defending its interests there and was practically reduced to the role of passive onlooker in the struggle between the Soviet Union and the United States for influence in the Middle East.

Painfully aware of their own weakness, many western observers tended in the late fifties and early sixties to overrate Soviet military strength; the Kremlin, needless to say, did nothing to dispel these fears. Its nuclear arsenal was at the time much smaller than commonly assumed; it began to catch up with America only in 1966, while its conventional strength in Europe was probably only half of the 175 divisions with which it was generally credited. But even if Russia's real military strength was not as formidable as commonly assumed, it kept the initiative in foreign policy, trying to force the West out of Berlin and attempting to establish missile bases in Cuba. Once their bluff was called by President Kennedy, the Soviet leaders retreated, and the West made a more realistic appraisal of Soviet strength. Moscow's foreign policy makers showed greater circumspection during the subsequent years, stressing in their speeches the great destruction that would be caused in a future war; hitherto they had been reluctant to deal with the subject. They accused the Chinese of reckless adventurism: Peking, they said, wanted to push America and Russia over the brink, believing that with the elimination of its two main rivals the road would be clear for the Chinese to dominate the world. But how, Khrushchev asked, could a real Marxist possibly argue that nuclear war was a paper tiger? Did the Chinese really think that bombs recognised class distinctions? Drawing the lessons of Cuba and Berlin, the Soviet leaders decided to acquire greater military mobility by developing their naval and air forces. By 1968 it was generally assumed that the Soviet Union would soon achieve strategic parity with the West, if that concept still had any meaning in the age of overkill.

The story of West-East contacts between 1955 and the present day is a series of frequent ups and downs. The great expectations of 1955 ('the spirit of Geneva') faded quickly as the meetings of heads of states and foreign ministers failed to produce any tangible results, and the invasion of Hungary seemed to quash all hope of an understanding. This was followed by several minor crises, and, in 1959, by a fresh upsurge of optimism following Khrushchev's visit to the United States. A new freeze was the result of the failure of the Paris summit in 1960. The Cuban missile crisis however cleared the air for a new détente which gave birth to the Nuclear Test Ban Treaty of August 1963. Khrushchev's successors seemed a little less enthusiastic about friendly relations with the West but they did not radically reverse his policy. It was the general belief in the western capitals between 1963 and 1968 that the 'Europeanisation of Russia' was an inevitable process. But developments inside Russia lent no support to this optimistic assessment, and the invasion of Czechoslovakia created new fears among Russia's neighbours. If, according to the Brezhnev doctrine of 1968, the Soviet Union was entitled to interfere in the affairs of its east European allies, what was there to prevent it giving military support in favourable circumstances to its partisans in the non-communist world? The Soviet leaders seemed to have no such plans for the immediate future; they went out of their way in an attempt to obliterate the unfortunate impression created by Czechoslovakia. Hungary, they must have reasoned, had been forgotten after a few years, and so would Czechoslovakia. But it was not at all certain that new sources of conflict would not develop. The peoples of eastern Europe had not become reconciled to Soviet interference and their striving for more freedom and national independence was bound from time to time to upset all calculations. There were, in addition, many other sources of conflict in West-East relations.

The Spirit of Geneva

Soon after Stalin's death the idea of a summit meeting was mooted as the most likely way to break the deadlock between the two blocs. Stalin's successors wanted a détente, but the new collective leadership needed time to agree on the form and substance of an approach. The idea of a summit meeting, to be followed by a conference of foreign ministers, had originated in the western capitals; it was welcomed by Marshal Bulganin, the then head of the Soviet government, once the struggle for power in the politburo had come to a temporary halt. At his meeting with Eisenhower, Eden, and Faure in Geneva in November 1955, the main topics on the agenda were Germany and control of nuclear weapons. Briefly, the Soviet aim was the removal of American bases from Europe, which it regarded as the main military danger; it was also Soviet policy to prevent, or at any rate to postpone, German rearmament. The Western powers, on the other hand, put the stress on the German question: without the reunification of Germany, they claimed, there would be no lasting peace in Europe. They were convinced that without the presence of American forces, and short of a substantial German contribution to NATO, western Europe would be unable to resist Soviet political and military pressure. But the Russians had lost what little enthusiasm they had had previously for the idea of German reunification; they wanted a neutral Germany and were opposed to free all-German elections which would have resulted in a certain communist defeat. On the other hand, they took the initiative with a sweeping proposal for an unconditional ban on all nuclear devices. The western powers were not eager to discuss this, being only too aware of Soviet superiority in conventional military strength, and since the Soviet blueprint made no provision for international inspection it was not difficult to find fault with it. To the Soviets the idea of foreign observers snooping around their military installations was utterly repugnant; they wanted to rest the unconditional ban on mutual trust. But the trust did not exist, and any such arrangement would have put the West at a clear disadvantage, for in the Soviet Union it would have been relatively easy to produce bombs and to hide them, but almost impossible to do so in the open western societies. President Eisenhower then suggested the 'Open Sky' plan as a possible solution to the question of inspection, but this was not acceptable to Moscow. The Geneva meeting and the subsequent Foreign Ministers' Conference ended with the participants – in the words of a British observer – still looking at each other across the Great Divide.

The meetings were not, however, a total loss, for they reflected greater willingness than before to look for common ground. The Soviet Union certainly showed greater readiness to normalise its relations with some of its European neighbours, notably Yugoslavia, Austria, and Finland. Khrushchev's visit to Belgrade in 1955 and Tito's mission to Moscow the following year signified the end of the bitter feud that had raged after Yugoslavia's expulsion from the Cominform. The Kremlin recognised in principle the existence of different roads to socialism, and while Soviet-Yugoslav relations were by no means undisturbed in the subsequent years,

Tito's right to pursue an independent policy was by and large recognised. A new serious crisis arose however in 1968 with the reassertion of Soviet military power throughout eastern Europe, when Yugoslavia felt itself directly threatened. Soviet willingness to conclude a peace treaty with Austria (the *Staatsvertrag*) ended a deadlock of almost ten years during which it had been Moscow's policy to maintain that the Austrian question could be considered only in the general context of the German problem. Suddenly the Soviet position changed: Austria undertook not to allow military bases on its territory and not to join alliances, whereupon the Soviet Union withdrew its forces and Austria regained full political independence.

Some western observers, greatly encouraged by this development, thought that the Austrian treaty could serve as a model for Germany. But this was an unrealistic assumption; Germany was the great prize to be won in the cold war. Its strategic position made it most unlikely that it could ever be neutralised. Chancellor Adenauer was as little inclined as the Russian leaders to make any substantial concessions. He was convinced that Moscow would have gradually to modify its attitude towards West Germany; in his eyes the Soviet Union was a colossus with feet of clay which would weaken, if not disintegrate, as a result of its internal contradictions and the growing pressure exerted by the 'Yellow Peril'. The changes inside the country after Stalin's death reinforced his belief; when a Soviet invitation to visit Moscow was extended to him in June 1955 he accepted, though with notable lack of enthusiasm, mainly perhaps to satisfy his domestic critics who had argued all along that no opportunity to reach an agreement with Russia should be missed. The Soviet Union wanted normal relations with West Germany but was unwilling to pay a high price. Adenauer's visit to Moscow led to a restoration of normal diplomatic and trade ties between the two countries, but there was no basic change in Soviet-German relations. It remained the only visit of a German head of government to the Soviet Union in the postwar period, and the one tangible result was the return of the last German prisoners of war from the Soviet camps. Some of Adenauer's critics later maintained that the old Chancellor was not flexible enough in his approach to the Soviet Union; there was a real chance for a new *rapprochement* with Russia, perhaps even a new Rapallo. But Rapallo, the often invoked symbol of the pro-Russian orientation in Germany in the early years after the first world war, had been a gesture, a demonstration, rather than a consistent policy. The Soviet leaders certainly would have liked to detach West Germany from the Western alliance but they had little to offer in exchange. The Warsaw Pact was based on the argument that the Soviet Union had to protect Poland, Czechoslovakia, and the other east European states against aggressive German militarism. This was the justification for the Soviet military presence in eastern Europe, and Moscow would not have been able to draw a united

Germany as a senior partner into its orbit without completely upsetting its whole system of pacts and alliances. Politically, a close alliance with a united Germany that had not opted for communism was not really feasible; it was a chimera hatched by ambitious but shortsighted ambassadors and beer table strategists.

Adenauer's visit to Moscow thus failed to bring a solution of the German problem any nearer; it continued to be the most important single issue in West-East relations in Europe. It would not necessarily have prevented a *rapprochement* between the two blocs as far as other aspects of relations were concerned, but with the sudden outbreak of rebellions in eastern Europe, the Russians concentrated on reasserting their hold over their own camp. This was clearly not the time for new initiatives in international relations, and western public opinion, which followed with great sympathy the stirrings in Russia's former satellites, would hardly have been receptive to any new Soviet moves. For the time being further top level negotiations were ruled out.

The Polish October

Boiling point was reached first in Poland. The economic and social consequences of Stalinism had given rise to intolerable tensions in all walks of life, and as political controls were slightly relaxed under the 'New Course' there was open talk about the shortcomings of the communist régime. The party leadership was deeply split; Bierut, Moscow's man, who had been both Prime Minister and First Secretary of the party, died suddenly during a visit to Moscow in the summer of 1956. Ochab, whom the Russians wanted as his successor, was a middle-of-the-roader; opposed to liberal reforms, he was nevertheless willing to compromise, realising that the country could no longer be ruled with Stalinist methods. The die-hards in the leadership, the so-called Natolin group, on the other hand, were firmly opposed to any basic change; they were willing to call on the Soviet army, if necessary, to suppress the reform movement. But these men were isolated; the masses were prepared to fight rather than to endure the tyranny any longer. The spirit of rebellion was infectious: in an act of open defiance, the Polish party leadership refused to re-elect to the politburo Rokossowski, the Soviet Marshal, who had been appointed by Moscow to function as Polish War Minister. The security police, having been purged of its Stalinist high command, was unwilling to support the Natolin group. The diehards could count on Pax, a non-communist Catholic organisation headed by Piasecki, a prewar leader of a pro-fascist organisation, who after his arrest by the Soviet secret police in 1944 had thrown in his lot with the Russians. But Pax, too, was a small isolated group, ostracised by the great majority of Polish Catholics.

The liberals were a minority in the party leadership but the middle-of-the-roaders were willing to enter into a tactical alliance with them, and they had the support of the overwhelming majority of the rank and file of the party. Students and writers played a leading role in giving expression to the discontent of the masses; Adam Wazyk, in his widely read and discussed 'Poem for Adults', castigated the failures and shortcomings which everyone knew, but no one had dared to condemn hitherto. *Po Prostu*, a student newspaper, suddenly gained great popularity by spearheading the fight for freedom. There were mass meetings and demonstrations in the streets of Warsaw and other Polish cities; everything indicated that the point of explosion was near.

It was in this critical situation that Gomulka's candidacy for the highest party post was first mooted and found an overwhelming response. When the eighth party plenum convened on 19 October 1956, the main points on the agenda were to co-opt Gomulka and three of his political supporters to the central committee, and to nominate him to the position of first secretary of the party. Wladislav Gomulka, a member of the Communist Party since 1926, did not have many allies among the leaders of the party. He was respected for his personal integrity, but his modest intellectual gifts and certain deficiencies and traits of character did not make him an eminently suitable candidate for the position. In the eyes of many Poles, however, he symbolised in 1956 the resistance to Soviet domination. He had fought in the underground during the war but was removed from the party leadership in 1949 and subsequently arrested as a 'national deviationist'. Released from prison in late 1954, he was not at first fully rehabilitated. Gomulka rejected the offer of some minor post, for he was convinced that in view of the split in the party leadership and the critical situation in the country his return to a key position was merely a question of time. For the rank and file party member Gomulka was the saviour, the man of the hour, and the anti-communists, i.e. the majority of the population, regarded him as the lesser evil in comparison with the Bierut-Minc faction which had ruled Poland since 1945.

The Soviet leaders were greatly worried about the turn events had taken in Warsaw and on the day the critical party plenum opened they arrived unannounced in the Polish capital. There were bitter recriminations: Khrushchev, Molotov, and their colleagues accused the Polish politburo of anti-Soviet propaganda and of many other sins in the communist calendar. But the Poles stood their ground against all attempts to interfere in their internal affairs. There were mass demonstrations in favour of Gomulka and the Soviet leaders must have realised within a very short time that the suppression of the 'Polish October' could be effected only through massive military intervention. Gomulka assured the Soviet leaders that Poland would remain a loyal member of the communist bloc and continue to support Soviet foreign and defence policies. He resisted the growing popular demand for the withdrawal of the Soviet troops from Poland. Very reluctantly the visitors gave their blessing to the new Polish leadership. It is not at all certain that they would not have opposed Gomulka's rise to power more actively but for the turn events had taken in Hungary. Moscow preferred to deal with one emergency at a time, and the situation in Warsaw seemed harmless enough in comparison with the rapidly unfolding crisis in Hungary. Gomulka and his supporters ousted the Stalinist clique from the politburo and proclaimed their own 'Polish road' to socialism. The tremendous wave of political activity all over Poland, on the crest of which they had seized power, was soon arrested; after the take-over Gomulka did all he could to regain control over political life. The Polish people was told that it had to be satisfied with the gains that had been achieved; Poland's geographical situation between the Soviet Union and communist East Germany narrowly circumscribed its freedom of action. The fact that Poland had acquired substantial territories that had formerly belonged to Germany also made the alliance with Russia a political necessity. Anti-Russian feeling had been in the past as strong as anti-German in Poland, but with the change in the European balance of power, Soviet paramountcy had to be accepted; the new official Polish ideology based itself on anti-Germanism as its main component.

Gomulka was widely praised at the time for providing responsible leadership, sparing his country a civil war and Soviet intervention. While making concessions to the Russians, he was able to secure for Poland a greater measure of freedom than enjoyed by any other communist country at the time. He induced the Soviet leaders to cancel the Polish debts and as a result of this and other measures the economic situation of the country began slowly to improve. He did not press for the collectivisation of agriculture (this was the one really unique feature of the 'Polish road'), and sought a *modus vivendi* with the Church, which was more influential in Poland than in any other east European country. The concessions made to the intellectuals were gradually withdrawn. *Po Prostu*, the journal which had played such a central role in the struggle against the Stalinists, was suppressed in October 1957. Leading Polish intellectuals left the Communist Party in protest against the reimposition of cultural controls. They had mistakenly expected that the new régime would follow a radically different course, even though Gomulka had made it clear from the very beginning that he was opposed to both dogmatism (Stalinism) and revisionism, i.e. the demand for more freedom. The great hopes raised by October thus slowly faded away: Poland still remained for some years the freest 'Popular Democracy', and the East German leaders were worried that the 'destructive influence' of Polish ideas would contaminate the younger generation in their country. But Gomulka gave full and loyal support to the Russians even against Tito, and the Soviet leaders had no reason subsequently to regret the approval given to him in 1956.

As hope gave way again to disillusionment and cynicism in Poland, the new leadership became isolated. There had been only a brief encounter between the Polish *pays réel* and *pays légal* during the critical days of October. But since Gomulka was in effective control of the army and the security forces, and since the public had become more and more apathetic, there was no scope for an active opposition movement. The intellectuals were in opposition to the régime, but lacking mass support they made little impact on the public at large. Within a decade after October the Gomulka régime, once the most liberal and progressive by east European standards, was to become a pillar of orthodoxy in the communist camp.

Revolution in Hungary

Communism in Hungary did not succeed in enlisting mass support during the early years of its rule. Imposed on the country by the Soviet army, the Communits Party barely managed to cling to power. Its economic policy resulted in a considerable lowering of living standards and the disaffection of the great majority of the population. There was no active opposition to the régime because of the terror, but once the fear lessened a revolutionary situation was bound to arise. The revelations about the crimes of the Stalin era at the Soviet Communist Party congress in 1956 greatly weakened the self-confidence of the old leadership. The most discredited members of the government, such as Rakosi, were dropped in July 1956 and some minor concessions were made to popular opinion: it was the classical example of a bad government making half-hearted attempts to reform itself in order to weather a coming storm. Instead of appeasing the masses, this policy gave a powerful impetus to the opposition movement. The intellectuals and the students demanded freedom of criticism, while old party members now released from prison insisted on basic policy changes such as the democratisation of political life and the removal of all old Stalinists. The ferment in Poland also had a great impact on developments in Hungary; during the second half of October the revolutionary agitation reached its climax. On the 23rd all political meetings and demonstrations were banned and when this order was defied, the AVH (secret police) opened fire on the crowds. In protest the workers joined the struggle, revolutionary committees were set up throughout Hungary, and the troops that were sent to defend the régime refused to obey and fraternised with the rebels. In desperation the Hungarian government called on the Soviet troops stationed in the country to intervene, but the Russians were not prepared at this stage for an effective military operation against the insurgents. The revolutionary movement spread like wildfire, the supporters of the old régime disappeared overnight, freedom of speech was restored, and the borders of Hungary were opened for the first time in a decade.

The Hungarian government and Communist Party were still led at that stage by Rakosi's closest collaborators such as Gerö, who made a belated attempt to reassert their authority in the face of the rising protest movement. These diehards were opposed to the return to power of Imre Nagy, who symbolised liberal communism in the eyes of most Hungarians. Nagy had been Prime Minister in 1954, was dismissed and purged the year after and restored to party membership only in October 1956. Events in Hungary moved within a few days much faster and much farther than in Poland. The Stalinists did succeed in containing the revolution; Nagy became head of a coalition government in which some of the traditional parties such as the Smallholders were also represented. To some observers this seemed the beginning of a return to a democratic multi-party system. In his negotiations with Moscow Nagy demanded the withdrawal of the Soviet troops, Hungary's release from the Warsaw Pact, and recognition of its neutral status between East and West. Such manifestations of independence by a former satellite were of course quite unacceptable to the Kremlin and only hastened the decision to invade Hungary.

A great many explanations have been provided for the success of the Poles and the failure of the Hungarians in 1956. Nagy, to be sure, did not always act decisively, nor did he receive much help from his own supporters; the insurgents did not lay down their arms even after the Stalinists had been routed, and the ultimative demand for Hungary's neutralisation was a bad tactical move. But even with the benefit of hindsight it is difficult to see how Nagy could have acted differently. The revolutionary movement in Hungary was even more intense than in Poland, but it did not have sufficient time to organise itself and to work out a clear policy. The old party leadership had resisted the movement for reform up to the last moment, thus making a revolutionary outburst inevitable.

The international situation, the involvement of Britain and France in the Suez operation, may have further contributed to the Soviet decision to intervene; it certainly made the suppression of the Hungarian revolution easier as far as world opinion was concerned. But events in Czechoslovakia 12 years later showed that not too much importance should be attributed to these factors; even if liberal communism had been far more restrained, even if Nagy had been more cautious and if the demand for leaving the Warsaw Pact had not been advanced, the Soviet leaders would in all probability still have opted in favour of military intervention. World public opinion does not count for much in Moscow's eyes if basic Soviet interests are involved. Nor was the Soviet Union impressed by Hungary's call for help to the United Nations, and the support for Hungary given by Peking, Belgrade, and Warsaw was purely platonic.

Hungarian resistance continued for a few days after the attack by Soviet tanks on 4 November, but it was a fight against overwhelming odds; having admitted defeat, the Hungarian government sought asylum in the Yugoslav embassy in Budapest. The military battle had easily been won by the Soviet forces, but the political aim of the intervention was more difficult to attain. The Stalinist old guard could not be called upon to form a new government; middle-of-the-road collaborationists were needed, able and willing to work with the Soviet Union for the 'normalisation' of the situation. They found such a man in the person of Janos Kadar, an old communist who in background and orientation had much in common with Gomulka. One of the few party leaders of working-class origin, he had not been in the Soviet Union during the war and had been arrested and imprisoned during the purge of the early fifties. In 1956 he was one of the leading liberal communists; as such he joined the Nagy government, and he was not even among those who opposed the decision to renounce the Warsaw Pact. Then, suddenly, within a few hours he changed sides, declared that counter-revolutionary forces were taking advantage of Nagy's weakness, and established a counter-government which appealed for Soviet intervention to give legitimacy to the invasion. Kadar's sudden change of heart has not been satisfactorily explained to this day; it has been said that he had been chosen by the Soviet leaders to be Rakosi's successor well before the revolution, but that the uprising had interfered with the orderly execution of this plan.

The task facing Kadar after the suppression of the uprising was not an enviable one. Having been carried to power by the Soviet troops he lost all popular support. In the eyes of all but a handful of his compatriots he was a quisling who had sold his country to the Russians. Kadar governed by martial law; the rule of the political police was restored, strikes were suppressed by mass arrests, leading writers were given long prison sentences. Nagy and the members of his government left the Yugoslav embassy, having been promised that nothing untoward would happen to them, only to be arrested outside the building. They were tried in secret, and only much later did it become known that several of them, including Nagy, had been executed.

The Soviet invasion and the ensuing counter-revolution caused a wave of indignation all over Europe. Passions were running high and for some months it seemed as if the Soviet invasion had destroyed forever the chance of a *rapprochement* between East and West, and that it also marked a great divide in the history of the communist camp. Cynical observers predicted that Hungary would soon be forgotten and subsequent events proved them right. The invasion did not have a great impact outside western Europe; most Asian and Middle-East countries abstained in the United Nations from voting for the withdrawal of the Soviet troops. A few west European communists left their parties in protest, but the communist camp soon recovered its balance and the Soviet decision to invade Hungary was universally accepted. After a suitable interval western statesmen resumed their contacts with Moscow; as far as they were concerned this had been an internal affair within the Soviet sphere of interest; the idea of responding to the appeal for help by the Nagy government had never been seriously considered, for no one wanted to risk a world war for Hungary. The 180,000 Hungarians who left the country after the Soviet invasion were welcomed in the West and received much sympathy; after a few months they, too, were forgotten.

A comparison between Kadar and Gomulka shows many parallels in their early careers but wide divergencies in their policies after 1956. Gomulka came to power on a wave of resistance to Moscow, while Kadar was imposed on his country by the Soviet army. The circumstances under which Kadar gained power could hardly have been less auspicious, but ten years later Hungary was beyond doubt the freer country. While Gomulka had steadily moved towards the reimposition of tight controls and the suppression of all democratic stirrings, Kadar had followed a more liberal policy, removing the leading Stalinists from their posts, deideologising daily life, concentrating on economic development and the raising of living standards. After 1963 those Czech, East German, and Polish communists who wanted more freedom began to look to Budapest, for Hungary went further than other communist countries in its opening to the West and in its economic reforms. Kadar's government, which at first had been among the most vulnerable in east Europe, gradually became one of the more stable régimes. This was not necessarily an indication of its popularity, but, on the contrary as many observers have pointed out, a sign of growing public apathy. After the heroic struggle of 1956 more and more Hungarians understood that in view of their geopolitical position there was no hope that real independence would be restored to their country in the near future: the Soviet Union would not give up its hold. The realisation of these basic facts made for despair and cynicism but also for the reluctant acceptance of a state of affairs that was not likely to change in the foreseeable future. The revolutionary spirit exhausted itself and gave way to a mood of *attentisme*. Kadar's régime did not succeed in appeasing the Hungarian people, let alone in infusing any enthusiasm among them, but it managed to neutralise public opinion in the country, which was no mean achievement after the defeat and the bloodletting of 1956.

Suez

While the eyes of the world were still focused on Warsaw and Budapest, Britain and France became involved in an ill-starred military expedition that was to end in utter failure and a severe loss of prestige. Earlier that year the United States had decided to withdraw its promised financial aid for the Aswan dam in retaliation against the anti-western policy pursued by Colonel Nasser. The Egyptian leader reacted in July 1956 by nationalising the Suez Canal, a step viewed with the gravest concern in London and Paris. Prime Minister Eden thought that British influence would be destroyed if Nasser was permitted to get away with such 'Hitlerian techniques'. The reaction in Paris was if possible even more violent, in view of Egypt's help for the Algerian rebels. The Suez Canal was an international waterway, but since Nasser had barred Israeli ships from passing through it, what would prevent him from closing it to ships from western nations? Nasser was threatening the 'imperialists' with death and destruction, and the leaders of western Europe were well aware that their industrial development depended to a large extent on regular oil supplies from the Persian Gulf. It was feared that once their lifeline was cut their economies would be paralysed.

The British and French governments tried without success to enlist the help of other states, but for the Americans the Canal was of only minor importance; they preferred to stay aloof and opposed any military action against Nasser. Other nations argued that since ownership of the Suez Canal was anyway to pass into Egyptian hands in the late nineteen-sixties, one might as well put up with Nasser's action and try to reach a settlement. Two conferences in London and the establishment of an Association of Canal Users brought no tangible results; Dulles thought that the management of the Canal ought to be taken out of the Egyptian hands, but he had no practical suggestions as to how this could be done. It was decided to recall the western pilots but this proved to be wholly ineffective; they were quickly replaced by Egyptian and Soviet bloc nationals who managed without great difficulty to keep the traffic moving. The dispute was then submitted to the Security Council, and Mr Hammarskjöld tried unsuccessfully to work out a solution acceptable to both sides. But Nasser was not in a mood to compromise; his gamble had paid off; with Russian support and American reluctance to get involved in the conflict, he had little to fear. His policy was tremendously popular inside Egypt. For a century the country had been a pawn of the big powers; now for the first time it had a leader who stood up to western pressure and threats and reasserted Egyptian independence. This was the feeling in Cairo and the other Arab capitals; almost overnight Nasser emerged as the undisputed leader of the whole Arab world.

When the diplomatic moves had failed Eden and Mollet (the French Prime Minister at the time) began to discuss military action against Egypt; subsequently Israeli leaders were also called in. Israel felt acutely threatened by Nasser who had sworn to destroy the Jewish state; the Egyptians had also closed the Straits of Tiran to Israeli navigation. Egypt moreover had established on its territory bases for irregular armed units which were used for hit and run attacks across the Israeli border. During 1955 and 1956 the number of these incidents multiplied and most Israelis felt that the situation had become intolerable. The Arab leaders did not heed Israel's warnings that it would not put up with the blockade and the armed incursions. Taking an extremely grave view of the situation, the Israeli leaders grasped the opportunity to have indirect British and French support for a military operation against Egypt. There certainly was 'collusion' between Israel and Britain and France; how far it extended has not been fully established. The Israelis attacked on 29 October 1956 and within a few days routed the Egyptian army in the Sinai peninsula. The British and French governments announced that they would intervene to separate the two armies, but the execution of their plan was little better than its conception, or perhaps the speed of the Israeli victory had taken the planners by surprise. British paratroopers landed in Suez and Port Said only on 5 November and by that time both London and Paris were already under heavy pressure to withdraw. Inside Britain liberal and left-wing opinion regarded the Suez operation as disastrous folly, a return to the days of gunboat diplomacy and imperialism. In the United Nations Britain and France were isolated, Washington was extremely displeased, and a note from Bulganin, the Soviet Prime Minister, contained a hardly veiled threat to bomb London and Paris. This Soviet warning came only after it was already clear that Britain and France would in any case withdraw their forces, and it was therefore not taken seriously; American pressure constituted a far greater danger. London's financial position was precarious, and it could hardly afford to antagonise Washington. Britain stopped military operations one day after the Israelis had accepted the UN ceasefire order. Great American pressure was also exerted on Israel, and on 8 November Ben Gurion decided to withdraw his troops from all the territories that had been occupied. The Israelis gained ten years respite from this war. True, Egyptian hostility did not diminish and Israeli ships were not permitted to use the Suez Canal, but the Egyptians did not interfere with Israeli ships in the Gulf of Aqaba, and the presence of the United Nations observers team (UNEF) which kept guard on the border from the Egyptian side prevented the outbreak of major clashes. Ten years later, in May 1967, Nasser decided that the time had come to demand the withdrawal of UNEF and to close the Gulf of Aqaba again, and thus triggered off the chain of events that led to the third Arab-Israeli war.

The Anglo-French action against Egypt had been based on a double miscalculation. Eden and Mollet had exaggerated the damage Nasser's policy was likely to cause to their interests; at the same time, they overrated their own ability to defeat Nasser's designs. Nasser had far-reaching ambitions, aiming ultimately at the establishment of a great pan-Arab empire from the Atlantic to the Persian Gulf. But Egypt, one of the poorest countries of the world, was a brittle foundation for such big-power aspirations. For this reason, if for no other, the comparisons with Hitler, freely bandied about at the time, were grossly misleading. Nasser's wild speeches, his whole style which was reminiscent of the dictators of the thirties, had been taken far too seriously. As subsequent events were to show, he failed to impose his will on his fellow Arabs and Egypt's military forces did not make much headway against Yemen's tribes, let alone against the Israeli army. The Egyptian régime was strong on propaganda, but weak in most other respects. It is in fact doubtful whether Nasser would have lasted for many years after 1956 but for the Anglo-French attack. He faced a great many difficulties at home and was suffering setbacks abroad. But his success in resisting the military attack of two major European powers gave him immense domestic credit and made him a great hero far beyond the confines of the Arab world. The defeat of the Egyptian army by the Israelis was explained as the result of collusion between them and the western powers; alone, it was argued, the Israelis would never have dared to invade Egypt, and had they attacked they would have been routed.

The failure of the Suez operation precipitated the loss of the last British and French positions in the Middle East and North Africa. But the French difficulties in Algeria and the trouble the British faced in Aden had not been instigated by Egypt. Nasser assisted the rebels, but they were not his creatures; sooner or later the former colonial powers would have been compelled to surrender their last positions. The Suez defeat caused Eden's resignation and it made many people in Britain and France aware for the first time of the limits of Europe's power in the world. The two super powers kept watch on their spheres of influence, and they could afford to defend their interests if necessary by force of arms. Britain and France on the other hand had descended to a minor league and had to adjust both their aims and their policies to their new standing in the world.

West-East Relations 1956 – 1961

After the failure of the summit meeting in 1955 and the east European and Suez crises, there was an interval in negotiations between Moscow and the West. Bulganin resumed his correspondence with Eisenhower in March 1957, suggesting a new approach to a nuclear test ban in the form of a moratorium on tests for two or three years under the control of an international commission. In October 1957 a new plan for a demilitarised zone in central Europe was submitted by Adam Rapacki, Poland's Foreign Minister, no doubt with the Soviet Union's blessing. In the meantime NATO forces in Europe had been equipped with tactical nuclear weapons and the disarmament problem assumed ever growing urgency. Experts from West and East met in Geneva in July 1958 in the first of a series of conferences to deal with ways of controlling nuclear tests and measures to prevent surprise attacks. These negotiations lasted more than five years; they covered both policy issues and technical problems such as the establishment of observer posts and the composition of the commission that was to supervise the control system. The West favoured a neutral chairman but the Russians, who had developed an intense dislike of Dag Hammarskjöld, the Swedish Secretary-General of the United Nations, maintained that only nations could be neutral, but not individuals. After protracted debates and countless blueprints that were submitted, discussed, and rejected, the ice was suddenly broken in August 1963 and a nuclear test ban agreement signed, not because the experts had at long last found an ingenious formula, but as the result of a change of heart in the Kremlin.

The year 1958 began with several promising Soviet moves designed to reduce international tension, but it ended with a Soviet ultimatum on Berlin which precipitated a new and exceedingly serious world crisis. Bulganin had suggested in January 1958 a new summit conference; the western leaders, with the failure of 1955 still fresh in their minds, insisted that this should be preceded by a foreign ministers meeting to establish whether there was sufficient common ground for the success of a summit meeting. Following up its peace offensive, the Soviet government announced in March the unilateral suspension of nuclear tests for the duration of six months. The impact of this move on the West was smaller than expected, for the announcement had come, as Eisenhower pointed out in his reply to Bulganin, just after Moscow had completed a series of tests of unprecedented intensity. Dissatisfied with the lack of progress and under new pressure to regain the foreign political initiative, the Kremlin veered in the autumn to a more militant line. Khrushchev, who had become the chief Soviet spokesman, made it known in November that the situation in West Berlin was a serious and acute threat to peace that could no longer be tolerated, and announced that the Soviet Union would hand over its functions in West Berlin to the East German government at the end of six months; it was willing to accept either the demilitarisation of West Berlin or a solution within a general German peace treaty, but it was not ready to put up any longer with the status quo. The Soviet Union had frequently pressed for a change in the status quo in central Europe, but this was the first time that it came in the form of an ultimatum.

The small western garrisons in Berlin did not of course constitute a military threat to the eastern bloc. Politically, the existence of a western island in the middle of East Germany was no doubt a constant irritant for the communists. It was an anomaly, but so was the division of Germany which the Russians did not question. Berlin was also the weakest point in the western pact system and the Soviet decision to concentrate pressure there was only natural, given the premises of Soviet foreign policy. Militarily, the western powers could not defend Berlin against an attack and it must have seemed doubtful whether they would be willing to risk a wider conflagration for the sake of the former German capital. Not a few people in western Europe and also in the United States were in favour of a retreat from Berlin if only a face saving formula could be found. The Germans, they argued, had after all provoked the war and had lost it; wasn't it only fair that they should pay this price too? The western position in West Berlin, they argued, was untenable, and if a lasting understanding could be bought at the price of surrendering Berlin, wasn't it advisable to explore the Soviet proposal? This in brief was the basic dilemma facing Eisenhower, and later on Kennedy. Eventually America decided against a retreat, for while the surrender of Berlin would have been a severe blow to West Germany and a grave setback for the whole Western Alliance, there was no certainty that it would have brought a détente with the Soviet leaders any nearer. It was more probable that a western retreat from Berlin would have encouraged the Soviet Union to apply political and military pressure in other trouble spots in the hope that the western leaders would show as little resistance elsewhere. After the building of the wall in 1961 the Berlin crisis faded for several years into the background. For the Soviet leaders the risks of brinkmanship were too high; they, and the East Germans, continued to lodge protests and warnings from time to time but there was no attempt to dislodge the western powers by force. They were confident that in view of its isolation the western position in Berlin would gradually wither away.

Among the factors that may have induced Khrushchev to de-escalate the Berlin conflict, relations with China were probably paramount. After 1959 this conflict came to preoccupy the Soviet leadership more and more, and it was clear from the beginning that the danger from the East was not just political and ideological in character. Soviet attempts to change the status quo in central Europe were also counterproductive, inasmuch as they impressed on the United States the need to increase and improve its defences. These rearmament programmes became more expensive every year for all concerned, but the Soviet economy, with a much smaller GNP than the United States, felt the strain even more acutely. Soviet foreign policy blew hot and cold alternately between 1958 and 1962, which confused western observers no end, but there was probably less deliberate intent in this than was commonly assumed at the time. There were conflicting domestic and foreign pressures on the Soviet leaders, their priorities changed from time to time, and Khrushchev's mercurial temperament no doubt also contributed to the sudden changes.

Nineteen fifty-nine was a year of great optimism, of constant coming and going between the world's capitals in anticipation of another summit meeting which was to break the stalemate. Richard Nixon, then American Vice-President, visited the Soviet capital, as did Harold Macmillan, the British Prime Minister. Among the visitors to Washington were Kozlov and Mikoyan, two senior members of the Soviet politburo. In September Khrushchev himself went for the first time to the bastion of capitalism and at Camp David had several long talks with President Eisenhower. The atmosphere was cordial but not much substance emerged from these conversations. Khrushchev could obviously not discuss with Eisenhower his difficulties with Mao, nor was he free to make any suggestions about an atom-free zone in Asia. He ridiculed the rumours about the differences between Moscow and Peking; he and Mao were good friends, he said, the two nations would always stand together in any international dispute. Eisenhower, on the other hand, had to take into consideration the views of his European allies about Germany and Berlin. Both West Germany and France were opposed to raising the Berlin issue. De Gaulle was in fact most reluctant to give the American President any mandate to speak on behalf of the West, and he had grave doubts about the uses of a summit meeting. Khrushchev withdrew his ultimative demand for a settlement on Berlin, suggesting a new scheme for complete disarmament within a period of four years. Soon after his return to Moscow he announced substantial cuts in the Soviet armed forces. The road seemed clear for a new summit meeting which, it was decided, should take place in Paris in May 1960.

The prelude to the Paris meeting was highly inauspicious: on the eve of the meeting, on 1 May, a U2 high altitude American spy plane was shot down over Soviet territory; the American government, instead of denying all knowledge as it is customary in such cases, tried to defend its action, and a few days later the President himself accepted full responsibility for the incident. With this the summit meeting was doomed; Khrushchev declared immediately after his arrival in Paris that he would walk out unless the

President apologised, punished those responsible, and promised to discontinue the flights. The flights were stopped; with the development of earth satellites such missions had become obsolete and unnecessary. But Eisenhower could not of course apologise. And so after a few days, amid bitter recriminations, the conference ended in total failure and Khrushchev withdrew the invitation for a visit to Moscow which he had extended to Eisenhower the year before.

The U2 affair was, to put it mildly, clumsily handled by the Americans, but such flights had been routine for a number of years, and since the Soviet leaders were no doubt aware of them, it seemed that the incident was for Khrushchev merely a pretext to back out of the conference. What then was his real reason? Since his meeting with Eisenhower at Camp David the Chinese had officially declared that any international agreement (including one on disarmament) arrived at in their absence would not be binding to them. As a result Khrushchev's hands were tied; he could not negotiate with the West without sacrificing the unity of the communist camp. In the Soviet politburo, too, there seem to have been doubts about the wisdom of another summit meeting. At Camp David there had been distinct hopes that the West would make concessions over Germany and Berlin. The British government was inclined to look for a compromise with the Russians, and Eisenhower himself had admitted on one occasion that the situation in Berlin was 'abnormal'. But during the succeeding months the western position on Germany again hardened; it was realised in the western capitals that they were about to strike a bad bargain. The Russians had little to offer in exchange: East Germany was no longer expendable and it was obvious that the Soviet Union would not withdraw its forces from the DDR or from the other east European countries, regardless of western concessions on Berlin and West Germany. For Moscow the situation had suddenly become unpromising and Khrushchev was now very angry about America and President Eisenhower personally, whom he had previously described to the Soviet people as a man of 'wise statesmanship, courage and will power'. This anger was real enough; Khrushchev's whole design for a détente with the West, his patient work over many months, was now in ruins. Another year was to pass before he resumed the dialogue with the new American President. But the meeting with Kennedy in Vienna in June 1961 was very different in spirit from the talks at Camp David. The political barometer had fallen; the Soviet delegates had walked out of the Geneva disarmament conference and at the United Nations, banging his shoe, Khrushchev had reminded his listeners that Russia had nuclear weapons and rockets. Russia was sure of its strength, he said; it no longer feared an American attack. On Berlin, he presented Kennedy with a new ultimatum: he would sign a separate peace treaty with East Germany by the end of the year if no German treaty was forthcoming. Khrushchev was out to frighten Kennedy; the new American President gained the impression that the Soviet leaders were willing to risk a nuclear war to get their way on Germany. The underlying Soviet assumption was that counsels were still divided in Washington about the advisability of a showdown with Russia over Berlin, and that fears within the Atlantic Alliance, in particular in Britain and Italy, made for a greater readiness to accept Soviet demands. The Soviet threats were not, however, altogether convincing, for Moscow's relations with China were deteriorating steadily, the Soviet hold over the communist bloc loosening, and there was no certainty that a world crisis would help to restore the unity of the camp and reassert Soviet leadership. Above all, Khrushchev misjudged the American temper. The Americans were not to be pushed out of Berlin, out of Germany, and ultimately out of Europe under pressure; threats made them angry, less inclined to meet the Russians half-way. The Vienna meeting ended in disagreement all along the line and the American President left the Austrian capital in a sombre mood. He said that he had realised on that occasion that words like war, peace, aggression, justice, democracy and popular will, had very different meanings in West and East. Kennedy was determined to act with great caution but above all the meeting had impressed on him the need for firmness in his dealings with the Russians.

The most striking feature of West-East relations during the fifties and early sixties is the fact that throughout the whole period the initiative remained with the Soviet Union. The Soviet leaders pursued a dynamic policy even in unfavourable conditions; they initiated new moves, unleashed crises, published ultimatums, if necessary made sudden concessions even when the situation on the domestic front or within the communist camp was far from stable. Western statesmen, by contrast, seemed lackadaisical, even lethargic; sometimes they reacted with vigour to Soviet moves, but seldom took any major initiative. Dulles had a consistent foreign political concept but it was better suited to the period before 1956 than to the years following, when European politics came again into flux. Kennedy's advisers developed a grand design which foundered quickly. Western statesmen stumbled from one crisis to the next since their thinking was purely defensive, based on the acceptance of the status quo and the division of Europe into spheres of influence. This the Soviet leaders took for granted, but in contrast to the West they did not hesitate to create opportunities to improve their position beyond their agreed sphere. The western lack of dynamism was not rooted in the personal shortcomings of its leaders; democracies in times of peace always act more slowly and with less vigour than dictatorships, and they seldom have clear and consistent foreign policies. The American leaders had to take into account the wishes and dislikes of their European allies to a far larger extent than Moscow considered the desires of its clients, and this too greatly hampered their freedom of action. Europe's inability to develop a common foreign policy was the main stumbling block; national interests had again proved stronger than common European or Atlantic policies that had, in principle, been agreed upon. Nor is it certain that a more dynamic, purposeful, and adaptable western foreign policy would have been able to prevail over Soviet resistance. Moscow was firmly resolved not to accept any solution of the German question contrary to its own interests, and since these were diametrically opposed to those of the West, there was little room for new initiatives and diplomatic manœuvres. It is doubtful, therefore, whether any opportunities were missed by the West. Greater initiative and drive might have had a cumulative effect in the long run; for Soviet attitudes, too, were subject to change, and greater western firmness might have induced the Soviet Union earlier on to desist from its attempts to expand its sphere of influence in central Europe.

The position of western leaders was weakened moreover by the emergence of a substantial domestic opposition unwilling to give them the benefit of doubt in the confrontation with the Soviet bloc. In these circles it was widely believed that the cold war had ended with Stalin's death, and that defence spending could therefore be substantially reduced. As the years passed a new generation of thinkers appeared maintaining that the West bore most of the responsibility for the deterioration of relations within Stalin's Russia in 1945–8, while others claimed that there was no cold war – it was a convenient myth conjured up by the military-industrial complex to suppress popular liberation movements all over the world. In this new climate of opinion the cold war seemed both an unwanted distraction from domestic policies and a bore, and there was a growing number of people who thought that if ignored it would disappear.

Germany and Berlin 1958 – 1962

The German issue continued to overshadow all other European problems even after the cold war had abated. The Russians regarded Germany as the key in the struggle for Europe and their spokesmen laboured the issue relentlessly; Germany was the main danger to world peace, a hotbed of militarism and fascism, a military and political danger to the Soviet Union, and to all its neighbours in West and East. This Soviet policy aroused a great deal of bewilderment in the West where, 15 years after the end of the war,

Germany in the eyes of many was still on probation and there was much criticism of Adenauer and his successors, but no one familiar with the German situation would have argued that Germany was again about to become fascist, and that West Germany constituted a military threat to anyone in Europe. The Soviet leaders were not known as men given to hysteria, and there was no reason to doubt that they were fully aware of the real situation in Germany and their own crushing military superiority. As a result more and more western observers reached the conclusion that the Soviet leaders were deliberately exaggerating the German danger so as to strengthen their own position in both West and East Europe. In terms of political warfare it had much to recommend it : there was envy of the German economic miracle and a great deal of political uneasiness among Germany's western neighbours. Poland and Czechoslovakia had been occupied by the nazi armies during the war ; both, but especially Poland, had suffered greatly, and memories of those years were still alive. Since the West German government had not yet formally recognised the territorial changes that had taken place in eastern Europe after the war, there was still the fear that it might one day claim what it had lost in 1945. A close alliance with Russia seemed the only guarantee for Poland to keep what it had acquired. There was a great deal of unreality in all the polemics about the Oder-Neisse line, because as a result of the division of Germany this was now East Germany's, not West Germany's frontier, and it was not of the slightest practical consequence whether or not West Germany recognised it. But with nationalist passions running high, Polish and, to a lesser extent, Czech fears were an important political factor, and the Soviet Union did its best to keep them alive and to impress on its allies that they would be no match for West German *revanchism* without constant Soviet protection. By not officially recognising the territorial changes of 1945 West Germany thus played into Moscow's hands.

The Soviet approach towards Germany was not however wholly Machiavellian. The defeat of the Russian army in the 1914–18 war, and the near defeat in 1941–2, had left deep traces in the Russian consciousness. Propagandist considerations apart, and despite the fact that the Soviet Union had become a super power while Germany was virtually defenceless, there was an inbuilt tendency to magnify the German danger. In the Soviet view NATO without Germany was not a serious adversary ; with Germany it was a factor that could not be ignored. The maximum aim of Soviet policy in Europe was therefore to detach Germany from the western Alliance. On three occasions, in 1952, in 1955, and again in 1964, attempts were made to open a dialogue with Bonn. It is not entirely clear how serious Stalin was in 1952, but it is almost impossible to believe that he would have agreed to dismantle the communist régime in East Germany, and short of this there was no hope for German reunification. In 1955 the Soviet leaders were simply probing German intentions but did not make any substantial promises, and in 1964 Khrushchev was overthrown before he could enter into serious negotiations. These three overtures apart, it was Soviet policy to isolate Germany, to prevent German rearmament, and to thwart systematically all hopes for German reunification. Long-term aims were also attributed to this policy, for it was likely to result in a growing feeling of frustration inside Germany which would eventually undermine the democratic character of government and lead to the growth of extremist movements either on the left, or more probably the right, which would be more inclined to leave the Western Alliance and to make a deal with the Soviet Union.

Germany's eastern policy was not very effective in counteracting Soviet designs. The expellee organisations bitterly opposed any official declaration concerning the lost territories, which would have contributed towards a reconciliation with Poland and Czechoslovakia. Both the leaders of the CDU and the Social Democrats were deeply reluctant to antagonise potential voters among these circles. A new initiative to improve relations with eastern Europe was taken only in 1969 following the electoral victory of the Social Democrats that year. Even the great coalition which came into being in 1966 inexcusably failed to take decisive action in this direction.

Germany's freedom of action in eastern Europe was narrowly circumscribed by the Hallstein doctrine, formulated in December 1955, which made known to all neutral and non-aligned countries that West Germany would regard diplomatic recognition of East Germany as an unfriendly act, for it would be interpreted as accepting the division of the country. The thesis that East Germany was not a sovereign state and that West Germany alone had the right to represent Germany (*Alleinvertretung*) greatly complicated Germany's position, for whatever the lawyers said about the continued juridical unity of Germany as a state, *de facto* there were now two countries in existence, and West Germany found it increasingly difficult to induce other countries to ignore the DDR. The Hallstein doctrine meant that for many years West Germany could have no diplomatic representation in the capitals of eastern Europe, for the communist régimes naturally recognised East Berlin. Bonn also exposed itself to various kinds of blackmail in Asia, Africa, and the Middle East as a result of clinging to the doctrine long after it had outlived its usefulness. The Hallstein doctrine was never officially dropped but gradually ignored: West Germany had excepted the Soviet Union right from the beginning and in 1966 it declared its willingness to have diplomatic ties with all east European countries.

With Adenauer's resignation there were gradual changes in Germany's eastern policy. Bonn began to pay more attention to relations with its eastern neighbours: representatives of Krupp and other leading German firms were frequent visitors to their capitals and official German trade missions were established in Prague, Bucharest, and Budapest. There was a great deal of bridge building even though the sceptics kept arguing that trade could never be a substitute for a clear policy. There was a gradual change also with regard to East Germany, a greater tendency to accept the status quo in the DDR and to help make it more human. A policy of 'little steps' towards normalisation was mooted by one school of thought expecting a change for the better through a gradual *rapprochement* (*Wandel durch Annäherung*), and it was argued that Germany should concentrate its efforts on the Popular Democracies since for the time being there was little hope of inducing the Soviet Union to change its policy *vis-à-vis* Germany. On the other hand there was the view that the road to eastern Europe ran via Moscow, and that all attempts to bypass the Soviet Union were doomed to failure. There were also many pessimists who thought that a *rapprochement* with the East, however desirable, was simply not feasible. Such fears were not altogether unfounded: Pankow saw a greater threat in West German friendliness than in its hostility, and the more concessions Bonn was willing to make, the more demands came from East Berlin. East Germany announced that reunification was out of the question; a loose confederation was the most it was willing to consider, but only after sweeping political, economic, and social changes had been carried out in West Germany.

For many years Bonn was criticised, and not altogether without reason, for the inertia of its eastern policy and its unwillingness to adopt the western policy of détente *vis-à-vis* the communist camp. At last there came a change, when in 1967 it was announced that the Munich agreement of 1938 was considered by Germany null and void, and various proposals were made for a reduction of both western and eastern armed forces in Germany. Bonn also expressed its wish to sign a treaty with the Soviet Union and all other east European countries renouncing the use or threat of force (*Gewaltverzicht*). It was largely the Protestant churches and the Social Democrats who brought about the change in the political climate inside Germany which made this reorientation in its eastern policy possible.

The initiative of 1967–8 was warmly welcomed in western capitals but not in Moscow, Warsaw, or East Berlin. There Bonn's initiative was violently denounced as an act of political aggression which increased international tension, and it was later thought to have contributed largely to the Soviet decision to invade Czechoslovakia:

The East German leaders feared that any improvement of relations between Bonn and their communist allies would eventually lead to their growing isolation. The Polish communists, remembering their recent conflict with the Catholic Church on the possibility of a reconciliation between the German and Polish peoples, were convinced that anything which weakened the fear of Germany would undermine the Polish people's willingness to rely solely on Russian protection, and with it the basis of their own rule. And the Soviet leaders concluded that Bonn's active participation in the détente was a far greater threat to their own security than its former rigidity – because it might isolate their East German bastion, cause differences within their alliance, and reduce the common fear of 'a new Hitler' that was its strongest popular cement (R. Löwenthal).

It is one of the great ironies of contemporary history that the West German 'opening to the East', demanded by its allies and by liberal opinion inside the country, had such disastrous consequences. If the West Germans had not left the decision to modify their eastern policy so late, the communist governments would have been compelled to look for other, much less plausible pretexts to intervene in the affairs of their allies. They would have found it more difficult to conjure up the spectre of German *revanchism* had Bonn officially recognised the changes in the political map of East-Central Europe after 1945. This German readjustment was, after all, inevitable and once this had been accepted in principle there was no turning back even after the Czech disaster.

During the late fifties and early sixties Berlin was the focus of West-East tension in Europe. After the division of Germany, West Germany had treated it as one of its *Länder*, though young Berliners were not obliged to serve in the Germany army, and there were several other important exceptions designed to pacify the Russians. East Germany, on the other hand, treated Berlin as part of the Soviet zone and, in violation of its four power status, established its capital there. Since 1947 the communists disputed the legal rights of the western powers to have a garrison in West Berlin and insisted on its demilitarisation and neutralisation. The Soviet ultimatum of November 1958 demanded the end of the occupation status of West Berlin and the implicit recognition by the western powers of the East German government. It was, as Philip Windsor has pointed out, not a sudden departure from Soviet policy and it did not yet hold the threat of a separate peace treaty with East Germany. This new element was introduced by Khrushchev only later, when it emerged that the western allies were unwilling to make any substantial concessions.

Soviet pressure was stepped up during the second half of 1960 and reached its climax in the early summer of the following year. In July, in a speech at the Moscow Military Academy, Khrushchev announced that in view of increasing international tension all manpower reductions in the Soviet armed forces would be suspended and the Soviet military budget increased by one third. The NATO Council meeting a few days later made it clear that the West would not give up its position in Berlin; the French were the most outspoken in their refusal to consider a recognition of the DDR. Ulbricht, the East German leader, had promised the western allies certain guarantees if West Berlin became neutral, but at the same time told his fellow Germans that with the conclusion of a separate peace treaty his government would exercise sovereignty over West Berlin as well. On 16 July John McCloy, a former American High Commissioner in Germany, arrived in Moscow as President Kennedy's personal envoy but from his talks with Khrushchev no hope for an agreement emerged; an Italian attempt to negotiate was no more successful. Then, during the first week of August, Khrushchev began to act. At a meeting of the Warsaw Pact countries it was decided to close the frontier between East and West Berlin. This was a risky step but the Soviet leadership no doubt felt itself compelled to take action; having insisted for so long that the Berlin problem had to be solved, they had at last to show some progress. For East Germany it was indeed a real emergency. The DDR was meant to be the showcase of socialist achievements for the whole of Germany, yet far from attracting the West Germans, it lost each week many thousands of its citizens who preferred the freedom (or the fleshpots) of the West. During the last week of July 1961 10,000 East German refugees appeared in the West Berlin reception centres, and on one single day, 7 August 1961, more than two thousand registered. This was not just a matter of loss of prestige for the DDR, for unless the stream of refugees was stopped the whole East German economy was likely to be paralysed. On two different occasions, in June and July 1961, Ulbricht had still declared that there was no intention to close the border and to build a wall. But the communist leadership was now a prisoner of its own escalation of the Berlin crisis; the more pressure it applied the more it swelled the stream of refugees, for everyone sensed that it might be the last opportunity to escape.

During the night of 13 August units of the East Germany army closed all crossings from East Berlin to the West, and in the subsequent days a wall was built along the Soviet sector. This was in violation of the four power status which provided free access to all parts of the city and it came as a great shock to West Berliners and West Germans. There was an immediate outcry for counter-measures; surely the West would not remain inactive in the face of such a flagrant violation of international law? Dean Rusk, the American Secretary of State, condemned the building of the wall and other western spokesmen denounced it also in no uncertain terms. Lyndon Johnson, then Vice-President, was dispatched to Bonn and Berlin and, trying to reassure the Germans, declared that the communists would fail in the long run because they had put themselves against the forces of history. But the Germans in their present mood were not satisfied with references to the distant future; as the news was received of the circumstances in which East Germans had found their death while trying to cross the border, the general excitement reached a climax. But the western powers were not prepared for military counteraction; they had contingency plans for a Soviet-East German take-over of the whole city, but not for cutting off the eastern part of the city.

According to the western concept, East Berlin was part of the Soviet sphere of influence within which the communists had full freedom of action. They were not willing to risk a military clash; only when faced several days later with new threats such as interference with air transport and with American patrols in East Berlin did they react with greater firmness, announcing that any act of aggression would be resisted. Khrushchev and Ulbricht were not willing to escalate the crisis any further; the idea of a separate peace treaty was dropped for the time being and tension was gradually permitted to die down.

The communist leaders had every reason to be satisfied with the outcome of the crisis. They had not achieved all they wanted, but the building of the wall contributed decisively to the consolidation of the East German régime; the official explanation given out by East Berlin (that the wall had to be erected to prevent the infiltration of western diversionists) was hardly meant to be believed and from a propagandist point of view the wall was not exactly the pride of Ulbricht's régime. But the long-term political gain was substantial; the refugee stream was halted; only a few daring spirits succeeded at great risk in crossing into the West after 13 August. The East German government overcame the economic problems caused by the mass exodus and grew far more self-confident and assured. In West Germany, on the other hand, the seeds of distrust *vis-à-vis* its western partners were sown; if America was incapable of resisting Soviet encroachments in Berlin, would it be willing to defend West Germany against an all-out attack? President Kennedy in a speech in November reiterated his support for German reunification on the basis of self-determination; during a visit to Berlin he declared to great acclaim that 'we were all Berliners'. But confidence in America was shaken and not a few Germans were now more willing than before to ponder the implications of Gaullism.

Gaullism, Europe, and the United States

General de Gaulle came to power for the second time in 1958, and it soon appeared that he had his own concept of Europe on which he was not willing to compromise. The General, never an admirer of the 'Anglo-Saxons', had been deeply hurt by their behaviour towards him during the war years. A proud man, he had not forgotten the snubs and the slights, real and imaginary, to which he had been exposed in exile. But it was not of course simply a matter of personal resentment; de Gaulle stood uncompromisingly for French self-interest and he was convinced that there was little common ground between his country and Britain and America. His concept of international politics was essentially eighteenth century in inspiration; ideology played little if any part in it. For this reason he was not likely to be impressed by the alleged Soviet threat, and the need for Atlantic or European unity appeared much less urgent to him than to his contemporaries. Such an outlook was intriguing, if only because it was so different from everyone else's, and many foreigners admired the General's utter self-confidence in a world of uncertainties, his Olympian calm, his majestic style. His views on many topics were so out-of-date and irrelevant that they seemed occasionally ultra-modern. De Gaulle put much of the blame for the ills of contemporary Europe on the decisions taken at Yalta and Potsdam, partly because France had not been represented there, partly because these conferences had perpetuated the division of Europe into two rigid power blocs, and the intrusion of the two non-European super powers. He had no sympathy with the attempts to create European political unity, and initially he was also opposed to the Common Market. The blueprints of the Eurocrats were for him flights of fancy in the style of the Arabian Nights, and he compared their work for a European federation with the efforts to create Volapük, the artificial language. About the advantages of economic cooperation he later changed his mind; all European countries had derived great benefits from it, and none more than France. But he was not willing to be party to the various political and military unification schemes.

His differences with the Americans emerged clearly when he met Secretary of State Dulles soon after having again become President of the Republic. This was more than a dispute about a specific line of policy; it was a basic conflict. The Americans regarded France as a European power in the same sense as Germany or Italy, whereas in de Gaulle's eyes France's place was with the world powers. To underline his disagreement with the Americans and to stress France's independence, de Gaulle gave instructions in March 1959 to withdraw from NATO Mediterranean Command all French naval units that had been assigned to it. Since these were few in number, the decision was of no great consequence; it was, as so often with de Gaulle, the gesture that mattered. His decision also established a new pattern, often to be repeated in subsequent years. De Gaulle opposed the American schemes for the defence of Europe partly because he doubted Washington's capacity to lead the alliance in view of its inexperience and lack of vision, but also because American national interests were not identical with those of Europe. De Gaulle foresaw some of the basic problems of the balance of terror; no one could know when or how one or the other of the great nuclear powers would use their weapons. It seemed as the nineteen-fifties drew to their close that all the concepts about the defence of France and of Europe and even a third world war that had been considered basic at the inception of NATO were already out of date. The alliance of the free world, the reciprocal commitments of Europe and the United States, could not in the long run preserve European security unless (to quote de Gaulle) there existed in the Old World a 'bastion of power and prosperity of the same order as that which the United States constitutes in the New World'.

De Gaulle was touching on a real dilemma. The doubts he expressed about the future of the American commitment in Europe were real, and so was the necessity to strengthen the old continent's capacity to defend itself. Unfortunately, de Gaulle contributed little towards this aim; on the contrary, he seemed fairly resolved to sabotage all such attempts. Europe, as he conceived it, included both western and eastern Europe ('Europe to the Urals'), for the European countries, despite all ideological differences, had more in common with each other than with America and Russia. England would perhaps one day become part of Europe, but it was not yet ready to be admitted. It was a grand design, but since it ignored the power realities of the nineteen-sixties it was bound to fail. Europe, as de Gaulle envisaged it, was to be a loose federation of independent states (*L'Europe des patries*, as he was misquoted); the attempts to establish a supranational 'High Authority', acting on majority decisions, he thought premature if not utopian; the sovereign state was still the basic unit and could not be expected to surrender any of its prerogatives. For this reason he insisted on a French nuclear deterrent, however diminutive, and he despised the British for having virtually signed theirs away at Nassau in 1963.

De Gaulle's European policy was based on close cooperation with Germany. He loyally supported Germany against Soviet and east European pressure, but expected in return German concurrence with his own European projects. The other Common Market countries he hardly ever bothered to consult; the new Europe he envisaged was to be based on the Paris-Bonn axis, with West Germany, as befitting, taking a back seat. It was not a policy likely to endear him to many Europeans. French defence policy was based on the correct assumption that there could be no real independence, let alone big power status, without a nuclear deterrent. For this reason de Gaulle needed his *force de frappe* and he persevered against much domestic opposition and Washington's refusal to help him. He insisted on the project despite the great cost (about one billion dollars a year) and its very limited military value. Had it developed as originally planned, French nuclear capacity would have been in 1975 equal to the load of a single American B52, but the economic crisis of 1968 caused a slowdown in the project.

The American political and military schemes, developed during the nineteen-sixties, found in de Gaulle an implacable foe. He regarded them as hardly-veiled attempts to subjugate Europe, and he was firmly resolved not to be an American satellite. America, to be sure, talked about partnership, but it had never clearly defined it. Instead it evolved half-baked projects such as the ill-starred MLF – a scheme for establishing multilateral, seaborne mixed-manned nuclear forces, a supranational, and therefore in de Gaulle's eyes, artificial creation. France's foreign policy veered more and more towards a neutral position. In 1965 it left SEATO, the South-East Asian equivalent of NATO, and it ceased to participate in NATO's European manœuvres. In March 1966 de Gaulle announced that French forces would be withdrawn from the Treaty Organisation, and French officers from NATO command, and the headquarters of the organisation was accordingly transferred from Paris to Brussels. The Alliance was not to be dissolved, but as far as France was concerned it was to be put on ice. As a result of this show of independence *vis-à-vis* America, France's prestige soared in the uncommitted countries, and de Gaulle was given a cordial reception in the Soviet Union in June 1966; previously the Soviet leaders had viewed the Paris-Bonn axis with undisguised hostility. Kosygin returned the visit in December 1966, and again there was a warm welcome and many professions of friendship. But as some of de Gaulle's critics had predicted, the newly acquired prestige was largely spurious. Once the banquets, the speeches, and all the other pomp and circumstance were over, some minor cultural and economic agreements were all there was to show. De Gaulle became accustomed, as one of his critics noted, to playing a game of poker without cards. There was a great deal of unreality in so many of his initiatives; his whole policy was based on the assumption that there was a stable balance of power and that France would in any case be defended in an emergency by the Western Alliance. He deliberately ignored the fact that not much would have remained of the balance of power had other western countries behaved in a similar way. The limits of French influence appeared perhaps clearest of all in relations with Algeria which, despite the French cultural tradition and massive economic help from Paris veered more and more to the Soviet Union. If France could not retain its influence in its former North African department, how much less likely was a lasting French impact in eastern Europe or Latin America?

Official Washington showed surprising patience about de Gaulle's attempt to undermine American influence in various parts of the world, and the French assault on American monetary policies and the dollar. This Gaullist opposition helped to draw attention to some of the main weaknesses of American's grand strategy. The French suggestions for disengagement in Europe were not all devoid of merit, and the General's approach to world politics, however quaint and antiquated, had a consistency and sometimes a grandeur which commanded the respect even of his bitterest enemies. But it totally failed to present any realistic alternatives, for it overrated French strength and Europe's capacity to defend itself without America's help. The reckoning came in the summer of 1968 when the student revolt demonstrated how brittle Gaullist rule was. The uncertainty created by the domestic unrest led to the near collapse of the franc; the monetary crisis showed that France was in immediate need of massive foreign help, especially from West Germany and the United States. The Soviet invasion of Czechoslovakia and the change in the balance of power in the Mediterranean revealed that French foreign and defence policies had been based on mistaken assumptions. The whole concept of a gradual disengagement to overcome the division of Europe, drastically reducing both American and Soviet influence suffered a fatal blow despite valiant French attempts to behave as if nothing had happened. 'Europe up to the Urals' (or to the Ussuri?) again receded beyond the distant horizon.

The European Community

The efforts to create a European supranational political authority had failed in 1954; France was at the time preoccupied with the war in Vietnam, and the other countries concerned in the initiative were not really willing to give up their sovereignty. The realities of the nation-state proved stronger than the seemingly abstract concept of a united Europe. But the endeavour to establish a Common Market and free-trade zone in Europe continued. West Germany, Italy, France, and Benelux joined forces to establish a new European community on 1 January 1958. During the first decade of its existence the chief problems confronting the Six were whether any European states other than the founder members should also be admitted, and how much freedom of action should be given to the administration of the Common Market headed at the time by a West German, Professor Walter Hallstein. The two main decision-making organs in the Community were the Council of Ministers and the Commission. The former was composed of the foreign ministers of the respective countries representing the national interests, with a voting system which gave more votes to the big countries than to the small. In the Commission on the other hand the permanent, supranational element prevailed, the Eurocrats representing the common interests of the organisation.

The existence of the Commission and its powers was a source of great annoyance to de Gaulle; the abdication of sovereign rights was a dangerous deviation from his concept of a 'Europe of the fatherlands'. De Gaulle's hostility was partly shared by Professor Erhard, Adenauer's successor who, while favouring close European cooperation, was also critical of the Commission's attempts to enlarge its sphere of influence. In 1965 de Gaulle forced a showdown; the Community was immersed at the time in difficult negotiations about its agricultural policies. France did not accept the proposals worked out by the Commission and suddenly presented it with an ultimatum: unless a solution acceptable to France was adopted within a given period, France would withdraw and boycott further meetings of the Community. While the issue at stake, agricultural financing, was certainly important for France, de Gaulle's real aim was to prevent any further strengthening of the Commission and to forestall any possibility that France would in future be outvoted by its partners. At a press conference he made his position abundantly clear: when the Treaty of Rome had been negotiated France had been weak, its partners had taken advantage of this weakness, and as a result certain mistakes had been made which had to be corrected. France, needless to say, was not alone among the Six in fighting for its national interests, but none did it so relentlessly and with so little consideration for its partners. De Gaulle's point of view was strictly utilitarian; the overriding consideration was always the extent to which France was likely to profit from its collaboration with the Community. The patience of France's partners was wearing thin; they had too often been angered by de Gaulle's cavalier attitude and there was no willingness to give in to the French ultimatum. Even the Germans had serious misgivings; their delegation at the time was headed by Foreign Minister Schroeder who was not one of de Gaulle's admirers. France faced the possibility that the majority would use its absence to invite Britain to fill the vacant chair. At this stage de Gaulle decided to compromise and the French delegates returned to Brussels. They had to make some concessions but succeeded nevertheless in weakening the Commission and tilting the balance of power within the Community: all really important issues were to be decided in future by the foreign ministers. The dangerous trend towards supranationalism had again been checked.

The economic success of the Community compelled its critics to reconsider their attitudes towards it. The Soviet Union and the east European governments had asserted that the Common Market was bound to fail in view of the inexorable competition between the capitalist countries described by Lenin many years before. This thesis had to be modified in the light of the achievements of the Common Market, and the communist theoreticians soon found a new explanation: the collective interest of neo-capitalism was after all stronger than the divisive trends among its components. The American government had never underrated the prospects of the Common Market; there was some apprehension in Washington that it would succeed only too well and become a formidable threat to the United States. But it was also realised that a strong Europe was clearly more in the American interest than a weak and divided continent, even if individual branches of the American economy were to suffer as a result.

The European countries who had stayed out or were left out when the Common Market was founded had second thoughts, too. EFTA, the European Free Trade Area, founded in the summer of 1959, was much less ambitious and comprehensive than the Community; it did not, for instance, aim at the coordination of the foreign trade of its member states, nor did it want to establish common economic, financial, and social policies. Having missed the opportunity to take the initiative for a European Common Market in the early fifties, Britain reluctantly reached the conclusion that EFTA could be only a temporary stage on the road towards closer integration. The Macmillan government announced in July 1961 that it wanted to initiate negotiations with the Six about joining the Common Market. It applied officially soon after, and so did Sweden, Switzerland, and Austria. In the first postwar decade most Labour leaders had been convinced that the Treaty of Rome was a mere trade agreement, designed to prevent the adoption of socialist policies on the continent, whereas most Conservatives resented (like General de Gaulle) its political implications – the fact that it was eventually meant to be the basis of a supranational political institution which would involve the abdication of British sovereignty in some fields. The idea that foreigners would have a decisive say in shaping British domestic and foreign policies was quite intolerable to most Englishmen. But gradually the political and economic climate began to change. The limitations of Britain's postwar role and the loosening of the ties with the Commonwealth became more obvious, and the European idea kindled the imagination of many British public figures. This enthusiasm was not, of course, altogether disinterested; the economic success of the Six was the main attraction and persuaded many that it would be easier to solve Britain's own difficulties within the wider European framework. But it was equally true, as Macmillan told de Gaulle during a visit to Paris, that Britain had been genuinely converted and that it now looked to a European future. There were major stumbling blocks: Britain wanted safeguards for the protection of its special interests, such as agriculture, the ties with Commonwealth countries (in particular Canada, Australia, and New Zealand), and lastly there was the future of EFTA to be considered. Britain did not want to desert the Seven without reaching an agreement about the other EFTA members which wanted to join the Common Market. The British representatives made it clear that they did not suggest a basic modification of the Treaty of Rome. Nevertheless their insistence on conditions was a mistake; it would have been wiser to apply without any preconditions, for from inside the Community they would have been able to influence Common Market policies. But in view of French opposition it is unlikely that even an unconditional application would have been more successful. The negotiations dragged out for a long time and finally broke down after General de Gaulle's famous press conference in January 1963 at which he announced that Britain was not yet ready to join the Community. This declaration greatly annoyed the other members of the Community who were more favourably disposed and who, in addition, had not been consulted by the French. De Gaulle had not initially opposed the British application, for he assumed that Britain was not serious about joining. Only when he realised that there had been a real change of heart in London did he come out squarely against the British initiative. His basic public argument was that Britain, by tradition and by political and economic interest, was not really a part of Europe. The General's vision of Europe was essentially Carolingian and he deeply distrusted a country that was far too close to the United States for his taste, almost an American 'Trojan Horse'. De Gaulle wanted to keep the Community small; 'interdependence' and 'integration' were words without meaning for him. One day, he said, Europe would be an imposing confederation, but meanwhile he did all he could to torpedo the federative efforts. In the last resort de Gaulle was not worried by Britain's different cultural traditions or political interests but by the fact that it would have constituted a serious rival to French leadership of the Community.

All other members of the Common Market were in favour of Britain's entry but they were powerless to overcome the French veto. Erhard, Schroeder, and Brandt did not regard the French-German alliance as an end in itself, but they could not, or would not stand up to de Gaulle. Adenauer and Kiesinger were Francophiles, but they too had misgivings about de Gaulle's policy and would have preferred a European Community including Britain. Faced with a French ultimatum they gave in, for a Europe without France was unthinkable.

Prime Minister Wilson again tried to break the deadlock in 1966–7 by reapplying for membership without any preconditions. But the Labour government was no more successful than its Conservative predecessor: the General would not budge. Britain then suggested without much success various other schemes to circumvent French opposition, such as a technological union and new approaches to European defence. Meanwhile groups of continental 'Europeans' considered ways and means to achieve closer political union: Jean Monnet's European action committee, and Spaak, the Belgian Foreign Minister, submitted various plans; other schemes were prepared by official and semi-official German and French bodies (such as the Fouchet Committee). But these attempts to pick up the threads of 1954 were in vain; after long and fruitless discussions all these projects had to be shelved. Greece and Turkey eventually became associate members of the Community, and a special relationship was established with some African and Middle-

East countries. Neutral countries were not considered for full membership because (it was argued) they were not free agents and could not participate in the movement towards closer political union which, at least in theory, remained the aim of the Community.

France was not the only obstacle and there is no certainty that closer political unity would have been attained, but there was a real chance to make substantial progress in the late fifties and early sixties. De Gaulle's stubborn opposition destroyed one of the great hopes of the postwar world; temporarily it strengthened France's position but it weakened Europe as a whole and again gave free rein to the growth of nationalist movements and the resurgence of many old rivalries. If western Europe remained politically impotent despite its spectacular economic recovery, this was to a great extent the responsibility of the old man in the Elysée with his colossal vanity and his policy of grand gestures who wanted for his country a role far above its real strength.

West-East Relations: from Cuba to Czechoslovakia

The Cuban crisis was the watershed that marked the end of an acute phase in the cold war and opened a new era of détente. It is not quite clear what induced Khrushchev in summer 1962 to establish rocket bases in Cuba. It is unlikely that it was meant to act as a deterrent, defending Cuba against an American invasion. Perhaps the Soviet leaders intended to use the bases for bargaining with the Americans; perhaps Khrushchev hoped to extract a high price for their withdrawal, such as an American retreat from Berlin or at least from Turkey. On 14 October, firm evidence was received in Washington of the establishment of launching pads, and on 22 October President Kennedy made his first announcement. It was, as a Soviet commentator put it at the time, the most dangerous week since the second world war and it ended with a Soviet defeat and a setback for Khrushchev who had been personally responsible for what even the Chinese hardliners called a dangerous policy. Moscow had clearly underrated American resolution; the crisis made the Soviet leaders aware of American superiority in arms systems, and compelled them to re-examine their strategy. Russia clearly needed a breathing space to catch up with American ICBM strength and it had to improve its strategic mobility. The Soviet leaders had also to reconsider their policy vis-à-vis China: Chinese attacks were no longer restricted to specific aspects of Soviet policy; they exceeded in vigour and bitterness anything that had ever emanated from the West. In a conversation with Japanese socialists, Mao declared in August 1964 that the Soviet régime was imperialist, that it had annexed parts of Rumania, Poland and East Germany, driving out the local inhabitants. Mao said that he was willing not to press the Mongolian issue for the moment, but justice demanded that Moscow immediately return the Kurile islands to Japan. The Chinese comrades, in other words, had moved far beyond Mr Dulles in their attitude towards the Soviet Union.

It was generally believed at the time in the capitals of the West that the détente would produce long-term changes in Soviet aims; the Soviet leaders would increasingly occupy themselves with the urgent domestic and economic problems facing them. The international situation seemed to give credibility to such assumptions: a bipolar balance of power had emerged, and there was more and more tacit cooperation between the superpowers on a variety of subjects. America and Russia together with their European allies seemed to be moving towards a 'wider community of developed peoples'. America signed the test ban treaty in 1963 and tried unsuccessfully to obtain universal agreement for a non-proliferation treaty. There was growing impatience in the United States with western Europe after Kennedy's grand design had been torpedoed by General de Gaulle and the MLF scheme had been like-wise turned down. As American interest shifted to South-East Asia, the need for an American-Soviet dialogue seemed far more pressing to Washington than the apparently fruitless attempts to work out a lasting political and military arrangement with western Europe. This was the period of bridge building which, it was hoped, would lead to a gradual abatement of West-East conflicts and to negotiations on European security. The Soviet position had changed little, whereas the West had moved steadily towards acceptance of the Soviet terms 'even at the expense of progress towards such positive goals of Western policy as German reunification, European integration and Atlantic partnership' (Pierre Hassner). On the theoretical level new ideas were developed to show that industrial society in West and East had acquired strongly similar features and would eventually converge. This was the period of 'disengagement' and 'peaceful engagement', of increasing cooperation and interpenetration; some western observers already anticipated an American-Soviet alliance against the 'yellow peril'. There was a curious parallelism between the two superpowers, with America bogged down in Vietnam, incapable of winning a war against a much weaker enemy, and the Soviet Union seemingly powerless to prevent the disintegration of the communist bloc. Neither superpower seemed able to impose its will upon its centrifugal European allies despite their economic and military superiority. It was, as subsequent events were to show, a false symmetry, but this was barely noticed in the West at the time. There was clearly no immediate military danger to western Europe, and the Soviet Union had obviously given up hope that the Western communist parties would be able to seize power in the foreseeable future. Khrushchev was overthrown in October 1964, but his successors seemed determined to continue, in broad outline, his foreign policy. France made it known on every possible occasion that the identity of interests with the other western powers had shrunk even more. As the Soviet threat diminished, General de Gaulle saw the emergence of a new European balance of power: western Europe alone would soon be able to act as a counterforce to the Soviet Union. De Gaulle seemed willing as his critics saw it to sponsor a Franco-Soviet European security pact which would give Moscow limited hegemony in Europe with France as her junior partner to exclude the Anglo-Saxons and to control the Germans. France saw the primacy of policy endangered by NATO strategy, which overimposed unity and, generally speaking, limited its freedom of action. Since there was no acute danger of war, France did not want American bases on its own soil. It disapproved of American policy in Vietnam and other parts of the world. The critics of the Gaullist concept maintained that the General's complicated schemes aimed at 'Europeanisation' would in fact cause the Balkanisation of Europe and thus both increase the danger of war and create a greater Finland, making the continent far more exposed to Soviet pressure.

Similar separatist trends developed in other European countries and developed into a general NATO crisis. American strategy planners with their changing ideas about deterrence and flexible response, faced increasing scepticism in Europe. America wanted to withdraw part of its forces from Europe and urged the European governments to improve their mobilisation system and strengthen their conventional forces. Those in Europe who wanted to get rid of American bases but still insisted on the American umbrella in case of an attack, seemed not to mind if NATO was greatly weakened, or even dissolved, but at the same time they were reluctant to increase their own defence spending: in fact they wanted the best of both worlds. The Vietnam war was unpopular in Europe from the beginning and became even more so; it was the rallying point of the opposition forces among the younger generation. The countries of western Europe were drifting aimlessly, as they usually do when not facing an acute crisis, but it seemed to cause little concern for the disarray in the West appeared to have a beneficial effect on the East, strengthening the independence movement among Russia's former satellites. Perhaps de Gaulle was right after all in assuming that the split of Europe into two warring camps would eventually be overcome by the European countries requiring greater independence.

The decline of NATO was highly gratifying from the Soviet point of view, but its effects on communist Europe were definitely not. Nor were developments in the third world encouraging either: Kwame Nkrumah, one of Moscow's great friends in Africa, was overthrown, Indonesian communism all but disappeared, and in 1967 Egypt and Syria, Moscow's allies in the Middle East, suffered a major defeat. In Greece a revolutionary situation had existed for some time, but before the left could exploit it a right-wing military dictatorship was established. Taken separately these incidents hardly mattered; seen in a wider perspective they seemed to constitute a dangerous shift in the global balance of power: 'imperialism' seemed everywhere on the offensive, the tide was running against the communists. Inside Russia there were gradual changes: Khrushchev's style had annoyed his colleagues and it played an important part in his downfall, but there were also policy differences. Khrushchev, they thought, had gone too far in 'appeasing' the West; in his later years he even seemed to have envisaged a deal with West Germany shortly before he was overthrown. He had not given sufficient support to the Soviet army command for its plans and this policy too was reversed after his downfall. Defence spending rose substantially after 1965. Destalinisation was gradually discontinued and stricter controls reimposed. This in turn had direct repercussions on Soviet foreign policy, for a tough domestic policy could not be maintained for long without influencing Russia's relations with the outside world, not because the Soviet leaders had remained ideological fanatics but (in the words of Richard Löwenthal) because the distrust with which a despotic régime watches the peoples under its rule is inevitably projected on to the outside world, preventing a genuine solution of major issues in dispute and a genuine agreement on its place in the world.

The discussion about military policy during the years of the détente reflected the policy dilemmas facing the Kremlin. It remained the supreme Soviet aim to achieve strategic parity with America and ultimately superiority: the years of détente were put to good use in this respect. But at the same time there was growing awareness in Moscow that the scientific-technological revolution made it necessary to re-examine the question of war as an instrument of policy. According to their Chinese opponents the Soviet leaders had retreated from Lenin's (and Clausewitz's) teaching that war was a continuation of politics, they had 'gone soft' and been awed into 'capitulationism' towards the West through fear of nuclear war. The Soviet leaders certainly wanted to avoid the dangers of a major military conflict, and they were also aware of the fact that small wars could easily escalate into big ones. To that extent the détente was from the Soviet point of view not just a tactical temporary retreat made in order to catch up with American nuclear capability; the basic dilemmas of a major confrontation were likely to persist even after attaining parity of military superiority. Russia and America had one overriding common interest, namely to ensure their survival. This did not mean however that all conflict was to be evaded in future; the new Soviet military doctrine as it developed during the middle sixties did not for instance rule out support for national liberation wars. One influential Soviet school of thought claimed after 1966 that with the growth of Soviet military power greater risks would have to be taken, for a policy of détente *tout court* was likely to erode the ideological cohesion of the world communist movement and undermine Soviet prestige in the third world. It was dangerous to accept the doctrine that victory in nuclear war was impossible; to do so would spread fatalism, even defeatism among the faithful. The Soviet leaders did not question the necessity of great prudence in their relations with the United States, but they refused to accept the policy of détente as a constraint on political and military initiatives in areas presumed to be of less than vital interest to the Americans. Such initiatives were to proceed according to the 'rules of the game' that had been established; but these rules were fairly vague and as far as Moscow was concerned they were bound to change as Soviet military capability continued to grow.

Brezhnev and Kosygin accepted the statement of the military lobby that the all round strengthening of the armed forces had been neglected under Khrushchev and decided to reallocate resources. The military budget went up by five per cent in 1966 and by eight per cent the year after. These were the published figures; there is reason to believe that the real increases were higher. In 1965–6 a small Soviet fleet was stationed in the Eastern Mediterranean and subsequently expanded. The Soviet leaders justified these measures by referring to the worsening world situation and to the increasingly aggressive character of 'imperialism'. At a conference of European communist parties in Karlove Vary in Czechoslovakia the militant spirit found expression in resolutions describing the United States as the most aggressive imperialist power aiming at world domination. The removal of American bases from Europe and the American Sixth Fleet from the Mediterranean was described as the most urgent aim in the political field. At the same time a campaign for a new system of European collective security was launched. This scheme, as the Soviet Union envisaged it, accepted the territorial status quo in Europe and made provision for replacing NATO and the Warsaw Pact by a comprehensive security system to be guaranteed by all European states, and by the Soviet Union and the United States. From the western point of view the project had several fatal flaws; it did not, for instance, affect the bilateral agreements between the communist states: the Soviet army could still remain on the Elbe while the Americans would have to withdraw from Europe with the dissolution of NATO. The scheme would have given official sanction to Soviet hegemony in Europe; nevertheless some west European governments were willing to consider the Soviet proposals as a basis of discussion. The Middle-East war in 1967 and the Czechoslovak crisis of 1968 interrupted this dialogue.

Soviet influence in the Middle East had grown steadily during the sixties; the governments of Egypt and Syria, of Algeria and the Yemen, moved closer to Moscow, whereas the ties between Turkey and Iran and the West became much looser. But despite this growing involvement the Soviet Union had only limited control over the actions of its new friends. The extent of Soviet responsibility for the Syrian war scare in May 1967 which triggered off the war between Israel and the Arab states has not been clearly established; it is doubtful if the Soviet Union would have been able to prevent the war even if it had wanted to. Nor could it, according to the rules of the game, give direct military support in 1967 to its allies in the Arab world, provided America did not intervene in the conflict. The war which ended in a defeat for Egypt and Syria did not weaken the Soviet position in the Middle East, but it had repercussions in eastern Europe which were undesirable from the Soviet point of view. Moscow's onesided support for the Arab governments was not popular with all European communists. The leading west European communist parties supported the Soviet line without much enthusiasm, and as a result relations between them and the left in their countries became more strained. Even in eastern Europe there was some support for Israel and a great deal of *Schadenfreude* that the Soviet Union had suffered a defeat by proxy, and this by an adversary that had been consistently underrated. Worse yet, the Israeli victory gave a great uplift to the latent mood of revolt in Czechoslovakia and Poland. It constituted an additional link in the chain of misfortunes that befell the Soviet Union on the international scene in 1965–7.

One faction in the Soviet leadership had for some time advocated a more militant line in both domestic and foreign policy, and its influence grew as the result of the new setbacks. Kosygin went to the United States in June 1967 but his talks with President Johnson at Glassboro were inconclusive. The old understanding between Moscow and Washington to avoid any direct confrontation continued in force, but the Soviet Union was no more able to help America to extricate itself from the Vietnam morass than the United States was able to assist Russia in the Middle East. Washington still wanted to improve relations with the Soviet Union; Lyndon Johnson was almost pathetically eager to visit Moscow during the last months of his presidency and to have a summit meeting with the Soviet leaders. General political considerations apart, Johnson no doubt wanted to refurbish his image as a peace President which had been badly damaged in Vietnam. But the Russians in 1967–8 were no longer in the mood to oblige; the spirit of détente and cooperation had all but vanished.

In western Europe too there was growing pessimism as 1967 drew to its close. The Vietnam war had raised grave doubts about American priorities. It had always been taken for granted that Europe was uppermost in American priorities as regards the contest with Russia. With American military power and political interest so heavily engaged in South-East Asia, the defence of Europe suffered and the balance of power on the continent was bound to be affected. Fortunately from the west European point of view, Moscow did not show much vigour in exploiting the American weakness; moreover the unexpected crises in the Middle East and eastern Europe played havoc with Soviet plans. But it was unlikely that the Soviet leaders would remain inactive for long. The détente, as subsequent events were to show, had not solved any problems nor had the conflict become less bitter. The acute danger of war had disappeared, but so had western hopes for peaceful coexistence. There remained deep uneasiness about the shape of things to come.

Polycentrism in the East

Disarray and confusion were not limited to the Western camp: Under Stalin the communist system had been monolithic; ten years after his death it appeared irrevocably split, the once solid bloc a battlefield for ideological supremacy and political leadership. The differences between the various communist countries and parties seemed in some ways even more irreconcilable than West-East tensions because each believed itself to be the sole possessor of the means of grace, because each thought it was more authentically Marxist-Leninist, and because its sense of mission was so much more acute.

Throughout the Stalin era there had been but one major split: Tito had defied the Kremlin and had never recanted. There was a reconciliation between Moscow and Belgrade in 1955–6, but having tasted freedom the Yugoslavs insisted on maintaining their independent status. National communism was contained by the Soviet leadership in Poland in 1956 and suppressed in Hungary, but the unfolding conflict with China was a problem of a different magnitude.

Many reasons have been advanced for the rift between the two communist super powers between 1958 and 1963; Soviet unwillingness to help China with its nuclear programme and Chinese complaints about insufficient Soviet economic assistance and ideological divergencies. The Chinese leaders were opposed to Khrushchev's destalinisation and his 'revisionist' approach in both domestic and foreign affairs; they were not supported by Moscow in their dispute with India, and they had never renounced their claims to a number of territories in the Far East seized by the Russians in the nineteenth century. The conflict was not over the correct ideological interpretation of Marx and Lenin but over national interests, autonomy, and big power aspirations. Russian and Chinese quarrelled because they were dissimilar in national character, heirs to a markedly different cultural and social heritage and because their political and economic interests diverged. The fact that Peking claimed to be closer to Leninist orthodoxy was of no great significance; in 1956 they had taken a more liberal view on some issues than their Soviet comrades. When Tito quarrelled with Stalin in 1948, the Yugoslavs had been to the 'left' of the world communist movement; ten years later they were to its 'right'. The ideological orientation changed, the insistence on the right to autonomy remained. The terms 'left' and 'right' lost their relevance in the context of communist intra-bloc relations.

Attempts to patch up the differences between Moscow and Peking were made; the conference of the 81 communist parties in Moscow in 1960 worked out what Lenin would have called a rotten compromise, 'a confusion of incompatible political formulas' as one observer put it, which could only lead to the continuation of polemics, with both sides stressing their own part of the document until the inevitable happened and the polemics came into the open. Soviet experts were withdrawn from China; political, military, and economic cooperation between the two countries came to a standstill, and day by day the propaganda warfare reached new heights of vituperation. Peking accused Moscow of splitting the world communist movement while the Soviet Union tried to mobilise international support to isolate the Chinese. But adequate support was not forthcoming; some parties openly sympathised with Peking while others, although not identifying themselves with Chinese policies, were opposed in principle to excommunication because, as Togliatti, the Italian leader, put it in 1964, 'this contained the danger of a resurgence of authoritarian and sectarian methods of leadership in the individual parties'. The view gained ground that a central direction of the world movement, formerly essential, was now a thing of the past. Polycentrism (a term coined by Togliatti in June 1956) was, in other words, not a deviation but a necessary new stage corresponding to the new situation in the communist movement, a new development in its doctrine and its changing structure. From the Far East polycentrism spread to eastern Europe: Albania, the smallest communist country, was the next to defy the Soviet Union. Its leaders were among the very few who had not been brought to power with the help of the Russians but through their own exertions at the end of a long partisan war. Albania had no common border with the Soviet Union and there was little likelihood that its neighbours would agree among themselves to take common action against it. Tirana and Belgrade had been in bitter conflict since the late forties; this was outwardly ideological in character, since Albania was more Stalinist than Stalin, and continued to be so even after the dictator's death. The deeper underlying causes were easier to understand against the background of traditional Balkan rivalries; they concerned territorial questions and the fate of the Albanian minority in the Kosmet region of Yugoslavia. While relations between Moscow and Belgrade were strained, Albania remained a faithful member of the Soviet camp, but with the reconciliation between the two, it became restive, and in 1960–1 openly defiant. There was nothing in common between Tirana and Peking except their hostility to Soviet policies. Albania desperately needed a protector and found one in Chairman Mao, becoming in the process China's bridgehead in Europe. The political, military, and economic importance of the Peking-Tirana axis was not overwhelming; its most interesting feature was the powerful radio transmitter, broadcasting day and night bitter attacks on the American imperialists and their 'number one assistants', the Soviet revisionists.

Rumania was next in line to dissociate itself from Soviet policies. This country, like Albania, had been a faithful member of the bloc, but with the erosion of Soviet controls the Rumanian desire for a more independent policy collided with Moscow's centralising plans. The dispute was initially economic in character: Rumania opposed the Soviet-sponsored Comecon initiative to coordinate more closely economic relations between Russia and its east European clients, fearing that the new division of labour insisted upon by Moscow would greatly impede, if not completely frustrate, its own industrialisation programme. Much to Khrushchev's chagrin, the Rumanian leaders succeeded in thwarting his schemes and gradually adopted a more independent foreign political line. In 1964–5 Rumania was (to quote Adam Ulam) the only state in the world that could boast of the following combination of achievements: she was an ally of the Soviet Union, a friend of China, and the communist state whose diplomatic and commercial relations with the West had improved and expanded. The Prime Minister visited Peking and Paris; he and the new party leader Ceausescu admonished the Soviet and Chinese comrades to settle their dispute and at the same time expressed doubts whether the Warsaw treaty was still necessary. In 1967 Rumania was the only communist country, with the exception of Cuba, not to break off relations with Israel. Its independent course was however largely restricted to its foreign policy; desatellisation progressed much more quickly than destalinisation; the party and the police remained in firm control and Rumania was by no means in the forefront of the liberal forces within the communist camp.

The Sino-Soviet conflict caused a deep split in world communism which, but for China's virtual retreat from world politics during the 'cultural revolution', would have been even more complete. In Asia, the Mongolian party was almost the only one to remain solidly faithful to Moscow; the Indian party split, the Indonesian communist movement under Chinese guidance failed in its bid for power, and the others were closer to Peking than to Moscow. Most of them were at one stage or another antagonised by China's strange and apparently aimless hostility, but this did not necessarily make them more friendly towards Russia.

The Chinese found new admirers in western Europe; small pro-Maoist factions split away from the communist parties but not one of these became a factor of political importance. The main danger facing the Soviet Union in western Europe was of a different character: the demand for greater autonomy and 'right-wing revisionism'. The Italian communists were in the vanguard of this movement, the ones to press most strongly for their own road to socialism. A considerable gap had always existed, as a historian of Italian communism once wrote, between their theoretical positions and their actual policies; their line had for a long time been moving towards an adaptation to western society which the party had come to accept far more than its theoretical position would seem to allow. The Italian communist leaders were strongly attacked in 1956 by their French comrades who argued unity was a precondition for the victory of communism and that polycentrism would open the door to factionalism. The real quarrel was not however about polycentrism but about the use made of the new autonomy. Togliatti and the younger leaders of his party wanted to submit the Stalin era to a searching critique and to draw from it far-reaching conclusions for the future. The French party, on the other hand, had always been more Stalinist in character, more rigid and less willing to respond to change. At one time or another it had attracted many intellectuals but gradually antagonised most of them. In the middle fifties the Italian party began openly to criticise certain Soviet policies; it took the French party more than a decade to gather sufficient courage to do the same.

The Sino-Soviet split caused a great deal of disarray in European communism although there were not many open defections. The east European states remained faithful to the Soviet line, but there were misgivings about the policy followed by Khrushchev and his successors. Poland and Hungary for instance favoured a more conciliatory attitude. In western Europe the divisive tendencies were reinforced by differences of opinion on other topical issues, of which the Common Market was one. The initial communist attitude had been one of total rejection, but as the economic benefits of the European Community became manifest there was greater readiness to accept the new economic framework and to work for political and social change from within. It was by no means true that European communism had become social democratic in inspiration, as some of its left-wing critics maintained. But as Soviet control over the camp weakened, European political traditions began to reassert themselves, and the communist parties realised that it had been a mistake to copy Soviet policies slavishly and to apply them in countries with different political traditions. According to the Leninist theory of revolution it was impossible to take over the bourgeois state from within; the west European communists did not deny the validity of this contention for countries lacking democratic traditions and they interpreted the historical role of Stalinism in this light. But they were no longer willing to accept such generalisations as binding on all countries irrespective of the degree of their political, social, and economic development. The communist parties of Britain and Holland, of Sweden and Austria and Switzerland, and even the Spanish and Greek parties in exile, all criticised Soviet policy at the time of the Czechoslovak crisis in 1968. This was not a sudden eruption, nor were these parties willing to draw far-reaching conclusions, but it certainly reflected the ferment that had begun to work years before. The basic issue was whether the world communist movement should have a centre and accept its discipline. Moscow insisted on its leading role as deriving both from its great revolutionary experience and from its power, but many communist parties dissented, stressing that the Soviet experience had negative as well as positive aspects, and that Soviet power had on occasion been misused. The secretary-general of the Spanish Communist Party declared ruefully in November 1968 that while a certain détente had been achieved in the cold war, acute tension, a kind of new cold war, had developed in the communist camp: 'It is sad to see that when the words "socialist commonwealth" are spoken they do not refer to the commonwealth which the fourteen states (where communist parties are in power) should form, but only to five states (the Soviet Union and her four allies who invaded Czechoslovakia). It would seem as if the socialist commonwealth were a piece of cloth inexorably shrinking.' The same centrifugal trend could be observed among communist parties outside Europe: Castro went his own way and communist groups in Latin America, Africa, and the Middle East declared their neutrality in the struggle between Moscow and Peking, or even openly criticised the Soviet Union. There was a great revolutionary potential in these areas, but the orthodox pro-Soviet communists profited less from this than various radical national socialist groups who, outflanking them on the 'left', found their inspiration in Peking and Havana, Paris and Algiers. Ché Guevara in defeat was a more attractive revolutionary hero than the Moscow *apparatchiks* with their nuclear arsenal.

The Soviet leaders tried without much success to counteract these divisive tendencies and to restore the 'unity of the camp'. For years they invested great efforts in schemes to convene a world conference to paper over the deep splits that had arisen. While continuing the attempt to keep at least the appearances of communist ideological unity, the Soviet leaders reluctantly reached the conclusion that fear, 'material interest', and political dependence made for more loyal allies than ideological conviction. The conflict with China, and later on the Czech crisis, showed them that they could no longer take the loyalty of the 'camp' for granted, whereas 'client states' such as Egypt and Syria which had never subscribed to their version of Marxism-Leninism gave them full support. In the last resort the question was, as Humpty Dumpty said, which was to be master: the Soviet Union claimed the right to intervene in the affairs of other communist states if 'socialism' was in danger. But as the other parties were quick to point out, who was going to decide whether socialism was in danger? What if China reached the conclusion that the communist ideal was being betrayed in the Soviet Union? At its conferences in 1957 and 1960 the world communist movement had adopted resolutions affirming the socialist principles of completely equal rights, respect for territorial integrity and national independence, and non-intervention in each other's domestic affairs. These were unrealistic resolutions, given the unequal distribution of power within the communist camp and the fact that these principles had never been adhered to in the past. But in the past the pretence at least of equality and non-intervention had been maintained. The new leaders did not have Stalin's authority and the decision taken by his successors to drop appearances was bound to provoke resistance. Moscow could still rely on the support of certain sections of the movement, backing the Soviet Union partly out of self interest, partly out of fear, but it could no longer command the respect and admiration of millions of revolutionaries outside the Soviet Union; the invasion was in fact tantamount to abdicating all ideological legitimacy.

Polycentrism was the result of national differences whose existence the communist leaders had always in theory admitted, and for which they had made allowances in their tactics. But in practice substantial differences in approach were always discouraged if not roundly condemned. Yugoslav observers, who have had more time than others to ponder these questions, have stated in their theoretical writings that communism is not a magic formula which will do away with conflicts and contradictions. Edvard Kardelj has drawn attention to a point first made many years before by the social-democratic critics of bolshevism – that the starting point of each country on its road to socialism is of paramount importance for its subsequent development. If the starting point was very low, it was more than likely that political backwardness would be perpetuated and even canonised as part of the great heritage of the past. One neo-Marxist school of thought in the West asserted, on the other hand, that it was all a question of productive forces, and interpreted the development of world communism from Stalin to Khrushchev and beyond in terms of improving living standards that would more or less automatically lead towards more freedom. There was no doubt a grain of truth in this argument; the fact that the Chinese found their supporters mainly in the more backward areas of the world, with Albania as their only European bastion, was hardly altogether accidental. Unfortunately, while backwardness breeds tyranny, it has yet to be proved that a rise in the standard of living leads in itself towards democracy. The economic progress made in the Soviet Union or East Germany in the fifties and sixties has so far found no reflection in the political character of these régimes. 'Economic determinists' apart, opinion in the West ranged from the prophets of an inevitable clash among communist powers to those who denied the very possibility of conflict on the ground that since all communists agreed on essentials, any dispute among them could be of a tactical nature only. The late Franz Borkenau was virtually alone in predicting, shortly after the Chinese communists came to power, that a conflict between Moscow and Peking was inevitable because totalitarian régimes were bound to extend their absolute control as far as they could; the unity of the communist camp could be based only on domination, not on equality, and discord was bound to arise. To this 'law' of totalitarian rule another might be added, that there is no room at the top for more than one man, or one small group of men.

To many outsiders the dispute between Khrushchev and Mao, between Tito and Hoxha, between Togliatti and Thorez, seemed perhaps trifling. A Hindu might at the time have reached similar conclusions with regard to the quarrel between Luther and Leo x. There was in theory no reason why communists should not coexist on the basis of mutual toleration despite differences of opinion; but tolerance is a state of mind notably absent from missionary movements, and from their own point of view the communists rightly feared it; a slackening of the dynamism of the world movement, of its revolutionary zeal and fervour, would have incalculable consequences. If factions were officially recognised on the international level, it would not be long before similar factions were established in each communist régime and party. The unity of the régime would be disrupted, real party democracy would be restored, and the communist parties would gradually become the same as other parties; for obviously there could be no iron discipline at home if anarchy became the rule within the world movement. This would have been the end of communism as known during the first half of the century; communist parties would have continued to exist, radical, even revolutionary in character, but they would have shed the heritage of tyranny. The Soviet leaders and with them the Poles, the East Germans, and the Bulgarians, were firmly resolved to contain the danger.

Revolution 1968

All the discussions about détente and its long-range consequences were based on one assumption which seemed safe enough at the time: that the internal situation was everywhere reasonably stable, unlikely to undergo sudden and violent change in the foreseeable future. The fifties and the early sixties had been the quiet years; the status quo was rarely questioned; there were strikes but their aim was not the overthrow of the system. Students were apolitical and almost suspiciously quiet; the revolutionary impetus had faded away. Political observers noted the 'end of ideology', and forecast the arrival of the technocratic society. There was convergence in the political thought of left and right; differences of opinion persisted about priorities and about ways and means, but the consensus was wider than in any previous period. Suddenly, to everyone's astonishment, the assumptions about the exhaustion of political ideas were challenged by a wave of student revolt which affected the whole of Europe in 1967–8. It should perhaps not have come as a complete surprise, for Europe had a tradition of youth revolt and the conflict between the generations had often assumed a political character. Students had played a leading role both in the Russian revolutionary movement and in the early phases of European fascism. There had been signs in the late fifties indicating a growing spirit of revolt among the younger generation – the Aldermaston marches in Britain advocating nuclear disarmament, the French movement in support of Algerian independence and the prominent part played by students and young intellectuals in all the revolutionary movements in eastern Europe. Later on, resistance to the Vietnam war spread from America to Europe and became the main force of political activity among the young generation, but it was not regarded as a serious challenge to any western government. In Latin America or Turkey students have succeeded in overthrowing governments, but no one believed that this could happen in the open societies of the West. It was generally assumed among the older generation that the negative lessons of the nineteen-thirties and the world war, European revolution and counter-revolution, and the sacrifices they entailed were still so fresh in memory that no one would risk similar disasters by propagating a policy of violent change. This ignored the simple fact that a new generation had grown up for which all these experiences, Stalin and Hitler alike, had little meaning, and for whom history started around 1960. This could be observed most clearly in France, where many small sects on the extreme left were preaching violence, *groupuscules* consisting of Trotskyists (of various persuasions), Maoists, Castroists-Guevarists, anarchists and others engaged in hairsplitting disputes about revolutionary tactics. They seemed to have been relegated to Trotsky's famous 'dustbin of history'; few expected that they would receive a new lease of life not as the result of an 'objective revolutionary situation', but with the advent of a new generation willing to give extremist politics a new chance.

After several years of growing political activity and radicalism among French students, the first major confrontation occurred in November 1967 with the strike of sociology teachers and students at the new university of Nanterre near Paris. In February 1968 Paris students struck, demanding the removal of restrictions on movement between boys' and girls' hostels, and Molotov cocktails were thrown at some buildings, taken as symbols of the capitalist system, by members of a small ultra-radical group of *enragés*. Meanwhile the leadership of UNEF, the national students union, had passed into the hands of a militant group; Cohn-Bendit, Sauvageot, and Geismar first achieved prominence during those hectic weeks. There was growing unrest but it seemed to be confined to the universities and to concern their internal affairs. There was no sign of a national crisis when Prime Minister Pompidou left on an official visit to Teheran in early May, yet within a few days the situation changed completely. Student demonstrations and attempts to take over university buildings were broken up by the police; dozens of students were injured and others arrested. This in turn led to bigger demonstrations and more intensive police repression. The police, unaccustomed to street fighting on this scale, behaved with unnecessary violence; according to a poll taken during this period four-fifths of the population of Paris sympathised with the student protest movement which, it was commonly believed, concerned long overdue university reforms. Cohn-Bendit and his comrades seemed suddenly to have found a mass basis for their cause. They thought that by deliberately provoking police violence they would be able to show up the real, brutal face of the régime and its repressive character. Within the next few days it became clear that they were not really interested in reforming what most of them thought was long past reform; they stood for the destruction of the old university and regarded education, rightly from their point of view, as a marginal problem. Revolution was now the real issue. The rebels from Nanterre and the Sorbonne had the support of the teachers' federation which declared a sympathy strike; the left-wing Catholic trade unionists (CFDT) and many intellectuals also rallied to their side. On 13 May hundreds of thousands of Parisians demonstrated against the Gaullist régime; all over France action committees came into being; the workers joined the general movement against the advice of the Communist and Socialist parties and the CGT. Student Soviets were established in most universities. The state of high tension, of revolutionary expectation, was reminiscent of the atmosphere in Petrograd in 1917. Michel Butor and Nathalie Sarraute stormed the Society of the Men of Letters; footballers, television stars and even young rabbis joined the cultural revolution. On 13 May the Sorbonne was occupied by the students; four days later ten million workers were striking, and on the 18th de Gaulle returned post-haste from his state visit to Bucharest. What had started as a happening had turned into the most serious challenge his régime had ever faced.

There was no revolutionary situation in France in the early summer of 1968, but there was certainly a great deal of discontent and restlessness. The paternalism of the Gaullist régime, its empty phrases, social and economic failures, the mandarinism still dominating academic life, and a great many other negative aspects of French society had antagonised wide sections of the French people. The economic situation was, everything considered, not worse than in most countries, and compared with Spain, not to mention eastern Europe, France was still a haven of freedom. But many Frenchmen were not in a mood to engage in such comparisons; what mattered to them was that they had a great many grievances and that their expectations had not been fulfilled. This reaction came as a great shock to leading Gaullists and de Gaulle was disgusted; 'reforms yes – bed-messing no', the General is said to have declared soon after his return. By that time the leaders of the political opposition – the communists, the socialists, Mendès-France and Mitterrand–had joined the revolutionary bandwaggon and it seemed doubtful whether the Gaullist régime would survive. Authority was breaking down everywhere, the reins of government, central and local, appeared to be slipping, the bourgeoisie seemed paralysed by fear. The General himself appeared to have lost heart as the crisis reached its climax during the last days of May. The government negotiated with the CGT and reached agreement, conceding substantial wage rises to industrial workers. Much to everyone's surprise, the agreement was turned down by the rank and file and thus the deadlock was complete. On 29 May de Gaulle left Paris for an unknown destination and there were rumours that he was about to resign. He went in fact to Baden-Baden to consult the general commanding French troops in West Germany. Having assured himself of his loyalty, he returned to the capital in fighting spirit. In a very brief television appearance the next afternoon he announced that, having a mandate from the people, he would not resign. The National Assembly would be dissolved and new elections held on 23 June. The General also called for civic action everywhere and at once in defence of the Republic against the threat of communist dictatorship. Within minutes a million supporters shouting 'La France aux Français' and singing the Marseillaise filled the streets of Paris in a march on the Place de la Concorde. The Minister of the Interior telephoned all regional prefects asking for firm and immediate measures to put down any disturbances. It took only a few hours for the anti-revolutionary party to regain confidence, while all vigour seemed to have gone out of the left. Gradually the workers evacuated the factories and the students left the colleges which they had seized. The ultra-radical student groups were outlawed and the communists, accused by the General quite undeservedly of having plotted revolution, retreated everywhere. The June elections brought victory to the party of order while all left-wing parties lost votes. Within the left there were bitter mutual recriminations, directed above all against Cohn-Bendit and his comrades who with their ultra-radical slogans, their adventurism, and their thoughtless violence had antagonised wide sections of the public which had in the beginning sympathised with their cause. Yet many felt that Gaullism's victory was hollow; the student movement had only too effectively revealed its weakness. It seemed doubtful that it would overcome this blow to its prestige; the financial crisis six months after the May events showed that the repercussions were by no means over.

The events in France gave encouragement to the student movement in many other countries, but nowhere else did student revolt trigger off a mass movement; its impact, despite the great publicity it received, was on the whole limited to the universities. The German student movement spearheaded by the Socialist SDS had its traditional stronghold in West Berlin, the freest and most progressive of all West German universities. In its early stages its demands mainly concerned *Mitbestimmung*, co-determination, but leadership of the movement as in France soon passed into the hands of the most radical sections: the moment their demands were granted, they presented new ones, until study in some faculties came to a standstill. There was also a growing tendency to engage in street fighting. In June 1967 Berlin students demonstrated against the Shah of Persia then on a visit to the former German capital. In the course of the riots that ensued one student was shot by the police; he became the martyr of the movement which as a result of this incident gained many new adherents. In February 1968 the radical student groups launched a major campaign against Axel Springer, head of Germany's biggest newspaper concern. Springer's newspapers were violently hostile to the student movement and everything it stood for. This campaign had the support of many liberals who thought that the concentration of so many newspapers in the hands of one press lord was a danger to democracy. Other SDS initiatives were less successful; the attempt to engage in revolutionary violence met determined resistance in a country in which the consequences of the politics of violence were still well remembered. In Berlin the student movement had more to fear from the irate population than from the police; in view of Berlin's exposed position the students' antics were regarded by most of its citizens as a real danger to its freedom.

The German student movement was the most highly ideological in character; students of theology, sociology, and literature produced many books and pamphlets to prove that the old order was corrupt to the core, and that only total rejection of neo-capitalism (or late capitalism as others called it) would open a road to a better world. Some gravitated towards Soviet communism, but the majority drew their inspiration from revolutionary movements in the third world. In some respects it was an almost uncanny repeat performance of the noble-savage fashion that had swept Europe two centuries earlier. With all their rejections of modern social science, the rebels had become hopelessly enmeshed in the philosophical and sociological jargon of the day, and most of them were quite unable to express themselves clearly and precisely. For this reason, if for no other, they found it difficult to communicate with those sections of the population who had not been fortunate enough to read Marcuse, Bloch, Adorno and other masters of contemporary thought. Rudi Dutschke, the most prominent leader of the movement, was shot and badly wounded by a mad youngster; there were fresh demonstrations and an attempt was made, not too successfully, to put the blame on Springer and the Bonn government. The public response was not encouraging and as a result the centre of their activities was transferred back to the universities where their position was incomparably stronger.

The Italian student movement first gained prominence in April–May 1966, when several big demonstrations were staged in Rome which ended in rioting. The second and bigger wave of youth revolt lasted from November 1967 to the following summer and spread throughout Italy. The students demanded higher grants and better facilities in the universities but, as in the other European countries, their protests turned into a revolt against bourgeois society *tout court*. In Spain students were in the forefront of the struggle for the overthrow of Franco's dictatorship. A poll carried out in 1963 had shown that 77 per cent of them were not interested in politics, but in the following years radicalisation made quick progress. Demonstrations in open defiance of the authorities began in February 1965; Barcelona university was first closed in April 1966 and by spring 1968 the movement had affected all Spain. The political impact of the student movement in Britain was in comparison much more limited; on various occasions students seized university buildings and many of their demands for university reform were accepted. But with the exception of the demonstration in October 1968 against the war in Vietnam, they did not succeed in mobilising substantial public support for their wider political aims.

The student movement made itself heard and seen at one time or another in most European countries, even in eastern Europe, where it faced a totally different political situation, described elsewhere in the present study. About the mainsprings of the movement in the West there was general agreement: the number of students had trebled or even quadrupled since the war, there was overcrowding, and facilities were often quite inadequate. The internal structure of the universities was antiquated, too much of the medieval mumbo-jumbo still persisted, the administration and/or the professors ruled autocratically, and the students' demand for some form of co-determination was by no means unreasonable. It was surely no coincidence that almost all the leaders of the extreme groups were students of sociology and political science, of theology and philosophy. These fields were in a state of crisis which was reflected in the private frustration of the students who had failed to receive an answer to the questions preoccupying them. It was only natural that a young generation should turn against its predecessor, confident that it would have done much better. On an even deeper level there was dissatisfaction with the modern consumer society and a chiliastic urge in the tradition of the messianic hopes of former ages.

When all these factors have been mentioned there remain many question marks about the cultural and political aims of a movement, that, in view of its diffuse and inchoate character, are all the more difficult to answer. There were from the very beginning doubts about the genuine seriousness of the movement; the element of 'happening', of histrionics, the acting out of fantasies, was strongly marked. There was a great deal of talk about revolution but no one seemed to want to seize power. Perhaps it was an act of self preservation on the part of the student leaders who were dimly aware that in a post-revolutionary dictatorship power would not have remained for long in their hands. Liberation was the main slogan, but it was liberty only for like-minded people; the chief enemy of the young rebel of the sixties was not the fascist or the Stalinist, not even the conservative, but the liberal with his all-pervasive repressive tolerance. The movement claimed to be rationalist in character, a 'second enlightenment', yet there was much evidence of the opposite – the uncritical acceptance of myths, the rejection of historical experience (for history showed so clearly the limits of revolutionary movements). The movement put everything in question, but questioning its own basic beliefs was taboo. In its ideology it tried to combine incompatible ingredients such as utopianism and decadence, freedom and dictatorship, Marcuse's one-dimensional pessimism and Mao's revolutionary optimism. The adulation of some of its heroes was reminiscent of the cult of certain film stars.

The political character and direction of the movement were not easy to assess, even if one ignored the marginal groups that had decided to opt out of society altogether. Few outside observers accepted the ideological manifestos at face value; many doubted whether the movement was in the tradition of the radical left, and some called it left-fascist in orientation, although, unlike fascism it did not rate nationalism as the supreme value. Historical comparisons were freely drawn and similarities with the children's crusade, the anabaptists and the populists were emphasised at one stage or another. Yet in the last resort the movement was *sui generis*; never in recent history had rejection been so total and never had a movement of total rejection been taken so seriously. Above all, never before had the abdication of the older generation been so complete. Many intellectuals, uncertain of themselves, their values and their ideas, were only too willing to follow the crowd, to accept new ideas just because they were new, having decided that the young must be right simply because they were young. A new intellectual style became fashionable, in which fervent assertion replaced rational discussion and the search for truth. A youth revolt subculture developed which showed interesting parallels with the Chinese cultural revolution, but for the fact that it frequently took the material benefits of the affluent society for granted.

Some of the more farsighted leaders of the movement realised that the power in the advanced countries was so solid, the means of repression at its disposal so manifold, that the attempt to wrest power from its hands was hopeless. The whole system was so deeply rooted that it seemed doubtful whether basic changes could be effected even in the unlikely event of a successful revolution. Hence the great hopes attached to the revolution in the third world; there, as Frantz Fanon claimed, a new beginning, radically different from the decaying West, was still possible. Only gradually did it dawn on them that the third world revolutions had little if any guidance to offer advanced societies facing totally different problems. But if it was impossible to overthrow the established order in the advanced countries of the West, there was certainly a good chance of paralysing it. Life there had become fantastically complex and for that reason more vulnerable than ever before. If a few strategically placed obstacles could bring traffic to a standstill in a big town during the rush hour, could not a few determined revolutionaries through their actions paralyse not just the universities but public life in general? Society had become very tolerant. Its adversaries had more to fear from the blandishments of the television companies than from police repression, for they were given a free run of the media of mass communication. The more extreme their views, the more publicity they were likely to receive. Yet in the long run society was bound to defend itself against anarchy not because it was the victim of ideological manipulation but because the great majority of the population had an interest in the maintenance of law and order and had no trust in a future society engineered by the Dutschkes, Cohn-Bendits, and Tariq Alis. But they and their followers were not greatly worried by the possibility of a right-wing, authoritarian reaction, for they hoped that this would only further exacerbate the crisis and that their cause would benefit therefrom.

The central dilemma confronting the revolutionary youth movement was that their demand for absolute freedom collided with complex political-economic realities limiting freedom and democracy. Their quarrel was not just with neo-capitalism but with modern social systems in general, for they all contained strong elements of repression. Despite its radical political demands the European revolutionary movement of the sixties was, as in America, basically motivated by cultural discontent. It rejected alike the emptiness of mass culture and the higher idiocies of intellectual fashions; the charge levelled against it, that it lacked positive content, was therefore largely irrelevant. It was romantic in inspiration and romantic movements are always based on a mood rather than a programme. It could act in given situations as a catalyst of the general discontent which in periods of prolonged peace seems to be inherent in human existence. It could provoke a 'confrontation' with the system, it could in certain conditions seriously weaken it. But it had no alternative to offer and it was therefore, in the last resort, bound to be a failure.

The Invasion of Czechoslovakia

The communist seizure of power in Prague in February 1948 was a turning point in Europe's postwar history; 20 years later the Soviet invasion of Czechoslovakia similarly had a profound effect on European politics. Czechoslovakia is the one east European communist country with democratic traditions and it has been oriented towards the West during most of its recent history, an orientation that was not incompatible with feelings of Slav solidarity. The western tradition was firmly suppressed after 1948 but it had not been altogether uprooted and it re-emerged with the relaxation of political controls in the early sixties. Czechoslovakia was one of the last communist countries to engage in destalinisation, but the process was halted midway; 'liberalisation' was permitted to proceed much farther in the economic field than in political and cultural life. The thaw of 1961-2 was followed by a refreeze, the progressive cultural periodicals were either discontinued or put under strict political control. There was general disillusionment with communism, and this in a country in which the party had once been highly popular. Writers and students continued to maintain that since there had been no basic change in the structure of the political system there were no guarantees that the 'mistakes of the past' (to use the official euphemism) would not be repeated. The economic situation was going from bad to worse and there was growing resentment among the Slovaks of the Prague leadership which accused them of separatism instead of showing understanding for their specific problems. Power rested in the hands of Antonin Novotny, for many years First Secretary of the party and at the same time President of the Republic, who had been deeply implicated in the crimes of the Stalin era. Student demonstrations in Prague in November 1967 concerning living conditions in their hostels were brutally suppressed by the police and thus triggered off a wide sympathy movement. By itself the student protest would have remained as ineffective as the demonstrations of Warsaw students in spring of 1968, but it coincided with an acute crisis in the party leadership; the 'liberals', supported by the Slovaks, had a majority in the central committee and they used the opportunity for an all out attack on the constant violation of internal party democracy by the Novotny faction. Novotny and the conservatives were relieved of their functions in early January 1968 and a new leadership established under Alexander Dubcek, formerly First Secretary of the Slovak party. Their declared political programme was the democratisation of public life, 'so that every honest citizen believing in socialism and the unity of the country feels that he is being useful and counts for something' (Dubcek). The new action programme published in April stated that socialism must provide 'for a fuller assertion of the personality than any bourgeois democracy'. The new course had wide popular support; it was accompanied by the demand that the National Assembly, which for so many years had been a mere rubber stamp, should decide important political issues, and that the crimes of the fifties should be thoroughly investigated and those responsible for them punished. The censors themselves suggested the abolition of censorship in March and a freedom of expression prevailed, unprecedented in any communist régime. There was no intention to retreat from socialist principles in industry and agriculture, but economic reforms (such as decentralisation) were to be promoted more vigorously than in the past. While trying to expand trade links with the West, the new leaders repeatedly declared that the basic orientation of Czechoslovak foreign policy was towards the Soviet Union; there was no intention of leaving Comecon or the Warsaw pact. Addressing the central committee on 1 April 1968, Dubcek stated: 'We must continue to build up our army . . . as a firm link in the alliance of the Warsaw pact armies.'

There was no reason to doubt these professions of loyalty, yet the new Czech leaders encountered hostility among their communist allies almost from the beginning. Without at first directly attacking them, the Soviet press began to suggest that the internal situation in Czechoslovakia was very serious because 'anti-socialist elements', behind a screen of democratisation and liberalisation, were advocating a 'return to the bourgeois republic of Masaryk and Benes'. Gomulka, the Polish leader, was no doubt much displeased by the slogans shouted by Warsaw demonstrators: 'We want a Polish Dubcek.' But the leading voice in the hostile chorus was taken by the East Germans, who claimed that imperialism was trying to detach Czechoslovakia, against the wishes of its people, from the eastern bloc by

means of 'ideological subversion'. They were the first to accuse the Czech
leaders of not opposing this process and in some ways of assisting it. The East
German leaders feared that the new Czechoslovak leadership would
establish diplomatic relations and expand economic ties with West Germany,
and thus weaken East Germany's position in world affairs and even inside the
communist bloc. They feared even more that the call for 'socialism in freedom', if not suppressed, would soon reverberate in their own country. The
Soviet attitude was one of extreme displeasure, but officially at any rate it was
still one of non-interference in Czechoslovakia's internal affairs. By early May,
however, a high ranking Soviet officer was reported for the first time to have
suggested military intervention to assist loyal Czech comrades in their
struggle against the anti-socialist elements. During May Moscow clearly
became more concerned; the free public debate developing in Czechoslovakia
suggested to them that the Prague leadership was losing its grip. The disclosures about the crimes of the Stalin era were moreover extremely embarrassing, since they involved Soviet officials. Above all, the purge was beginning
to reach those elements in the party, the army and the secret police, on which
the Kremlin had been able to count in the past.

Liberalisation in Czechoslovakia coincided with a marked hardening in
Soviet policies, both domestic and foreign, and it was therefore all the more
provocative from the Soviet point of view. Facing the separatist tendencies
in so many communist countries, with Albania now firmly arrayed in the
Chinese camp and Rumania moving towards independence in its foreign
policy, it seemed imperative to take immediate action against the further
disintegration of the Soviet camp. Czechoslovakia's deviation must have
appeared to Moscow far more dangerous than Rumanian separatism, for
Rumania had no common border with any western country. Domestic
liberalisation moreover had been no more marked in Rumania than in the
other bloc countries, whereas the new spirit of freedom in Prague was bound
to be infectious, to spread to other east European countries, and eventually
perhaps infiltrate the Soviet Union itself, undermining the existing political
system. The repeated accusations concerning the growing influence of 'anti-
socialist elements' in Czechoslovakia were untrue, and those responsible for
making them knew it; but the Soviet leaders, Gomulka, and Ulbricht, were
no doubt correct in claiming that events in Czechoslovakia constituted a real
danger, not to socialism, but to the men at the helm in Moscow, Warsaw, and
East Berlin. This was the real substance behind the declarations about
revisionism, the dangers of counter-revolution, and the security of the camp.
There were additional considerations: the Soviet Union was unwilling to give
Prague the large hard-currency credits which the Czechoslovak leaders had
asked for to ease their economic troubles, but was even less willing to consider
the possibility that the Czechoslovaks would turn to the West to obtain the

necessary help. It was, however, neither economic nor military considerations which tipped the balance in favour of intervention; the overriding consideration was political.

A decision was taken, probably in late May, to bring to an end the Czechoslovak experiment of 'socialism in freedom'. There were reports of Soviet troop movements in Poland and during the second half of May Marshal Grechko visited Prague, announcing that Warsaw pact command staff exercises would be held in Czechoslovakia in June. Repeated assurances by the Czech leaders of their firm friendship and alliance with the Soviet Union did nothing to allay Soviet distrust; Moscow had decided that the process of democratisation was to be stopped and this could be effected only by a change in the leadership. The Russians, needless to say, would have greatly preferred to achieve their aim peacefully, by political pressure rather than a full scale military invasion. It was clear that military action would not involve any major risk, in view of the understanding with America about the division of spheres of influence, and it could be taken for granted that the West would refrain from action, as it had done during the Hungarian crisis of 1956. But it was also certain that the decision to occupy Czechoslovakia would deepen the rift in the communist camp and was also bound to alarm the West. For a number of years Moscow had tried, not unsuccessfully, to persuade the European members of NATO that there was no Soviet threat and that the continued existence of the Atlantic alliance was the main obstacle to a real détente and a lasting peace. Given the disagreements among its west European members, their indecision, and other disruptive forces, there had been a reasonable hope that this line would be successful. Now Soviet military intervention would reawaken old fears, undo much of the Soviet diplomatic spade work, and give NATO a new lease of life.

The Soviet, Polish, and East German propaganda campaign against Czechoslovak reform policies was intensified during June and July. Brezhnev and Kosygin referred on various occasions to the parallel between Hungary in 1956 and Czechoslovakia in 1968. In mid-July the leaders of the communist countries, excluding Rumania and Czechoslovakia, met in Warsaw to discuss the danger of 'Czech revisionism', informing Prague at the same time that they had no intention of interfering in its internal matters, which, they said, would violate the principle of respect for independence and equality in relations between socialist countries. But this principle, they added, was not sacrosanct, for Czechoslovakia was now in danger of being torn from the socialist community, and such a situation was completely unacceptable. Various means were used to intimidate the Czech leadership: an antisemitic campaign was launched against the few Jews in leading positions in Prague to prove that revisionism was a Jewish disease. This stratagem had worked in Poland, but Czechoslovakia did not have the same strong antisemitic tradition; the allegation was too absurd to be believed. Later on *agents provocateurs* went to work, planting arms caches (which were said to belong to German *revanchists*) and using other techniques similar to those applied by the nazis before their occupation of Czechoslovakia in 1938–9. To intimidate the Czechs and Slovaks, the Warsaw bloc troops which had held manœuvres in Czechoslovakia were not withdrawn from the country until 3 August. Meanwhile the Soviet, Polish, and East German press emphasised the danger of massive West German intervention and 'international counter-revolution'. When this did not help, the Prague leaders were summoned to a meeting with the Soviet politburo (only two of its members had been left behind) at the border village of Cierna nad-Tisou. Again they did not budge. Dubcek was willing to give the Russians specific assurances about their legitimate defence interests, but he rejected all imputations of 'counter-revolution' and refused to discuss the Soviet demand for a purge of some of the country's progressive leaders. Several days later yet another meeting with the eastern bloc leaders. (except the Rumanians) took place in Bratislava.

The two gatherings did nothing to solve the basic conflict. The Soviets did not withdraw their ultimatum; they had not succeeded in driving a wedge between the Prague leaders; on the contrary, national unity in Czechoslovakia was stronger now than before. This made their experiment all the more dangerous from Moscow's point of view, and the propaganda campaign against it was stepped up. Moscow asserted that there was a witch hunt against loyal, pro-Soviet workers, and that the Prague revisionists were not carrying out the Cierna and Bratislava resolutions. In Moscow, the visits to Prague of Marshal Tito and Ceausescu, the Rumanian leader, in mid-August, raised the spectre of a revisionist bloc, a new 'Little Entente', and the Soviet presidium decided, apparently between 10 and 17 August, that since other methods of pressure had failed, the military occupation of Czechoslovakia was now to proceed. How deep differences of opinion in the Kremlin went is not known, though some Soviet leaders undoubtedly had more misgivings than others. It was clear that a high price would have to be paid. Many foreign communist parties, including some of the most influential, like the French and the Italian, had expressed support for Dubcek and warned Moscow against the invasion. There was a real dilemma, but weighing the alternatives, there could be no doubt in the minds of the Soviet leaders. The continuance of the new course endangered the existence of all the conservative régimes in the bloc, whereas the propagandist setback caused by the invasion would not be lasting; after a few months world public opinion was bound to forget and so would the dissenting communist parties. It had been that way after the suppression of the Hungarian revolt 1956, and there was no reason to assume that the pattern would not repeat itself. To give more plausibility and legitimacy to their invasion on 21 August, plans were made for the establishment of a quisling government in Prague which was to ask the fraternal Soviet people and their allies to give them military assistance against internal and external enemies. It is not known what went wrong in the political preparation of the invasion, but when the Soviet troops entered Czechoslovakia their generals seemed to have no clear political directives. In the Security Council Moscow at first claimed that the invitation came from the Czechoslovak government, but in fact the Soviets found no one willing to collaborate with them; they arrested Dubcek, Cernik, Smrkovsky and the other leaders, but Svoboda, the President, refused to dismiss and replace them. When Svoboda rejected the demand for the appointment of a new leadership handed to him by the Soviet ambassador the scene shifted to Moscow. Svoboda, together with several potential collaborators, was invited to meet the Soviet Presidium, but he insisted on the presence of the arrested leaders. On their arrival, after having been in the hands of the Soviet political police, they were neither physically nor psychologically in the best condition to stand up to Brezhnev, who is reported to have threatened their country and them personally with the direst consequences if they failed to comply with Soviet demands. With one dissenting voice they accepted the Soviet ultimatum: Soviet troops were to be stationed for an indefinite period on Czechoslovak soil, censorship was to be restored, the 'notorious rehabilitation campaign' was to be discontinued, the economic reforms watered down. Generally speaking, coercion was again to replace popular consent as the basis of communist rule. True, the Russians paid lip service to the reform programme with which, they said, they did not want to interfere; nor were they anxious to restore Novotny to power; he was too discredited to fulfil any useful purpose. They assumed, not without reason, that they would gradually be able to replace Dubcek and the other progressives by more pliant leaders, and that eventually the new middle-of-the-roaders, under Soviet pressure and to ensure their own political survival, would suppress 'revisionism' altogether. Gomulka had acted that way after 1956, and there was every reason to assume that events in Prague would follow a similar course.

The occupation of Czechoslovakia came as a great relief in Warsaw and East Berlin; troops from both countries took part in the military operation. The participation of German troops was not, to put it cautiously, in good taste; but then Ulbricht and his colleagues had never been bashful men. Hungarian units also took part, but Budapest clearly felt ill at ease; memories of 1956 lingered on. The Soviet leaders, for want of more convincing arguments, claimed that history would justify their action, but meanwhile Chou En-lai, the Chinese Prime Minister, called the invasion the most barefaced example of fascist power politics. The Albanians spoke about 'fascist aggression', the Yugoslavs expressed extreme concern about the 'illegal occupation' of Czechoslovakia and mobilised their army, while the Rumanian leaders called it a 'flagrant violation of the national sovereignty of a socialist country'. The new Brezhnev doctrine was based on the principle *Le Marxisme c'est moi*, implying that Moscow did not recognise the sovereignty of other communist countries; this was bound to be interpreted by some of Russia's neighbours as a direct threat to their independence, perhaps even their very existence. Soviet attitudes towards Bucharest and Belgrade became threatening; for several weeks it appeared that the occupation of Czechoslovakia might be followed by the invasion of Rumania and possibly Yugoslavia. Faced with Soviet threats, the Rumanian leadership made a tactical retreat, refraining from adverse comment on Soviet policies. The Yugoslavs on the other hand remained defiant. Their country was not a member of the Warsaw Pact, and they were determined to resist an invasion regardless of the consequences. The Soviet leadership was aware of this and realised that the appearance of their troops on the shores of the Adriatic would have caused even greater alarm in the West and probably provoked counter-measures. If there had been a plan to settle accounts with Tito and Ceausescu it was dropped for the time being.

The Soviet action was sharply condemned in the western capitals but the policy of the governments remained one of studious non-interference. As far as they were concerned this was a purely internal affair between the Soviet Union and one of its allies. In Washington and Paris official circles played down the long-term consequences of the Soviet invasion. President Johnson continued to talk about a summit meeting, since the West-East détente had priority in his eyes. Michel Debré, the French Foreign Minister, thought it unwise to close a road simply because an accident had taken place. In the United Nations the Arab governments and some Asian countries opposed any condemnation of the Soviet action. For their part the Soviet leaders, soon after the immediate storm had subsided, launched a new diplomatic offensive aimed at persuading the West that the events in Czechoslovakia were not an obstacle to a normalisation of relations between West and East. It seemed as if they had after all been correct in assuming that the international repercussions of the occupation would be shortlived and not very profound. But in fact they underrated the long-term effects of the invasion, which was bound to be a turning point in European postwar history. The military balance, to be sure, had hardly been changed; the number of Soviet troops stationed in Czechoslovakia was relatively small and did not constitute a major danger for the West. But most of the western assumptions underlying the détente had been disproved, and this in the long run could not remain without consequences. It had been believed that as a result of the détente the era of bipolarity would come to an end (if it was not already over), that the centrifugal, disintegrative trends in both blocs would gradually lead to the shaping of a new European political system. De Gaulle and others were convinced that the Soviet threat to the West had diminished, if not altogether disappeared, and that as a result there was a good chance for the reunification of Europe-to-the-Vistula, if not to the Urals. It had been assumed that as the result of the gradual Europeanisation of the Soviet bloc, Russia would be willing to grant its allies a larger degree of freedom and independence, provided of course that its elementary security interests were not affected.

The Czechoslovak crisis demonstrated that there was no symmetry in the course of developments in West and East; the Soviet Union welcomed the disintegration of the western bloc but was not willing to tolerate any such trend within its own camp, even if reflected in no more than the replacement of a conservative communist leadership by a more liberal one in a client state. The Brezhnev doctrine furthermore implied that the communist seizure of power in any country was an irreversible event, a claim that was bound to have far-reaching consequences for the political fortunes of the communist parties in the West. Even if the Soviet decision to intervene was regarded as a defensive action it opened disturbing perspectives. Was it certain that the Soviet leaders would in future rule out altogether military action outside their sphere of influence if the risks were small? The occupation of Czechoslovakia implied a change in the balance of power in Europe because America, unlike the Soviet Union, was not in a position to reassert its hegemony over dissenting west European allies. Russia on the other hand had the power to do so, and its leaders were not impeded by scruples in suppressing without hesitation any manifestation of independence. This in a way was an admission of weakness, for it meant that the Soviet Union could not rely on ideological persuasion but had to resort to force of arms to safeguard its position. In a long term view this was a disturbing sign which should have caused heart searching in the Kremlin, but as far as the immediate situation was concerned it did not make the slightest difference.

The invasion put an end to the hopes for gradual change in eastern Europe; it now appeared that the initiative for any basic change in the character of the communist régime could come only from Moscow. There were no indications that such a change could reasonably be expected in the foreseeable future. The events of 1968 meant that Soviet hostility towards political systems different from its own had not abated and that, barring totally unforeseen circumstances, the cold war would continue for an indefinite period.

Internal Developments 1955 – 1969

BRITAIN: FROM CHURCHILL TO WILSON

The Conservatives replaced Labour as Britain's ruling party in 1951 and remained in power for the next thirteen years. But their policy did not differ radically from that pursued by their predecessors and rivals. Labour was still basically the party of the working class while the Tories broadly speaking represented the upper and middle classes. The socialist programme envisaged the nationalisation of the key sectors of the national economy while the Conservatives, at least in theory, stood for economic freedom, minimal state intervention, and the defence of the traditional ideas of Toryism. (The Liberals still polled several million votes but under the British electoral system had ceased to play an important role; their representation in parliament was reduced to less than a dozen.) The doctrinal position of Conservatives and Labour seemed diametrically opposed but in practice there was a great deal of common ground on issues of vital national importance such as foreign policy and defence, while the harsh realities of Britain's financial situation reduced the number of economic choices open to Labour and Conservatives alike ('Butskellism'). The more farsighted Conservative leaders realised that their party had to adapt itself to the welfare state if it was to maintain its position in British political life. They did not abolish or reduce the social services that had been introduced by Labour, and of the nationalised industries only road transport and steel were denationalised by Churchill after his comeback in 1951 (steel was again nationalised when Labour returned to power in the sixties). The Tory governments built more houses than Labour and Macmillan's 'wind of change' speech indicated that the Conservatives had accepted the loss of empire with all its consequences. The leadership of the party was passing steadily from members of the aristocracy to representatives of the middle class; Eton and Harrow old boys still predominated in the Tory cabinets, but graduates of Oxford and Cambridge constituted an almost equally high percentage of Labour's front bench.

Churchill suffered a stroke when in office; his illness was kept secret at the time but in April 1955 he had to retire. Anthony Eden who succeeded him had been intimately involved for many years in the conduct of British foreign policy; his experience in other branches of government was limited. He had been expected to replace Churchill one day and his selection came as no surprise. Ironically, it was in his own field of specialisation, foreign affairs, that Eden failed; but for Colonel Nasser's nationalisation of the Suez Canal and the inept way Eden handled the ensuing crisis, his government might have lasted many more years. As tension mounted Eden showed lack of judgment and, more surprising in an Englishman of his background, a lack of sang-froid. At the height of the crisis he suffered a breakdown and was replaced by Harold Macmillan, who had a great deal of political experience in both the domestic and foreign fields; in the twenties and thirties he had been one of the chief spokesmen of progressive Toryism. Under his leadership the Conservatives survived the humiliation of Suez without major ill effects.

Britain's main problems in the years following were domestic in character, and in this respect Macmillan's government was by no means a brilliant success. The rapid turnover at the Treasury (Thorneycroft, Selwyn Lloyd, Heathcoat Amory, et al.) was an indication of the continuing financial difficulties. But there was fitful economic progress and while the spirit of Britain during the late fifties was not one of buoyant optimism, a feeling of confidence returned after the economic setbacks of the late forties and the political shocks of the middle fifties had been overcome. The small Conservative majority of 1951 rose at the elections of 1955 and increased again in 1959; the position of the Tories seemed almost unassailable. But if the standard of living had risen, expectations had grown even faster; the British people became increasingly weary of heavy taxation, wage stops, higher bank rates and mortgage charges. The Conservative leadership showed signs of fatigue and the feeling spread that Labour ought to be given another chance. The Profumo scandal and several other incidents further damaged the prestige of the Macmillan government and the Prime Minister, sensing that public opinion (including important segments of his own party) was turning against him, decided to resign in October 1963. This was about one year before the next general election was due, and Sir Alec Douglas-Home's cabinet had therefore the character of a caretaker government. Douglas-Home was a High Tory and has been a member of the House of Lords, an unlikely choice for Prime Minister in the twentieth century. But the policies he followed hardly differed from those of his predecessor, which again showed that the freedom of manœuvre of both prime minister and governing party had become very limited indeed. Douglas-Home had been the candidate of a small but influential group within the Conservative party for whom Butler (the leader who had been thought most likely to replace Macmillan) was too radical and therefore unreliable. Douglas-Home's election caused a great deal of resentment inside the party and the demand gained ground that the succession should in future be decided by open democratic vote. In these inauspicious conditions Douglas-Home did surprisingly well, and though his party was defeated in the elections of October 1964, Labour returned to power with a majority of only 13 seats over the Tories.

Labour had been in a state of profound internal crisis throughout the nineteen-fifties. After the resignation of Attlee the mantle of the leader passed to Hugh Gaitskell, an economist by training, an Oxford don and wartime civil servant. Gaitskell's personal integrity was widely respected and his intellectual competence, especially in his own field, was beyond doubt. But he lacked dynamism and the charisma of a born leader capable of inspiring his followers and winning new suporters to his cause. Above all, he had to face bitter opposition inside the party, for Labour was virtually split during most of these years and the fundamentalist left attacked the leadership for allegedly betraying socialist principles. The left stood for full nationalisation and a strictly controlled economy, and for neutralism and disarmament in foreign affairs. The difficulty with the left-wing programme was not so much its extremism as its unreal character: a political programme, however extreme, has a chance of eventually succeeding if it is attuned to political realities and exigencies; that of the Labour left was not, for Britain's economic difficulties could clearly not be cured by the medicines suggested by these circles. While almost everyone in Britain preferred peace to war, and friendship with all nations to tension and crisis, praiseworthy sentiments are not sufficient to resolve international conflicts. The nuclear disarmers went each Easter on their Aldermaston protest march; the Labour Party conference regularly voted each year to abolish nuclear arms, and anti-Americanism made some headway in the country. Unilateralism had its attractions, but was it practical politics for a party in power? When Labour was again called on to form a government, yesterday's rebels soon found themselves pursuing the very policies they had denounced not long before, and they in turn came under attack from a new generation of radical critics.

These battles lasted for several years and in the end, under Gaitskell's patient leadership, the party slowly closed its ranks, realising that it would be condemned to stay in the political wilderness for ever unless it ceased its internal strife. Then, with better prospects in sight, Gaitskell suddenly died. The two main candidates for the succession were George Brown, an indefatigable, highly extrovert and somewhat erratic party stalwart of working-class background, and Harold Wilson, like Gaitskell an economist by training, a former Oxford don and wartime civil servant. Wilson at an early age had been President of the Board of Trade but, together with other left-wing ministers, resigned in protest against some of the government's policies.

Wilson showed greater tactical skill than Gaitskell; his decision to dissolve parliament early in 1966 resulted in a much larger majority for Labour and thus provided a secure basis for carrying out the Labour Party election programme. But soon the government was overtaken by a series of economic emergencies and within two years it had lost most of its popular support, while Wilson's personal prestige declined even more sharply. The government seemed to totter from one disaster to another – the devaluation of sterling in November 1967 was only one of a series of major blows. Even the most secure Labour seats were no longer safe in the by-elections of 1967 and 1968; much of the blame was put on the Prime Minister personally; Wilson, his many critics argued, had not made the full seriousness of the latent economic crisis known to the people and seemed incapable of acting decisively at the right time. While much of this criticism was justified, it was an oversimplification to put all the blame on the Prime Minister and his entourage: Britain's difficulties were largely structural. Both the City of London with its periodical jitters provoking unnecessary monetary crises, and the trade union leadership with its unwillingness to cooperate in the modernisation and streamlining of Britain's economy, bore a heavy share of responsibility. The resignation of Frank Cousins, head of the largest trade union, was typical of the lack of support for the government from within its own ranks. But it would be invidious to single out individual culprits: no government could have worked wonders while the country failed to earn its way in the world.

The Conservatives would have been even more successful in making political capital of Labour's weakness but for the dissension of their own ranks. The leadership had passed after Douglas-Home's resignation to Edward Heath, who however failed to carry much conviction. Within the party there were wide-ranging differences of opinion on such issues as immigration, Rhodesia, the social services and incomes policy. Some imaginative measures had been taken by the Tories when in government to cope with the economic situation, such as the establishment of the National Economic Development Council in 1961 in which business, trade unions, and government cooperated in shaping economic policy. Unfortunately this new body did not gain the influence it was hoped it would acquire. The establishment of a National Incomes Council was also envisaged, but failed to come into being owing to the refusal of the trade unions to participate.

Foreign affairs played a comparatively minor part in Britain's crisis: the decolonisation of the empire continued as Ghana and Nigeria gained independence in the fifties. They were followed by the East African countries, Malaya (1957) and Singapore (1959). The West Indian Federation established in 1958 foundered in 1962. More serious from Britain's point of view was the breakdown of the Central African Federation in 1963, for it led two years later to the Rhodesian crisis. The majority of white settlers refused to surrender their position to the Africans, claiming that such a policy would lead to a state of chaos similar to the situation in the Congo. The British government applied economic sanctions in accordance with UN resolutions, but the African countries, now Britain's Commonwealth partners, demanded in addition the use of force against the Rhodesian Prime Minister, Ian Smith, and his régime. There was little popular sympathy for military action in Britain, and the Wilson government tried to steer a middle course between the two extremes as the Rhodesian issue came to play temporarily a role out of all proportion to its intrinsic importance in British politics. Elsewhere the transfer of power presented fewer difficulties: Malta became independent in 1964, and also British Guyana, the last African colonies and, after a prolonged struggle and civil war, Aden. Despite strong Spanish pressure Britain was not willing to surrender Gibraltar. In Cyprus and South Arabia the British exodus was followed by bitter internal strife: the consequences of the British decision to leave the Persian Gulf will not be clear for years to come. The Commonwealth Prime Ministers continued to meet from time to time but these were social occasions rather than events of great political consequence. There was reluctance to sever ancient ties altogether, and it was thought that the old framework could still be of some limited use. But membership in the Commonwealth in these conditions had almost lost its meaning; there were exchanges of opinion but no binding decisions.

Britain's foreign and defence policy had to be modified in the postwar era in the light of the country's diminished resources and reduced status in the world. It was a complicated and often painful adjustment; military positions east of Suez were gradually given up and the army on the Rhine reduced. Conscription was abolished and a small professional army was entrusted with the defence of Britain and its shrinking commitments abroad. Britain produced its own nuclear devices but did not have the financial strength to compete with the United States and the Soviet Union in the missile race. The construction of Britain's own rocket, Blue Streak, had to be given up in 1960 because it proved too costly. The common Anglo-American project for the production of Skybolt rockets was also discontinued and Britain became almost entirely dependent on the Polaris submarine and American rockets and aircraft to give even token credibility to her deterrent.

Successive governments showed in their foreign policy a great deal of caution and notable reluctance to engage independently in any major initiative. Such prudence was in marked contrast to de Gaulle's striking but ultimately futile ventures. Conservatives and Labour shared the conviction that reason should prevail in world affairs and violence not be used to solve conflicts. There was much willingness to mediate between East and West, North and South; to look for a compromise was the recommendation to all antagonists. The Americans, some Englishmen argued, had the power and the money but lacked the experience to act wisely in complicated international situations, and they would therefore benefit from British advice. But the special relationship between London and Washington which had existed during the second world war and had lingered on during the decade after faded away. American foreign policy lacked resolution rather than advice, of which there was more than enough, and the Soviet Union preferred to talk to Washington directly without intermediaries. Macmillan's visit to Moscow and Wilson's more frequent trips were therefore of no great political consequence; nor did the often heralded expansion of British trade with the Soviet Union ever materialise. While individual British firms no doubt benefited from trading with the Soviet Union, the overall trade balance was unfavourable to Britain for most of the time.

Unlike the United States, Britain had established diplomatic links with China, but the hope of improving relations with Peking and exerting a moderating influence was not realised. British diplomats and journalists were harassed and kept under house arrest in China, and London could do little to alleviate their lot or effect their release. The Foreign Office tried to improve relations with individual communist countries, but since their freedom of action was strictly limited the immediate value of these contacts was not great. The attitude of the communist countries certainly did not give much encouragement to the British left, and sympathies for the third world also began to fade. Nehru had died and not much remained of the spirit of Bandung. The record of Sukarno and Nkrumah, of Nasser and Ben Bella, did not inspire much enthusiasm, while Mao's policy made sense only to the staunchest believers in his cause. Castro, Ché Guevara, and Ho Chi Minh still had their admirers in some circles but these were distant idols, hardly of much relevance to the conduct of British policy.

The belief of sections of the British establishment in its historical mission of playing Greeks to the Washington Romans had a parallel in the conviction of the radical left that socialist movements abroad were expecting British moral guidance. Such assumptions contained a grain of truth, for there existed a traditional reservoir of goodwill towards Britain in Europe as well as in other parts of the world. These hidden assets are not to be belittled, but they did not make it any easier for British policymakers (and the British people in general) to come to terms with their new vastly reduced status in the world. This was the main challenge facing Britain in the fifties and sixties; not an easy one to meet, in view of Britain's leading role in the past and the inclination to hanker after lost power and splendour. Feelings of resentment *vis-à-vis* the United States and West Germany were more pronounced however among the literary intelligentsia than other sections of the population. There was bound to be a great deal of dissatisfaction in this difficult period of transition; sometimes it found expression in unexpected directions, such as the resurgence of nationalist and separatist movements in Scotland and Wales and the revival of religious strife in Ulster. If Labour had not done well there was no certainty that the Tories would have done any better. Some critics put the blame for Britain's malaise on the people as a whole ('suicide of a nation'), but less alarmist observers, too, wrote with growing concern about the consequences of inefficiency and the fact that the country despite all warnings was still living beyond its means. There were frequent complaints about the absence of a common national purpose and the general preoccupation with individual (or sectional) material interests. This feeling of malaise, combined with political frustration and economic stagnation, caused a great deal of heart-searching. The world success of the Beatles, the exploits of Sir Francis Chichester sailing the oceans in his 'Gipsy Moth', and stories in American news magazines about swinging London were not sufficient to dispel the mood of dejection. Seen in a wider perspective, the problems besetting Britain were part of a general trend afflicting in various degrees of intensity all developed countries. They were aggravated by the specific problems of a country that had been overtaken by others not as the result of a traumatic defeat in war but as a consequence of long-term political and economic trends, partly at least, beyond its own control. In its long history the British people had emerged from worse calamities with flags flying, revealing sterling qualities of calmness and determination. But then it is always far easier to mobilise a nation to cope with a sudden emergency than with a long drawn out creeping crisis such as it faced after the second world war.

FRANCE: THE FIFTH REPUBLIC

As government followed government in rapid succession in the middle fifties, France seemed to be heading towards the brink of disaster. Since no single political party had a majority, all governments were coalitions and thus carried in themselves from the beginning the seeds of dissolution. There was growing anger among Frenchmen of all classes about a system of parties and politicians that was unable to provide a minimum of political stability. Economic progress was more substantial than appeared at first sight, but inflation deprived many Frenchmen of its fruits. The state of affairs was somewhat reminiscent of Germany before 1933: the Fourth Republic was steadily losing the last shreds of its authority, until in the end hardly anyone was willing to lift a finger in its defence. The extremes gained ground: the communists, and on the other hand the Poujadists, who at the general elections of 1956 obtained at their first attempt 50 seats in parliament. Together, the two could effectively block most initiatives of the democratic centre.

The colonial wars were the greatest immediate danger to the survival of democracy in France. The Mendès-France government had liquidated the bloody and protracted war in Indo-China; Tunisia became independent in

1956, and even before that, in 1955, the Moroccan imbroglio had been settled by permitting the Sultan to return to his country from exile. Algeria was the greatest problem of all; the insurrection there had broken out in November 1954, only a short while after the end of the war in Indo-China. When the revolt began fewer than 50,000 French soldiers were stationed in Algeria; in two years that figure was doubled, and later on increased to 350,000. The French army had to withdraw part of its contingent from NATO to cope with the attacks carried out by the Algerian Liberation Movement (FLN). Government after government (headed by Edgar Faure, Felix Gaillard, Guy Mollet, and Bourgès-Maunoury) was unable to bring to a successful conclusion a war which was fought with increasing bitterness on both sides. France was deeply split on the issue; at first a majority of Frenchmen were strongly opposed to a retreat from Algeria for, unlike Indo-China or Morocco, this was not a colony but a part of metropolitan France and, incidentally, also the home of one million Frenchmen.

As the FLN received substantial support from the neighbouring African and Arab countries, the French army felt increasingly frustrated in its military actions and 'pacification' programme. Its commanders claimed that their hands were tied and that they did not receive full support from the Paris politicians. The army had the enthusiastic backing of the local French population and of individual French leaders such as Bidault, the former head of the MRP, and Soustelle, de Gaulle's former lieutenant, who bitterly opposed any retreat from 'Algérie Française'. As the war entered its fourth year there was a shift in public opinion and more and more Frenchmen admitted that there would have to be a negotiated peace. The right and the *Pieds Noirs* (the French Algerians), on the other hand, were determined not to surrender the Algerian position and prepared for a war to the bitter end. Terrorist acts became a daily occurrence in both Algeria and metropolitan France, with the OAS (*Organisation de l'Armée Secrète*) leading the fight against 'defeatists and traitors'. When Pierre Pflimlin, believed to favour a negotiated settlement, was asked to form a new government in May 1958, tension reached a climax. On 13 May, the French army in Algeria was in open revolt; in Corsica local 'committees of public safety' were established in defiance of government authority.

In this acute crisis many eyes turned to de Gaulle; his leadership alone seemed acceptable to a majority of Frenchmen and thus a guarantee against the outbreak of civil war. De Gaulle accepted the call on condition that he would be given a free hand to deal with the emergency; he was not willing to share power with parties and politicians. His views on Algeria were by no means clear and he did little to clarify them. The army expected him to give them full support to continue the war; General Salan, the Commander in Chief in Algeria, had proclaimed de Gaulle chief of state even before the politicians in Paris had made up their minds. But de Gaulle seems to have been sceptical about the chances of military victory and was willing to make major concessions to the FLN. His main efforts were at first directed towards strengthening his own position. He ruled by decree; the political parties were not suppressed but they lost effective power. Under the new Constitution the President had the right to appoint the Prime Minister and to dissolve Parliament, and effective control over defence and foreign policy was in his hands. He was directly elected by the people for a period of seven years and made repeated use of a popular referendum, thus further reducing the importance of parliament. When the deputies opposed the appointment of Georges Pompidou, de Gaulle's candidate, as Prime Minister, the President simply ignored the decision and reappointed him the following day. Some of his governments were composed of Gaullists in combination with leaders of other groups (Guy Mollet, Giscard d'Estaing), but the key positions were always in the hands of his own faithful followers; Michel Debré, Georges Pompidou, and Couve de Murville could be relied upon to carry out unquestioningly the General's instructions. Before 1968 the Gaullists never obtained an absolute majority of votes but they were the strongest party, and the new electoral system provided them with a safe parliamentary base. The new Constitution had been welcomed by 79 per cent of all Frenchmen in a plebiscite in September 1958; there was every reason to believe that the Fifth Republic had a firmer and more secure basis than its predecessor.

The Algerian problem had not yet however been solved; the war continued while various schemes to give Algeria greater autonomy or semi-independence were elaborated, discussed, and rejected. These plans did not satisfy the FLN but they infuriated the protagonists of Algérie Française. In January 1960 the French army in Algeria rebelled when General Massu, one of its heroes, was recalled by de Gaulle. A more serious showdown came in April 1961, when a number of generals (Salan, Jouhaud, Challe, and Zeller) openly defied the General. By that time, however, public opinion in France was solidly behind de Gaulle; it seemed hopeless to continue the war, and the acts of terrorism carried out by the OAS in metropolitan France did not endear its perpetrators to the population at large. The insurgents might have succeeded in overthrowing an old style cabinet and dictated their policy to the country, but de Gaulle, who did not fail to appear in a general's uniform in his effective television appearances, was a much more formidable antagonist and in the face of resolute resistance the rebellion quickly collapsed. De Gaulle's Algerian policy received the support of 90 per cent of all Frenchmen in a referendum in 1962, and the army, albeit somewhat reluctantly, followed suit.

Negotiations with the FLN in Evian (in Switzerland) dragged on for a long time, but in March 1962 agreement was at last reached. Algeria became independent, most of the French Algerians migrated to France and were absorbed without much difficulty in its political and economic life; the dire predictions about a fascist backlash did not materialise.

At the end of the Algerian war de Gaulle was at the height of his power. France for the first time in many years had a homogeneous government providing effective leadership. It was not a democratic régime by the standards of the Third or Fourth Republic, but the negative experience of parliamentary government with its shortcomings and abuses was still fresh in everyone's mind and the Gaullist slogans of stability, tradition, and progress thus fell on welcoming ears. The economy continued to improve after the devaluation of the franc in 1958; in this respect de Gaulle was reaping the fruits of the initiatives undertaken by his predecessors. There were some rumblings on the left and the extreme right; communists and socialists established a Federation of the left, but the communists, despite their tightly knit organisation and their formidable electoral basis, did not constitute a serious challenge to the régime. They were in full accord with de Gaulle's anti-American policy, and in later years the President sometimes found more sympathy for his foreign policy among the communists than in the ranks of his own party. There was opposition among the centre groups against Gaullist foreign and domestic policies but Lecanuet, the leader of these forces, polled only 15 per cent of the vote in 1964, in comparison with de Gaulle's 44 per cent and the 31 per cent given to Mitterrand, who represented the left-wing Federation. But behind the outward façade of stability a slow process of erosion of the Gaullist régime was setting in. The General's main interest was focused on defence and foreign policy. His anti-NATO line and blocking of Britain's entry into the EEC were criticised by many Frenchmen. Even among de Gaulle's own followers some failed to see any purpose in his foreign policy; others, shocked by the growing cost of an independent French deterrent, began to regard it as a mere waste of money. The dictatorial style, the grand gestures which bore so little relation to France's present needs, irritated a growing number of young Frenchmen. In 1967 the first signs of an incipient crisis could be detected; in the parliamentary elections of March 1967 the Gaullist share of the vote fell to 38 per cent. Separatist trends were reported from Brittany, there was growing student unrest and increasing dissatisfaction among the working class. The economy had recovered in 1966–7 from the crisis of 1963 (and the measures taken by the government to combat it), but the stabilisation programme and the price freeze were only partly successful, and real wages grew only slowly. It became increasingly obvious that the achievements of the government were lagging sadly behind its promises. *Paris s'ennuyait*: impatience grew and with it unwillingness to put up much longer with the General's paternalist régime.

The events of May–June 1968 have been described above: they were part of a general European trend but to almost everyone's surprise they found their most acute and dramatic manifestation in the European country that was believed to be more stable than the rest. De Gaulle once more defeated his challengers and some of whom, such as Mitterrand, were discredited as the result of the confrontation. But although de Gaulle had prevailed, not without some difficulty, against Cohn-Bendit, the shortcomings of his régime had become only too manifest. The Gaullist government did not find it at all easy to cope with the economic consequences of the *événements*. The General's idiosyncratic style and splenetic utterances, his disregard for his own ministers, as shown in his handling of the Israeli arms embargo, became a source of embarrassment to his own party. There was, in short, a growing feeling in 1969, that he had outlasted his usefulness and his decision to withdraw from the political scene was welcomed by a majority of Frenchmen. His place in history will be debated for a long time. Probably no other Frenchman would have been able to liquidate the war in Algeria in the way he did, and it was his great merit to have provided a period of stability after the uncertainties of the Fourth Republic. Under his leadership France had recovered, but the whole political régime was tied up with his own person. By clinging to power too long, de Gaulle put in question the achievements of the earlier years of his rule.

GERMANY: ADENAUER AND AFTER

While the German question preoccupied the chancelleries of Europe and America, German domestic affairs were a model of tranquillity. The Adenauer years were uneventful; there were no striking gains, other than economic, and no great crises. The old Chancellor was averse to experimenting in either foreign or domestic policy; he believed in guided democracy, Germany's political history in his own lifetime having taught him the dangers of excessive freedom. In the German postwar Basic Law (*Grundgesetz*) an effort was made not to repeat the mistakes of the Weimar Republic. The electoral system put a premium on stability, favouring the two big parties, the Christian Democrats (CDU) and the Social Democrats (SPD). The Liberals (FDP) were all along a poor third, and the other parties either failed to overcome the five per cent hurdle for representation in parliament, or counted for little even if they did. Adenauer was bitterly attacked by his critics for lack of imagination, the paternalist attitude towards his own countrymen, the invariable pro-Western attitude which prevented any *rapprochement* with the East. Adenauer believed that Germany needed a long time to recover its equilibrium. The fifties were a period of political stagnation which provoked boredom rather than dissent; it alienated the intellectuals, not the working class. This *immobilisme* certainly helped to perpetuate the division of the country, and Germany's faithful adherence to the Atlantic alliance limited its freedom of manœuvre in foreign affairs.

On the credit side of the balance sheet was the fact that millions of refugees from the East were absorbed, that the century-old enmity with France was buried, that the new German army (*Bundeswehr*), unlike its predecessors (*Reichswehr* and *Wehrmacht*), was firmly integrated into the democratic order and no longer the breeding ground for dangerous dictatorial tendencies. Adenauer's policy corresponded in many ways to the German postwar mood, with 'Above all no experiments!' as its first commandment. A more elastic policy towards East Germany and the Soviet Union would certainly have made it more difficult for Moscow and East Berlin to attack West Germany as the main danger to peace, but it would hardly have caused any substantial change in their relations. Given the political aims of the communist powers, the conflict was irreconcilable, no settlement possible on mutually agreeable terms.

Adenauer's policy, despite its lack of inspiration and excitement, had a great deal of popular support. In the general elections of 1957 the CDU received for the first time an absolute majority – 270 seats in the Bundestag out of a total of 497, with 169 for the SPD and 41 for the Liberals. Four years later the first signs of a decline in CDU fortunes appeared, stemming perhaps not so much from any major failure on the part of the government as from the feeling that new men and new ideas were needed. In the elections of 1961 the share of the CDU declined to 45 per cent, whereas the Social Democratic poll rose to 36 per cent. The Christian Democrats, while still the biggest party, had again to look for outside support to form a coalition and thus to lay themselves open (as they saw it) to political blackmail. The elections of 1961 thus foreshadowed the end of the Adenauer era.

The success of the Chancellor's rule during the nineteen-fifties had a profound impact on German society and should be measured not only by the extent of electoral support given to his party. The changes that took place in SPD policy were also the outcome of Adenauer's successes. Up to the late fifties the Social Democrats had toyed with neutralism and, in theory at least, continued to put the emphasis on the class struggle and a radical socialist policy, including a far-reaching nationalisation programme. In 1958–9 the party leadership realised that in view of the unchanging Soviet and East German hostility, neutralism was no longer a practical proposition, and in their new (Godesberg) programme they undertook a drastic revision of their domestic policy. The party of the working class was to be transformed into a broad popular movement appealing to all sections of the population. Under the leadership of Willi Brandt and Herbert Wehner, formerly a leading communist and therefore particularly disliked by his ex-comrades, the party made a major effort to win the confidence of those sections of German society which in the past had rejected Social Democracy as dangerous and irresponsible. In this way the SPD laid itself open to attacks from the left, especially from the younger generation and the intellectuals. But these radical forces, though militant and highly vocal, constituted a small minority, whereas support by at least part of the middle class was essential for any electoral breakthrough, as the SPD victory in 1969 showed.

The President of the Republic played a much less important role in the postwar German political system than in the Weimar period. He served as a symbol, giving legitimacy to the system, but had little influence on shaping current policies. Theodor Heuss, a highly cultured South German of impeccable liberal background, admirably fulfilled this task and was re-elected for a second term; the election of Heinrich Lüebke in 1959 was one of Adenauer's less successful schemes; Lüebke, a ponderous North German, gradually became the butt of much sarcasm as the result of maladroit gestures and speeches, and he was further discredited when it appeared that his political past during the nazi era had not been so blameless as was at first thought. Franz Josef Strauss, the South German leader of the Christian Democrats, was at the centre of another political storm; greatly annoyed by often unfair attacks in *Der Spiegel*, an influential news magazine, the then Minister of Defence gave instructions for the arrest of some of its correspondents on suspicion of betraying military secrets. This high-handed action aroused great indignation; those arrested had to be quickly released, and Strauss's political career seemed at an end. But with his political base in Munich still intact the Bavarian leader, one of the most talented and certainly the most dynamic political figure to have emerged in the fifties, spent a few years mending his fences and eventually returned to Bonn as the holder of a key economic portfolio in the Great Coalition of 1966. Ludwig Erhard, Vice-Chancellor under Adenauer, was the most popular figure in the CDU government; the portly architect of the economic miracle embodied for many Germans stability and prosperity. His critics called him a 'rubber lion', doubting his capacity to act decisively in a time of crisis. Adenauer tried to sabotage Erhard's election as his successor, and after Erhard had been elected in April 1963 by the CDU despite the retiring Chancellor's opposition, Adenauer continued his attacks.

Erhard remained Chancellor for a little over three years, and his reign was, broadly speaking, as uneventful as that of his predecessor. The new Chancellor was less enthusiastic than Adenauer about de Gaulle's European policies, and would have preferred to see Britain join the Common Market; he was also somewhat more conciliatory towards the Soviet Union. But he lacked the firmness to stand up to de Gaulle and as Bonn's options in eastern

Europe continued to be limited there was no substantial advance towards a *rapprochement* with the East. There were indications of an economic recession in 1965 as domestic orders levelled off, and the growth rate during 1966 fell to a mere three per cent. The recession was not the result of any major mistake or miscalculation on Erhard's part; it was common to almost all European countries. But having been accustomed to uninterrupted economic growth since the end of the war, the Germans took it much harder than the others, and consequently it had wider political repercussions. The confidence so recently gained disappeared almost overnight, and Erhard became the first victim of the changing mood. In October 1966 the Liberals withdrew from the coalition, giving as their official reason their opposition to Erhard's budget which provided for tax increases. Their decision reflected the loss of confidence sometimes bordering on near hysteria, which affected wide sections of the people, not excluding Erhard's own party. Faced with growing opposition inside the CDU, Erhard resigned in November 1966 and was replaced by Kurt Kiesinger, who was to head the first Great Coalition in the history of postwar Germany.

Kiesinger, Swabian by origin, had made his name in local politics; he was a firm believer in the alliance with France and, like Erhard, a Protestant. Willi Brandt became Vice-Chancellor and Foreign Minister; Schroeder, who had been a member of most governments since the early fifties, was appointed Minister of Defence, while Strauss and the Social Democrat Schiller, were made responsible for Economic Affairs. Herbert Wehner and Gustav Heinemann, who became Minister of the Interior, were other leading Social Democrats to join the cabinet. The CDU had opted for the great coalition in view of the gravity of the economic crisis. Aware of the decreasing popularity of their party, they wanted to share responsibility. For the Social Democrats the decision to enter the government was not an easy one, and a substantial number disagreed, arguing that by accepting responsibility for dealing with a crisis which was not of their making, the Social Democrats were tying their own hands and in the long run were bound to suffer a reverse. The party leadership, on the other hand, was convinced that the opportunity was too good to be allowed to pass; it was their only chance of demonstrating that the Social Democrats had a constructive contribution to make and could be entrusted with the management of the affairs of state.

The Great Coalition quickly overcame the economic crisis but failed to make use of its authority in foreign policy. It had been argued for a long time that neither CDU nor SPD could afford to recognise the Oder-Neisse line for fear of the influence of the refugee organisations and electoral setbacks. The Great Coalition offered a unique opportunity to break out of this vicious circle, but it was not taken.

As the immediate crisis passed, an increasing number of critics argued that a strong opposition was needed for the functioning of a healthy democracy; the Free Democrats were hardly equipped to fulfil this task. There was a distinct danger that the radical forces on right and left would exploit the situation. The rise of the right-wing NPD, led by Adolf von Thadden, raised the ghost of the Nazi party. The NPD did comparatively well in the traditional strongholds of national Socialism, Lower Saxony, Franconia, parts of Hesse, polling between five and ten per cent in local elections. Its support was mainly in small towns among the middle-aged lower middle classes, but it also had some backing in other age groups and social strata. It was difficult to generalise about the mass basis of the party, apart from the fact that it was fundamentally a negative phenomenon reflecting a variety of discontents and that it represented a reassertion of the nationalist spirit in Germany.

While many former nazis belonged to the NPD, its ideological orientation was closer to the pre-1933 conservatives than to the Hitler movement, and it certainly lacked the dynamic character of National Socialism. On the extreme left the German Communist Party became legal again in 1968 under a new name (DKP), but it attracted even fewer followers than the NPD. More striking were the activities of the various anti-parliamentary factions on the extreme left (APO), most of them militants of the student movements. These groups too were small in numbers but their strategic concentration in the big cities, their constant attempts to provoke the authorities and the establishment, attracted an enormous amount of publicity. Their ideological beliefs were a curious mixture of Marxism with strong utopian-anarchist elements and ideas that had traditionally been a preserve of the extreme right (élitism, *Kulturpessimismus*, the cult of violence, opposition to liberalism and 'repressive tolerance'). Their activities had a considerable impact on life in the universities but hardly affected national politics, apart from provoking a great deal of hostility and probably quite unwarranted fear.

Two decades after the end of the war Germany had regained an uneasy equilibrium but not yet its self-confidence; the longing for stability at almost any price was still very strong and there was an inclination to magnify every crisis, political or economic. Many Germans had not yet accepted the fact that a democratic régime usually means living without panicking with unresolved conflicts and through crisis situations.

ITALY: CHRISTIAN DEMOCRACY AND THE 'OPENING TO THE LEFT'

Christian Democracy remained the leading force in Italian as in German politics throughout the postwar era. But the Democrazia Christiana (DC), with a smaller electoral basis than the German CDU, could not provide stable government, and after de Gasperi had left the political scene it lacked a leader whose authority was accepted unquestioningly by the whole party. In the ten years after de Gasperi's death there were no fewer than 12 governments; a certain measure of stability returned only with the installation of the first Moro government in December 1963. Influential sections of the DC made great efforts to establish an opening to the left (*apertura a sinistra*), trying to induce the Nenni Socialists to give up their alliance with the communists and join the government coalition. They needed additional parliamentary support, for in the elections of 1953 they and the small parties supporting them failed to obtain an absolute majority. The right-wing (Pella and others) regarded the proposed opening with deep misgivings, opposing in principle any major concession to the left. In 1955 it seemed for a moment that the *apertura* would come into being despite their opposition; Gronchi, a left-wing Christian Democrat, was elected President of the Republic with the votes of both socialists and communists. A year after, following the revelations made by Khrushchev at the twentieth congress of the Soviet Communist Party, Nenni decided to dissociate himself from the communists and to renew his collaboration with the Saragat group which had split away several years earlier. But this policy did not find sufficient support in Nenni's own party; the veteran socialist leader was outvoted in 1957 by left-wing opponents and the *apertura* was dropped for the time being.

Scelba and Segni headed uneasy coalition governments in which both the Saragat socialists and the right-of-centre liberals participated. These were followed by Zolli's caretaker government from May 1957 to July 1958; it was based on the DC alone and thus depended on parliamentary support from parties outside the government. In the elections of May 1958 the Christian Democrats improved their position, but with 42 per cent of the total vote they were still dependent on the backing of at least two of the smaller parties. The communists, who had not yet fully recovered from the shock of the invasion of Hungary, polled 22 per cent; the Nenni socialists improved their position with 14 per cent of the total, and the Saragat groups was a poor fourth, with little more than four per cent. After the elections Fanfani formed a government with Saragat's help; it lasted only six months; a dynamic and highly ambitious leader belonging to the DC left wing, Fanfari antagonised a great many influential people within his own party. Saragat on the other hand was afraid that his party's participation in a minority government would further weaken its position. Subsequent cabinets (Segni, Tambroni, and again Fanfahi) were drawn exclusively from the ranks of the DC; their dependence on outside support and the constant changes ruled out any consistent policy. There was a prolonged crisis in 1960 when the liberals decided no longer to support the DC. In March 1962 Saragat's Social Democrats and the small Republican party joined yet another cabinet headed by Fanfahi. The Social Democrats urged the Christian Democrats to make another effort to gain Nenni's support. Conditions seemed auspicious, for in the Vatican too the idea of an *apertura* had won new adherents. Moro, the party secretary, was no less eager to establish a left-centre coalition, but for a long time there was little progress because Nenni was still the captive of the opponents in his own party of any such cooperation. Only after many setbacks his views were accepted at a party congress in December 1963. The socialists then joined the Moro cabinet (with Nenni as deputy Prime Minister), while Nenni's left-wing opponents broke away and established their own organisation (*Partito Socialista Italiano di Unità Proletaria*). Nenni and Saragat again joined forces in 1966, almost 20 years after their ways had first parted.

Throughout all these years there was hardly any change in the internal balance of power. The share of the Christian Democrats fell to 38 per cent in the elections of 1963, and increased a little, to 39 per cent, four years later. The Communists progressed from 25 to 27 per cent in 1967, but the United Socialists party (PSU) did less well than anticipated, obtaining only 14.5 per cent of the total vote.

Italy's economic progress continued throughout this period despite constant government crises and reshuffles, and the DC received some credit for these achievements. At the same time there was widespread dissatisfaction with administrative inefficiency and many complaints about corruption and nepotism. The continuing great influence of the clergy also caused resentment and indirectly affected the DC. Despite greater prosperity, the number of strikes increased, reflecting growing working-class unrest. The operation of Italian democracy was far from perfect; the rule of the apparatus and of the party secretaries provoked much criticism; Italy, it was argued, was a partitocracy, its structure more appropriate to neo-feudalism than to a modern democratic state.

The Italian Communist Party was well placed to profit from the political malaise. More than any other west European communist party it showed initiative and tactical skill as, for instance, by dissociating itself on occasion from Soviet policy or even criticising it openly. Togliatti in his testament had gone further than other communist leaders in condemning Stalinism; Luigi Longo, his successor, followed a somewhat more orthodox policy. Italian communists remained in the forefront of the liberal forces in the camp of world communism as shown by their opposition to the Soviet invasion of Czechoslovakia. But the transformation of the PCI into a 'normal' radical socialist and democratic party, as had been predicted by some observers in the nineteen-fifties, seemed at best a distant prospect.

Successive Italian governments were strong advocates of a détente in international politics, and Fanfahi in particular occasionally toyed with neutralist policies. But there were few illusions in Rome about Italy's role in the world; it was clear that even in North Africa and the Middle East, the traditional spheres of Italian interest, there was only limited scope for an independent Italian policy. The dispute over Trieste and Venezia Giulia having been settled in 1954 in agreement with Belgrade, the problem of South Tyrol (Alto Adige) came to the fore. This region had been part of Austria before 1919; of its 380,000 inhabitants, about 220,000 were German-speaking. They resented the lack of cultural autonomy and the encouragement given by the government to the migration of Italians into the area, thus further weakening the position of the Tyrolese, and as the demands of the South Tyrolese met no response, extremists among them launched a terrorist campaign which caused tension between the Austrian government and the Italians.

SPAIN: THE FRANCO ERA

General Franco, whose days seemed to be numbered at the end of the second world war, continued to rule Spain for another quarter of a century. The country's economy stagnated, wages were abysmally low, social services almost non-existent; less than one per cent of the budget was allocated to education, but the régime nevertheless succeeded in suppressing all political opposition. The economic situation slowly improved in the later fifties and the sixties; American credits and French and German investments acted as a spur to industrialisation, and the rapidly growing influx of millions of tourists constituted another major source of income. Above all Spain needed social reform: of six and a half million peasant holdings, five million were of one hectare or less, while 9,000 big landowners each held 100,000 hectares or more. Social inequality in the towns, too, was more marked than in any other European country, but the government showed no intention of tackling these problems. Official complacency was criticised without much effect by the more far-sighted sections of the Catholic Church. There were widespread strikes in Catalonia and in the Basque country in 1951, and again in 1956–7, when unrest also affected Madrid. The strike movement in April and May 1962 began in the Asturian mines and quickly spread to other parts of the country; it had the tacit support of 'Catholic Action'. The government had to give in to some of the strikers' demands; the Caudillo complained bitterly that the Catholic lay groups had been taken over by the communists. Ferment among workers, university students, and the separatists, in Catalonia and the Basque country continued throughout the sixties until, in January

1969, a state of emergency was proclaimed to enable the government to cope with this increasingly serious challenge to its rule.

The main weakness of the opposition was its internal division: the monarchists did not see eye to eye with each other, the democratic left ('Democratic Union') competed with Gil Robles' right-wing front, and no one wished to cooperate with the communists. The government tried to appease its opponents by making certain concessions: the military courts were abolished in 1963 and a new press law was introduced which gave the Spanish press somewhat greater freedom than before; the workers received the right to strike, albeit narrowly circumscribed, and greater tolerance was shown to the minority religions. In 1969 the teaching of the Basque language was at last permitted in state schools. The Organic Law of 1966 provided for the division of executive powers between the head of state and parliament, and for the free election of 100 (of the 600) members of parliament; two representatives were to be elected from each province. Political parties were still banned, but compared with the situation in the early postwar years these reforms marked a great advance. The Law was approved in a plebiscite by 96 per cent of the population.

Spain was still a kingdom without a king, since General Franco was opposed to the restoration of the monarchy in his lifetime. Within the monarchist camp the Carlists fought the Bourbons with the government preferring the latter. The Carlist candidate was expelled from Spain by the government in December 1968. The Bourbons were divided into supporters of the more liberal Don Juan, the Pretender (the younger son of Alfonso XIII, the last king of Spain), and those who backed Don Juan Carlos, his son. The Church, the Falange, and the army were the traditional pillars of Franco's régime, and the Caudillo maintained himself in power by playing off one against another. But these forces, too, were troubled by infighting; there was a generational conflict in both church and army; the younger officers wanted both the modernisation of the régime and quicker promotion, and the younger clergy did not wish to be closely identified with the régime. The Falange, fascist in inspiration, has not succeeded in putting its own imprint on Spanish politics and society. It had gradually been eased out of the government, though some of its leaders kept key positions in the provinces and the state-sponsored trade unions. A minority within the Falange moved towards the left; the majority was engaged in defending the positions it had gained in the forties and fifties. Both the Catholic hierarchy and the anti-clerical Falange were opposed to the powerful Catholic *Opus Dei* movement. *Opus Dei* had the support of many younger economists and technocrats, the ministers of commerce and finance belonged to this group whereas the bishops were fearful of its modernist zeal and pro-European enthusiasm. The Falange on the other hand stood for a corporative state and opposed the 'liberal-capitalist spirit' of *Opus Dei* which, they claimed, undermined the foundation of the régime. The official state-sponsored trade unions were challenged by workers' associations (*comisiones obreras*) which had developed in illegality and gradually attained considerable influence. The battle for the recognition of these organisations, as well as the independent student associations, became after 1965 the focus of the struggle between government and opposition. Basque nationalism also intensified its fight against the Franco régime; after the assassination of the police chief of San Sebastian in August 1968 a state of emergency was declared which lasted many months.

General Franco was more successful in his foreign policy. As the danger of a United Nations boycott passed, many countries established normal relations with Madrid. While the Fourth Republic had closed the border with Spain, de Gaulle sought to have closer links with Franco; Couve de Murville, the French Foreign Minister, went to Madrid in 1964 and in January 1969 Michel Debré went on a similar mission to the Spanish capital. General Franco maintained close relations with Castro's Cuba notwithstanding the ideological gulf between the two régimes and the fact that he thereby incurred American displeasure. Franco supported the Arabs against Israel and he negotiated with various Soviet delegations which visited Spain in the nineteen-sixties. In 1962 Spain first applied for membership in the Common Market; this was for both economic and political reasons the most important aim of Spanish foreign policy, for membership would have given great additional strength to the régime.

THE NETHERLANDS AND BELGIUM

The Netherlands lost their colonial empire after the second world war; West Irian, their last major possession in South-East Asia, was given up in 1962. Decolonisation was a great psychological shock but neither Holland's economy nor its domestic policy was greatly affected. The Socialists (*Partij van de Arbeid*) and the Catholic People's party, each polling fairly regularly about 30 per cent of the vote at consecutive general elections, formed a coalition under Willem Drees, the socialist leader, which lasted until 1958, when the Conservative parties (which included the two Protestant parties, the Christian Historical Union, and the Anti-Revolution party) replaced the socialists in the government. Relations between the parties had been poisoned as a result of the prolonged crisis of 1956, when it took almost four months to form a new government. The main cause of the malaise in Dutch politics was the deep rooted confessionalism which permeated all aspects of Dutch society; schools and hospitals, even radio stations, and almost all other associations, were strictly divided on confessional lines. To surmount this division became the main task of Dutch politics, but the vested interests were not easily overcome and no party could find a remedy.

The socialists returned to power for a short time within a coalition government in 1965–6. Both they and the Catholics lost votes in the general election of 1967; the socialists were weakened by the defection of a pacifist, anti-NATO group, while a radical faction split away from the Catholic party in 1968. A new element on the political scene appeared with the Farmers' party, founded in 1959, and the Amsterdam Provos, predating by a few years the upsurge of the European new left, added colour and excitement, if not many constructive political ideas, to Dutch political life.

Internal dissension in Belgium, complicated by the national conflict between Flemish and Walloons, was far more bitter than in Holland. The Flamands had been defeated in their bid for the return of King Leopold III, and they felt their national identity endangered by the steady encroachment of the French language. The Walloons on the other hand complained about economic discrimination; many of them supported the Socialist party. The socialists, under the leadership of Huysmans, Spaak, and Van Acker, were represented in all the early postwar governments but were ousted in 1949 when the Christian Socialists, having gained almost 48 per cent of the total vote, took over. The Socialists returned to power in 1954 and tried to push through a new school and language law which caused a great deal of trouble, reminiscent of the German *Kulturkampf* in the late nineteenth century, culminating in street demonstrations and disturbances. After years of struggle a spirit of compromise prevailed; the Christian Socialists under Gaston Eyskens replaced the Socialists in 1958, but formed a coalition with them in April 1961. It tried to find a solution to the language dispute by freezing the linguistic borders dividing the country into four main regions and granting them a large measure of cultural autonomy. This policy, intended to put Flemish fears at rest, did not however have the desired result: the Liberals opposed it and with the quarrel about the character of Louvain University which later spread to Brussels, the conflict became more bitter than ever. Both the Socialists and the Christian Social party suffered substantial losses in the elections of 1967, while the Liberals made considerable gains. Belgium was the country in which a general strike had first taken place; another such strike in 1960 showed that there was again much dissatisfaction among the industrial working class. The country's economic progress was less than that of its neighbours. Heavy industry and, in particular, the coal mines, faced difficult problems of adjustment in the postwar period.

The Eyskens government decided in 1958 to give independence to the Congo, but since under Belgian rule little had been done to educate a native élite capable of running the country, decolonisation soon ran into trouble.

The mutiny of the black troops, Lumumba's murder, the secession of Katanga and other provinces, and the ill-fated Belgian intervention in Katanga, were stages in the disintegration of Belgium's former colony. It took years to overcome a crisis that in its early phases could certainly have been halted. As Brussels gained new importance as a European centre, the seat of both the Common Market headquarters and NATO, as well as other international organisations such as Euratom, some of the old spirit of confidence returned to the country.

SCANDINAVIA

The Nordic Council established in 1951 provided a framework for close cooperation on all levels between the Scandinavian countries. There were of course limits to such coordination in foreign policy: Finland was exposed to direct Soviet pressure and had to refrain from any political moves likely to irritate Moscow. Norway and Denmark, which had been victims of nazi aggression during the war, opted for collective security by joining NATO. Sweden, which had remained neutral, decided not to join any power bloc. All the Scandinavian countries made great economic progress, and considerable advances on the road to the complete welfare state, with Finland, the poorest country, in each case lagging behind; all except Finland were monarchies and in all (again except Finland) the Social Democrats played a leading role; in Sweden they were in power without interruption throughout the whole postwar period.

Finland had not shared the fate of the east European countries and had not been incorporated into the Soviet Union, though Russia clearly regarded it as part of its own sphere of influence. The Soviet leaders distrusted the Finnish Social Democrats and insisted on keeping them out of the government. Their chosen instruments were Paasikivi, President of Finland up to 1956, and after that Kekkonen, also a leader of the Agrarian party. To ensure Kekkonen's election, Moscow openly intervened in 1956 in Finnish politics as it did on several other occasions during the postwar period. At a time of crisis the Russians usually referred to the provision for joint consultations in the Soviet-Finnish defence treaty, which meant in practice the right to send troops into Finland. The Finnish Communist Party was fairly strong, polling around 20 per cent in most elections, but since its abortive attempt to stage a *coup d'état* in 1948 the democratic parties, except Kekkonen's Agrarians and the Simonites, a breakaway group from the Social Democrats, refused to cooperate with them. Since the Russians, on the other hand, insisted until 1966 on keeping the Social Democrats out of the government, Finnish politics became very complicated and it was almost impossible to find a stable government majority; there were no fewer than 25 different cabinets between the end of the war and 1966.

Sweden, by contrast, was a model of stability. The Social Democrats under Prime Minister Erlander dominated its politics throughout the whole postwar period. The Swedish Communists, one of the most liberal communist parties in Europe, were too few to have any decisive impact on national policies; the centre parties, among whom the Liberals were the strongest, seemed more than once near the verge of success, but the Social Democrats always mustered enough strength in the decisive tests. They suffered losses in the elections of 1956 but improved their position in 1958 and 1960. There were fresh signs in the sixties of a decline of Social Democratic influence, but the centre parties suffered a fresh setback in the elections of 1968: unlike the socialists in Norway, who had been ousted in 1955 after many years in power, the Swedish Social Democrats increased their vote, a reflection of their success in economic and social policy; Sweden became in the postwar era both the richest and the most egalitarian European country. It was also a laboratory for the observation of some of the side effects of the welfare state. Boredom, as Schopenhauer noted, is an evil not to be taken lightly. In addition to Sweden's non-involvement in power blocs there was a strong neutralist undercurrent in public sentiment, not confined to the Social Democrats; there was much sympathy for victims of tyranny, especially in far away countries. Swedish policy towards Germany before 1945 and *vis-à-vis* the Soviet Union after the second world war had been more restrained.

In Denmark, too, the Social Democrats were the leading political force; their share in the elections throughout the postwar period remained more or less steady at 40 per cent, with only minor fluctuations. Under Hedtoft, H. Chr. Hansen, Viggo Kampman, and J.O.Krag, they were represented in almost all postwar governments, either alone or in cooperation with other parties; they were in opposition between 1950 and 1953 when they were replaced by the liberal Peasant party (Venstre). An interesting phenomenon without parallel at the time in any other European country was the emergence of the Socialist People's party, founded by Axel Larsen, in 1958. Larsen, the former leader of Danish communism, having been excommunicated by Moscow, established his own political group, drawing votes away from the Social Democrats and all but annihilating the official Communist party. His group polled 11 per cent of the vote in the 1966 elections and became overnight an important factor in Danish politics, since the Social Democrats, lacking a working majority, badly needed his support. Larsen's party took a neutralist, radical socialist line, but its success did not last as radicals and moderates within its ranks began to fight each other. The Danish economy showed signs of strains after 1966; following sterling, the kroner too, had to be devaluated. Economic problems contributed to the fall of the Social

Democratic government; after the elections of 1968 it was replaced by a coalition of the centre groups under the leadership of Baumgard, head of the Radical Venstre, which had seceded from the Venstre.

Norway had been more severely affected than either Sweden or Denmark by the war, and most of the efforts during the first postwar decade were devoted to economic reconstruction. Once this task was successfully accomplished under the leadership of the Social Democrats headed by Gerhardsen, and the groundwork had been laid for a welfare state on the Swedish pattern, the party's fortunes began to decline. It was also weakened by the defection of a left-wing group, the pacifist Socialist People's party. In 1965 the Socialists were forced into opposition following the formation of a new government by the four centre parties.

AUSTRIA AND SWITZERLAND

For 20 years Austria was ruled by a coalition of the Christian Social party and Social Democrats, the two parties which virtually monopolised Austrian politics. Between the two world wars they had bitterly fought each other but the experience of the nazi *Anschluss* had made them discover common ground. After the country had regained its independent status in 1945 the leaders of both parties realised that in view of Austria's exposed position concessions on both sides were imperative to prevent fresh disasters. An elaborate and slightly ridiculous system was evolved by which all official positions from top to bottom were distributed between nominees of the two parties in fixed proportions. The system was cumbersome and often wasteful, but it worked with some success until 1966 when, following a crisis among the socialists and a small shift in the balance of power, the Christian Social party felt strong enough to terminate the coalition. The party, ably led during the postwar period by Figl and Raab, Gorbach and Klaus, took great care not to deviate to any major extent in its foreign or domestic policy from the broad lines established during the long years of coalition.

There were few, if any, changes in Swiss domestic policies. The position of the leading parties, the *Freisinn* (liberals), the Social Democrats, and the Conservatives remained unchanged. In pursuance of its traditional neutrality, Switzerland did not join the United Nations though it was represented in several organisations sponsored by the UN such as UNESCO. In view of the underlying political character of the Common Market, Switzerland could not join this organisation either but decided to participate in EFTA. The Swiss policy of neutrality had evolved in an age in which it could be assumed that all sides would respect it. In the second world war, however, Switzerland escaped occupation largely by good luck and by its readiness to defend itself. The implications were not lost on Swiss citizens, and the principle of neutrality was questioned after 1945; in these changed political conditions, greater stress than ever before was put on national defence.

GREECE

From the end of the civil war until 1955 Greece was ruled by a conservative government under Papagos. This was succeeded by a coalition of centre and right-wing forces led by Karamanlis who, after a great deal of electoral manœuvring and manipulation, received a small majority. The position of the ruling coalition was weakened by the Cyprus conflict, the unpopularity of the royal family and the army command, and such incidents as the assassination of the left-wing deputy Lambrakis by right-wing elements. In the 1963 elections George Papandreou's Progressive Centre Union (EPEK) received more votes than Karamanlis's ERE. Since Papandreou did not however have an absolute majority but would have been dependent on the support of EDA (a communist front organisation), he called for new elections in 1964 in which his group obtained an absolute majority. The conservative forces were bitterly opposed to EPEK which they accused, quite unfairly, of 'communist leanings'; the army command feared that Papandreou would subject them to a political purge and prevailed on the King to refuse the Ministry of Defence to the leader of the liberals. Papandreou in response mobilised the masses against the court and the right-wing forces. To forestall yet another electoral victory by the liberals, a group of officers carried out a *coup d'état* in April 1967 and established a right-wing military dictatorship. Most politicians were removed from positions of influence, some were arrested while others escaped abroad. King Constantine tried without success to curb some of the excesses of the new régime, after the failure in December 1967 of a highly amateurish counter coup, he too went into exile.

THE SOVIET UNION: KHRUSHCHEV AND HIS SUCCESSORS

After Stalin's death political power in the Soviet Union passed into the hands of a small group of his closest associates. With Beria's arrest and execution, and after the fall of Malenkov, Nikita Sergeevich Khrushchev emerged as the strongest contender for power. He had been less in the limelight than most other members of the Presidium but once elected first secretary of the party in September 1953, his faction became strongly entrenched in the party apparatus. Khrushchev in turn was overthrown in 1964 but those whom he had ousted remained in the political wilderness. He was replaced by new men who had not yet reached front rank in Stalin's lifetime. After 1953 some of the worst excesses of the Stalinist system ceased, but many basic features remained and hopes for radical change and a far greater measure of freedom did not materialise. Khrushchev favoured destalinisation within limits, but after his fall this policy was gradually abandoned. His appointment as first party secretary did not at first attract much attention, for in Stalin's time the party had lost much of its earlier influence. But within a few years Khrushchev gained control of the Central Committee, and many regional key positions were also in the hands of his appointees. At the same time the party as a political factor greatly increased in importance as Stalin's private apparatus was dissolved and as the secret police were brought under the control of the party leadership.

Khrushchev gave the key speech at the Communist party's twentieth congress in 1956; though unpublished in the Soviet Union, this speech was of momentous importance, for it was the first time that a Soviet leader had openly talked about the crimes of the Stalin era. Everyone had known about them, but it had been unthinkable to mention these things in public, for Stalin had been the party, and the party had always been right. Khrushchev's revelations were highly selective: he mentioned only the Stalinists who had been wronged by Stalin, not his political opponents within the party, let alone his non-communist victims. Khrushchev moreover put all the blame on certain negative traits in Stalin's character, which was at best a superficial explanation for a highly complex phenomenon. The deeper causes of Stalinism he did not touch, nor did he suggest any remedies that would make a recurrence impossible. What Khrushchev told his comrades and fellow countrymen was, in fact, that Stalin had been a bungler, and during his later years a madman with criminal tendencies, but that the new leaders were good men and could be trusted.

The secret speech came as a profound shock. The conservative elements in the party, men like Molotov, but also many in the middle and lower ranks, were bitterly opposed to the new policy. They, too, were critical of certain aspects of Stalinism but they did not question the system as such and they feared that by disavowing Stalin the very legitimacy of Soviet rule was being undermined. For, once the principle of infallibility was given up, his successors, and indeed everyone from top to bottom in the line of command, was likely to be criticised in future, and this was bound to put into question the whole political system. Destalinisation was also likely to create havoc in Russia's relations with its allies and satellites; there were many reasons for the conflict with China, and in particular for the Hungarian rising in 1956 and the unrest in Poland, but the events at the twentieth party congress were perhaps the most important single factor. While antagonising his rivals in the Soviet leadership, Khrushchev at the same time weakened their position, for his speech caused a great deal of heart searching within the party with regard to its own past, and gave further impetus to the release of Stalin's surviving victims from prison and labour camps. Since Khrushchev's rivals in the Presidium had been more deeply involved than himself in the purges and terror, they were put on the defensive: they could not get rid of him without turning back the wheels of history, and this in view of the general mood in the party seemed well nigh impossible after the twentieth congress. Molotov lost his job to Shepilov, one of Khrushchev's men, and as the result of the great confrontation in the Presidium in June 1957 the entire old guard was routed. The 'anti-party group', as it was called after its defeat, consisted of Molotov, Kaganovich, Malenkov, Bulganin, and Voroshilov, as well as Saburov and Pervukhin, the economic experts. They were all opposed to Khrushchev's economic policy and had many other grievances as well. Since they had a majority in the Presidium, their victory, and the replacement of Khrushchev by Molotov, had seemed a foregone conclusion. But Khrushchev fought back, mobilising the Central Committee in which his supporters were in the majority. The Central Committee was in theory the highest policy-making body, but it had largely been ignored by the leaders in the past; the reassertion of its authority constituted a significant shift in the internal balance of power. Some of Khrushchev's rivals were immediately dropped; others, such as Bulganin and Voroshilov, were ousted later on. They were all disgraced but there were no arrests or executions; the victims of the purge were shifted to minor positions outside Moscow: Molotov, for instance, became Soviet ambassador to Mongolia.

This was the end of collective leadership; after June 1957 Khrushchev could pursue without hindrance his reforms such as the abolition of the Machine-Tractor Stations in agriculture and the establishment of *Sovnarkhozy*, regional economic councils, as the basic unit in the national economy. By 1959, when the twenty-first party congress was held, the Soviet Union was again ruled by one man, though Khrushchev was subject to far more constraints than Stalin. The congress was called to adopt the Seven-Year Plan; according to Khrushchev the country was now entering a new phase in which material abundance and with it communism was at last within reach. To achieve this Khrushchev demanded greater stress on agriculture and light industry. But while output in Soviet agriculture rose by 50 per cent between Stalin's death and 1959, there was only a small increase thereafter, and this in turn had a direct impact on food supplies and the standard of living.

Khrushchev's foreign policy was not an outstanding success either; the building of rocket sites and the transfer to Cuba of a substantial nuclear arsenal was considered a reckless adventure even by the Chinese hawks. After the confrontation with America Khrushchev changed his line and became a protagonist of peaceful coexistence. His cuts in military spending antagonised the powerful military lobby. The attitude to Germany became more threatening than ever, yet towards the end of his reign Khrushchev seemed inclined to seek a *rapprochement* with Bonn. He quarrelled with Nasser but subsequently made him a 'Hero of the Soviet Union' without consulting the Presidium; he also made major loans and arms shipments available to Egypt. Relations with China deteriorated during the Khrushchev era and there were further defections from the Soviet camp as the battle for hegemony over world communism reached a new climax.

The intellectuals found at times a powerful though inconsistent ally in Khrushchev in their struggle for greater cultural freedom; Khrushchev personally read Solzhenitsyn's book on life in Soviet labour camps and authorised its publication. This was an important breakthrough, for it opened the way to a whole new literature dealing with aspects of the past that had hitherto been taboo. Such liberalism had its limits. Khrushchev warned the intellectuals that he would not hesitate to have them shot if they overstepped the boundaries and endangered (as the Hungarian writers had done) the very foundations of the régime. On other occasions he behaved in an almost incredibly boorish manner, denouncing all modern influences in the arts, the cinema and music, and unleashing a minor witch hunt against the perpetrators of avant-garde art. Destalinisation too followed a curiously inconsistent pattern. Many, but by no means all of Stalin's victims were rehabilitated, most of them posthumously; the twenty-second party congress in October 1961 brought further revelations and gave a powerful fresh impetus to this movement. Symbolically, Stalin's remains were removed from the mausoleum in the Red Square and reburied at the Kremlin wall. Yet every now and then the movement was reversed and those who had gone too far in their condemnation of the 'cult of the individual' were severely reprimanded. Like postwar Germany, the Soviet Union faced a major problem in coming to terms with its own past, but since the country had not been defeated in the war, and many of the old leaders were still in power, the inhibitions and the vested interests militating against any radical change were far more powerful than in Germany.

The main topic of the twenty-second congress was the adoption of a new party programme envisaging in some detail the transition to communism. The state would finally wither away and would be replaced by various public and communal organisations; the party, however, would still retain its central role in Soviet society. Soviet citizens were promised a radiant future: there was a boastful streak in Khrushchev's personality and the fact that so many of his promises had not come true did not deter him from making fresh predictions. In June 1957 he had declared that the Soviet Union would within four years overtake America in the production of meat, butter, and milk. In 1961 he announced that Soviet productivity would rise to the American level by 1970, which meant of course that the country would be outproducing the United States, for Russia was more populous. These and similar pronouncements did not go down very well in the Soviet Union, for everyone knew that they were unrealistic. Among the intelligentsia there was a great deal of contempt for the leader who was regarded as little better than an uneducated, uncouth *muzhik*. Popular reaction too was often negative. A great purveyor of anecdotes, Khrushchev himself became the butt of many jokes, but not a few of those who had ridiculed him later on came to regret it. Everything considered, the Khrushchev years were not bad ones for Russia : considerable economic progress was made, and, above all, there was reason to believe that gradually more freedom would be allowed. The intellectuals in particular were to look back in later years with nostalgia to the relative cultural freedom of Khrushchev's rule. The cult of Khrushchev, whose seventieth birthday in 1964 was made an occasion of official rejoicing, was mild and relatively harmless. With all his weaknesses and inconsistencies Khrushchev was an agent of freedom and progress in Soviet postwar history. He attacked Stalin, though he would not and could not attack the system that had produced Stalin. But in comparison with his successors his record shines brightly.

Most of the Stalinist old guard were eliminated under Khrushchev, and while some of their policies were rehabilitated after his fall in 1964 none of them made a political comeback : they were too old and discredited, and their seats were taken by new men. Mikoyan, who was on good terms with Khrushchev, survived his fall but was bowed out in 1966, more or less gracefully, and Voroshilov and Shvernik too, became honorary pensioners and disappeared from the political scene. Suslov, who had the reputation of an ideologist, remained a member of the inner circle, but Brezhnev and Kosygin rose more rapidly, and until a stroke put an end to his public career in 1963 Frol Kozlov seemed the Soviet leader most likely to succeed Khrushchev. Brezhnev had won his spurs as a party organiser, while Kosygin's career had been in the economic field. Two Ukrainians, Podgorny and Shelest, also came to the fore ; the former was a protégé of Khrushchev who survived the fall of his protector and became president of the Soviet Union; the second was like Kozlov and Brezhnev a conservative and a hardliner. Perhaps most significant was the rise of younger party leaders such as Polyansky (born on the day of the October Revolution), Voronov, Mazurov, Shelepin, and Semichastny. The two last named had been leaders of the Komsomol, the Soviet youth organisation, who were subsequently given leading positions in the political police. These men, together with a few others, constituted the top leadership in the early sixties and it was their decision to depose Khrushchev in October 1964.

Khrushchev's prestige had suffered as the result of the Cuban defeat; there was resentment among the military men as well as the party '*apparatchiki*': Khrushchev's attempt to divide the Communist party into an industrial and an agricultural branch was obviously impractical and was soon abandoned. Above all there was dissatisfaction with his arbitrary style of work, which caused much irritation and impatience and contributed to his downfall. The conspirators made use of Khrushchev's absence on holiday to proclaim Brezhnev first party secretary and Kosygin head of the Soviet government. On 16 October 1964, it was announced that Comrade Khrushchev had resigned because of his 'advanced age and deteriorating health'. Soon the attacks on him began; he was made responsible for all the economic shortcomings and other failures in Soviet foreign and domestic policy. After a while the attacks ceased and he too became an unperson, like so many other Soviet leaders before him.

Brezhnev and Kosygin, the leading spirits in the new team, did not make any drastic policy changes. Domestic policies were pursued more or less as before – indeed, the absence of any new ideas and initiatives was perhaps the most significant feature of the post-Khrushchev era; there seemed to be no definite policy and no clear purpose. Destalinisation was gradually stopped, there was no further rehabilitation of Stalin's victims. In April 1965 Brezhnev gave the signal for the rehabilitation of Stalin and Zhdanov, and their policies were again praised. There was some further economic decentralisation but care was taken not to engage in any radical reform. The twenty-third party congress in 1966 brought no surprises either; the Soviet régime went on existing as it were by its own momentum: some leaders were promoted and others lost ground, there was a slow but steady rise in the standard of living and the country gathered strength in the military field. But politically it was now weaker than ever before in its history – a conservative society with a superstructure of revolutionary phraseology. The appeal of Soviet communism was almost non-existent beyond its own borders; it could reassert its authority, as in the case of Czechoslovakia, only by force of arms.

Soviet foreign policy became more similar in character to that of Ivan Kalita and Ivan the Terrible than of Lenin. Neither the handling of the Middle-East crisis in 1967 nor of the Czech crisis the year after inspired much confidence in the new leadership. The political weakness, the many conflicts inside the Soviet bloc and within the Soviet Union, were not conducive to a policy of détente with the West, even though the Soviet leaders wanted to prevent major military confrontation with the United States. At least some among them seemed to believe that the rot which had afflicted the communist world in the sixties had to be stopped and Soviet military strength reasserted. But there were obvious limits to Soviet action in central

Europe, for any intervention in Germany was bound to lead to a head-on collision with NATO. The 'grey areas', such as Yugoslavia and the Middle East, which lay outside both the western and the Soviet sphere of influence, thus became the main danger zones in world politics.

On the home front there was no danger of an immediate crisis; intellectual ferment was easily suppressed by arrests and stiff prison sentences, as in the Sinyavsky-Daniel case. There were manifestations of dissatisfaction and criticism among the intelligentsia, but a censorship far more severe than in Tsarist times and a well functioning secret police prevented all but the most courageous spirits from openly voicing dissent. There were indications of the continued existence of national antagonisms between the peoples of the USSR, but these too were seemingly kept well under control. The long-term prospects were less reassuring: the erosion of the official ideology created problems for which no solution was in sight. A generation earlier millions of communists had genuinely believed in the truth of their doctrine and in Stalin's infallible wisdom. Now official communist ideology was no longer taken seriously except by those officially entrusted with the propagation of the faith and by the poor in spirit. Few people in Russia envisaged any change in the prevailing economic order, and most no doubt were good Soviet patriots. But Soviet communism had set out with greater hopes and ambitions; it had wanted to build a richer, freer, and more progressive society than any previous one in history, to be a beam of light to all the oppressed throughout the world. These dreams had certainly not come true: the Soviet Union had become a going concern but not in the way the founders had imagined it. Its industry had made great progress and Russian citizens had a higher living standard than before 1917. Russia's place in the world had become stronger and its military power was impressive. A new society had been created but it inspired little enthusiasm.

EASTERN EUROPE: LIMITED INDEPENDENCE

East Germany

Throughout the whole postwar period East Germany remained the Soviet Union's most faithful client. While the other east European countries showed in varying degrees signs of independence, East Germany after the suppression of the revolt of 1953 gave no cause for Soviet complaints. The presence of 20 Soviet divisions, first as an occupying force, later under the provision of the Warsaw Pact, effectively guaranteed the status quo. As far as the East German leadership was concerned, loyalty to the Soviet Union was genuine: Ulbricht and his colleagues needed Soviet protection more than any other communist régime in eastern Europe, both because of the inferior position of the DDR *vis-à-vis* West Germany, and because of the unpopularity of their rule. For these reasons they could not afford to make any substantial concessions to the people and their régime remained the most orthodox in eastern Europe. They were perturbed by the 'liberal excesses' of the Khrushchev era, and banned certain books published in the USSR in the early sixties. There was continuity in the political leadership: for 25 years Ulbricht remained at the helm, and while there were frequent changes under him, including defections to the West and suicides, his own position was never seriously threatened. The prewar communist generation was gradually replaced by younger men who had not been involved in the political storms of the twenties and thirties. Stoph and Honecker became the most likely candidates for the succession, while technocrats such as Ewald, Jarowinsky, and Mittag were not without success in running the economy. During the fifties the DDR had not been able to keep pace with the rapid development of the West German economy, and the propaganda about the advantages of the socialist planned system had sounded hollow. After 1962, and in particular after the sixth party congress in 1963, the SED (Socialist Unity Party) adopted a more flexible economic policy which soon began to show results. Within the next five years the DDR became the country with the highest living standard in Comecon and its industry the best developed outside the Soviet Union.

The economic achievements gave greater confidence to the leadership, even though the absence of a genuine mass basis continued to act as a brake. The building of the Berlin wall in 1961 closed the escape route to the West and, together with the establishment of a sizeable standing army (the National People's Army), stabilised the position of the régime. The most difficult task of the East German leaders was to inculcate a feeling of separate national identity in their subjects, most of whom still believed that the division of Germany was artificial and would not last. The leadership on the other hand stressed on every occasion that West Germany was not merely a foreign country but the main enemy, that the division would be lasting – unless communism came to power in West Germany. At first they found it difficult to oppose openly the movement for German reunification, but since the West Germans refused to deal with them they could, in fact, champion the cause of German unity without being seriously challenged. In the sixties a less rigid policy was adopted in Bonn which greatly alarmed the East Germans, who regarded it as far more dangerous than the earlier boycott. As a result they became more intransigent and the demand for German unity disappeared from their political programme.

The government tried to gain diplomatic recognition throughout the world and to combat West Germany's claim to be Germany's representative. It achieved some success in the third world, though major countries such as

Egypt and India, heavily indebted to the Soviet bloc though they were, were reluctant to grant East Berlin diplomatic recognition. Ulbricht's visit in Belgrade in 1966 was intended to improve relations with the non-orthodox forces in the communist world. The democratic revival in Czechoslovakia in 1968 awakened old fears in East Germany and Ulbricht was reported to have been among those who brought pressure on the Soviet leaders in favour of intervention. Young people in East Germany, Ulbricht said during a visit to Czechoslovakia in 1968, were not engaged in revolutionary, destructive activities; they were singing merry songs.

Poland

The great promise of the Polish October (1956) was followed by long years of bitter disappointment. Some of the worst economic bottlenecks were overcome as the Soviet government extended aid to Warsaw and as American credits were made available. About 80 per cent of the agricultural cooperatives established during the Stalin era were dissolved after 1956 and this had in the short run a beneficial influence on output. But agriculture remained backward; the distance between town and country did not diminish. For many years Poland continued to have a passive foreign trade balance and the zloty remained one of east Europe's weakest currencies. The tension with the Catholic church did not abate; Cardinal Wyszinski was permitted to visit Rome but the Polish bishops were severely attacked by the Warsaw government when, together with the German bishops, they appealed in 1966 for an effort to overcome national antagonisms by a spirit of goodwill. Any such attempt at reconciliation with 'German *revanchism*' was anathema to Gomulka and the other Polish leaders. Enmity towards Germany was a pillar of Polish policy, any attempt to reduce tension was even more dangerous than questioning communism. Influential circles in the Polish leadership also tried to make antisemitism ('Zionism') part of official Polish ideology. Jews had always been numerous and prominent in the communist movement in Poland and some of them had been in leading positions in the early years of the régime. After Stalin's death most Jewish communists joined the liberals, whereas the 'Partisans' headed by General Moczar, following a national communist line, tried to remove them from the party. They argued that Jews were not trustworthy; having spent the war years abroad and having entered Poland in 1944 with the Red Army, they were little better than foreign agents. The Partisans deliberately exaggerated the part of the Jews in Polish politics; there were only about 30,000 of them left in Poland after the war and Moczar used the issue as a stratagem against his rivals, the Gomulka faction, in the struggle for power. This open recrudescence of antisemitism culminated in a wholesale rewriting of history; according to the new official version

Poles had helped the Jews during the nazi occupation but the Jews had brought the disaster upon themselves by collaborating with the enemy. A commission for the supervision of Jews and of anti-Jewish propaganda was established; it was abolished in December 1968 following the unfavourable publicity these activities attracted abroad. In March 1968 students demonstrated in Warsaw for more freedom and a more independent, more national policy. The government, greatly disturbed by the ferment in neighbouring Czechoslovakia, undertook severe reprisals and a major purge ensued. Many leading figures in Polish intellectual life, and not a few in politics, were dismissed from their posts; the majority were of Jewish origin and they were all branded as 'Zionists'. The Moczar group used the opportunity for a major onslaught on the Gomulka faction which, it claimed, had shown a lamentable lack of toughness all along *vis-à-vis* Poland's enemies. Gomulka was pushed on to the defensive; at one time his political survival seemed in question, but eventually he outmanœuvred his opponents, mainly no doubt because the Partisans were somewhat suspect in the eyes of the Russians. Their exalted anti-Germanism and antisemitism would have passed, but their whole approach was basically nationalist and there was reason to fear that sooner or later they would turn also against Russia in the time-honoured Polish tradition.

Poland in the sixties was a deeply unhappy country despite the improvement in the economic situation since the early fifties and notwithstanding the fact that some of the worst social inequalities had disappeared. But, more than in the neighbouring countries, the communist régime had failed to grow roots in the country and few believers in the cause of communism were left even within the ranks of the party. Communism remained in power because no other régime would have been acceptable to the Soviet Union. Such a situation vitiated the deep seated Polish longing to reassert their national identity and to live in freedom; it was bound to lead to cynicism and frustration.

Hungary

While Soviet troops continued to be stationed in Hungary, the Kadar government pursued a relatively liberal course after the suppression of the popular uprising of 1956. Some of the country's leading writers were released from prison under the 1960 amnesty. Kadar and his government were among Khrushchev's closest supporters; they fought both left-wing and right-wing deviations. The exclusion from the Communist party of Rakosi and Gerö in 1962 was meant to reassure the population that there would be no return to the bad old days of Stalinism. In its foreign policy, too, Hungary tried to steer a moderate course; its relations with Yugoslavia were fairly cordial, and while it had to participate in the invasion of Czechoslovakia in 1968, it did so without conviction and with a minimum of fanfare. Most of the government's efforts were concentrated on the economy. After experiencing difficulties in agriculture and several years of stagnation in industry, there was a new upswing as the economic reform programme got under way. Under their programme, first adopted in 1965, productivity was raised, foreign trade with both West and East expanded, and investment steered towards the most profitable sectors. The previous planning system was largely abolished; firms were judged on the basis of their profitability, and the income of both managers and workers was tied to productivity. Hungary went further with its economic reforms than any other east European communist country with the exception of Yugoslavia. This gave rise to misgivings among its conservative neighbours, including the Soviet Union, which feared that sweeping economic reforms would in the long run stimulate the demand for more political freedom.

Czechoslovakia

For a decade after Stalin's death Czechoslovakia remained the least changed of all his satellites. The big Gottwald monument symbol of the old era, was removed only in 1961 from one of Prague's central squares, and very reluctantly at that. Political conservatism was paralleled by economic stagnation and gave rise to much popular discontent. Czechoslovakia had been industrially the most developed country in eastern Europe, and the one with the closest ties with the West; the isolation imposed on it was as acutely felt as the wretched economic situation. There were internal conflicts in the party leadership, culminating in 1962 in the arrest of Rudolf Barak, a former Minister of State Security. In this struggle for power, ideological considerations did not play a major part and there was little hope for a substantial improvement. When the Communist party had seized power in 1948 it had a mass following, in sharp contrast to Poland and Hungary; large sections of the working class and many intellectuals were among its supporters. Fifteen years later communist militancy had given way to disillusionment and despair, which pervaded even the higher ranks of the party and government apparatus. Communism had been tried and, as was now admitted, had been a failure.

Under Prime Minister Lenart an economic reform programme was launched in 1966 on the lines proposed by Professor Ota Sik, a leading economist. This project provided, as in Hungary, for changes in the system of planning and a larger output of consumer goods. But given the deteriorating economic situation, the success of the scheme depended on substantial Russian credits, which Prague failed to obtain despite all efforts and remonstrances. Czechoslovakia wanted closer political and economic relations with western Europe, but these links were vetoed by Moscow. The developments leading to the rise of Dubcek and the Soviet invasion have been described: the military occupation of the country proceeded smoothly but the political solution of the crisis desired by Russia proved more difficult than in Hungary 1956. Direct military rule by the Soviet occupation forces was not desirable for political reasons; gradually the conservatives returned and ousted the progressives. While strengthening the Soviet hold over Czechoslovakia and removing the danger of defection, the consequences of Soviet policy could easily be foreseen: deep frustration which sooner or later would again cause an acute crisis and deepen the split inside the communist camp.

Rumania

Rumania was among Stalin's most faithful satellites; measured by economic performance it was among the least successful. After the arrest and purge of Anna Pauker and Vasile Luca who had led the party during the Stalin era, Gheorgiu Dej emerged as the outstanding figure in the country. Together with his closest assistants Chivu Stoica and Apostol, he was in effective control of party and state up to the time of his death in March 1965. The Russian occupation forces left Rumania in 1958. Earlier Bucharest had been released from paying reparations to Russia, which removed a serious obstacle to her economic recovery. The mixed Soviet-Rumanian companies for the exploitation of the country's natural wealth were also dissolved, much to Bucharest's relief. The withdrawal of the Russian troops gave a great boost to the self-confidence of the leaders, who gradually became more independent in their foreign and economic policy. The domestic scene was hardly affected by the new course. In 1960 they adopted a programme envisaging the further rapid development of heavy industry; this brought them into conflict with the industrially developed Comecon countries which had other plans for the division of labour in eastern Europe. The Sino-Soviet dispute made an opening for more freedom of manœuvre than ever before and Gheorgiu Dej was not slow to make the most of it. Cultural relations with the Soviet Union were reduced to a minimum, and the Rumanian press published open attacks on Soviet historians for having belittled the role of the Rumanian people in the struggle against nazism and for justifying the annexation of Bessarabia by Russia in 1812 as a progressive step. Bessarabia had been returned to Rumania in 1918, but again seized by the Soviet Union in 1945, and it remained an explosive issue. In April 1964 the Central Committee of the Rumanian party adopted a resolution stressing the equal, independent, and sovereign character of each socialist state; this was tantamount to a Rumanian Declaration of Independence. There were complaints in the east European capitals that the Rumanians were no longer fulfilling their obligations under the Warsaw treaty, which gave rise to a great deal of mutual recrimination.

The turn towards national communism made the régime more popular than before, despite the fact that domestic policy was scarcely affected by the process of de-Sovietisation. The economic upswing which had begun in the late fifties also strengthened the position of the communist leaders, and when Nicolae Ceausescu succeeded Gheorgiu Dej there was no question that he would pursue policies similar to those of his predecessor. Ceausescu, the son of a peasant and a prewar member of the communist youth movement, was co-opted to the politburo at the early age of 37, and quickly asserted himself against his rivals of the old guard; the most serious competitor, Draghici, formerly Minister of Internal Security, was deposed in April 1968 and the other members of the anti-Ceausescu group had publicly to recant. Ceausescu's policy resembled in some respects that followed by Khrushchev. By reopening the trials and purges of the Stalin era, by rehabilitating Patrascanu, a former secretary of the party who had been executed in 1954, and Luca, he implicated the party old guard and incidentally also Gheorgiu Dej, and reinforced his own position. It was a difficult balancing act: Ceausescu welcomed the nationalist revival on the domestic scene but did not want to lose control over it. He wanted to pursue an independent line in foreign affairs but was aware that he could defy the Soviet Union only up to a certain point. Bucharest approved the Czechoslovak democratic revival in 1968 and condemned the Soviet invasion, more perhaps because it welcomed a strengthening of the communist club of independents than out of sympathy for what was happening in Prague. Faced with a stern Soviet warning and the possible danger of Soviet military intervention under the guise of Warsaw pact manœuvres, Ceausescu had to retreat from his exposed position. But there was little doubt about the basic mood of the country and its leadership: national communism was there to stay.

Conclusion

For a continent that has been declared dead many times during the last thousand years, Europe has shown a surprising capacity for survival. Prophets of doom have appeared and found a public eager to listen to their message not just during the last generation or two but throughout the history of European civilisation: Spengler and his successors were preceded by a whole army of Cassandras in the seventeenth, eighteenth, and nineteenth centuries who announced that Europe had reached the state of old age and that society was in the last stages of corruption. Among the Romantics of the nineteenth century it was *de rigueur* to contrast the social harmony of the past with the materialist individualism and universal preoccupation with material gain of modern times. During the last decades of the nineteenth century the feeling of decay and decadence became overpowering among the literary intelligentsia, and their message was echoed between the two world wars, probably with greater justification. Moralists have always exaggerated the defects of their age; the less history they know the greater their inclination to regard the sickness of their society as unique and incurable.

There was good reason for profound pessimism in 1945, and not just because Europe had lost its pre-eminent place in the world. The relative decline was a long drawn out process that had begun several decades earlier with the end of the colonial age, the rise of new super-powers, and as a consequence of political, economic, social and demographic processes. Few Europeans were disturbed by the fact that their continent was no longer the political centre of the world at the end of the second world war. The crisis facing Europe was far more acute, for the very survival of the continent was at stake. As a result of two European civil wars, of fascist rule and nationalist madness run wild, Europe was politically dislocated and on the verge of economic collapse; it displayed all the signs of cultural exhaustion. Eastern Europe had been incorporated into the Soviet system and had lost its independence. The small- and middle-sized states of western Europe were incapable of defending themselves and seemed no longer viable, politically or economically. There was more reason than ever before to predict the continent's impending demise.

Events since 1945 have again belied these prophecies: the astonishing economic recovery resulted in an era of prosperity unprecedented in

European history. This affluence was not limited, as so often in the past, to a relatively small section of the population. The welfare state and the rapid spread of higher education made it possible for larger sections of the population to participate actively in political and cultural life. Europe to be sure was still beset by constant political crises but so was the rest of the world, including the new super-powers. The difficulties facing the Afro-Asian countries, in whom some saw the great hope of the future, were so massive in scale as to make those experienced by Europe appear almost insignificant. There was no prospect that these countries would overtake and outstrip the West; the real danger was that they would fall even further behind in their political, cultural, and economic development. With the progress made by Europe in the 25 years since the end of the war, it moved right back into the centre of the international stage; from its earlier preoccupation with third world affairs, both American and Soviet policy was gradually reorientated towards Europe.

Room for self-satisfaction there was not, for the division of the continent remained and large parts of it were still deprived of even the basic elements of freedom. The Europeanisation of the Soviet Union made agonisingly slow progress, and at times it appeared as if it was making no headway at all. The flame of freedom was burning more brightly in eastern Europe, but these countries remained under strict Soviet control and their freedom of action was narrowly limited. The countries of western Europe faced a great deal of internal discontent because their achievements, as usual in democratic societies, fell short of expectations. They made progress towards economic integration, but hardly any towards political unity. The lesson of two world wars, of fascism and Stalinism, seemed to have been in vain; nationalist passions and vested interests, or simply the force of inertia, prevented the close political and military cooperation which would have contributed so much to the further progress of the continent and have made it possible to defend itself without constant dependence on outside military help.

The new prosperity gave rise to self-confidence and optimism, but, as so often in past history, it also produced signs of demoralisation and decay. The welfare state freed many millions of people for the first time from immediate worries about food and shelter, but the energies thus released were not necessarily channelled towards the higher things in life; they provoked boredom and encouraged destructive impulses. There was a new *fin-de-siècle* mood, a sense of spiritual suffocation, of lack of purpose such as had been felt before 1914 by many who welcomed the outbreak of war as liberation. The affluent society was not necessarily conducive to greater sanity, nor did it weaken the forces of darkness and unreason. These phenomena were common to all advanced societies, but this did not make them any less of a problem for Europe. Britain and France, West Germany and Italy still had to find an answer to the stultifying effects of a mass culture that catered for the lowest common denominator and had grown immensely in influence with the expansion at the other end of the spectrum of the mass media. Western Europe faced a sick avant-garde culture manifested in music and painting, in literature, the theatre and the cinema that encountered scarcely any hostility from a gullible and docile public or from critics so fearful of being called old fashioned that they treated every idiocy seriously. The list of danger signs is far from complete, but what age in European history has been quite free of them? Not decay but the resilience, the will to survival, that Europe displayed after 1945 constituted the great novelty, and a source of renewed hope for its future. Far from dying in convulsions as Sartre had predicted, Europe has shown a new vigour which has astonished friends and foes alike. European ideas and techniques have spread to all corners of the earth and European civilisation is still the model for the entire world. The age of European political predominance has ended but no other centre has so far wrenched from Europe the torch of civilisation. In a wider sense the European age has only begun.

Bibliography

WORKS OF REFERENCE

Europa Yearbook London (yearly).
L.L.Paklons: *European Bibliography* (1964).
H.Pehrson and H.Wulf: *The European Bibliography* (1965).
H.L.Roberts: *Foreign Affairs Bibliography, 1942–1952* (1955).
United Nations: *Statistical Yearbook* (yearly).

PART I

GENERAL WORKS

R.Aron: *The Century of Total War* (1964).
M.Beloff: *Europe and the Europeans* (1957).
J.Calmann (ed.): *Western Europe* (1966).
J.Freymond: *Western Europe since the War* (1964).
S.R.Graubard (ed.): *A New Europe* (1964).
J.A.Lukacs: *The Decline and Rise of Europe* (1965).
Royal Institute of International Affairs: *Surveys and Documents*.
A.Sampson: *The New Europeans* (1968).
H.Seton Watson: *Neither War nor Peace* (1960).

YALTA, POTSDAM, THE BEGINNING OF THE COLD WAR

Gar Alperowitz: *Atomic Diplomacy: Hiroshima and Potsdam* (1965).
R.Aron: *Le Grand Schisme* (1948).
Herbert Feis: *Churchill, Roosevelt, Stalin: The War they Waged and the Peace They Sought* (1957).
Herbert Feis: *Between War and Peace: The Potsdam Conference* (1960).
Herbert Feis: *The Atomic Bomb and the End of World War II* (1966).
D.F.Fleming: *The Cold War and its Origins* (1961).
André Fontaine: *Histoire de la Guerre Froide* (1965, 1967).

L.J.Halle: *The Cold War as History* (1967).
M.F.Hertz: *Beginnings of the Cold War* (1966).
Gabriel Kolko: *The Politics of War* (1969).
Jean Laloy: *Entre Guerres et Paix* (1966).
W.H.McNeill: *America, Britain and Russia: Their Cooperation and Conflict 1941–1946* (1953).
Chester Wilmot: *The Struggle for Europe* (1952).

DIPLOMATIC MEMOIRS

Dean Acheson: *Sketches from Life* (1961).
James F.Byrnes: *Speaking Frankly* (1947).
Winston Churchill: *The Second World War*, vol. VI *Triumph and Tragedy* (1953).
Jan Ciechanowski: *Defeat in Victory* (1947).
Correspondence between the chairman of the Council of Ministers of the U.S.S.R. and the President of the U.S.A. and the Prime Ministers of Great Britain during the Great Patriotic War of 1941–1945 (1957).
The Memoirs of Cordell Hull (1948).
Stanislaw Mikolajczyk: *The Rape of Poland – Pattern of Soviet Aggression* (1948).
Robert E.Sherwood: *Roosevelt and Hopkins* (1948).
Harry S.Truman: *Memoirs* (1955).

THE WAR CRIME TRIALS AND THE POSTWAR PURGES

Robert Aron: *Histoire de la Libération de la France* (1958).
E.Davidson: *The Trial of the Germans* (1967).
P.H.Doublet: *La Collaboration* (1945).
C.Fitzgibbon: *Denazification* (1969).
Henry L.Mason: *The Purge of Dutch Quislings – Emergency Justice in the Netherlands* (1956).
L.Nogueres: *La Haute Cour de la Libération 1944–49* (1965).
P.Novick: *The Resistance versus Vichy* (1968).
Les proces de la Collaboration (the verbatim reports of the trials of Pétain, Laval, Maurras, de Brinon and others).
Paul Sérant: *Les vaincus de la Libération* (1964).

GREAT BRITAIN AFTER THE WAR

C.R.Attlee: *As it Happened* (1954).

Janet Beveridge: *Beveridge and his Plan* (1954).
R.H.S.Crossman (ed.): *New Fabian Essays* (1952).
Hugh Dalton: *High Tide and After* (1962).
J.E.D.Hall: *Labour's First Year* (1947).
Harry Hopkins: *The New Look* (1963).
R.B.McCallum and A.Readman: *The British General Election of 1945* (1947).
Herbert Morrison: *An Autobiography* (1961).
Alan Ross: *The Forties* (1950).
Michael Sissons and Philip French (ed.): *Age of Austerity* (1963).
Ernest Watkins: *The Cautious Revolution* (1950).
Francis Williams: *Ernest Bevin* (1952).
C.M.Woodhouse: *British Foreign Policy since the Second World War* (1962).

ITALY

G.Andreotti: *De Gasperi e suo tempo* (1956).
A.Battaglia *et al*: *Dieci anni dopo: 1945–1955* (1955).
Ivanoe Bonomi: *Diario di un anno* (1947).
Muriel Grindrod: *The New Italy* (1955).
Norman Kogan: *A Political History of Post-War Italy* (1966).
Giuseppe Mommarella: *Italy after Fascism* (1964).

FRANCE

Raymond Aron: *Le Grand Schisme* (1948).
Raymond Aron: *Immuable et changeante: de la IVe à la Ve République* (1959).
Robert Aron: *Histoire de la Libération de la France* (1959).
Joseph Barsalou: *La Mal Aimée: Histoire de la IVe République* (1964).
Jacques Chapsal: *La Vie Politique en France depuis 1940* (1966).
Maurice Duverger: *Les Partis Politiques* (1958).
Jacques Fauvet: *Les Forces Politiques en France* (1951).
Jacques Fauvet: *La IVe République* (1960).
Edgar Furniss: *France – The Troubled Ally* (1960).
Charles de Gaulle: *Memoirs de Guerre*, 3 vols (1955, 1959, 1960).
Catherine Gavin: *Liberated France* (1955).
François Goguel and Alfred Grosser: *La Politique en France* (1964).
Stanley Hoffmann (ed.): *In Search of France* (1963).
Herbert Luethy: *France Against Herself* (1955).
Henri Michel: *Les Courants de la Pensée de la Resistance* (1962).
André Siegfried: *De la IIIe à la IVe République* (1956).

David Thomson: *Democracy in France* (1958).
Alexander Werth: *France 1940–1955* (1956).
Philip Williams: *Politics in Post-War France* (1965).

GERMANY

Konrad Adenauer: *Memoirs* (1966, 1968).
Fritz René Allemann: *Bonn ist nicht Weimar* (1956).
Ruediger Altmann: *Das Erbe Adenauers* (1960).
Michael Balfour: *West Germany* (1968).
Klaus Boelling: *Republic in Suspense* (1964).
Wilhelm Cornides: *Die Weltmaechte und Deutschland* (1961).
Hans Dollinger (ed.): *Deutschland unter den Besatzungsmaechten* (1967).
Thomas Ellwein: *Das Regierungssystem der Bundesrepublik Deutschland* (1965).
Raymond Elsworth: *Restoring Democracy in Germany* (1960).
Fritz Erler: *Democracy in Germany* (1965).
Theodor Eschenburg: *Staat und Gesellschaft in Deutschland* (1960).
J.F.Golay: *The Founding of the Federal Republic of Germany* (1958).
Wilhelm G.Grewe: *Deutsche Aussenpolitik der Nachkriegszeit* (1960).
A.Grosser: *Western Germany from Defeat to Rearmament* (1955).
A.Grosser: *Die Bonner Demokratie* (1960).
W.F.Hanrieder: *West German Foreign Policy 1949–1963* (1967).
Theodor Heuss: *Aufzeichnungen 1945–47* (1966).
Richard Hiscocks: *The Adenauer Era* (1966).
Albrecht Kaden: *Einheit oder Freiheit* (1964).
Gerhard Loewenberg: *Parliament in the German Political System* (1966).
Peter Merkl: *The Origins of the West German Republic* (1965).
Paul Noack: *Deutschland von 1945–1960* (1960).
Tilman Puender: *Das bizonale Interregnum* (1966).
Hans Peter Schwarz: *Vom Reich zur Bundesrepublik Deutschland* (1967).
G. Stolper: *Deutsche Wirtschaftsgeschichte seit 1870* (1964).
F.J.Strauss: *The Grand Design* (1965).
F.Roy Willis: *The French in Germany* (1962).

EAST GERMANY

Stefan Doernberg: *Die Geburt eines neuen Deutschland 1945–1949* (1959).
Stefan Doernberg (ed.): *Beitraege zur Geschichte der sozialistischen Einheitspartei Deutschlands* (1961).
Horst Duhnke: *Stalinismus in Deutschland – die Geschichte der sowjetischen Besatzungszone* (1955).

C.J.Friedrich (ed.): *The Soviet Zone of Germany* (1956).
Peter Nettl: *The Eastern Zone and Soviet Policy in Germany 1945–1950* (1951).
Ernst Richert: *Das Zweite Deutschland* (1964).
Carola Stern: *Ulbricht* (1963).
Carola Stern: *Portraet einer bolschewistischen Partei* (1957).

EASTERN EUROPE

R.R.Betts (ed.): *Central and South East Europe* (1950).
J.F.Brown: *The New Eastern Europe* (1967).
Z.Brzezinski: *The Soviet Bloc: Unity and Conflict* (1961).
L.A.D.Dellin (ed.): *Bulgaria* (1957).
F.Fejtö: *Histoire des Democraties Populaires* (1969).
S.Fisher Galati (ed.): *Romania* (1957).
Ygael Gluckstein: *Stalin's Satellites in Europe* (1952).
J.Hajda: *A Study of Contemporary Czechoslovakia* (1955).
E.Halperin: *The Triumphant Heretic* (1958).
Richard Hiscocks: *Poland. Bridge for the Abyss?* (1963).
St Kertesz: *The Fate of East Central Europe* (1956).
J.Korbel: *The Communist Subversion of Czechoslovakia* (1959).
Werner Markert (ed.): *Jugoslawien* (1954).
Werner Markert (ed.): *Polen* (1959).
Fred W.Neal: *Titoism in Action* (1958).
Hans Roos: *A History of Modern Poland* (1966).
Hugh Seton Watson: *The East European Revolution* (1950).
N.Spulber: *The Economics of Communist Eastern Europe* (1957).
Hansjakob Stehle: *The Independent Satellite* (1965).
E. Taborsky: *Communism in Czechoslovakia 1948–1960* (1961).
Adam Ulam: *Titoism and the Cominform* (1952).
F.A.Vali: *Rift and Revolution in Hungary* (1961).
R.L.Wolff: *The Balkans in our Time* (1956).
Paul Zinner (ed.): *National Communism and Popular Revolt in Eastern Europe* (1957).
Paul Zinner: *Communist Strategy and Tactics in Czechoslovakia 1918–1948* (1963).

CHRISTIAN DEMOCRACY

Werner Allemeyer: *Christliche Demokratie in Europa und Lateinamerika* (1964).
J.Calbrette: *La Crise Actuelle du Catholicisme Francais* (1957).
Ernst Deuerlein: *CDU/CSU 1945–1957* (1957).

Mario Einaudi and François Goguel: *Christian Democracy in Italy and France* (1952).
M.P.Fogarty: *Christian Democracy in Western Europe* (1957).

CHURCH AND STATE IN ITALY

A.C.Jemolo: *Church and State in Modern Italy 1850–1950* (1960).
Leo Valiani: *L'Avvento di de Gasperi* (1949).
L.C.Webb: *Church and State in Italy 1947–1957* (1958).
Richard A.Webster: *The Cross and the Fasces: Christian Democracy and Fascism in Italy* (1960).

COMMUNISM IN EUROPE

Raymond Aron: *The Opium of the Intellectuals* (1957).
F.Borkenau: *European Communism* (1953).
David Caute: *Communism and the French Intellectuals* (1964).
M.Einaudi (ed.): *Communism in Western Europe* (1951).
J.Fauvet: *Histoire du Parti Communiste Francais* (1964–65).
G.Galli: *Istoria del Partito Comunista Italiano* (1958).
W.Griffith (ed.): *Communism in Europe* (1964).
D.G.Kousoulas: *Revolution and Defeat: The story of the Greek Communist party* (1965).
Leopold Labedz (ed.): *Revisionism* (1963).
Branko Lazitch: *Les Partis Communistes d'Europe, 1919–1955* (1956).
George Lichtheim: *Marxism in Modern France* (1966).
Charles A.Micaud: *Communism and the French Left* (1963).
A.Rossi: *Physiologie du Parti Communiste Francais* (1948).
Neal Wood: *Communism and the British Intellectuals* (1957).
C.M.Woodhouse: *Apple of Discord* (1948).

SOVIET UNION

Robert Conquest: *Power and Politics in the USSR* (1962).
Edward Crankshaw: *Russia without Stalin* (1956).
D.J.Dallin: *Soviet Foreign Policy after Stalin* (1961).
B.D.Datsiuk (ed.): *Istoria SSSR* (1963).
Isaac Deutscher: *Stalin* (1966).
Milovan Djilas: *The New Class* (1957).

Merle Fainsod: *How Russia is ruled* (1965).
Wolfgang Leonhard: *The Kremlin since Stalin* (1962).
Boris Meissner: *Russland im Umbruch* (1951).
Boris Meissner: *Sowjetrussland zwischen Revolution und Restauration* (1956).
Boris Meissner: *Das Ende des Stalin Mythos* (1956).
Alec Nove: *The Soviet Economy. An Introduction* (1961).
R.W.Pethybridge: *A History of Postwar Russia* (1966).
B.N.Ponomarev (ed.): *Istoria Kommunisticheskoi Partii Sovetskovo Soyuza* (1959).
Georg von Rauch: *A History of Soviet Russia* (1960).
Leonard Schapiro: *The Communist Party of the Soviet Union* (1960).
Harry Schwartz: *The Red Phoenix* (1961).
Hugh Seton Watson: *From Lenin to Malenkov* (1954).
Michel Tatu: *Power in the Kremlin* (1969).
Bertram D.Wolfe: *Communist Totalitarianism* (1961).

EUROPEAN UNION

E. Benoit: *Europe at Sixes and Sevens* (1961).
M. Camps: *The European Common Market and American Policy* (1956).
J.F.Deiau: *The Common Market* (1960).
Lord Ismay: *Nato, the First Five Years* (1954).
U.W.Kitzinger: *The Challenge of the Common Market* (1962).
G.Lichtheim: *The New Europe* (1963).
R.Mayne: *The Community of Europe* (1962).
B.T.Moore: *NATO and the Future of Europe* (1958).
Roy Price: *The Political Future of the European Community* (1962).
A.H.Robertson: *The Council of Europe* (1956).
H.A.Schmitt: *The Path to European Union* (1962).
Howard K.Smith: *The State of Europe* (1949).
G.L.Weil: *A Handbook of the European Economic Community* (1965).
Theodore H.White: *Fire in the Ashes* (1953).
A.J.Zurcher: *The Struggle to Unite Europe* (1958).

PART II

THE CULTURAL SCENE

C.Freeman and A.Young: *The Research and Development Effort in Western Europe, North America and the Soviet Union* (1965).

H.Kahn and A.Wiener: *The Year 2000* (1967).

M.Kranzberg and C.W.Pursell Jr: *Technology in Western Civilisation*, Vol. II (1967).

Walter M.Abbott (ed.): *The Documents of Vatican II* (1966).

Carlo Falconi: *Pope John and his Council* (1964).

Hans Kung: Theological Currents in Europe Today, in S.Graubard (ed.) *A New Europe?* (1964).

Emile G.Leónard: *Histoire Generale du Protestantisme*, Vol. III (1964).

Xavier Rynne: *The Second Session* (1964).

Xavier Rynne: *The Fourth Session* (1966).

S.Paul Shilling: *Contemporary Continental Theologians* (1966).

Robert Brustein: *The Theatre of Revolt* (1964).

Martin Esslin: *The Theatre of the Absurd* (1962).

Laurence Kitchin: *Midcentury Drama* (1960).

Penelope Houston: *The Contemporary Cinema* (1963).

F.Pige: *La Television dans le Monde* (n.d.).

Wilson P.Dizard: *Television. A World Review* (1966).

Ben B.Seligman: *Main Currents in Modern Economic Thought* (1962).

M.F.Sciacca: *Philosophical Trends in the Contemporary World* (1964).

I.M.Bochenski: *Contemporary European Philosophy* (1956).

D.C.Watt (ed.): *Contemporary History in Europe* (1969).

W.Laqueur and G.Mosse: *The New History* (1967).

J.F.Cramer and G.S.Browne: *Contemporary Education* (1965).

Anthony Kerr: *The Universities of Europe* (1962).

World Yearbook of Education (1965).

Paul Henry Lang and Nathan Broder: *Contemporary Music in Europe* (1968).

Rene Huyghe: *The Larousse Encyclopaedia of Modern Art* (1965).

W.Haftmann: *Painting in the Twentieth Century* (1965).

U.Apollinio et al.: *Art since 1945* (1968).

Pierre de Boisdeffre: *Une Histoire Vivante de la Litterature Française d'Aujourd'hui* (1958).

M.A.Burnier: *Les Existentialistes et la Politique* (1966).

David Caute: *Communism and the French Intellectuals* (1965).

M.Stuart Hughes: *The Obstructed Path, French Social Thought in the Years of Desperation 1930–60* (1968).

Gaetan Picon: *Panorama de la Nouvelle Litterature Française* (1949).

Antonio Viscardi: *Storia della Litteratura Italiana* (1960).

Jean Amery: *Preface to the Future. Culture in a consumer society* (1964).

Hans Braun: *Deutscher Geist zwischen Heute und Morgen* (n.d.).

Kenneth Allsop: *The Angry Decade* (1958).

E.P.Thompson (ed.): *Out of Apathy* (1960).

Gleb Struve: *History of Soviet Literature* (German edit. 1958).

George Gibian: *Interval of Freedom. Soviet Literature during the Thaw 1954–1957* (1960).

Max Hayward and Leopold Labedz: *Literature and Revolution in Soviet Russia 1917–1962* (1963).

Priscilla Johnson: *Khrushchev and Soviet Art. The Politics of Soviet Culture 1962–1964* (1965).

Tibor Meray and Tamas Acsel: *The Revolt of the Mind* (1960).

Helen Ssachno: *Der Aufstand der Person. Sowjet Literatur seit Stalins Tod* (1965).

Harold Swayze: *Political Control of Literature in the USSR 1946–1959* (1962).

PART III

ECONOMIC AND SOCIAL TRENDS

Paul Alpert: *Twentieth Century Economic History of Western Europe* (1967).

J.F.Dewhurst, John O.Coppock, P.Lamartine Yates and associates: *Europe's Needs and Resources* (1961).

ECE: *Economic Planning in Europe* (1965).

Charles P.Kindleberger: *Europe's Postwar Growth* (1967).

A.Maddison: *Economic Growth in the West* (1964).

OEEC: *Economic Progress and Problems* (1951).

OEEC: *Europe and the World Economy* (1960).

OECD: *Economic Growth 1960–1970* (1966).

OECD: Economic (country) surveys by the OECD published yearly.

M.Poston: *An Economic History of Western Europe* (1967).

A.Shonfield: *Modern Capitalism* (1965).

United Nations: *Statistical Yearbook 1967* (1968).

United Nations: *Economic Survey of Europe 1948* – published yearly, 21 volumes appeared up to 1968.

United Nations: *Some Factors in Economic Growth in Europe during the 1950s* (1964).

W.S.Woytinsky and E.S.Woytinsky: *World Population and Production* (1953).

AREA STUDIES

Michael Shanks: *The Stagnant Society* (1961).

Andrew Shonfield: *British Economic Policy since the War* (1958).

PEP: *Growth in the British Economy* (1961).

Ludwig Erhard: *Germany's Comeback in the World Market* (1954).

N.J.G.Pounds: *The Economic Pattern of Modern Germany* (1963).
Gustav Stolper: *The German Economy: 1870 to the Present* (1967).
Henry C.Wallich: *Mainsprings of the German Revival* (1955).
Banco di Roma: *Review of the Economic Conditions in Italy*. Bi-monthly.
Shephard B.Clough: *The Economic History of Modern Italy* (1964).
George H.Hildebrand: *Growth and Structure in the Economy of Modern Italy* (1965).
Joseph La Palombara: *Italy: the Politics of Planning* (1966).
John Ardagh: *The New French Revolution* (1968).
Herbert Luethy: *France Against Herself* (1955).
PEP: *French Planning; Some Lessons for Britain* (1963).
Gordon Wright: *Rural Revolution in France* (1964).
Abram Bergson (ed.): *Soviet Economic Growth* (1953).
A.Bergson and S.Kuznets (ed.): *Economic Trends in the Soviet Union* (1963).
Naum Jasny: *Soviet Industrialisation 1928–1952* (1961).
Michael Kaser: *Comecon* (1965).
J.M.Montias: *Central Planning in Poland* (1962).
Alec Nove: *The Soviet Economy* (1965).
Frederic L.Pryor: *The Communist Foreign Trade System* (1963).
Harry Schwartz: *The Soviet Economy since Stalin* (1965).
Alfred Zaubermann: *Industrial Development in Czechoslovakia, East Germany and Poland* (1958).

SOCIAL CONDITIONS

B.Abel Smith: *An International Study of Health Expenditure* (1967).
A.Brodersen: *The Soviet Worker* (1966).
Colin Clark: *The Conditions of Economic Progress* (1958).
D.V.Donnison: *The Government of Housing* (1967).
S.Eltz: *Health and Pension Insurance in Sweden* (1963).
Walter Galenson: *Trade Union Democracy in Western Europe* (1961).
David Grannik: *The European Executive* (1962).
Pauline Gregg: *The Welfare State* (1967).
Alex Inkeles and Kent Geiger (ed.): *Soviet Society* (1961).
International Labour Organisation: *The Cost of Social Security 1949–57* (1961).
International Labour Organisation: *The Cost of Medical Care* (1959).
Bernice Q.Madison: *Social Welfare in the Soviet Union* (1968).
S.Mallet: *La Nouvelle Classe Ouvrière* (1962).
OECD: *Tourism* (1967).
OECD (C.Freeman and A.Young): *The Research and Development Effort* (1965).

United Nations: *Incomes in Postwar Europe* (1967).
United Nations: *Annual Bulletin of Housing and Building Statistics.*
United Nations: *1963 Report on the World Social Situation.*
United Nations: *Demographic Yearbook.*
U.S. Department of Health, Educational Welfare: *Social Security Programs throughout the World, 1964* (1964).
F.Zweig: *The Worker in the Affluent Society* (1961).

PART IV

COLD WAR, DÉTENTE, WEST–EAST RELATIONS

Coral Bell: *Negotiation from Strength* (1963).
Alastair Buchan: *Nato in the 1960s* (1965).
Alvin Cottrell and James Dougherty: *The Politics of the Atlantic Alliance* (1964).
Die Internationale Politik. Jahrbuecher der Deutschen Gesellschaft fuer auswaertige Politik 1961, 1962.
Jacques Freymond: *Western Europe since the War* (1964).
Norman A.Graebner: *Cold War Diplomacy* (1962).
Henry Kissinger: *Nuclear Weapons and Foreign Policy* (1957).
Henry Kissinger: *The Troubled Partnership* (1966).
Joseph Kraft: *The Grand Design* (1962).
Walter Laqueur and Leopold Labedz: *Polycentrism* (1962).
George Lichtheim: *Europe and America* (1963).
John A.Lukacs: *A History of the Cold War* (1961).
Philip Moseley: *The Kremlin and World Politics* (1960).
Robert Osgood: *Nato: The Entangling Alliance* (1962).
Paul Seabury: *The Rise and Decline of the Cold War* (1967).
Ronald Steel: *The End of Alliance* (1964).
Hugh Seton Watson: *Neither War nor Peace* (1960).
J.W.Spanier: *American Foreign Policy since World War II* (1960).
Survey of International Affairs (Royal Institute of International Affairs – 1956–1958, 1959–1960, 1961).
Adam Ulam: *Expansion and Coexistence. The History of Soviet Foreign Policy 1917–1967* (1968).

EUROPEAN UNITY: THE SIXTIES

Nora Beloff: *The General Says No* (1963).
Kurt Birrenbach: *The Future of the Atlantic Community* (1963).

Miriam Camps: *Britain and the European Community 1955–63* (1964).
Miriam Camps: *European Unification in the Sixties* (1967).
Miriam Camps: *What Kind of Europe* (1965).
François Duchène: *Beyond Alliance* (1965).
Walter Hallstein: *United Europe* (1962).
Stephen Holt: *The Common Market: The Conflict of Theory and Practice* (1967).
Uwe Kitzinger: *The Challenge of the Common Market* (1962).
Max Kohnstamm: *The European Community and its Role in the World* (1964).
Richard Mayne: *The Community of Europe* (1963).
William Pickles: *Britain and Europe: How much has changed* (1967).
John Pinder: *Britain and the Common Market* (1961).
John Pinder: *Europe against de Gaulle* (1963).
Roy Price: *The Political Future of the European Community* (1962).
Michael Shanks and John Lambert: *Britain and the New Europe* (1965).

GERMANY AND BERLIN

Willi Brandt: *The Ordeal of Coexistence* (1963).
Heinrich von Brentano: *Germany and Europe* (1964).
Zbigniew Brzezinski: *Alternative to Partition* (1965).
Gerald Freund: *Germany between two Worlds* (1961).
Alfred Grosser: *The Federal Republic of Germany* (1964).
John Mander: *Berlin: Hostage for the West* (1962).
Geoffrey McDermott: *Berlin, Success of a Mission* (1963).
James L. Richardson: *Germany and the Atlantic Alliance* (1966).
Ernst Richert: *Das zweite Deutschland* (1964).
Jean Edward Smith: *The Defense of Berlin* (1966).
Hans Speier: *Divided Berlin* (1961).
Walter Stahl: *The Politics of Postwar Germany* (1963).
Franz Joseph Strauss: *The Grand Design* (1965).
Ference A. Vali: *The Quest for a United Germany* (1967).
Philip Windsor: *City on Leave: A History of Berlin 1945–62* (1963).

GAULLISM

Edward Ashcroft: *De Gaulle* (1962).
Edgar Furniss: *France – The Troubled Ally* (1960).
P.M. de la Gorce: *De Gaulle Entre Deux Mondes* (1964).
E. Jouve: *Le Général de Gaulle et la Construction de l'Europe* (1967).
Roy Macridis (ed.): *De Gaulle, Implacable Ally* (1966).

E.Mannoni: *Moi, Général de Gaulle* (1964).
Roger Massip: *De Gaulle et l'Europe* (1963).
Armin Mohler: *Die fuenfte Republik* (1963).
C.Purtschet: *Le Rassemblement du Peuple Français* (1965).
David Schoenbrun: *The Three Lives of Charles de Gaulle* (1966).
Heinrich von Siegler: *Kennedy or de Gaulle?* (1966).
J.M.Tournoux: *La Tragédie du Général* (1967).
P.Viansson-Ponté: *Les Politiques* (1967).
Alexander Werth: *De Gaulle* (1965).

POLYCENTRISM IN EUROPE

Donald L.M.Blackmer: *Unity in Diversity. Italian Communism and the Communist World* (1968).
Zbigniew Brzezinski: *The Soviet Bloc* (1967).
R.V.Burks: *The Dynamics of Communism in Eastern Europe* (1961).
Edward Crankshaw: *The New Cold War: Moscow v. Peking* (1963).
Alexander Dallin (ed.): *Diversity in International Communism* (1963).
François Fejtö: *The French Communist Party and the Crisis of International Communism* (1967).
David Floyd: *Rumania: Russia's Dissident Ally* (1965).
John Gittings: *Survey of the Sino-Soviet Dispute* (1968).
William E.Griffith (ed.): *Communism in Europe* Vol. I (1964).
William E.Griffith: *Albania and the Sino-Soviet Rift* (1964).
William E.Griffith: *The Sino-Soviet Rift* (1964).
William E.Griffith: *Sino-Soviet Relations* (1967).
G.F.Hudson *et al: The Sino-Soviet Dispute* (1961).
Leopold Labedz (ed.): *International Communism after Khrushchev* (1965).
Richard Loewenthal: *World Communism: The Disintegration of a Secular Faith* (1964).
Twenty-second Congress of the Communist Party of the Soviet Union (1962).
Twenty-third Congress of the Communist Party of the Soviet Union (1966).
Plenum of the Central Committee of the CPSU, June 18–21, 1963 (1964).
Donald S.Zagoria: *The Sino-Soviet Dispute 1956–61* (1962).
Paul E.Zinner (ed.): *National Communism and Popular Revolt in Eastern Europe* (1956).

NATIONAL SECURITY AND ARMS CONTROL 1961–67

Raymond Aron: *The Great Debate* (1965).

Robert A.Bowie: *Shaping the Future* (1964).
Alastair Buchan and Philip Windsor: *Arms and Stability in Europe* (1963).
Hedley Bull: *The Control of the Arms Race* (1965).
Morton H.Halperin: *Limited War in the Nuclear Age* (1963).
Arnold L.Horelick and Myron Rush: *Strategic Power and Soviet Foreign Policy* (1966).
William Kaufmann: *The McNamara Strategy* (1964).
Robert S.McNamara: *The Essence of Security* (1968).
James L.Richardson: *Germany and the Atlantic Alliance* (1966).
Thomas C.Schelling and Morton H.Halperin: *Strategy and Arms Control* (1961).
Arthur M.Schlesinger: *A Thousand Days: John F.Kennedy in the White House* (1965).
Glenn H.Snyder: *Deterrence and Defence* (1963).
Theodore C.Sorensen: *Kennedy* (1965).
Timothy W.Stanley: *Nato in Transition* (1965).
Jeremy J.Stone: *Containing the Arms Race* (1966).
Thomas W.Wolfe: *Soviet Strategy at the Crossroads* (1965).

DÉTENTE

Georg Bluhm: *Détente and Military Relaxation in Europe* (1967).
Neville Brown: *Arms without Europe* (1967).
Zbigniew Brzezinski: *Alternative to Partition* (1965).
Harold van B.Cleveland: *The Atlantic Idea and its European Rivals* (1967).
Pierre Hassner: *Change and Security in Europe* (1968).
Stanley Hoffmann: *Gulliver's Troubles* (1968).
Jean Laloy: *Entre Guerre et Paix* (1966).
Jean Laloy: *Western and Eastern Europe* (1967).
George Liska: *Europe Ascendant* (1964).
George Liska: *Imperial America* (1967).

REVOLUTION 1968

Tariq Ali (ed.): *New Revolutionaries* (1969).
René Andrieu: *Les Communistes et la Révolution* (1968).
Raymond Aron: *La Révolution introuvable* (1968).
J.J.Brachier and B.Oelgart: *L'International Etudiante* (1969).
A.Cockburn and R.Blackburn: *Student Power* (1969).
Daniel Cohn-Bendit: *Obsolete Communism : the Left-wing Alternative* (1968).

David Cooper (ed.): *The Dialectics of Liberation* (1969).
R.Debray: *Revolution in the Revolution* (1967).
H.M.Enzensberger (ed.): *Kursbuch 13 et seq.* (1968).
Lewis Feuer: *The Conflict of Generations* (1969).
André Glucksmann: *Stratégie et Révolution en France 1968* (1968).
Jens Hager: *Die Rebellion von Berlin* (1967).
Leopold Labedz: 'Students and Revolutions' in *Survey*, July 1968.
Seymour M.Lipset (ed.): *Student Politics* (1967).
Tom Nairn: *The Beginning of the End* (1968).
Lucien Rioux and René Backmann: *L'Explosion de Mai* (1969).
Nikolaus J.Ryschkowsky: *Die linke Linke* (1968).
Erwin K.Scheuch (ed.): *Die Wiedertaeufer der Wohlstandsgesellschaft* (1968).
Patrick Seale and Maureen McConville: *French Revolution* (1968).
Michel Thurlotte: *L'Hypothèse Révolutionnaire* (1969).
Alain Touraine: *Le Mouvement de Mai ou le Communisme Utopique* (1968).
UNEF et SNE: *Le Livre Noir des Journées des Mai* (1968).
Alain Schnapp and Pierre Vidal-Naquet: *Journal de la Commune Etudiante,* (1969).
René Vienet: *Enragés et Situationnistes dans le Mouvement des Occupations* (1969).

EASTERN EUROPE IN THE FIFTIES AND SIXTIES

J.F.Brown: *The New Eastern Europe* (1966).
R.V.Burks: *The Dynamics of Communism in Eastern Europe* (1961).
St. Fischer Galati: *Eastern Europe in the Sixties* (1963).
H.Hamm: *Albania – China's Beachhead in Europe* (1963).
St. D.Kertesz: *Eastern Europe and the World* (1962).
M.J.Lasky (ed.): *The Hungarian Revolution* (1957).
H.G.Skilling: *Communism, National and International* (1964).
P.Windsor and A.Roberts: *Czechoslovakia 1968* (1969).
Z.A.B.Zeman: *Prague Spring* (1969).

THE SOVIET UNION AFTER 1956

Z.Brzezinski: *Ideology and Power in Soviet Politics* (1967).
R.Conquest: *Russia After Khrushchev* (1965).
Carl A.Linden: *Khrushchev and the Soviet Leadership* (1966).
H.R.Swearer and M.Rush: *The Politics of Succession in the USSR* (1964).
Adam Ulam: *The New Face of Soviet Totalitarianism* (1965).

Index